Plight of Indian Muslims After Partition

Habibur Rehman

ATLANTIC
PUBLISHERS & DISTRIBUTORS (P) LTD

ATLANTIC
PUBLISHERS & DISTRIBUTORS (P) LTD
7/22, Ansari Road, Darya Ganj, New Delhi
Tel.: +91-11-4077 5252, 2327 3880
E-mail: orders@atlanticbooks.com
Web: www.atlanticbooks.com

Reprint 2026

Published by Atlantic Publishers & Distributors (P) Ltd.

Printed & bound in India by Atlantic Print Services

Preface

Muslims of India are extremely grateful to Dr. Manmohan Singh and Shrimati Sonia Gandhi for instituting the Sachar Committee because the Report of the Committee not only absolved Muslims of the charges of appeasement levelled by their adversaries, but also highlighted their pathetic conditions at the hands of the governing structure and convinced the civil society of India that Muslims are a miserable lot. In many ways they are worse than the Scheduled Castes, Scheduled Tribes and the Backward Classes. It also emphasized the need for affirmative and positive actions to bring Muslims at par in the mainstream within a meaningful time horizon. However, Muslims lament that no efforts were made by the Government and the wellwishers of the minority community to deal with the trauma and anguish suffered by them since the Partition of the country, especially after the publication of the Report for diagnosing the maladies and suggesting their remedial measures.

This venture is a humble effort to place before the general public, the Muslims, the majority community and the Government, the actual conditions of the community so that something meaningful can be done for them. We know that a wide variety of policy measures and initiatives have been taken by the Government for the amelioration of minorities in India, but the general impression among Muslims is that these are mere cosmetic in nature as the development deficit between them and others is widening. The findings of the Sachar Committee Report are alarming as they convincingly prove that all is not well with the Muslims of India. Muslims indeed are a miserable lot. They are already under siege due to lack of education, shrinking political space, divisions and sub-divisions, discrimination and deprivation and deliberate pauperization and are being pushed into becoming a new class of super dalits to fill the vacuum created by the upward movement of the lower classes. Affirmative and positive steps are needed for the redressal of their grievances and solution of their problems. Admittedly, they could not reap the benefits of development vis-à-vis others during the last sixty years and are struggling with several social, economic, political and cultural issues affecting their identity, security, livelihood, status and dignity. Due to lack of equity, absence of equality of opportunities and transparency and want of inclusive approach they could not be brought within the pluralistic mainstream of the country. Consequently, they are educationally worse than the Scheduled Castes and Scheduled Tribes, economically behind the Backward Classes, socially isolated, politically divided and culturally suffocated. Their representation in Government jobs and private sector is minimal; they are conspicuous by their absence at the top level, especially in panchayats, zila parishads, assemblies and parliament; the doors of banks and financial institutions are half closed for them and they are meeting their two ends by serving as mechanics, artisans, transport workers, labourers, farmers, petty shopkeepers and hawkers.

There is no doubt that all perceptions of Indian Muslims are not true, many may be based merely on hunches but certainly they have not been built on vacuum. Muslims are certainly striving under heavy stress which results in frustration, anger and dejection but they cannot put the whole blame for their state of affairs entirely on the Government or the majority community. They will have to think patiently where have they faltered and the majority community too has to be sympathetic to their genuine problems, and it becomes the duty of the state to see that they get their due. Unfortunately, Muslims' charges of unfair treatment have some element of truth which gives rise to a feeling of being discriminated against and so the situation continues to deteriorate.

As always happens in situations of this type, people generally do not reach the bottom of the situation but involve themselves in mutual ceaseless recrimination, mutual accusation and war of attrition with the result that they fail to adopt corrective measures. The purpose of the present endeavour is neither fault-finding nor to create ill-will between communities and people nor to pamper any segment of the minority community or dent any section of the majority community or blame the Governments but to put the case history of the conditions of Muslims in the light of Sachar Committee Report and put their feelings and perceptions before the majority and minority communities as well as the Central and State Governments of the country and the people of India in general and the Muslims in particular, so that they may find a solution to this problem through peaceful, democratic, constitutional and humanitarian means in the interest of all people, failing which the situation would continue to deteriorate and cause immense damage and harm not only to the secular web of our society but also stall the growth and development of the country.

The book is a description of the life of Muslims after the Partition of the country. It would not only be appreciated by all the sections of the minority community but also be looked with compassion by various segments of the majority community as well as by the Government, intelligentsia and the wellwishers of Muslim community. It would be read with interest by the commoners as well as the students and teachers of various disciplines, especially political science and sociology.

Habibur Rehman

Acknowledgements

I am grateful to Eng. S.V. Subramanyam, Mr. Syed Farookh Ahmed, Eng. P.K. Kapoor and all eminent geniuses whose contributions helped me to give a proper shape to the endeavour. I am also thankful to my wife Masarrat Habib, daughter Dr. Sitwat Khan, son Eng. Bilal Habib, son-in-law Dr. Jamshedur Rahman Khan, daughter-in-law Dr. Reshma Mukhtar, grand son-in-law Dr. Danish Kazmi, grandson Master Basil Habib Khan and grand-daughters Dr. Areeba Kazmi Khan, Eng. Abeer Khan, Ms Rahma Habib Khan and Ms Rifa Habib Khan and all other wellwishers who helped me in shaping of this work.

Habibur Rehman

Contents

	Preface	*iii*
	Acknowledgements	*vii*
1.	Muslims' Perceptions and Apprehensions	1
2.	The Turbulence and Agony of Post-Partition Period from 1947 to 1971	45
3.	Stability, Pressure Tactics and Apprehensions	98
4.	Strain and Stress Exerted by the Right-Wing Extremist Parties	130
5.	The Contemporary Phase of Assertion, Depression and Contemplation	161
6.	Policy Measures to Tackle Radicalism	215
7.	The Socio-Religious Structure of Muslim Community	258
8.	The Economic Deprivation of Muslims	284
9.	Hindus and Muslims are the Two Sides of the Same Coin	347

1

Muslims' Perceptions and Apprehensions

India since time immemorial has been considered a land of peace, progress and prosperity. It was renowned for its magnificent art, wonderful architecture, rich culture and glorious past. Once upon a time, this piece of land was called a 'Golden Land' wherein flew the rivers of milk and honey. Indians were heralded for their scholarship, piety, fellow-feelings and large-hearted tolerance. The glimpses of India's glory and grandeur are spread throughout the length and breadth of the country. Several rulers and emperors from foreign lands stormed the country as invaders but influenced by its enchanting beauty many of them ultimately accepted it as their final and permanent abode. The country saw many ups and downs, defeats and victories and settling and unsettling of its vital cities, towns and their surrounding areas. However, the mid-night of 15 August 1947 was the unique night in the life of the country in the sense that it was indeed the 'tryst with destiny' when a moment came in the life of Indians, though rarely in history, when they stepped out from the old to the new, when an age ended, and when the soul of Indians, long suppressed, found utterance, but alas! it was the mixture of blessings and miseries. It gave Indians freedom but side by side divided the country into India and Pakistan on communal lines. In one stroke of pen brothers were separated from brothers and friends became enemies and there was such a chaos and confusion in the country which was never seen before. Indian Muslims who were the integral and composite part of the cultural and social milieu of the Indian society were fractured. Those who lived in India became a minority and those who migrated to Pakistan became refugees but thanks to the Indian Constitution and the sagacity of the far-sighted Indians that the polity of plurality, ethos of diverse culture and the principles of unity in diversity and multiplicity in uniformity were enshrined in the Constitution and the nation was committed to the equality of citizens and the state was made responsible to preserve, protect and assure the rights of minorities in matters of language, religion and culture. The various clauses of the Constitution have been so intelligently crafted that in a pluralistic and multi-ethnic and multi-culture country there is neither any dichotomy between the minorities and majorities nor an inevitable conflict among various socio-religious groups, though it cannot be denied that some of the minorities and the depressed sections of the society in the country often perceive discrimination and neglect because of their weak position and unique identity and meager number and also due to the very fact that religious, ethnic and marginalized sections of the society in almost all the countries of the world often feel open or discreet discrimination against them. Since Independence, India made remarkable progress in the fields of agriculture, industry, defence, environment, space research, telecommunication and service sectors. It narrowed down inter-personal, inter-regional and inter-sectoral inequalities and achieved significant growth and development along with improving the quality of human life by spreading literacy, removing diseases and ignorance and improving the standard of living of the people. Merely through the excellent managerial qualities, technical superiority, financial acumen and the dexterity of its people it carved out a place amongst the most developed nations of the world. In the race for super power India is far ahead of many mighty powers. Despite multi-dimensional and multi-farious progress there are indications that not all socio-religious communities and the neglected parts of the society have shared equally the fruits of progress. A wide variety of policy initiatives have been taken by the government for the development of the minorities but the general feeling among most of the Muslims is that these are cosmetic in nature since despite the process of accelerated growth, the development deficit between them and others is increasing. There is general perception among many Muslims that there seems to be some fears among various sections of the society that the consequences of empowerment of Muslims by giving them special benefits would strengthen communal politics in the country. This factor as well as the lack of necessary will on the parts of the Central and State Governments due to vote bank politics appears to have largely dented the development process among minorities in the country.

The country being one of the largest secular democracies of the world is committed to the betterment of the minorities. In 2009, the Supreme Court asked the Orissa Government to protect minorities or quit. The Bench headed by the Chief Justice of India K.G. Balakrishna, which included justices Markandey Katju and P. Sathasivam, specifically highlighted the fact while dealing with atrocities on Christians in Orissa that we are a secular country. We cannot allow persecution of minorities. No minority community should be insecured in the country. Pandit Jawaharlal Nehru said once that if India was to be a secular, stable and strong State then our first consideration must be to give absolute and fair place to our minorities. However, despite all good intentions on the part of the well-wishers of the country, it seems that very little could be done for the betterment of the minorities of the country especially the Muslims. Deprivation, poverty, ignorance and discrimination may be found among other segments of the society too for there are several sections which are not fully satisfied with the due process of justice and equity. Since our main aim is to focus on Muslims we would like to keep the focus on the conditions of Indian Muslims only. Our objective is neither fault finding nor to create ill-will between communities and people nor to pamper any segment of the minority nor dent any section from the majority or blame the government but to put the case history of depressing section of Muslim community as well as its feelings and perceptions before the Indian masses and the leaders of the country so that they may themselves diagnose the diseases and prescribe suitable remedies. For prescribing a reasonable cure within a meaningful time horizon, it is imperative for us to know what the community feels and what are its pressing needs and pinching problems. Besides, those ruling the country should also know that things are perhaps not in good shape as far as minorities are concerned. They should not only take affirmative steps but also ensure that justice is not only done to the marginalized segments of the minority community but it is also abundantly and transparently seen and felt by all the sections of the depressed society that it is being done. The Sachar Committee has done a commendable work. The Government of India especially the Congress President Shrimati Sonia Gandhi and the Prime Minister of India Dr. Manmohan Singh deserve highest appreciation for removing the tag of appeasement from the neck of Indian Muslims. The Chairman and the members too deserve praise from the Indian community in general and Muslims in particular for rationally and dauntlessly analyzing the conditions of Indian Muslims and pin-pointing and suggesting remedial measures for their redressal. As the statistics and facts and figures given in "social, economic and educational status of the Muslim community of India" a report prepared by Prime Minister's High Level Committee, Government of India (Cabinet Secretariat) under the Chairperson: Justice Rajindar Sachar, are authentic and that have been accepted by the nation, the author has used them profusely to explain the pitiable conditions of Indian Muslims. Since the statistics somewhere has become unwieldy, hope the learned readers would bear with him.

Before analyzing the trauma and anguish of Muslim community, it should be kept in mind that there are several factors which have contributed in the worsening of the conditions of Indian Muslims during the period of nearly sixty years. The most important among them is the historical stigma. It is most astonishing that many Indians often talk of the preceding one thousand years as a dark period of slavery with disgust which includes the Muslim rule as well as the rule by British. Many of them seem to have no soft corner for Muslims for they consider them as the progeny of those Muslim rulers who in their opinion subjugated Indians for centuries and caused immense harm to their culture, institutions and religion. Besides, Muslims unfortunately inherited the British-time legacy of communal discord between Hindus and Muslims and ironically the blame of creating Pakistan too was wholly and solely put on them which reduced their size and influence in this part of the sub-continent. Moreover, nearly five million Muslims mostly from Northern India and the isolated segments of Southern India migrated to Pakistan which robbed the community of its potential leaders, administrators, intellectuals, elites and the well-wishers most of whom were civil servants, teachers, traders, doctors, engineers, professionals and legal luminaries. In addition to it, after the worsening of India-Pak relations and the complaints of step brotherly treatment of non-Muslims by the Government of Pakistan, it appeared that it was certain that the Muslims in India were bound to be vulnerable. Besides, it is also alleged that it was the sheer apathy and ineptitude from the side of Indian Government at the Centre and the State Governments at provincial levels that most of the Muslims were not provided with adequate security and the desired equity and the meaningful equality of opportunity in the fields of health, education and employment which paralyzed them during the course of time. Likewise, the communal riots during post-partition period created ill-will between minority and majority communities which in turn closed the doors for Muslims' betterment. Similarly, the venomous perception of certain right wing and reactionary officials and the hardened attitude of a few anti-Muslim parties and the speeches, actions and reactions of some of the fanatic leaders and organizations from the majority community in the country highlighting the so-called Muslim appeasement came in the way of Muslims' growth and development. Furthermore, the perceived bias by certain right wing political parties in power at the Centre as well as at regional levels against the community under the ideological influences too dented their development. It is also true that the communal atmosphere that was generated after Shah Bano case and which ultimately resulted in the demolition of Babri Masjid in 1992, created a wide gulf between the majority and minority communities. The 1993 Mumbai Blast in retaliation to the demolition of the mosque worked as fuel to the fire. The international anti-Muslim and anti-Islamic atmosphere and the terrorism emerging from certain radical Muslim countries also affected the fate of Muslims adversely. The lack of credible middle class among Muslims and the failure on the part of Muslim community to throw plausible leadership in mainstream political arena resulted in their low participation in governance of the country. The siege mentality of the community made Muslims defunct and as a consequence of which their spirit of adventurism, philanthropy and dynamism got back seat and instead of solving their problems by their own might, they looked towards others. Muslims developed in them guilt conscience, fear psychosis and bias towards several segments of the majority community as well as the governing structure which kept them away from the centre of power. Certain proactive acts, speeches, utterances and proclamations of irresponsible leaders from both the sides of the corridor especially during Babri Masjid movement created bad blood in the country. Recently, the involvement of certain radical Muslim elements in terrorist activities from among a minor section of Muslim community and the participation in similar terrorist acts by the like-minded hard core activists from the fringe section of the majority community spoiled the atmosphere of peaceful co-existence. Lastly, some of the biased national and international media played havoc and painted Muslims dark. All these factors and many more finally resulted in their down fall as a consequence of which in several segments Muslims are far behind even Scheduled Castes and Scheduled Tribes. Speaking generally, the present climate in the country is such that several Indian Muslims including many educated, progressive and enlightened lot as well as the religious people and the general masses mostly feel helpless and aggrieved seeing the pathetic conditions of Muslims in various parts and segments of the country. Many of the affected people who face the music very often conceive that not only are they being discriminated, isolated, humiliated and victimized but their constitutional rights are jeopardized and they feel unwanted and second class citizens in their own land. This perception based on facts or mere conjecture is not good for the health of the country as the country is like a body, all parts of which needs to be healthy. The paralysis in any part of the country is bound to affect the health of the whole country. It is an admitted fact that the depressed, regressive and the unsatisfied minorities are a bane to the country, the countrymen have a right to know where the things have gone wrong and where the shoe pinches so that the affirmative and positive steps may be taken to redress the genuine grievances of the minorities. This study is a humble attempt in that direction. To begin with we would like to quote the observations of Justice B. Vithyathil and Ghanshyam Shah on the 1971 Thalassery riots as they would help the learned readers to perceive and appreciate the agonies and mindsets of the Muslims of India. Justice B. Vithyathil stated, "so far as minorities are concerned, it is the feeling among them that they are not getting justice, that they are discriminated against in matter of appointments in the Public Services, that they do not get equal protection of the law and that their religion is in danger, that prompts them to rally around religious organizations of their own". In the words of political scientist Ghanshyam Shah, "to be a Muslim in contemporary India is to face constant fear and insecurity, discrimination and humiliation. You have to prove your patriotism every now and then. Rule of law, the soul of a democratic civilized society, is frequently violated by the state, more so in the case of the deprived and dispossessed. This is irrespective of the party in power, be it the Congress, the BSP or BJP; and even CPM. The violation of the rule of law is not an aberration, confined to certain states but it is widespread and frequent; it is almost being legitimized. Fake encounters in which the officers have willfully killed the alleged 'accused' are legitimized by a few political leaders. More shocking, such officers are celebrated by self-styled, non-partisan 'intelligentsia' in places like Gujarat; ironically for 'peace' and 'security'." In the following sections we are giving the overview of the conditions of Muslims which would provide some support to the assertions of Justice Vithyathil and Ghanshyam Shah.

The Numerical Profile of Indian Muslims

Muslims are surely a minority in the context of a huge Indian majority but the significant fact is that despite being a minority, the combined strength of Muslims in India is more than the strength of several European countries. Among the Muslims of the world they are the largest, exceeded only by Indonesia and Pakistan and close to the population of Bangladesh. After partition, their population came down from 25% to merely 10% as they were reduced to 47 million out of 439 million total population after the division of the country. Muslims are still the second largest religious group in India and thus the largest religious minority. According to 2001 Census, Muslims are over 138 million out of 1028.6 million or they constitute 13.4% of total population. Presently, they are nearly 150 million. Many unofficial estimates claim that Muslims range around 20%. It is generally alleged by Muslims that they have been shown less than what they are by purposely discounting their number by some of the vested census enumerators. Certain irresponsible and fanatic anti-Muslim groups generally claim that Muslim population has reached 30%. Incidentally, Muslims are not a homogeneous class as generally perceived by many despite their religious equality. They too have castes, sub-castes and classes. During 2004-05, Muslim Scheduled Castes constituted 0.8%, Muslim Scheduled Tribes 0.5%, Muslim Other Backward Castes 39.2% and Muslim Higher Castes 59.5% of total Muslim population which is revealed from Table 1.1.

Table 1.1: Distribution of Population of each Religion by Caste Categories

Religion/Caste	SCs	STs	OBCS	Others	All
Hindu	22.2	9.1	42.8	26.0	100
Muslim	0.8	0.5	39.2	59.5	100
Christians	9.0	32.8	24.8	33.3	100
Sikhs	30.7	0.9	22.4	46.1	100
Jains	0.0	2.6	3.0	94.3	100
Buddhists	89.5	7.4	0.4	2.7	100
Zoroastrians	0.0	15.9	13.7	70.4	100
Others	2.6	82.5	6.2	8.7	100
Total	**19.7**	**8.5**	**41.1**	**30.8**	**100**

Source: Sachar Committee Report, Table 1.2

However, if we look as a whole towards the Muslims irrespective of their castes and classes, we find that most of them fall within the backward segments of the society. As per 2001 Census, 30.74 million Muslims live in Uttar Pradesh followed by 20.24 million in West Bengal, 13.72 million in Bihar, 10.27 million in Maharashtra, 8.24 million in Assam, 7.86 million in Kerala, 6.99 million in Andhra Pradesh, 6.79 million in Jammu and Kashmir and 6.46 million in Karnataka. There are 4.79 million Muslims in Rajasthan, 4.59 million in Gujarat, 3.84 million in Madhya Pradesh and 3.47 million in Tamil Nadu. Incidentally, their number is merely 1.62 million, 1.22 million 1.01 million, 076 million, 0.41 million and 0.38 million in Delhi, Haryana, Uttrakhand, Orissa, Chhattisgarh and Punjab respectively. In percentage terms, 67.0% Muslims live in Jammu and Kashmir, 30.9% in Assam, 25.2% in West Bengal, 24.7% in Kerala, 18.5% in Uttar Pradesh, 16.5% in Bihar, 13.8% in Jharkhand, 12.2% in Karnataka, 11.9% in Uttaranchal, 11.7% in Delhi, 10.6% in Maharashtra, 9.2% in Andhra Pradesh, 8.5% in Rajasthan, 6.4% in Madhya Pradesh, 5.8% in Haryana and 5.6% in Tamil Nadu. Their percentages in Orissa, Chhattisgarh and Punjab are only 2.1%, 2.0% and 1.6% respectively. According to 2001 Census in 13 districts of Uttar Pradesh, 12 districts of West Bengal, 8 districts of Bihar, 4 districts of Jammu and Kashmir, 3 districts of Maharashtra, 3 districts of Assam and one district each of Andhra Pradesh, Gujarat and Karnataka, the Muslim population ranges between 29.9% to 98% of the total population of those districts. Apart from these fifty highly concentrated Muslim districts, there are 22 districts where the Muslim population varies between 37,35,380 to 10,17,495. Likewise, there are 17 districts where the population ranges between 9,77,943 to 7,03,596. Similarly, there are 31 districts where the population fluctuates between 6,96,126 to 5,15,124. In the same way, there are 30 districts where Muslim population is found between 4,97,516 to 3,83,204. Not only this, 35.7% Muslims live in urban areas and 64.3% in rural areas and they are found in every important activity of the country. It is the beauty of Indian Muslims that the entire landscape from Kashmir to Kanyakumari is dotted with mosques, sufi shrines, makatibs and madarsas. The call for prayer can be heard from Amritsar to Sunderbans. Muharram is observed with solemnity by Hindus, Muslims, Shias and Sunnis in Lucknow, Aligarh, Jodhpur, Patna, Kolkata, Indore, Mumbai, Chennai and many other cities of the country. Hindus and Muslims relish Diwali, Holi and Eid festivals with love and compassion and the sweet smell of Sufi Islam and the fragrance of Hindu saints can be felt from Himalaya to Indian Ocean. The men, women, children and old visit Taj Mahal, Red Fort, Charminar, Imambaras, Humayun Tomb and Jama Masjid with grace and glamour. It is the misfortune of Muslims that despite their past glory being intact they are passing into the worst phase of their history.

Muslims are proud of being Indians. They resemble with other Indians as water resembles with water. Being Indians they are the integral part of the country's tolerant and progressive civilization, though they have some social, cultural and religious distinctiveness being the followers of Islam. Their peaceful nature and meekness is reflected in the fact that since long ordinary and elite Muslims have distanced themselves from the destructive, terrorist and disruptive activities when similar acts were widely prevalent in a few Muslim and non-Muslim countries. Despite the terrorist assaults, on Jama Masjid Delhi, Mecca Masjid Hyderabad, Dargah Ajmer Sharif and many mosques in Malegaon and others which were affected by the unruly and fanatic elements from among the adversaries of Islam with the clear intention of inflaming communal feelings not a single case of rioting was noticed from any part of the country. Muslims showed the same maturity which was shown by the majority community in the wake of terrorist attacks on Raghu Nath temple, Akshardham temple and in various sensitive places in Varanasi, Delhi, Jaipur, Ahmedabad and Mumbai. India is perhaps the lone country where as many as 6000 Muslim theologians from various parts of the country gathered at Hyderabad and expressed their anguish and disgust and showed their unqualified support against terrorism. There is probably no country elsewhere in the world where ulemas or religious heads and the educated, illiterates, the rich and poor, the high and the low as well as all segments of Muslims stood against terrorism on such a large scale. Indians are proud of the diversity which is prevalent in the country among various segments of the society. The uniqueness among various sections of the society including that of Muslims has evolved over centuries. It was because of the slow-stretched out process spread over centuries that explains the persistence of a wide spectrum of Islamic, pre-Islamic and even anti-Islamic customs, ceremonies and values among Indian Muslims. As long as 1780s, Muslims celebrated Eid, Diwali and Holi along with their Hindu brothers. Much more significant is the fact that militancy has never found a strong civil support among Muslims at any stage of their historical development. The commendable development is that the new generation of Muslims is coming out of the siege mentality with which the older generation had lived for long. It does not have any guilt conscience. It has its own agenda for growth and development. It is ready to fight for its own constitutional rights in the atmosphere of peaceful co-existence. The seeping realization that peace, progress and prosperity lies in reaching out to other communities and segments rather than sulking in isolation or living in ghettos auger well for both Hindus and Muslims as well as for the welfare and the well-being of the whole country. The laudable aspect is that the perception of the new generation from among the majority community towards the young generation of Muslims is changing fast. They do not consider Muslims as aliens and totally responsible for the partition of the country. They do not doubt their integrity and have soft corner for their genuine demands. They want to bring Muslims within the main stream without destroying their social, cultural and religious identities. In spite of all these healthy developments, one thing is certain that Muslims are lagging in all the spheres some of which are being cursorily discussed in the following sections.

Educational Backwardness

The process of introspection is certainly on and many Muslim intellectuals and the meaningful and enlightened non-

Muslims as well as several right-thinking politicians and statesmen from various segments of Indian society too are worried due to the miserable and pathetic conditions of Muslims. Education is the main source of empowerment and enlightenment. Through proper and meaningful education, we can round the sharp corners of one's personality. It is through education that cultural handicaps are toned up and work ethics is sharpened, work culture is developed and transcendental perception for introspection is created among people. Without education one is dumb, deaf and blind. Unfortunately, Muslims have forgotten the significance of education. They consider it merely as the source of getting bread and butter but fail to realize that it leads both to piety and prosperity. The Holy Book asks them to ponder over the created process with a view to acquire knowledge about the creation and the Creator. The Holy Prophet told them to acquire knowledge even if they had to go to China. However, the figures show that educationally Muslims lag behind the Scheduled Castes, Scheduled Tribes, other minorities, higher castes and others. If we look into the figures of last fifty years we find that they have trailed behind many sections of Indian society in educational field. For instance, in 1948 the percentage of Muslims who completed at least primary school was 18.2 compared to 8.8 for SCs/STs and 27.8 for all others. However, after 53 years the percentage for Muslims in 2001 was 60.9 compared to 61.4 for SCs/STs and 79.3 for all others. Likewise, the percentages of urban males and rural males which were 43.4 and 21.8 in 1948 compared to 33.4 and 13.1 for SCs/STs and 66.7 and 31.6 for all others reached to the levels of 71.3 and 58.9 in 2001 compared to 80.2 and 66.1 for SCs/STs and 89.6 and 80.8 for all others. The condition of Muslim women too is also highly unsatisfactory. The percentage of Muslim urban and rural females who completed at least primary school in 1948 was 13.9 and 4.0 compared to 7.5 and 1.6 for SCs/STs and 34.1 and 7.4 for all others. The same reached the levels of 70.9% and 47.8% in 2001 as contrasted to 74.8% and 47.0% for SCs/STs and 88.1% and 67.6% for all others. The Technical Note covering age specific education levels into Time Trends also shows that Muslims are inferior to all others and they lag behind the SCs/STs in the field of primary education.

Technical Note

Table 1.2: Distribution of Population Completing at least Primary Education by Religion

Age Group	Muslim	SCs/STs	All others
14-15	57.8	60.1	77.6
16-17	60.9	61.4	79.3
18-19	58.4	55.9	75.5
20-24	54.7	49.0	71.4
25-29	47.3	40.2	64.7
30-34	41.0	32.2	59.0
35-59	33.6	23.1	50.4
60+	18.2	8.8	27.8

Source: Sachar Committee Report, Table 4.2

In the same way, the percentage of Muslims who completed at least middle school was 8.6 in 1948 compared to 3.8 for the SCs/STs and 15.7 for all others. After more than fifty years, 40.5% Muslims had completed at least middle school up to 2001 compared to 41.3% SCs/STs and 62.7% for all others. The position of urban and rural Muslim males and urban and rural Muslim females too was disgusting. The percentages for urban and rural Muslim males were 25.5 and 9.4 compared to 19.2 and 5.1 for SCs/STs and 50.3 and 15.2 for all others which in 2001 reached to 49.6 and 37.3 for Muslims, 59.8 and 43.7 for SCs/STs and 76.7 and 62.0 for others respectively. Similarly, in 1953 nearly 5.45% Muslims in West Bengal, Kerala, UP, Bihar, Jharkhand, Karnataka, Maharashtra, AP, Gujarat, MP and Tamil Nadu had completed at least metrics compared to 2.1% SCs/STs and 11.0% all others but after forty eight years their percentage in 2001 reached to the level of 23.9 compared to 21.1 for SCs/STs and 42.5 for others. The urban and rural Muslim males lagged behind SCs/STs during this period for their percentages which were 18.3 and 5.0 in 1953 compared to 12.8 and 2.6 for SCs/STs, reached to 36.1 and 22.0 in 2001 compared to 42.1 and 24.5 for SCs/STs.

Two separate studies conducted by UGC based on NSSO data of the 61st round during 2004-05 revealed that Muslim OBCs with 6.73% Gross Enrolment Ratio (GER) were far behind Hindu STs with 6.95%, Hindu SCs with 7.37%, Hindu OBCs with 10.45%, Christian STs with 11.14% and Christian SCs with 23.53% Gross Enrolment Ratios. Likewise, the upper Caste Muslims with 8.27% GER were far behind Hindu High Castes with 24.28%, Christians with 25.19% and Sikhs with 17.81% GER. In the same way, the Muslim OBC males with 8.22% Gross Enrolment Ratio were lagging behind Hindu ST males with 8.83%, Hindu SCs with 9.0%, Hindu OBCs with 12.89%,Christian STs with 8.76% and Christian SCs with 11.89% GER. The condition of Muslim OBC females was also not satisfactory. They with GER 5.16% were behind Hindu SCs with 5.55%, Hindu OBCs with 7.78%, Christian STs with 13.11% and Christian SCs with 32.59% Gross Enrolment Ratios. Similarly, if we analyze the condition of Muslim males and females in the urban and rural areas we find that they are trailing behind in various segments of the society. For instance, the urban Muslim male OBCs with 9.68% Gross Enrolment Ratio were lagging behind Hindu STs with 26.08%, Hindu SCs with 15.96%, Hindu OBCs with 22.64%, Christian STs with 33.52%, Christian SCs with 20.8% GER. In the same way, the upper caste Muslims with GER 12.6% in urban areas were trailing behind in Hindu urban upper castes with 37.69%, Christians urban STs with 33.52% and Christian urban SCs with 20.8%GER. In urban areas the non-SC Sikh women were on the top with 39.69% GER followed by High Caste Hindus with 37.69%, Hindu OBCs with 17.86%, ST Hindus with 16% and Muslim females at the bottom with 12.6% Gross Enrolment Ratio. The urban Muslim females were hard hit as their GER was 5.02% compared to 15.8% for Hindu STs, 10.72% Hindu SCs, 17.86% Hindu OBCs, 46.7% Christian STCs and 25.89% Christian SCs. Actually, the Christians, Hindus and Sikhs were far ahead of Muslims in matters of Gross Enrolment Ratio. Even Christian SCs and STs were far superior to Muslims in the area of higher education. The Census data 2001 suggests that there were 23.9 lakh Muslim graduates and 2.7 lakh Muslim Diploma and

Certificate holders compared to 30.8 lakh and 4.1 lakh SCs/STs, and 32.2 lakh and 33.7 lakh all others. Likewise, the distribution across socio-religious communities revealed that there were 6.3% graduates and 6.8% diploma and certificate holders among Muslims compared to 8.2% and 10.2% for SCs/STs and 85.5% and 83.0% for all others. The younger generation of SCs/STs in the age group 6-17 was more literate compared to Muslims in 2004-05. The percentage of population completing at least primary education in the age groups 14-15 and 16-17 was 57.8 and 60.9 among Muslims compared to 60.1 and 61.4 for SCs/STs and 77.6 and 79.3 in all others. Thus, Muslims who were far ahead of SCs/STs in 1948 and 1953 made little progress in the field of education and lagged behind even the SCs/STs after a period of nearly half a century.

The current educational condition of Muslims is highly precarious. According to the 2001 Census, the literacy rate among Muslims was below the national average. The literacy gap between the Muslims and the general average was greater in urban areas and among women across the country. Muslims' lack of interest in education is reflected in their lower levels of admissions and the lower mean years of schooling for as many as 25% Muslim children in the 6-14 age group have either dropped out or have not seen the portals of learning. Since most of the Muslim children come from the poor and illiterate families, the drop out rates among Muslim children is highest at primary, middle and higher secondary levels compared to other socio-religious communities.

The condition of Muslims at higher secondary, graduation and post-graduation levels and in the fields of engineering, technology, management and medical fields too is frustrating. Only 4% under-graduates and 2% post-graduates are Muslims. The condition of Muslims with reference to acquiring degrees, diplomas and certificates is miserable which is revealed from Table 1.3.

Table 1.3: Graduates and Diploma Holders by SRCs (Census 2001)

SRCs	Number (in Lakhs)		Percentage of 20 years + Population		Distribution across SRCs	
	Graduates	Diploma and Certificate	Graduates	Diploma and Certificate	Graduates	Diploma and Certificate
Total	376.7	40.5	6.7	0.7	100	100
Muslims	23.9	2.7	3.6	0.4	6.3	6.8
SCs/STs	30.8	4.1	2.4	0.3	8.2	10.2
All others	322	33.7	8.8	0.9	85.5	83.0

Source: Sachar Committee Report, Table 4.2

Table reveals that Muslim graduates and diploma and certificate holders were merely 23.9 lakhs and 2.7 lakhs or 6.3% and 6.8% compared to 30.8 lakhs and 4.1 lakhs or 8.2% and 10.2% SCs/STs and 322 lakhs and 33.7 lakhs or 85.5% and 83.0% all others respectively. The probability of a Muslim completing his graduation is lowest among all the socio-religious classes. Unemployment rates among Muslim graduates too is highest compared to other castes. The irony of fate is that the disparity in acquiring the graduate degrees since 1970 in urban areas is widening between Muslims and others. Besides, the gap between Muslims and others is also increasing with the increase in the level of education. There are very few Muslims in IIMs, IITs and in the areas of super-specialties. Their attainment across various socio-religious communities is inferior compared to the upper castes, OBCs and other minorities and even to SCs/STs in many segments. The disheartening fact is that over years after independence the expansion of the educational opportunities have led to divergence of attainment levels rather than convergence between Muslims and others. Muslims have not benefited even from Jawahar Navodaya Vidyalayas and similar other schemes. One factor is clearly visible that due to affirmative action and positive discrimination SCs/STs and OBCs have made tremendous progress but the current generation of Muslims despite some progress here and there has lagged behind in the race of education due to their own lethargy as well as the lack of pro-active action on the part of the governing structures.

It would not be out of place to mention here that India is booming in knowledge sector. India has the third largest higher education system in the world next only to China and the USA. By the end of 2003 nearly 90 per cent of India's rural population had primary school within the distance of 1 km and 84 per cent population had upper primary schools within 3 km of their residence and the gross enrolment ratio in primary education between 1991 and 2003 had risen from 82 per cent to 95 per cent and in upper primary education from 54 per cent to 61 per cent which was commendable. According to the economist Jandhyala B.G. Tilak, the contribution of higher education to GDP growth in India's post-reform period remained between 27 to 30 per cent. India had nearly 311 universities and 15,600 colleges as of 2004. Of the 10.5 million students attending Indian universities 88.9 per cent enrolled for under-graduate programmes and 9.4 per cent for post-graduate degrees. India produces about 2.5 million graduates and 3,50,000 engineers every year. India's contribution in producing university graduates is 1.5 times the size of China and twice as large as that of the USA. India is the largest producer of engineers and the scientists in the world. The number of degrees awarded by various educational institutions in India as well as the engineering colleges increased by 70 per cent and 90 per cent respectively between 1990 and 2004. It is lamentable that despite this favourable image of India in the education sector Muslims are living within the education-shadow areas. There are few takers of reservation for Muslims in educational institutions. The sympathizers of Muslims from among the majority community contend that reservation is of no use for Muslims as it would absorb merely 2,000 students in IITs and IIMs and it would not solve the problem of 150 million disadvantaged sections of the society. In their opinion, the government should focus on primary education and it should spend more resources on enhancing the performance of the low performers without diluting the performance standards in higher education. They also favour the creation of a large number of preparatory institutions for such students so that the weak students from disadvantaged backgrounds may be provided extra coaching, nutrition and financial support so that they may become competition worthy. The suggestion is certainly praiseworthy but Muslims generally contend why two different sets of standards are suggested for similarly situated two types of Indians. Why Muslims are denied the privilege of reservation when SCs/STs and Backward Castes were uplifted through affirmative and positive discrimination rather than through preparatory and simulative efforts. In their opinion such suggestions are merely the ploy to keep Muslims backward.

Cultural Suffocation

We should keep this fact in mind that individually and collectively we are what our culture is and what our values are since we are governed by our culture and value system. Culture is mainly about our belief system, our priorities in life, things that we relish, things that we detest, how we behave, how we spend our time, money and resources and how we interact with others and what are our perceptions about life and death. Values shape our behaviour pattern and enhance hope, confidence, enthusiasm and commitment. They bring joy and sorrow and prompt us for hard work, discipline, honesty and integrity and generate concern for fellow beings and others. Societies and the communities survive as long as their culture and the value system survive. The moment their culture and values are throttled, the groups and individuals too lose their uniqueness and the identity. They become rolling stones which gather no moss. It is highly regrettable that many Muslims strongly feel that their cultural identity is in crisis. They have become more or less culturally bankrupt. They have a constant feeling that they are culturally suffocating for they have lost much of their elitist qualities, value-based etiquettes, cultural grace and dignified glamour. The fluency of Urdu, the decency of their dress code and the sharpness of their intellect are missing. Their distinctiveness in matters of communication skill, customs, traditions, dress, address, architecture, cultural connotations is the matters of the past. They lament that Islam and Islamic traditions which are the source of Muslim culture are at receivers end. Unfortunately, after 9 September 2001 till 25/26 November 2008 whatever happened in the world and

India in the name of terrorism and Jihad tarnished the image of Muslims and Islam. Many non-Muslims not only began to blame the whole Muslim community for the terrorist activities, they did not spare Islam and its teachings from the blame of terrorism.

Several Muslims believe that their unique identity and the religious distinctiveness seem to be in peril. Very few people relish seeing them in skull caps, lungis, sherwanis, shirts and trousers and their ladies are generally not looked with grace in their veils and the burqas. Likewise, in religious field their beards and the marks of prostrations on their foreheads are seldom appreciated by some of the reactionary cadre of Indian society. The Muslim caps, tehmads, kurta pajamas, and beards and the veils of Muslim women seem to have become the symbols of hatred, aversion and even danger for several non-Muslims in India and abroad. Many people in India and elsewhere have come openly against covering the heads and face by Muslim women forgetting the fact that parada or hijab is an integral part of Islam. Those Muslim women who believe in Islamic principles and values and who wish to adhere to them cannot discard the veil system in the name of human rights and empowerment of women in the same way as Muslim society cannot accept sexual misadventures between the same sexes as the landmark of freedom of sexes. It is quite interesting to note that many young and highly educated Muslim women have voluntarily covered their heads and bodies and have become practicing good women without any compulsion from the side of their elders merely due to the constant bullying and criticism of Islamic veil system and the prevailing nudity in various sections of the society. Likewise, many young and educated Muslim youths too have kept beards and they are following Islamic principles despite no encouragement or pressure from their families. It is disheartening to know that in matters of address and communication, Muslims have lost much of the soft and sweet smell of their mother tongue due to step-motherly treatment to Urdu. They are mostly recognized by their Urdu slant which is the mixture of Urdu, Hindi, Persian and Arabic. Similarly, their social distinctiveness which was marked by their cultural sophistication is now marked by their marriage customs, ethos, traditions and ceremonies. Ironically, some political parties and individuals and organizations give the impression as if they do not relish their uniqueness. Many a time they behave in such a manner as if they want to abolish their identities and individualities by abolishing their culture, customs and even their personal law which provides them some leverage in matters of marriages, divorces, maintenance, bequeaths and will and inheritance. Their mosques, mazars, graveyards and madrasas which provide them religious distinctiveness are often the targets of several anti-social elements. Many Muslims generally hesitate in expressing their free and frank opinions on certain vital national and international issues for they fear that they might be bracketed differently and might not be condoned as the people of the majority community are generally condoned for expressing their similar views on such matters in much stronger words. Likewise, it is alleged that sometimes certain eminent artists and skillful Muslims very often face public ire unnecessarily for their unique innovations and bold adventures in arts and crafts when their counterparts in majority community are usually forgiven and ignored for similar kinds of misadventures. Similarly, there are many businessmen, professionals and artists and traders who often complain about the excesses by the income-tax and other government departments. Some of them even consider such excesses as the ploy to dent their progress and development. In the same way, there are many meaningful Muslims who due to occupying important positions or being in the limelight very often lead a very cautious life for many of them fear that they are being watched by the state agencies. It is generally said by many Muslims that there are many government officials who claim that they had appointed larger number of Muslims during their tenure as government officials since they considered them capable and deserving. However, they had to face the music for their sound decision as the charge of communalism was imposed upon them for appointing larger number of Muslims. They lamented that when a non-Muslim appointed practically 100 per cent non-Muslims or majority of them, he was not questioned but if a Muslim did it he was caught. Over and above this, those who have confronted the police departments are generally very critical of the partisan behavior of the police personnels with reference to the petty criminals and the ordinary civilians. Many a time the media blows the news pertaining to certain lapses of law and order by a few distinguished Muslims out of proportions despite the fact that every day such incidents take place in the country as a routine matter. Mostly Muslims especially those who are poor and resourceless generally consider themselves strangers in government offices due to the near absence of Muslim officers, clerks and peons. Such perceived biases like the discriminations in educational institutions, government offices, health-care centres and other spheres as well as the non-willingness on the part of the landlords in respect of renting houses to Muslim tenants in non-Muslim areas are matters which only the wearers know where the shoes pinch. Several meaningful Muslims are worried due to the tag of appeasement and doubting their loyalty and integrity despite the fact that many of them are more loyal than the king. Many Muslims often complain that the police and the security agencies often pick some men with caps and beards on slightest provocation and unnecessarily harass them at their end. Several women folk in veils are sometimes treated disgustfully. Over and above this, it is stated that their contribution from history books and national mainstream is being systematically scratched and they are being projected as aliens and invaders. The cases of conceived and concealed discriminations are seldom highlighted by the Muslim intelligentsia due to the perceived fear of adverse reactions from the side of the state or civil society. Mostly they are discussed in drawing rooms or in private conversations. Sometimes the Urdu Press exposes such cases but rarely as a consequences of which the countrymen and the responsible people of the society who are opinion makers seldom know about them and they continue unabated. The author has tried to put before the general public what most of the Muslims feel and believe so that a solution may be found out. However, it is heartening to note that there are innumerable Indian citizens across party or religious lines who come openly in support of such Muslim men and women who are unnecessarily targeted being Muslims. They give befitting reply to the reactionary forces which helps Muslims to see the light at the end of the tunnel.

Muslims are convinced that Urdu which was the source of Muslim culture is a liability for Muslims. Its knowledge is practically of no use to them for through Urdu medium education one can neither get job nor earn his livelihood. Though the three language formula in the Hindi speaking states was perhaps meant to introduce Urdu, yet instead of Urdu we find that Hindi, Sanskrit and English are being taught in schools with the result that Muslim students do not know ABC of Urdu. There are very few Urdu dailies and magazines and there are very few buyers of Urdu books, consequently Urdu is vanishing from the scene. The Central Government and several State Governments have opened Urdu academies some of which are working nicely but many of them seem to be Shabby and need improvement. Save appointing a few Muslims and non-Muslims as chairmen, giving awards to some Urdu writers, conducting functions and publishing a few Urdu books these institutions appear to be doing practically too little for the promotion of Urdu. Wherever Urdu has been declared as the second language, the condition of Urdu is miserable. Several Urdu medium schools are without Urdu teachers and wherever Urdu teachers have been appointed, they are not Urdu-knowing persons. It is alleged that many vacancies of Urdu teachers have been filled by other categories of people. Urdu is somewhat surviving because of mushaeras, cinemas, gazhal and qawwalis. The misfortune of Muslim community is that Muslim children do not know Urdu hence they cannot perceive Islam and Islamic ideology because most of the Islamic literature has been preserved mostly through the medium of Urdu. Muslim children read Hindi literature and communicate with their parents in Hindi rather than Urdu. They are more conversant with Hindu culture than their own. The Hindu culture is affecting the conducts, behaviour patterns and ways of living of many Muslim students. Besides, the communal content of many school textbooks, the hostile atmosphere in some of the institutions for Muslims and projecting Muslim rulers as the invaders and the destroyers of Hindu religious places put Muslim students in odd positions and they begin to abhor the modern educational institutions. The frequency of communal riots across the country has torn them into pieces. They cannot dare to attend modern schools situated in predominantly Hindu areas due to the fear of communal clash. They have become the victims of inferiority complex for they mostly find Muslims depicted with negative contribution in their textbooks and they seldom find any Muslim worth mentioning in the list of enlightened, far-sighted and geniuses. Madrasas which provide them Islamic education have been blamed as the terrorist centres without any substantial proofs. The media and press has created the impression among the general masses as if all school going Muslim children go to Madrasas when the fact is that very few children among school going age go to Madrasas. Several Muslims believe that concerted efforts are being made even from the side of some of the governments to dilute Muslims' cultural identity by diluting the identity of Madrasas which are the fountains of Islamic culture. Besides, the condition of minority institutions is pitiable. Muslims find several obstacles in establishing and running schools and colleges. First of all they do not possess enough funds to buy the land and to establish the necessary infrastructure for schools and other institutions. Secondly, if they manage these facilities any how, they face bottlenecks and hurdles in getting recognition. Muslim University, Aligarh despite being a minority university has been declared as a national institution by law courts and the fate of Jamia Millia Islamia is also hanging in balance. Muslims believe that several attempts are being made to merge Muslim culture in the majority mainstream. The destruction of Babri Masjid and the fear of demolition of a few more mosques and attempts by some right-leaning historians to link some of the historical Muslim monuments with Hindu rulers are a cause of great concern for Muslims. Over and above this, some of the media which is owned and managed by the vested interests is playing havoc. It is highlighting and glorifying the Muslim batters and many Indian Muslims with atheistic and agnostic tendencies.

Besides, many issues like triple talaq, gender inequality, Fatwas, utterances of a few irresponsible Muslims which have adverse bearings upon Hindus are often blown out of proportions. It is highly frustrating to note that within sixty years Muslims have lost much of their cultural penetration, and as things are moving if positive and affirmative steps are not taken Muslims would soon resemble with all others as apples resembles with apples and bananas with bananas.

Social Isolation

Several Muslims especially the poor lot and the marginalized sections of Muslim community in India are generally isolated and neglected. Due to fear psychosis and hate campaign released against them by some of the vested interests many Muslims across the country have sought shelter from mixed localities to Muslim-dominated zones both in the rural and urban areas. After 1971 many educated Muslims had started moving out of the congested Muslim localities. They bought houses in predominantly Hindu colonies which were neat and clean and where educated and enlightened Hindus especially the government officials, businessmen and others lived. They found the space congenial and comfortable. The locals also came to know about them and a sense of belonging developed between them. Muslims benefitted a lot from their Hindu counterparts for they were in a better position to help them. Having seen the favourable climate in such localities many educated Muslims started moving towards the mixed localities in large numbers since they were previously feeling uncomfortable in ghettos. However, this was not relished by the anti-social elements. Thus, whenever any communal riot took place after 1971 the houses of Muslims in mixed areas were marked by the outsiders who were mostly hardened criminals. Despite the fullest support and all efforts of the saner Hindu neighbours they could not save some of the losses of their Muslim brothers. As soon as they came to know of any such eventualities they informed the Muslim neighbours, gave them shelter and even kept their valuables with them. However, since they had no control on the outsiders, they could not do much against the hooligans who were in large numbers and were bent upon violence and bloodshed. Fearing their safety in the mixed areas, the Muslims again reverted back to the Muslim congested areas. This made them the easy prey of the neglect by panchayats, municipal corporations and the government and semi-government agencies. One can see the miserable condition of Muslim areas even today. Depleted roads, poor lighting, water-logging, heaps of dirt and foul smell are the characteristic hallmarks of those areas where poor and depressed Muslims reside. Muslim areas are highly deficient in matters of civic amenities, infrastructural support, educational, medical and health facilities. On the contrary, it is alleged that they are highly taxed areas and have concentration of police posts and paramilitary organizations. Muslims are bitter about the government's so-called step-brotherly treatment towards the minorities. They contend that the local MLAs, MPs and the government officials ignored the development of Muslim areas and diverted the development funds to majority dominated localities for most of the MLAs and MPs belonged to the majority community. Undoubtedly, there are marked differences in matters of availability, accessibility and the utilization of social and physical facilities across various socio-religious communities but one thing is certain that Muslims are the most deprived lot. There is a clear and significant inverse correlationship between the proportion of Muslim population and the availability of infrastructural and other facilities. Other things being equal, the social and physical amenities decreased with the increase in the proportion of Muslim population. Generally, the Muslim concentrated towns including the important town of Aligarh fall in the neglected areas. Despite the existence of Muslim University, Aligarh and Aligarh being historically and socio-politically significant town, the area is one of the most neglected and dirtiest. Neither the Central Government has done any thing substantial for the development of Aligarh nor has the UP Government done anything significant for the improvement of the town. The towns like Agra and Meerut have been developed and linked with Delhi and Noida but Aligarh advertently or inadvertently has been left neglected due to the reasons best known to the governing structure. It has neither better road connections nor sanitation facilities nor drainage facilities. One can see heaps of dirt accumulating on road sides and worst type of Muslim slums in the vicinity of the city. More or less the same is the condition of all towns with substantial Muslim population. Similarly, the Muslim community is without any substantial access to basic amenities like education, medical, post and telegraph, pucca approach roads, bus stops, housing, sanitation, electricity, portable water and fuel for domestic purposes across the country. In urban and rural areas, the proportion of Muslim households living in pucca houses is much lower than the national average. More than half of the Muslim households throughout the country lack access to toilet facilities; this proportion is higher in rural areas. Muslims and the SCs/STs live in the least electrified villages. As their share decreases, the village electrification increases with the increase in the proportion of the Hindu general category. The use of electricity by Muslims is much lower than the all-India average. Ironically, in Muslim-dominated villages, the proportion of villages with no electricity increases as the size of the village falls and the share of Muslims rises. Muslims have least access to potable water compared to other socio-religious communities. Likewise, the use of modern fuel like LPG, electricity and kerosene for cooking purposes decreases as the share of Muslims increases and the villages become bigger in size. The survey conducted in South Indian States of Karnataka, Andhra Pradesh and Tamil Nadu showed only marginal deprivation in the Muslim-concentrated areas. However, the study conducted in the context of the Muslim-concentrated localities in Lucknow and its surrounding areas shows that compared to Muslim majority areas the areas inhabited by few Muslims have better quality of roads, sewage and drainage disposal system, sanitation and water supply. One often finds a school and a health centre in these areas which are absent in Muslim-dominated localities. Not only this, even the slums in Hindu-concentrated areas with little Muslim population were better equipped in matters of roads, sewage, drainage and water supply. As a general rule one can conclude that the condition of Muslims in matters of access to social and infrastructural facilities is somewhat comparable to Hindu OBCs and marginally better than SCs/STs but certainly worse than Hindu high castes, creamy layers of OBCs and STs and other minorities.

Table 1.4 shows the actual number of villages of different sizes with Muslim concentration lacking specified physical and social facilities.

Table 1.4: Number of Villages without Basic Facilities, All India 2000

Facilities	Small (Less than 1000 Population			Medium (1000-2000 Population)			Large (More than 2000 Population)		
	Within Muslim Population Share of								
	<9%	10-39%	40%+	<9%	10-39%	40%+	<9%	10-39%	40%+
	All India								
Education	44542	4676	4240	3667	1186	1078	906	423	382
Medical	193640	13051	11193	56813	9435	7130	18181	6191	4680
Post Office	168088	11670	11013	43838	7959	7111	11194	4398	4448
Bus Stop	172048	12410	10547	53199	10336	7898	22519	8859	6717
Proper Approach Road	133063	8496	7910	34124	5749	4970	10627	3644	3502
Number of Villages in the respective category	242549	16525	13840	103174	15648	11149	68537	18895	11763
% of Population (All)	87.7	6.8	5.5	23.2	2.6	74.2	26.7	3.3	70.0
% of Muslim Population	8.8	23.3	67.9	13.8	7.4	78.9	14.9	8.2	76.8

Source: Sachar Committee Report, Table 7.1

Table shows the actual number of villages of different sizes with Muslim concentration lacking specified physical and social facilities. A study of smaller, medium and larger villages in Assam, Bihar, Uttar Pradesh and West Bengal shows that in West Bengal where Muslims are 40%+ in villages with less than 1000 population, 827 villages are without schools, 1456 villages without medical facilities, 1946 villages without post offices, 1905 villages without bus stops and 1504 villages without proper approach roads. In medium sized villages with population ranging between 1000 to 2000 and with Muslim population 40%+, 236 villages are without schools, 965 without medical facilities, 1504 without post offices, 1605 without bus stops and 1109 without approach roads. As against this, in the larger villages with more than 40%+ population, 70 villages are without schools, 849 without medical facilities, 1272 without post offices, 1846 without bus stops and 1124 without approach roads. In the same way in Uttar Pradesh 2400 villages in smaller villages with 10 to 39% Muslim population were without schools, 4844 without medical facilities, 4543 without post offices, 5556 without bus stops and 2853 without proper approach roads. Such villages with 10 to 39% Muslim population in different categories in medium and larger villages were 674, 3988, 3485, 5487 and 2149 and 198, 2365, 1702, 4253 and 931 respectively. The position of Bihar is not much different. In Bihar there are 729 villages in smaller villages with 40%+ Muslim population without schools, 1329 without medical facilities, 1313 without post offices, 1371 without bus stops and 1098 without proper approach roads. These villages in medium and larger villages with 40%+ population in different categories are 253, 1091, 1036, 1148 and 869 and 100, 1208, 910, 1386 and 866 respectively. The situation in Assam seems to be slightly better for only 233 villages in smaller areas with less than 1000 population are without schools, 11646 without medical facilities, 1605 without post offices, 1278 without bus stops and 1093 without proper approach roads. With 40%+ Muslim population in the medium villages with population ranging between 1000 and 2000, there are 253, 1091, 1036, 1148 and 869 without schools, medical facilities, post offices, bus stops and proper approach roads respectively. Whereas the villages with more than 2000 population and with 40%+ Muslim population there are 8 villages, without medical facilities, 698 villages, without post offices, 767 villages, without bus stops and 652 villages without approach roads.

The ghettos have affected Muslims in several ways. Their women folk cannot dare to go beyond their localities to seek education, health care and employment. Parents do not send their girls to schools beyond their safe neighbourhood. Even they hesitate to send their sons to far off places due to the fear of communal riots and prefer to send them in Madrasas or minority ill-equipped schools within their vicinities. It is unfortunate that after communal riots and the spread in terrorism Muslims were compelled to leave their places where they were living for centuries. This has affected their livelihood and employability. They were doubly sufferers for when they moved from insecure areas where there were chances of frequent communal clashes, they got little value by the distress sale of their properties in such areas and they had to pay a price higher than the average in the Muslim concentrated areas due to increased demand for the properties in such areas. Needless to say that Hindus too do not want to live in Muslim dominated areas. They too prefer to live in Hindu concentrated areas. Those who were living within the communally sensitive zones have migrated to safe places. After bomb blasts in important cities of India even the housing societies dissuade the Muslims to acquire houses in predominantly Hindu vicinities. The ghettos have resulted in isolated Hindu and Muslim localities across the country which is not good for the health of the country. The seclusion between Muslims and Hindus has created mistrust and fears about each others. Many people do not dare to go to each others congested localities. Besides, the composite and tolerant culture which is created through peaceful co-existence is missing. Seclusion is giving way to exclusive and separatist culture which is not good for the health of the country.

Political Marginalization of Indian Muslims

Muslims feel that they are politically divided and marginalized. Despite being a force to reckon with they have no say in the political game plan of the country. They have been living in fear and a sense of guilt for the last sixty years. Politicians have been faithfully feeding them with their choicest diet of fear by showing the horror of right wing extremist parties and in return reaping their harvest cheaply and conveniently in the form of votes. They are the only people who seldom demand roads, water supply, electricity, sanitation, schools, hospitals, bank loans, jobs, comforts and luxuries for themselves and their children for they are convinced that after partition their rights have been dented. Regretably, it is this defeatist mentality of many Muslims that has provided a golden opportunity to other segments of the society to grab their share in governance as well as wealth and welfare. If we look at the general profile of the country, we would be amazed to observe that upper castes with nearly 20.9% share in total population as per 2004-05 seems to be controlling nearly 50% yield in the legislature, bureaucracy, judiciary, security agencies and the media of the country due to its competence and ability. The reservation quota at the level of the Centre and States has transformed the destinies of many Hindu SCs, Hindu STs and the Hindu OBCs. The 17.9% SCs with 15% reservation and 7.3% STs with 7.5% quota and the 34.5% OBCs with 27% allocation at the level of the Centre have gained much in educational and job sectors. However, Muslims with 13.4% share at the national level and 30.9% in Assam, 25.2% in West Bengal, 24.7% in Kerala, 18.5% in Uttar Pradesh, 16.5% in Bihar and 13.8% in Jharkhand, 12.2% in Karnataka, 11.9% in Uttrakhand, 11.7% in Delhi, 10.6% in Maharashtra, 9.2% in Andhra Pradesh, 9.1% in Gujarat, 8.5% in Rajasthan and more than 5% in Madhya Pradesh, Haryana and Tamil Nadu could not take any benefit from the government. There is no separate quota for Muslims both at the national as well as state levels. To provide cosmetic benefits some castes of Muslims have been clubbed with all OBCs but there too they could not get justice due to the non-representation of suitable Muslims in interview boards and selection committees. The SCs/STs and the backward castes could develop faster for each state has provided separate quotas for them. For instance, SCs have 22%, 21%, 20%, 19%, 18% and 16% reservation in West Bengal, Uttar Pradesh, Punjab, Uttrakhand, Tamil Nadu and Madhya Pradesh respectively. Likewise, Bihar, Karnataka, Delhi, Andhra Pradesh, Rajasthan, Haryana, Orissa, Himachal Pradesh and Chhattisgarh have provided 15% quota to SCs in their respective spheres. There are states like Maharashtra, Assam, and Gujarat which have provided reservation to SCs to the limits of 13%, 11%, 7%, and 7% respectively. Similarly, the STs have 27%, 20%, 18%, and 15%, 15% in Jharkhand,

Madhya Pradesh, Chhattisgarh, Assam and Gujarat. Besides this, Delhi, Rajasthan, Haryana, Orissa and Himachal Pradesh have provided 7.5% to STs within their jurisdictions. Over and above this, West Bengal has provided 6%, Bihar 1%, Karnataka 3%, Uttrakhand 4%, Maharashtra 7%, Andhra Pradesh 6%, Tamil Nadu 1% and Punjab 5% to STs. In the same way, the OBCs have 50% reservation in Tamil Nadu, 40% in Kerala, 34% in Bihar, 32% in Karnataka and 32% in Maharashtra. Similarly, Uttar Pradesh, Delhi, Gujarat, Rajasthan, Haryana and Orissa have provided reservation to the extent of 27% each for OBCs within their spheres. Besides, West Bengal has provided 7% quota to the OBCs, Assam 15%, Jharkhand 22%, Uttrakhand, 25%, Andhra Pradesh 14%, Madhya Pradesh 5% and Himachal Pradesh 14% to these castes. One can see to oneself that how easy it became for the SCs/STs and OBCs to develop so faster with the help of the affirmative actions by the Centre and the States. However, when Muslims demanded reservation, it was denied to them by saying that the Constitution of India does not allow reservation on the basis of religion and moreover any religion-based reservation has a potential to divide the country on the basis of religion. Where the fact is that reservation to the Hindu Scheduled Castes was given purely on the basis of religion. Initially, the Hindu Scheduled Castes were provided reservation in educational institutions and government jobs but the Scheduled Castes from among the Christians, Muslims, Sikhs and neo-Buddhists were not included in the category of reservation. Later on the Scheduled Castes from among Sikhs and neo-Buddhists were given the benefits of reservation but Christians and Muslims were excluded. Not only this, a provision was made that if someone from Scheduled Castes got converted to Islam or Christianity, he would lose the benefits of reservation. However, if he joined back the Hindu religion, he would be entitled to reservation. Since any discrimination purely based on religion was not commensurate with the spirit of Indian Constitution, the subject of reservation of these castes was placed under Ninth Schedule which was added to the Constitution as First Amendment to keep these matters beyond the jurisdiction of civil courts. The misfortune is that no political party seems to be in support of reservation for Muslims which does not auger well for a democratic and liberal country like India. Reservation in itself is not a healthy means to develop any community for through reservation only a small segment of the reserved category secures the benefits of the quota and the majority of the community remains out of its purview. Besides, the microscopic minority which is elevated by reservation separates itself from its roots and tries to merge itself with the higher and prosperous caste. Not only this, it also continues to take the benefit of reservation at the cost of the remaining backward segments of the community. Moreover, the bulk of people who acquire education or jobs are not as competent as those who come through competition. Over and above this, the reservation creates segregation, compartmentalization and ill-will amongst the communities. In addition to it, the communities under the reserved category lose confidence, courage and vigour and begin to depend upon the governments for their salvation. The government should think of other methods to lift the backward sections of the society so that they may not lag behind in the race of growth and development. However, once the reservation has been provided to certain sections of the society. Muslims too should be provided this facility being the backward and equal citizens of Indian society. Each party talks of Muslims' deprivation but when it comes to solution or reservation no body comes forward. It is very often claimed that Indian Constitution has provided some safety margin for cultural, religious and educational advancement of Muslims but most of the Muslims allege that when it comes to doing something practical obstacles are created by the vested interests at political, administrative, judicial and other levels to stop any special facility to Muslims.

Muslims' representation in the Parliament and the State Assemblies is meager. Out of 543 members in the last Lok Sabha, nearly 36 were Muslims but in the current Lok Sabha their number has fallen to 30 only when according to their ratio in total population of the country their number should have been somewhere near 80 to 100. The same is the position of State Assemblies. Besides, there is no formal and pro-active cooperation between various Muslim MPs and MLAs as a consequence of which their strength becomes meaningless for they are distributed in various parties and thus individually they can neither put any pressure in their parties nor at general level. There is a strong unity among the Scheduled Caste and Scheduled Tribe and backward caste MPs and MLAs across party lines as a result of which they are able to exert some pressure for the benefit of their respective castes irrespective of their party affiliations. Wherever Muslim MPs and MLAs have united across party lines for the Muslim cause the results have been encouraging. Thus, there is a strong need on the part of such functionaries to form a formal alliance under some senior persons or under some influential or meaningful persons so that the scattered MPs and MLAs may become a force to reckon with. If they do so, no political party would create any hurdle for there are precedences of such types of groups, combinations and alliances. Needless to say that many meaningful Muslims fear that the political climate of the country seems to be rough for Muslims because if Muslim dominated areas are reserved for women under women's 33% quota, there is every possibility that Muslims' percentage would further decline. Likewise, there are very few Muslims who are ministers, governors, ambassadors, chairmen, vice-chancellors, and heads of various commissions, committees and bodies. Many Muslims do not know whether it is a coincidence or deliberate act that either the left-oriented liberal Muslims find a top position in the government due to their so-called ultra secular image or those are absorbed to important positions in the government who have political connections or who live in or around Delhi or state capitals due to their strong lobbies irrespective of their talents and qualifications. Moreover, it has also been observed recently that some conservative and backward Muslims too have been placed on bodies like wakfs and minority commissions due to their emerging influence in the political arena. Mostly, the old and senior Muslims occupying higher positions in political parties or government structure are repeatedly put on the top or the vacancies are filled by those who have already occupied such positions in the past resulting in low number of new and dynamic Muslims on the top. It can be verified that a Muslim Governor of one state is being placed again and again as Governor of another state or a Muslim who has served as the minister, secretary, chairman, judge or ambassador is placed on important positions after retirement which blocks the future of competent and bright Muslims and close the doors for Muslim leadership to nurture at the top level. Mostly, the Muslims in Delhi and the capital cities who form nexus get government favours irrespective of their calibre and competence. Over and above this, those Muslims who have found a place for them in government they never allow any other competent Muslim near the centre of power due to the fear of being thrown out. It is because of this reason that today the Muslim leadership is conspicuous by absence and there is hardly any Muslim of any significance whom Muslims may approach or who may convey their grievances to the higher ups or governing structure.

Muslims also complain that in the name of delimitation of the boundaries, Muslim majority areas are reserved for backwards, women, Scheduled Castes and Scheduled Tribes to minimize Muslims' presence in the legislative bodies.

Table 1.5 shows the State Assembly Electoral Constituency/ Tehsil Reserved for Scheduled Castes with Relative Share of Muslim Population.

Table 1.5

Tehsil Name	SCs as % of Total population	Muslims as % of Total population
Uttar Pradesh : Reserved Assembly Constituency		
Hapur	23.4	28.6
Najibabad	23.0	49.2
Nagina	21.6	42.3
Koil	20.6	26.8
Khalilabad	20.4	32.1
Manakpur	16.5	18.1
Jansath	16.4	36.6
Faridpur	16.1	23.0

Bihar: Reserved Assembly Constituency		
Raniganj	21.3	28.7
Phulwari	18.8	21.8
Sakra	18.5	20.9
Chhatapur	16.9	18.4
Bagaha	14.4	16.9
Korha	14.2	37.3
Darbhanga	13.1	26.4
Mairwa	11.0	12.5
Dhuraiya	10.1	30.0
Basanti	38.6	41.2
West Bengal : Reserved Assembly Constituency		
Rajarhat	35.9	41.3
Nanoor	31.9	33.5
Kulpi	31.9	36.3
Ketugram-1	26.7	44.5
Sankrail	25.2	31.9
Keshpur	25.1	26.6
Khargram	23.6	51.3
Sagardhighi	17.8	62.2
Kaliganj	17.0	55.6

Source: Sachar Committee Report, Table 2.2

For instance, in West Bengal 10 Muslim dominated assembly constituencies, namely Basanti, Rajarhat, Nanoor, Kulpi, Ketugram-1, Sankrail, Keshpur, Khargram, Sagardighi and Kaliganj with Muslim population ranging between 62.0% and 43% have been reserved for SCs when the SCs population in these constituencies varies between 17% to 38% only. As against this, 10 constituencies in West Bengal such as Sitai, Haldibari, Jalpaiguri, Kaliaganj, Khajuri-II, Kharibari, Tufanganj-II, Bamangola, Galghata and Bongoan have been declared as unreserved where SCs population varies between 67.3% to 47.1% and the population of Muslims ranges between 6.3% to 32.0% only. Actually, the later should have been reserved for SCs rather than the former. Likewise, in Uttar Pradesh eight constituencies identified as Hapur, Najibabad, Nagina, Koil, Khalilabad, Mankapur, Jansath, and Faridpur having Muslim population ranging from 23.0% to 49.2% have been reserved for the SCs/STs and Marihan, Ghorwal, Lalganj, Hardoi, Misrikh, Sandila, Haidergarh,

Bakshi ka talab and Tahruli having SC/ST population ranging between 35.3% to 49.3% have been declared as unreserved which has blunted the chances of Muslims. In Bihar nine constituencies, namely Raniganj, Phulwari, Sakra, Chattapur, Bagha, Korha, Darbhanga, Mirwa and Dhuraiya with Muslim population varying between 16.9% to 37.3% have been reserved for SCs/STs and Dumaria, Banke Bazar, Dobhi, Manpur, Amas, Kuppa, Mohanpur and Sirdala having SC/ST population between 39.3% and 34.1% have been declared as unreserved. It is most unfortunate that Muslims despite existing in substantial numbers are at the receiving end when several other segments of the society with lesser numbers have gained much. There are fifty districts where Muslims range between 30% to 98.5% and 100 districts where they can decide the future of the contesting candidates. Muslim population in these districts varies between 400,000 to 3800,000. Table 1.6 shows number of districts by Muslim Population size and concentration as per 2001 Census.

Table 1.6

Muslim population in the district	Number of districts	Percentage of Muslims in the total population of the district	Number of district
1,000,000 or more	25	75 or more	9
500,000 to 999, 999	51	50 or more but less than 75	11
250,000 to 499, 999	104	25 or but less than 50	38
100,000 to 249, 999	125	10 or more but less than 25	182
50,000 to 99, 999	87	5 or more but less than 10	129
10,000 to 49, 999	95	1 or more but less than 5	147
Less than 10,000	105	Less than 1	77
Total	**592**	**Total**	**593**

Source: Sachar Committee Report, Table 3.1

It is believed that despite their sound numerical position Muslims find themselves helpless due to several reasons. First of all it is alleged that many political parties do not give tickets to Muslims due to the fear of losing elections because Muslims are generally scattered throughout the country and there are very few areas from where Muslims can be elected with some certainty. Besides, there are hardly a few Muslims who possess the necessary money, muscle, mafia and tongue powers to defeat the rival candidates. In addition to it, it is often alleged that Muslims are systematically denied their voting rights by not including their names in the voters list. In several states, many names in so many localities seem to be excluded from the voter lists. Over and above this, they find it cumbersome to get identity card or when they reach the polling booths, they find the atmosphere hostile due to communal climate or mafia influence at the level of villages. It is because of this reason that despite the fact that 37.7% Muslims are urbanites and there are nearly 150 constituencies where they can mark their presence, they are mostly defeated by the majority candidates because the contesting candidates play the communal card at the last moment to polarize the majority votes with a view to defeat the Muslim candidates. The political parties do not follow the strategy of nominating non-Muslims in the Muslim dominated cities and placing Muslims from the non-Muslim areas to avoid polarization. Thus, the lack of adequate Muslim representation in the Parliament, State Assemblies, local self-government bodies and similar other grass-root institutions has resulted in the political isolation of Muslims with disastrous consequences. Muslims are taken for granted by the political parties in the absence of Muslim leadership and non-existence of a credible Muslim party since they cannot punish the neglect on the part of these parties. In Jammu and Kashmir, the Muslims with 67.0% population could have their political parties such as the National Conference and PDF. The Kerala Muslims with 24.7% population too have shown maturity by rallying behind Muslim League which is their local secular party and efforts were also made in Assam with 30.9% Muslim population to have separate Muslim secular party which yielded good dividends. The Muslims of West Bengal with 25.2% population failed to float their own secular party with the result that their condition is miserable despite the fact that they are living under the shadow of the Communist Party which is supposed to be kind towards Muslims. The same is the fate of Muslims in Uttar Pradesh who are numerically the largest among Muslims in the country and constitute 18.2% of the total population but are depending upon the Congress, Scheduled Castes and the backward castes for support due to the lack of their own secular political party. The Muslims of Bihar despite being third largest Muslim population and Muslims of various other states having substantial Muslim population failed to take lesson from the stalwarts of the smaller regional parties like BSP, Samajwadi Party, Shiv Sena and RJD who despite representing lesser number of people compared to Muslims could reap rich political harvest merely due to the power of their unity.

Politically, Muslims of India became the victims of history. The last sixty years have proved miserable for Muslims after partition for the whole blame of partition was placed on the shoulders of Mohammed Ali Jinnah and the Muslims of India as a consequence of which the vested interests did not allow Muslims to reap the fruits of development. Whenever they demanded anything they were told to go to Pakistan, the country they had created. Fortunately, things are changing. People are increasingly realizing that partition was caused not by Jinnah alone but many Indian leaders and British Government too were equally responsible for the division of the country. Likewise, Hindus, Sikhs, Jains, Parsis and others were as guilty for creation of Pakistan as Indian Muslims. Even many important Indian Hindus have begun to say that Jinnah was a secular person and he never wanted the partition of the country. He wanted to remain within the domain of Indian Republic but it was due to some reactionary Hindus and Muslims and the vested interests in Congress and Muslim League and the British connivance that he was compelled to opt for Pakistan. The facts reveal that wherever Muslims were in large numbers and they were under Hindu domination such as Sindh, Punjab, Bengal and Assam, Muslim League flourished for Muslims in these areas never wanted to live under Hindu domination after independence. As against this, where Muslims were in majority and were in the controlling position like North West Frontiers, the Muslim League could not have much say. Likewise, where the Hindus were under Muslim zamindars and Muslim influence such as Uttar Pradesh and Bihar, the Congress found its fertile ground since the Hindus of these areas never intended to live under Muslim subjugation after securing freedom. Besides, there were many people in India who never wanted Muslims' active role in independent India for they abhorred the Muslim rule in the past. Moreover, the role of Muslim and Hindu zamindars and Muslim and Hindu capitalists was in favour of a separate state for themselves. Over and above this, the British were playing their own game plan so as to create such conditions that they might be called back to rule the country in the wake of failure on the part of Indians to rule their respective countries effectively. All these and many more factors were behind what happened in India on the eve of 1947. Without going into the merits and demerits of each case, it can be concluded that it is a healthy development that people in India are now examining the history of independence with critical eyes. It not only shows the maturity of Indian minds but also shows their pragmatism and search for truth and free enquiry. Soon a time would come when Muslims of India would be partly absolved of their guilt of creating Pakistan and they would get their due and no one would oppose their genuine demands by bringing the plea of Pakistan or by propounding the theory that if any special benefit is given to them it would further lead to the partition of the country.

Moral Frustration in the Community

The tragedy with Indian politics is that there is perhaps no internal democracy in most of the political parties of the country. The heads of several political parties decide the fate of their parties and the honest and sincere dissent is not welcome. There are very few who can dare to oppose the leadership with the result that the leadership of several political parties in India has been mostly surrounded by sycophants and controlled by the dominant families. The tendency to blindly follow the leaders or the heads has percolated to the bottom and many heads of government departments, educational institutions, health care centres, research organizations and many more in the country are functioning according to their whims and fancies. Unfortunately, those who dare to criticize constructively are generally shown the doors with the result that the major segment of Indian society is galvanizing around the proactive groups of the sycophants. Besides, the in-breeding and the promotion of family members in the political parties have acquired prominence in the same way as they are found in family business with the result that there has been the casualty of deserving persons and principles. Muslims are also frustrated due to the apparent dual morality and dual modes operating in the country for the majority segment and the minority sector, privileged and less privileged groups and reserved class and unreserved depressed classes. They appreciate the banning of anti-social and anti-people parties irrespective of their religious affiliations in the larger interest of the Republic but banning some and letting and allowing others with fanatic, aggressive, anti-social and anti-national designs pains them very much. Besides, they allege that they confront different standards of judgment in matters of providing jobs, dealing with communal disputes, coverage by media and in tackling disputed Muslim and non-Muslim properties. The modern society is a success-oriented society where nothing succeeds like success since success needs no explanation and failure has none. Thus, by hook or crook, every political party tries to achieve success by following cast, communal or religious cards and once it is successful, it is heralded as the champion in the society. Thank God that the conscience of the majority of the countrymen is above board. They can distinguish between good and bad but the tragedy is that they are in silent majority. The constructive discussions of the silent majority are confined merely to the extent of their drawing rooms and village chaupals. The vocal minority which matters is mostly conscienceless. The conscience of most of the petty politicians is tuned to the need of the hour. They judge matters from the point of view of their personal interests without any regard to moral judgment. They appear to do everything fair and foul suiting to the needs of their leaders, parties and the electorates without any regard to the interest of the country and the welfare of the people. If the appeasement of any community demands tougher and fascist anti-terror laws, such laws are generally passed to please the particular vote bank without any regard to their adverse impacts upon the other segments of the society as well as the country. Likewise, if the lenient laws suit some of the parties or segment they do not lag behind and plead for laws suiting to the appeasement of their electorates without any regard to the safety and security of the country. There seem to be no dearth of people who benefit by keeping silent for they feel that by doing this they please their supporters. Similarly, if some section, person or the segment of the society or political party can win elections by unleashing hatred against the people of one religion, region, caste or community or raising the public emotions by raising emotional issues, there is none to deter it from spreading hatred, killing people, destroying properties, demolishing religious places, looting honour and causing immense harm to innocent men, women, young and old save a select few. Muslims lament that if the extremists and criminals from the minority community cause terrorist activities the whole Muslim community is generally blamed by the unscrupulous section of the society but when any misguided segment of majority community kills people and indulges in violent and terrorist activities, causes bloodshed and havoc, there are some fanatics who glorify it and term such acts as honest reactions to atrocious acts committed by their counterparts. Besides, Indian Muslims are also highly perturbed in the way the encounters of a few Muslim youths are sometimes executed by police and paramilitary organizations to get honours, promotions and distinctions or to please their masters. Likewise, it pains them much when their madrasas are unnecessarily targeted for allegedly spreading unrest in the country without obtaining any proofs and evidences against such institutions.

The issue of reservation for Muslim SCs is perplexing the Muslims throughout the country since it is justified for Hindu SCs, Mazhabi Sikhs and neo-Buddhists but if Muslim and Christian SCs demand the same facility, they are denied the privilege of quota by citing legal lacunas. Certainly, there are Scheduled Castes among Muslims. The Muslim safai walas, mehtars, chamars, halalkhors, gadheris, gorkun, and lalbegis belong to Muslim Scheduled Castes and they are found in many states of the country but they have been excluded by the Constitutional (Scheduled Castes) Order, 1950. The order was amended twice, once in 1956 to include the SCs among the Sikhs and later in 1990 to include neo-Buddhists. Many Constitutional experts claim that the Order of 1950 is inconsistent with Articles 14, 15, 16 and 25 of the Constitution that guarantee equality of opportunity, freedom of conscience and protection of the citizens and protect citizens from discrimination by the state on ground of religion, caste or creed. Besides, many legal luminaries claim that the 50% quota kept for the general category is arbitrary and discriminatory for in essence it is benefiting the 20% higher castes at the cost of the minorities and other marginalized sections of the society. Moreover, if the 50% limit fixed by the Supreme Court was so sacrosanct, why was it allowed to touch 69% in Tamil Nadu, 60% in Jharkhand and 52% in Maharashtra. The benefit of reservation should have been given to Muslim and Christian SCs too on principle. Besides though reservation for Scheduled Tribes is religion neutral, yet Muslims have not benefitted by it although 99.74% Muslims live in Lakshadweep. Moreover, the reservation was not going to pose any problem due to its meager number for according to Census 1991, Muslim STs were 170428 out of 67758285 or merely 0.25% of total ST population. They were 0.5% of total Muslim population in 2004-05 and they were spread across the country. Similarly, Muslim SCs, were merely 0.8% of total Muslim population in 2004-05 but they were not provided any reservation under SC/ST category despite several efforts of the NGOs. In the same way, Christian SCs and STs too were meager compared to other SCs and STs, they were merely 0.21% and 0.77% of the total population respectively but they too were not considered.

In addition to it, Muslims are also bitter in the manner in which the reports of various riot commissions have been placed in cold storages, different measures of paying compensations and punishment were adopted, and the minorities were deprived several times of their just, equitable and constitutional rights. They were pained due to the shabby treatment meted out to them in the past at the hands of practically every political party. Their faith in state machinery had been shattered after having seen the fall of Babri Masjid and the post-Godhra after effects. They have not forgotten their adverse period during the days of George Bush when they were insignificant and meaningless. Over and above this, they are panicky that there is practically none to help them. There are only a few conscientious people who call a spade a spade. Muslims' hopes, however, have been pinned on the dynamic, sane and non-communal younger generation and the silent, liberal, secular and truthful silent majority and the insignificant vocal minority of enlightened, far-sighted geniuses from all the segments of the society for it is they who would reign the country in the long run and it is they in whose hands the minorities and majorities would be safe and secure. Their impact has started showing results in Gujarat and elsewhere and it is hoped that it would be difficult for the unsocial elements to go scot free after committing heinous crimes or atrocities on any section of the society.

Muslims are certainly in a fix. They find themselves in wilderness without any leader, helper and supporter. During the pre-partition days they had eminent personalities like Maulana Abul Kalam Azad, Hakim Ajmal Khan, Hasrat Mohani, Saifuddin Kitchlew, Allama Shibli Nomani, Badaruddin Taiyabji, Dr. Syed Mahmud, Maulana Mohammad Ali Jauhar, Maulana Shaukat Ali, Abdul Bari Firangi Mahal and Dr. Zakir Husain and a host of others. In the present scenario, there is a political vacuum. Muslims are not only leaderless but many of them also carry a burden of being called terrorists and anti-national. The loyalties of several Muslims are generally at stake, their sincere moves are doubted and they mostly feel alien and unacceptable in the country they love most. Till recently they were considered as the equal partners in the national reconstruction, strategic planning and policy formulation but with the partition of the country they became generally redundant, irrelevant and a burden on the national exchequer. They mostly complain of discrimination, prejudice and indignation. It is, therefore, imperative for our countrymen to know their feelings and perceptions in the light of their assertions and mind-set, even if all of them may not be correct with a view to solve their problems. If a large numerical minority equal to the strength of many Asian and African countries remains downtrodden, frustrated and dumbfounded, the country cannot prosper. Besides, poverty anywhere is dangerous everywhere and ignorance creates bad blood and misery and injustice breed hatred, violence and mistrust. A coherent, peaceful and cohesive society cannot be created purely on unity, uniformity or obliteration of differences of identity but it needs the independent development of various socio-cultural and religious systems in which tolerance, co-existence and interaction enrich the system and give it a needed strength. There is no doubt that all perceptions of Indian Muslims are not true, many of them may be based merely on hunches but certainly they have not been built in vacuum. Muslims are surely labouring under a heavy strain which gives rise to frustration, anger and dejection but they cannot put the whole blame for their state of affairs entirely on the government or the majority community. They will have to think patiently where they faltered and the majority community too has to be considerate and sympathetic to their genuine problems and it becomes the duty of the state to see that they get fair treatment. Unfortunately, Muslims' charges of unfair treatment have some content of truth which gives strength to their conviction and so the situation continues to deteriorate. As always happens in situations of this type, people generally do not reach to the reality but involve themselves in ceaseless recrimination, mutual accusation and war of attrition with the result that they fail to adopt corrective measures. The purpose of the present endeavour is not to find out the fault of this segment or that segment or to indulge in blame game but to convince the majority and minority communities as well as the central and the state governments of the country and the people of India in general and Muslims in particular that to find a solution to this vex problem through peaceful, constitutional, democratic and humanitarian means is in the interest of all people failing which it would continue to deteriorate and cause damage not only to the minority and majority fabrics of the country but also dent the growth and development of the country.

2

The Turbulence and Agony of Post-Partition Period from 1947 to 1971

Muslims' history in India is very long. They had settled in the coastal parts of the country during the seventh century prior to the invasions of Muslim rulers. Many of the local Hindus too had converted themselves to Islam due to the magnetic influence of the Muslim sufi saints during the eighth century, prior to the arrival of Muslim rulers and their retinue from Central Asia. However, after the partition of the country, their history is very short but written by the cruel marks of misery and frustration. Quantitatively, this period extends merely over a period of sixty years but qualitatively its agony is much sharper, deeper and widespread than the pains and turmoil of centuries for a day spent in misery and adversities is more painful and depressing than many years passed in luxuries and comforts. We can divide the transitional period of Indian Muslims after independence of the country broadly in three phases: the turbulent and agony period from 1947 to 1971 when Bangladesh was created; the stability, pressure tactics and apprehension period from 1971 to 1992 when the Babri Masjid was demolished and the contemporary phase of assertion, depression and contemplation which is continuing. In this section, we are analyzing the agony period from 1947 to 1971 which starts with the freedom of the country and culminates in the creation of Bangladesh.

The Large-Scale Migration of People Across Borders

When India became free on 15 August 1947, many Muslims especially in this part of the world who had perceived different visions about Pakistan became disillusioned for their several misconceptions pertaining to Pakistan were shattered. Most of the Muslims with Muslim League mentality were expecting that their cities, towns and villages would be included in Pakistan and the era of pleasure, happiness and progress would dawn upon them with the emergence of a newly created Muslim state on the world map but when the lines were finally drawn, they were miles away from the newly created country. The partition had divided the country into Bharat and Pakistan and it had brought freedom coupled with such agonies, worries and atrocities in both the countries which the people of undivided India had never imagined before. Delhi which was the capital of the country became unsafe within a few days. Many people who had been living there for centuries and who had intimate relations with each other became strangers and enemies for each other. Suddenly, the climate of Delhi changed with the change in the boundaries of the country. Night curfew was imposed from 28 August to 1 September 1947. Looting, arson and murders were widespread and men, women and children were being killed. The GT Express was stopped and it is claimed that most of the Muslims were butchered. Muslims of Timarpur, Lodhi Colony, the Lutyens, Ajmeri Gate, old cobbler's bazaar, Sabzi Mandi, Paharganj, Karol Bagh, Mehrauli, and airport were affected most. Even the crowded colonies of the old city where the poor lived too were not spared. Muslim Rajputs of Dhulkot near Palam airport were also attacked and they hurriedly emigrated to Pakistan. Several mosques were destroyed or taken over by the refugees from Pakistan in retaliation to their places of worships in Pakistan. Many bungalows and mansions of wealthy Muslims were forcefully occupied. It is alleged by many Delhi people that most of the damage to Muslims was caused by those non-Muslim lower class people who were known to them or who were either working with them or supplying them the commodities of daily needs as they were aware with the geography and the internal conditions of the locals. Many such people invaded Muslim localities in large number equipped with spears, swords and lethal weapons. Having seen the danger to their lives, honour and possessions people left their homes in large number and sought shelter in refugee camps in the Old Fort and Jama Masjid. By 1951, nearly 3.5 lakh Muslims had migrated from Delhi to Karachi reducing the Muslim population of Delhi from 33.22% in 1941 to 5.7% in 1951. It is claimed that Delhi Muslims were on the special agenda of the fanatics for they never wanted the excessive presence of the educated, rich and meaningful Muslims in and around Delhi, the new capital of independent India. On an average, 4500 Muslims boarded the train to Pakistan daily from UP. The cities which were affected most in Uttar Pradesh were Shahjahanpur, Aligarh, Meerut, Garh Mukteshwar, Muzaffarnagar, and Rohilkhand. Bharatpur, Alwar, Panipat, Sonipat, Gurgaon, Ghaziabad and Rewari, Rohtak, Ambala and near by areas of Delhi were the places from where the Muslims had practically migrate *en masse*. The same was the case of Punjab. The whole of Punjab and its princely states were on fire and bloodshed. In Bihar, emigration had begun in November-December 1946 due to rioting in Saran, Patna, Monghyr and Bhagalpur and nearly 5 lakh Muslims had shifted to East Pakistan. The Princely State of Hyderabad also saw migration of Muslims in large scale after police action. Nearly 500 Muslims a day went to Sindh through Khokhrapar. Many professionals and elites left from the Princely States of Rampur, Bhopal and smaller Muslim states. In Bihar and UP, very few Muslims were left in defence services, universities, government jobs, police and judiciary. In Hyderabad where Muslims were in large number, it is alleged that many of them were subjected to screening and some were removed, several demoted and a few were put in jails. Urdu ceased to be the official language and the medium of instructions in the state. The police departments, paramilitary units, government offices and business establishments in the affected areas had become defunct. The schools, colleges, universities and research institutes in communally sensitive areas had been closed. Refugees had occupied most of the educational institutions, cultural centres and religious places. As a matter of fact the things were in bad shape since whole of Northern India was burning. There were murders, lootings, rapes, arsons and bloodshed. Trains and buses were full of casualties, corpse were rotting on roads and properties were burning in broad day light. Pandit Nehru, Gandhiji and many secular leaders were watching the misfortune of the unfortunate people with their own eyes but despite their good intentions and meaningful efforts they could not help them. Pandit Jawaharlal Nehru wrote to Nawab of Bhopal on July 9, 1948, "Partition came and we accepted it because we thought that perhaps that way, however painful it was, we might have some peace to work along our own lines. Perhaps we acted wrongly. It is difficult to judge now. And yet the consequences of that partition have been so terrible that one is inclined to think that anything else would have been preferable. The partition has come, and it brought in its train other vast changes. There is no going back now to India as it was before the partition." The memoirs, eye-witness accounts, poems and short stories and historical accounts written by high-profile writers, poets, government officials, public figures and eminent personalities like Saadat Hasan Manto, Rajinder Singh Bedi, Ahmed Ali, Attia Hosain, Khuswant Singh and many others reveal the real tragedy faced by people of those days. These distinguished personalities have not only portrayed a fragmented and wounded Indo-Pak society engulfed in widespread violence but also highlighted the ill-conceived designs of those politicians who could not perceive human sufferings and failed to imagine the consequences of their own hurriedly chalked out plans despite sane warnings and signed death warrant of millions of people. Prof. Mushirul Hasan too has written aptly, intelligently and factually on various aspects of Muslims after independence in much detail from which the author too has immensely benefitted.

It is the cruel joke of history and the gimmick of times that the well cherished and well sought after freedom of the country brought incalculable miseries upon millions of people for with the declaration of independence communal riots started on massive scale in the newly created countries and a large-scale migration of people from India and Pakistan took place simultaneously on both sides of the borders with disastrous consequences. According to certain estimates from August 1947 to March 1948, nearly 4.5 million Hindus migrated from West Pakistan to India and about 6 million Muslims moved from India to Pakistan. Likewise, between 1950 and 1952 about 9 to 10 lakh Hindus entered India from East Pakistan and 4 lakh Muslims migrated from India to East Pakistan. Up to 1949 Muslims had left behind about crores of acres of land and lakhs of houses and properties and possessions as evacuee property. Likewise, the Hindus from Pakistan left behind their houses, properties and possessions worth crores of rupees. Caravans after caravans moved in opposite directions and left behind their elegant dwellings, lush green fields, bushy orchards, vast meadows; costly business establishments, valuable factories and spacious work places; pretty cupboards, gorgeous utensils, exquisite cutlery and trunks full of beautiful clothes, splendid ornaments and above all the lovely goats, cute sheeps, stunning buffaloes, angelic cows and charming calves herded and tied in the yards. Migrating Muslims had to leave behind their adorable mosques, reverent maqbaras, grand minarets; majestic dargahs of Khwaja Ajmeri, Nizamuddin Auliya and Ahmad Riza Khan Barelvi; admirable Imambaras of Lucknow, Jaunpur and Rampur and pleasing Taj Mahal, stunning Fatehpur Sikri and well-composed Humayun Tomb which they cherished most. They left behind graceful Aligarh Muslim University, pious Darul-Uloom Deoband, sublime Nadwa; superb Delhi, glorious Lucknow, lustrous Calcutta, magnificent Bhopal and splendorous Mumbai, holy Ganga, sacred Jamuna and vigorous Kaveri which were dearest to them. They left behind brilliant Firaq Gorakhpuri, eminent Jigar Moradabadi and the famous Asrar ul Haq Majaz; glamorous Dilip Kumar, grand Mehboob and royal Nargis; Maulana Azad the world fame statesman, Ali Miyan the towering personality and many dearest and loved ones whom they admired and cherished most. So did the Hindus. The industrious Punjabis, soft spoken Sindhis, melodious Bengalis, brave people of North West Frontiers and others left behind the charms of lofty Lahore, imperial Rawalpindi, picturesque Peshawar, palatial Karachi, imposing Hyderabad Sindh, impressive Dhaka, stately Chittagong and the memories of the sweet evenings and the rejoices of the refreshing mornings as well as their historical landmarks, precious heritages and the symbols of their grace and glory.

It is not appropriate as well as advisable to write in detail about what happened after partition of the country to the miserable people of both the countries for firstly, the present generation cannot conceive and appreciate why their elders despite being so close to each other behaved as they did and secondly they cannot imagine how horrible were those days and how much they suffered at each others hands and lastly, it possesses enough potentialities to arouse feelings on both sides of the borders. We have all sympathies for the martyrs of all communities who suffered untold miseries and our hearts weep for those innocents who sacrificed their lives, honour, liberties and possessions and faced humiliation and indignation as a consequence of India and Pakistan acquiring freedom. Admittedly, they were none other than our own dear and near, kith and kin and beloved and cherished ones. Millions of people whose ancestors had been living for centuries in their sweet homes had to leave their dwellings in hurry leaving everything to destiny. How painful and torturous it was to be uprooted from one's homeland, how hurtful and agonizing it was to see one's kith and kin separating, how aching and biting it was to see our own in shambles and how distressing and anguishing it was to see the honour and dignity of our own smashing, only the miserable and unfortunate know who had gone through the miseries and misfortunes of those times. Friends became enemies, custodians of law crossed all limits, men became barbarians and all norms of civilized society, all rules of moral conducts and all lessons of piety were thrown aside and the heaven wept bitterly, earth cried woefully and the Lord saw man falling to the lowest of the low. Those who came to India or went to Pakistan were indeed most unfortunate people. They had suffered so much at the hands of their own friends, neighbours, colleagues and the trusted ones that they could not imagine even in their dreams. Those who had survived and had to pass through the ocean of fire and blood also lost their control and in the fit of anger and revenge created such heart-breaking and atrocious and horrible problems for Muslims in India and Hindus in Pakistan that the pen fails to describe them in black and white. Many meaningful Indians and people with strong nerves have written with their bleeding pens about what happened at the terrible times of the partition but the author cannot muster courage to describe the condition of the pitiable people at the hands of their own brothers for no fault of their own save this that they belonged to different religions and professed different faiths. He had seen with his own eyes the miserable caravans of shattered people migrating from one country to another in deplorable conditions. He had witnessed the tears rolling in the eyes of the aged, frustration lit large on the faces of the youths and the clouds of fear hovering in the eyes of the innocent children. He had read the question marks prominently engraved on the foreheads of the miserable women, insecurity overshadowing the perceptions of the family heads and helplessness spreading its wings on the hearts, minds and the souls of the leaders, administrators and the social reformers. Indeed, it is difficult to imagine and conceive for the present generation of India and Pakistan and the world at large the horrors of post-partition days because whatever happened at that time was an exception in history.

However, since we have to convey some minor glimpses of those bad days to our posterity, we shall now briefly discuss only that part of the story which is relevant to Indian Muslims. This never means that the author is insensitive to what happened to Hindus in Pakistan. He was equally perturbed from the ghastly stories which he had heard from the refugees coming from Pakistan while he was helping them at Jodhpur Railway Station as a young chap along with his school and college fellows and his heart had wept bitterly after having heard what had happened to the innocent people of Pakistan who had to leave their homes with no fault of their own. He can only imagine how horrible must have been those days for the helpless and fractured Hindus of Pakistan. He has all sympathies for them but unfortunately he cannot pen down their agonies and tortures due to lack of knowledge on his part as well as due to the limited nature of the work. Our intention to write about the experiences of Muslims and Hindus during post-partition period is neither to arouse any feelings nor to blame any community, section or sect or group or any segment of the government but simply to let our younger generation know the mindset of the people from the majority and minority communities in those days of turmoil and turbulence. Those days were highly frustrating for those unfortunate Muslims who had migrated to Pakistan and those who had decided to stay in India and for those Hindus who had stayed in Pakistan and those who had come to India as refugees. There was hatred, indignation and mistrust of extreme type against the unfortunate people of those times which the present generation cannot perceive. The horrible and agonizing experiences and stories of torture, humiliation and persecution communicated by the refugees in India and the migrants in Pakistan boiled the blood of many emotional and short-sighted Hindus in India and proactive and reactionary types of Muslims in Pakistan as a consequence of which the helpless Muslims in India and powerless Hindus in Pakistan became the victims of their revenge and retaliation. The persecution was similar in nature but there was difference of degrees only. What happened in those days was a blot on the face of civilization and efforts should be made by every civilized group that similar things in the name of religion, culture or ideology may not happen in future.

Most of the Sindhis from Sindh came through the route of Khokra par or through sea to Mumbai and reached Jodhpur and Mumbai. From there few settled in Jodhpur and Mumbai and some migrated to Ajmer, Jaipur, Pune and many migrated to different parts of the country. Many of the migrating Sindhis had suffered immensely for they were the elites, traders and the masters in Sindh and were living gracefully, comfortably with honour and dignity. They had to leave everything behind. They suffered losses of lives too but in comparison to Punjab it was not so severe. As against this, many of the Punjabis who migrated from Punjab and Hindus who came from North Western Frontiers too were rich, prosperous, literate and powerful people. They were the backbone of Punjab and the Frontiers but in one stroke of pen they became paupers. Mostly, they had to pass through Punjab which was burning. They suffered physically, emotionally and materially. There was bloodshed on both sides of Punjab. Most of the Punjabi immigrants settled in Eastern Punjab, Haryana and Delhi and many moved to important cities of the country. The good point with the immigrants from Pakistan both Sindhis and Punjabis was that they did not beg but created their own place in the country merely by their hard work and genius and in a short period of time dominated the important markets and business segments of the country. Most of the progress, dynamism, modernization and change in outlook in this part of the world can be attributed to the progressive outlook of Sindhis and Punjabis. Many Bengali Hindus also migrated from East Pakistan but they mostly settled in and around Calcutta. Likewise, those Muslims who migrated to Sindh through Jodhpur and Khokra par from various parts of Uttar Pradesh, Rajasthan and Southern India suffered in the sense that they too had to leave everything behind but in physical terms their loss was not heavy as the atmosphere on this route was peaceful. They had suffered only in their own cities since their houses were looted, properties destroyed and they had to sacrifice their comforts and luxuries. However, those Muslims who migrated from Punjab, Haryana, Delhi, Uttar Pradesh, Rajasthan and Bihar through Punjab were the worst sufferers for they had lost everything which their ancestors had gathered over centuries. Besides the loss, they had to pass through blood bath in and around Punjab and Delhi. Most of the Muslims who went to Pakistan from Northern India were the cream of Muslim society. They were bureaucrats, judges, legislators, generals, police officials, traders and the elites. Their migration dented the destiny of Indian Muslims but they proved asset to the newly created Pakistan for these were they who helped in laying a somewhat stable foundation for Pakistan. Those Muslims who were poor or who had decided to remain in

India being attached to the root or soil remained where they were despite tortures and turmoils. Many Muslims migrated from Bihar, Assam and Orissa to East Pakistan but their number was not very large. It is worth noting that in comparison to Hindu migrants of India, many Muslim migrants in Pakistan were docile. They did not carve out their own place and remained refugees for most of the time.

The Intensity of Communal Riots

Communal riots took place in Uttar Pradesh, Bihar, Bengal, Assam and various parts of Central and Southern India from 1947 to 1977 with short intervals. Leaving aside millions of people who were killed on and around borders while migrating to India and Pakistan, if we analyze the communal situation in India we find that between 1954 and 1979 nearly 6000 communal riots took place in which nearly 5000 persons were killed and 30,000 were injured. The death toll in the 1980s was about 3500. In UP alone dozens of riots took place between February 1986 and June 1987 in which more than 150 people were killed and hundreds were injured who were mostly Muslims. In October 1989 nearly 1000 people were killed in Bhagalpur, majority of whom were Muslims. The communal riots were not uncommon during the Nehru era also but they were generally sporadic and localized and were controlled within few days. However, the riots that took place at Aligarh, Moradabad, Kanpur, Meerut, Hyderabad, Bhagalpur, Ahmadabad, Baroda, Mumbai and Surat and several other parts of the country were bloodier and more widespread and lasted for weeks. Those who were interested in residential and business properties of prime importance or wanted to settle their past scores or intended to get rid of their business rivals or nasty neighbours or were burning in fanatical hatred against each other ignited the riots in planned ways. Mostly, they themselves did not take part in these riots directly but instigated the most downtrodden sections of the society assuring them of their fullest support and the help of local administration. These marginalized and depressed sections of the society under the influence of liquor which was abundantly and freely provided to them took part in looting, arson and killings with a view to obtain the booty. Neither these culprits were caught nor the looted booty was recovered from them which perpetuated the riots in the country for a considerable period of time. In addition to it, there was no dearth of the rivals in business enterprises, political circle, religious arena and the unruly elements who also vent their angers and put their cities to flame. In the first stage, there was merely the burning and looting of the properties. Generally, shops and properties in the main markets and houses and factories in mixed areas were targeted, identified and systematically destroyed in broad day light allegedly in the presence of the police force. Muslims always complained that the mob was burning and looting their properties and the police and paramilitary forces were following them as if they were giving them protection and when they resisted they were targeted and suppressed ruthlessly by the supposedly partisan force. Muslims too did not lag behind. Wherever they could retaliate they destroyed Hindus' properties and factories in their own areas. Since Muslims were in small number and were ill-equipped and unfavourably placed they suffered much in comparison to Hindus. Initially, in the game of burning and looting, the Muslims tolerated passively due to fear and adverse reactions but when it took the shape of rape and killing, Muslims stood against the rioters but could not face the provincial constabularies which had been raised practically in every state to tackle law and order.

The Alleged Biased Role of Paramilitary Forces

It is alleged by many Muslims that these paramilitary units often adopted partisan approach and caused huge damage of lives and properties of Muslims. Muslims came openly against them and began treating them as their enemy number one. Muslims believe that major damage to the Muslims everywhere was caused by the mob in connivance with these paramilitary units. Muslims tried their best to persuade the State Government from deploying such units during the times of riots in their areas but in vain. Many a time, the Muslim youths clashed with the paramilitary units without caring for the consequences and suffered the loss of life and faced imprisonment. The worst aspect of the riots was that the society was generally divided on communal lines during the period of riots. It is said that most of the administration, the press, the intellectuals and the commoners used to be biased against each other and thought merely in terms of their own religions and communities. Besides, the local vernacular press played a very nasty role. It published baseless rumours about killing, arson and rapes and kidnapping especially of various virgins, maidens and women—old and young—which people believed and acted upon them resulting in horrors, havoc and confusion. The redeeming thing about these riots was that it was mostly an urban phenomenon affecting generally the Northern India. Mostly, the Southern and Central India as well as the rural areas were immune from these maladies. Riots certainly spread in many rural areas also just after partition and wherever they took place they were very furious and barbaric but soon Muslims left their homes where they were in minority and shifted to those areas where there were Muslim majority villages. They collectively faced the looters and killers and the riots in the rural areas were eventually stopped due to checks and balances as well as government efforts and the interference of the elders of the society. However, in the long run many Muslims migrated from the villages where they were unsafe to the nearby cities as a consequence of which the foundation was laid concerning concentration of people on communal lines in the country.

During the period of lawlessness, the religious places became the special targets of the rioters because the rioters on both the sides of the borders had heard from words of mouth or they had read in the print media that their adversaries were burning and destroying their religious places. Thus, in retaliation both the communities destroyed each others religious places. The anti-social element from India and those pro-active refugees who had come from Pakistan with bad memories destroyed Muslim mosques, dargahs, madrasas and erected houses, business establishments and recreation centres on the graveyards, wakf properties, mosques. Even today many mosques, madrasas, dargahs and Muslim religious organizations in Punjab, Haryana, Delhi, Rajasthan, Madhya Pradesh and various parts of the country have been occupied by non-Muslims and they are being used as houses, hotels, restaurants, and recreation centres. Many such institutions which were destroyed during post-partition days and which were not used by the local people are in their depleted shapes and no effort has been made either by the Muslims or government organizations to restore them into their original shapes. More or less the same is the situation in Pakistan. The Hindu temples, pathshalas, cremation grounds, religious institutions and gurudwaras of Sikhs, their cremation grounds and religious organizations which were deserted by the migrating people have been usurped by the perverted Muslims and they have converted them into houses, business establishments, restaurants and recreation centres. The temples and gurudwaras which were destroyed during the upheaval and which were not utilized by any are also in bad shape and the government and local Muslims, local Hindus and other organizations have done very little to restore them. The religious institutions could become the easy prey for nobody was there to protect them and they were abandoned first by their adherents and followers for they used to seek shelter in their homes or safer areas. The vested interest thought it better to capture such places due to several reasons. Firstly, they were easiest to acquire. Secondly, they were situated in the prime locations. Thirdly, they were erected on vast tracks of land. Fourthly, they were constructed on high plinth and the material used was also of high quality. Lastly, there was no claimant of such institutions. It is most unfortunate that the conscience of such people who have usurped these pious religious institutions on both sides of borders is dead. They did not think for a moment that once upon a time several heads and hearts bowed in reverence before their Lord where they are rejoicing in lust and worldly ventures and doing all sorts of activities ugly and dirty. Indeed, they are in utter ignorance and none can awake them from their slumber of vanity, ignorance and stupidity.

It is heartening to know that in these riots the role of Indian army remained exemplary. Muslims always had full confidence in the integrity, impartiality and transparency of the army and whenever the army arrived they felt relief. The army also dealt with criminals effectively and without any kind of bias and prejudice and brought the situation under control within no time. The Flag March of the army was an indication to the criminals and anti-social elements that enough was enough and now onward no violation of law and order would be tolerated. Generally, the soldiers from the units of Kerala, Tamil Nadu and Karnataka or Southern States were deputed in Northern India and the army men from the military units of Punjab, Haryana and Rajasthan were placed in Southern India. After having seen these units from other states and areas half of the problem was solved. Nobody could dare to take law in his own hands fearing these soldiers because none could expect any special favour from these people on the basis of caste or religion. It was because of the fear of the army that wherever these riots took fierce shapes, they were suppressed immediately by the intervention of the army. The tragedy was that the army was deputed very late after much struggle and political pressure. The State Governments mostly relied on their own police and paramilitary forces and never accepted that they were not in a position to quell the riots. The Centre too could not do much because the subject of law and order fell under the purview of the states. When the riots persisted despite employing police and paramilitary forces, Muslims used to complain to the Chief Ministers about the alleged partisan role of such forces but their request was generally set aside because the deployment of the army was not welcomed by the reactionary sections from the majority community. There were certain pro-active people from the majority community who used to supply food articles and sweets to the police and paramilitary personnel with a view to get their favour which created doubts and fear in the minds of Muslims. Finally, since the riots were not controlled by the state agencies Muslims used to request the Central Government to send the army. It was on the initiative of the Central Government due to pressure from various Muslim and non-Muslim MPs, local and national organizations that army was finally deployed in troubled areas. Another heartening thing was that there were enlightened and visionary Hindus and Muslims who used to call spade a spade. They always spoke against these riots and tried their best to suppress them without causing much damage.

Riots on Minor Matters

Initially, the riots used to take place on trifle matters perhaps due to mutual hatred towards each other and the charged communal atmosphere in the country and they used to last for a few days only. For instance, if two people quarreled on any matter such as paying riksha charges or buying and selling of goods, riot was inevitable if they belonged to two different communities. Supporters of the rivals in the garb of Hindus and Muslims with no connection whatsoever with the quarreling people save religious affinities, used to gather and turned the minor incidence into a major riot, causing deaths, arsons and lawlessness. First of all, the section 144 was promulgated and when the situation went out of hands curfew used to be imposed which created problems for the society and soon the saner people of both the communities with the help of administration used to come out openly and help the District Administration to bring the situation under control. As soon as the curfew was lifted the situation used to come under control and people used to move in the cities as if nothing had happened. They used to blame the anti-social elements of both sides for the riots which showed that by and large the Indian masses were peaceful and conscientious. Their fault was that they could not control a few vagabonds in their communities and used to come temporarily under their malicious influence. The unique thing about these riots was that the vagabonds from both the communities who killed people cold bloodedly and destroyed properties and indulged in rapes and revenges were not only heralded by their respective religious fellows but were also provided shelter, patronage, protection at the time of their arrests by the police. This gunda patronage proved very costly to both the sections of the society for in peace times these elements began to harass their own supporters to extract money by black mailing, kidnapping and creating mischief to them. It was the same unruly element which in the long run took the shape of the mafia, kidnappers and thugs and became the strong wing of several political parties. Initially, this anti-social element was Hindu and Muslim in denomination but later on it became cosmopolitan. There were Muslim rascals in the group of Hindu vagabonds and Hindu wicked in the chunk of Muslim criminals. They used to work in tandem and many riots and murders, lootings, rapes and acts of arsons were committed by these people only because the ordinary law abiding citizens could not dare to commit such heinous acts.

The Long Duration of Riots Dented the Intensity of Riots

It is interesting to note that as the frequency of riots increased, the duration of the riots also increased and it lasted for days and months. This new situation caused immense harm to the society. Those who had to supply their goods to outsiders or foreign countries failed to supply their goods in time and they lost their orders. Those who had to receive their goods through trains or trucks could not do so due to curfew hence they had to pay huge demurrages and their goods too used to get perished. Since the markets remain closed for longer period of time, the shopkeepers lost their livelihood and the laboureres starved due to lack of employment. The marriages could not be solemnized in time and many patients died due to lack of proper treatments. Many students lost their costly years, thousands of children suffered due to paucity of baby milk, several outsiders stopped marrying their children in such cities and tourists stopped visiting the riot-prone cities. Thus, the adverse impact of the riots was so severe that people realized that it was futile to participate in such riots for save criminals and the vested interests no body was gainer. They realized that by doing so no material change took place around their surroundings. Those who were living prior to riots were still there because they were the people who had decided to live in India and were not ready to leave their country at any cost. Those who had to go had already gone. A few deaths here and there and a few rapes and arsons, and lootings did not affect materially the inter-community interface. Consequently, sense prevailed upon the people who were tired of everyday riots, and the intensity of riots in Northern India decreased. Another factor which checked these riots was that a chunk of middle and rich rural class had migrated to cities due to uncertainty and lawlessness in the villages as well as to enjoy prosperity in the cities and provide education to their children. Consequently, the composition of population of the cities had changed. Since these rural people were not prone to communal virus, they dented the riots. Besides, due to several changes in the mindsets of the urbanites such as compulsions of urban life, impact of modern education and keen competition for livelihood the attitude of indifference was created in them for their community fellow who blunted the old caste and community affinities that could gather masses at the slightest provocation and cause riots. The affinities between various communities, religious groups and sects are weakening due to urbanization, increase in population and the need of the hour hence when two people of different communities, sects and castes quarrel nobody bothers about them and people ignore their misadventures. This discourages the vested interests to ignite the fire of riots. Over and above this, it had been seen that generally the students used to help directly or indirectly in fanning riots but with globalization they became active in acquiring better degrees and thus the student moments became docile. We do not find much agitation in the universities. Moreover, the old generation which had witnessed partition and which was affected by the turmoil of the division of the country is no more and a new generation has come on the scene which is not biased against their counterparts. With new economic era generating a rich middle class and providing better opportunities for work and pleasure and with the emergence of mighty malls, beautiful restaurants, attractive food joints and nice buildings people would never think of burning their beautiful cities in the fire of ignorance and wickedness. The media too has become active these days. It tries its best to expose the rioters as well as the administrative machinery which further helps in controlling the communal riots. Many ruling governments too have become cautious. They do not hesitate in suspending district and police officials in the wake of failing to control the riots which compels the administration to be alert and proactive. It has been stated that Dr. Manmohan Singh government is also bringing an Act in the Parliament to control the riots which would further discourage the rioters. Thank God riots are now the abrasions at least in Northern India. The judiciary and the human rights groups as well as the NGOs have become active and now it has become difficult for a rioter to go scot free. The Indian Military and the judiciary especially the High Court and Supreme Court Judges have played a prominent role to maintain law and order and in providing safety and security and justice to all the communities. During recent times, the role of Indian media has been commendable especially in Gujarat riot. Likewise, the NGOs have done tremendous service to minorities by fighting their cases and in bringing the culprits to book. Unfortunately, the riots have started in Southern, Central and Western India but it is hoped that the sense will prevail among people and the frequency of riots in these areas too would decline very soon.

The Redeeming Features of the Riots

The redeeming feature of the post-partition riots was that majority of the older generation was not involved in it. They had cordial relations between them and used to help each other in emergencies. Besides, thanks to the Rajas, Maharajas and Nawabs that most of the princely states except some of the states near Delhi and Punjab were free from the virus of communal riots. Southern India, excluding certain isolated pockets here and there, was immune from this malady. Severe communal riots took place only at such places where the refugees from Pakistan had migrated in large numbers. They affected certain volatile portion of the younger generation and people with rightist leanings as well as those who had some grudge against each other. Most of the local people had no complain against Muslims or Hindus since they had been living in peace with them for centuries. They could not imagine that a situation like that would ever happen in India. Besides, the intensity of riots was also dented due to the fact that the local businessmen over a period of time kept themselves aloof from the refugees as they were not happy with Punjabi and Sindhi businessmen because they were their main rivals. They had occupied the important places in the main markets and were competing with them due to their superior business techniques. The evacuee properties of those Muslim Zamindars, businessmen, rich Muslims and others who had migrated to Pakistan and which were located at the prime places were also allotted to them by the government. Over and above this, those businessmen who had come from Pakistan had government backing and support which had increased their competitive power. With the state patronage and their proactive approach, they captured almost all the important markets, mandis and business establishments throughout India in no time which were previously dominated by the local businessmen. It created heart burning among the local businessmen, since they could not relish the domination of the people coming from Pakistan. Moreover, the presence of the so-called refugees had created a stir in the local majority and minority communities because their lifestyle was liberal which was affecting their younger generations. Locals were averse to inter-caste marriages, co-education, free mixing, liberal customs and dynamic ethos. It is fact that the presence of the refugees ultimately changed the whole conservative complex of the Indian society at this side of the border the credit or debit for which goes to the immigrants. Another retrieving feature was that senior and higher government officials were above communalism. They had British background of neutrality towards any caste and religion and were serving honestly to restore law and order. Many of the middle level baboos and almost all the new appointees had been affected by the communal virus which was a cause of concern for Muslims of India. The peace could be restored in the country despite so much bloodshed simply because majority of people in India and Pakistan did not relish what happened in post-partition days.

In addition to it, the continuous occurrence of the riots mainly in the markets of Indian cities led to the establishment of various markets by Muslim lads in predominantly Muslim localities. Actually, it had become risky to buy goods and services from the main city markets due to the frequency of communal riots. Prior to these riots, Muslims throughout the country used to buy the goods of their daily requirements from the main markets of the cities which were mostly dominated by the businessmen of the majority community. However, as the frequency of the riots accelerated, it became difficult for Muslim men and women to purchase materials of their daily requirements from the main markets of the cities for many a time the riots used to take place suddenly and it used to be difficult for people to reach home safely. On several occasions, they were trapped and suffered heavy losses. Besides, since the riots used to last long, they had to depend upon the government machinery for the goods of their daily needs including baby milk and medicines. Thus, in order to overcome this difficulty, the Muslim shops which were conspicuous by absence, started flourishing in Muslim localities. As time elapsed, full-fledged markets developed in almost all the Muslim localities of the country. Initially, these markets were in rudimentary stage and served the needs of Muslims only but as time passed, they became specialized and even the non-Muslims started coming to these markets due to their unique styles, cheap prices and personal attention. The emergence of these markets not only solved the problem of Muslims but also provided them employment and developed in them the spirit of entrepreneurship which augured well especially for those Muslims who were not finding jobs in government, semi-government and private organizations.

The Minorities and the Majorities Looked Through Prism

The most disturbing aspect of the communal riots was that the Muslims and Hindus looked at each other with suspicion and disgust. India was a united nation. Their misfortune was that during the British period a prism of looking at people from communal angle was put on their perception and they began to see things from the point of view of Hindu interest and Muslim interest. The same prism ultimately led to the partition of the country. Initially, two wavelengths emerged from the prism in the shape of Bharat and Pakistan and soon the third wave emerged in the shape of Bangladesh. As time elapsed, many more wavelengths have come up in the shape of Scheduled Castes and Scheduled Tribes, Backward Castes, minorities, majorities, high castes and low castes, Brahmans, Yadavas, Biharis, Marathis and what not. Today, the situation is that there is no majority. All have become minorities. There is rivalry between various minority segments of the majority community and each one fears from the other segment of the Hindu society. When the Yadavas compare themselves with Brahmins, they find them in minority and hence they fear the Brahman domination. Likewise, when the Brahmans compare them with backward castes they find themselves in minority and thus they fear from the backlash of the backward castes. The beauty of these indigenous caste and class streams is that they flow like the small rivulets parallel and nearer to the national and international mainstreams at a safe distance while preserving their identities. If they are not disturbed or cautioned, they gradually and gradually converge towards the mainstream and the national stream and in doing so shed some of their individualities. However, if they are shaken or challenged, they become alert and make a loop and move away from the international and national streams and cautiously flow at a safe distance while preserving their identities especially those which were challenged by their adversaries. Muslims of India lost many of their distinctiveness such as dress, address, styles and their many social and cultural distinctiveness which were not challenged by their rivals for they silently and fearlessly moved along and nearby national and international streams and in doing so shed those individualities which were not challenged by their adversaries. However, the moment the issues like veil, talaq, maintenance, etc. were raised, they made the loop and went away from the mainstream and are cautiously moving preserving their family distinctiveness. Besides all, sometimes it so happens that two minorities moving near each other make loop simultaneously with each other and a very long gap is created between them. It happened in Orissa where the Christians and the Extremist Hindu sections were moving along with each other. However, when they feared each other, each one of them made a loop with each other and threw them too much apart from each other which finally led to the bloodshed. Since each and every caste and class is conscious of its narrow identity, new forces have emerged in the country which are strengthening revivalism, aloofness and uniqueness in each caste and class group. The assimilation of various sections of the society which was the by-product of industrial growth, modern education and dynamism and which was to bring people in the mainstream has been dented and people mostly feel proud in being called by their caste and class affiliations rather than by their larger Indian identities. These caste and class rivalry have created a fear psychosis in the country which is not good for the health of the country. Many caste groups are producing children in large number to increase their population with a view to strengthen their vote bank which is detrimental for the health of the country. Muslims are paying a heavy price for almost all the smaller Hindu castes or class groups are afraid of them for each one of them consider Muslims as a majority compared to them and they fear that being in large number of Muslims would overcome them one day. This helps the reactionary parties in uniting them against the Muslims. Whenever any question is raised about providing any concession to Muslims as a religious minority, the anti-Muslim parties succeed in throttling the move by convincing the various smaller sub-sects of Hindu society that Muslims are not a minority, instead they are a majority. Besides this, they incite them by emphasizing that such a move would strengthen Muslims' position vis-à-vis Hindus as a consequences of which the Muslims fail to get the support of various segments of the Hindu society and remain in their pathetic condition. Needless to say that Muslims are not a homogeneous group. There are castes and sub-castes among them also. There is rivalry between various Muslim sub-groups too. The Muslim backward castes feel that they are being dominated by Muslim higher castes and the Shias feel that Sunnis are dominating them. Thus, the need of the hour is to throw aside the prism which has distorted our vision and divided us in several caste and sub-caste groups so that we may look at the light of India in its natural form which has potentials to unite us on the path of our Indian identity.

It was in fact the impact of this distorted vision that during post-partition days mostly the government officials, civil society and even the meaningful people looked at Muslims from their coloured glasses and hence justice could not be done to them. Muslims not only suffered in communal riots but the blame of initiating the riots was also put upon them by various commissions and committees. Whenever and wherever communal riots took place some kind of administrative and seldom a judiciary enquiry was instituted by the State Governments since the subject of law and order fell within the purview of the states. First of all, the reports of these committees were either delayed unnecessarily or suppressed. Whenever they were made public, the blame was mostly placed on the minority community. It was concluded that since Muslims were under a sense of frustration, they were prone to anger and sporadic outbursts of vituperation which resulted in violence and destructive activities. Majority community, in their opinion, reacted in response to Muslims' misadventure. consequently, Muslims being in minority suffered more in comparison to Hindus. Speaking generally, most of the commissions maintained that Muslims wrongly blamed the majority community for subjecting Muslims to injustice and ignominy. They held that the majority community was merely striving for peace, secular attitudes and good moral behaviour and for national integration which were interpreted by Muslims as an attempt to overawe their sufferings and destroy their cultural and Islamic beliefs and ideas. Muslims were advised not to take part in ceaseless recrimination, accusations and war of attrition but shun their deep nostalgia and tribal memory of centuries when they ruled over India as kings and emperor and develop in them the sense that they are no more than equal citizens where they have to compete on the basis of merely their personal merit. It is strange that thousands of riots took place during the rule of Congress Government in which thousands of people were killed and injured and many were humbled and humiliated but hardly the criminals were jailed in sufficient number and seldom any meaningful compensation was given to many. In every riot Muslims generally suffered more compared to Hindus. The number of people arrested and tortured was generally much more from the minority community compared to those of their opponents. More than 28 Commissions were appointed to look into the causes and suggest remedial measures. Some of the important commissions were: Justice P. Jagmohan Reddy Commission, 1969 to enquire Ahmedabad riots, Justice D.P. Madan Commission, 1970 to look into the Bhiwandi riots, Justice P. Venugopal Commission, 1982 to probe Kanyakumari riots, Justice Vithathil Commission to go into the Tellicheri riots, Justice Narayan S.K. Ghosh and S.Q. Rizvi Commission, 1979 to explore Jamshedpur riots, Justice R.C.P. Sinha and S.S. Hasan Commission to analyze Bhagalpur riots, Justice Ranganath Mishra Commission to investigate into the 1984 Delhi riots and Justice Shrikrishna Commission to find facts about the 1993 Bombay riots. Almost all of them showed the passiveness and the connivance of the civil and police authorities with criminal element but no action was taken against any official. It is alleged by many Muslims that several major riots took place in Meerut, Maleyana, Hashimpura, Moradabad, Aligarh, Sambhal, Kanpur, Bhagalpur and Jabalpur perhaps with the connivance or complicity of many biased police officials and thousands of people were perished, properties worth crores of rupees were destroyed and rapes were committed but hardly any one was dealt with effectively to create deterrence or compensation of some significant nature was given to the victims. Actually, the atmosphere at that time was not congenial to Muslims. The Governments at the State level as well as at the Centre hesitated to do anything for the riot victims due to the pressure from the right wing extremist parties and the fear of losing the votes of the majority community.

The condition of the governments appears to be not much better even after the lapse of sixty years. Even today Muslims generally feel insecure and discriminated during the surcharge communal atmosphere. Communal tension or any untoward incidence is enough to create fear and insecurity among them across various states and regions. The lackadaisical and knee jerk approach of the government and the political mileage certain political parties seek to please majority and minority communities to secure their votes frustrate Muslims beyond redemption. Not only this, many a time the police and certain sections of the biased media exaggerate the role of Muslims in violent and destructive activities and underplay the involvement of the rival groups and organizations. The government inaction in bringing the culprits to book and the delay and the alleged discrimination in paying compensation to victims when they happen to be Muslims act as eye sores to the community. The recent mind boggling and heart-piercing one sided riot resembling ethnic cleansing or genocide happened in Gujarat during 2002, with supposedly police connivance and where the innocent men, women, aged and infants were butchered and where Muslim women became the special target of sexual violence. The episode shattered the faith of even those Muslims who were not affected by them and who were living miles away from such incidents. The lack of police presence in adequate strength and the supposedly connivance of the police force and the necessary will on the part of the state to fight the menace of communal virus have created fear psychosis in the minds of Muslims. They have mostly relapsed in the vicious circle. Consequently, their efforts to get higher education have dented, the literacy rate among Muslim girls has slowed down and their horizontal, vertical and diagonal mobility too has suffered adversely. The men in power know that Muslims are a worst lot but fail to do anything positive for them due to the fear of annoying the adversaries of Muslims. Similar facts created uncertainties in the minds of Muslims in the past too and up to 1971, most of the Muslims in Northern India were thinking that one day they will have to migrate to Pakistan. Nearly for twenty-five years, they remained in the state of mental siege and neither constructed new houses nor repaired the old ones nor started any meaningful new adventures. They survived on the basis of their old family businesses, professions, vocations and trades and never demanded government jobs, admissions for their children, bank loans or any other civic facility from the Central and State Governments save the protection to their lives, honour and properties. Basically, the Muslims were in the state of shock and depression and hence they did not exert much and remained silent observers. Even today, they are not pro-active. They seldom send their children to schools in large number and rarely demand any help or concession from the government as a consequence of which their share of prosperity is mostly usurped by other sections of the society and they have been constantly drifting towards poverty, ignorance and diseases. Thank God that the ramifications of communal riots are on the wane now and it is hoped that Muslims will come out of their siege mentality and participate in the mainstream as equal partners.

Muslim Victims of Hate Campaign

Just after partition nearly 45 million Muslims had stayed in various parts of the country due to their compulsions or sweet will. Those Muslims who stayed in India after the partition of the country suffered heavily due to the constant taunts of attributing extra-territorial loyalties, infidelity and unfaithfulness to them by a section of a reactionary and unruly wing of the majority community. Muslims were mostly blamed for the partition of the country and people scoffed at them by saying that "Muslims wanted to eat the cake and take away the plate too" or "they wanted to have their cake and eat it too". Muslims were often asked to go to Pakistan, the country of their choice. There was a diehard fanatic section amongst the majority community which was basically anti-Muslim in nature and which had also been affected by the atrocities committed to their brethren in Pakistan. This segment was not in favour of allowing Muslims to live in India. It used to call Muslims by bad names and talked in terms of "your Baber and our Sanga, your Akbar and our Pratap and your Aurangzeb and our Shivaji". Muslims too had their hard-core fanatics but they were not assertive. They were at the receiving end but did not lag behind in provoking Muslims. However, there was an enlightened and liberated section amongst Hindus and Muslims headed by Mahatma Gandhi who was doing everything for the safety, security and the honour of Muslims of India. The world knows that the same Mahatma Gandhi whom the Indians called the Father of Nation came openly against his own people for the protection of Indian Muslims. He ultimately became the target of the hatred of an extremist for having a soft corner for Pakistan and Muslims and lost his life on January 30, 1948. It was the hatred which caused the martyrdom of Mahatma Gandhi and it was the hatred that created bloodshed in various parts of the country. Wherever the immigrants went in Northern and certain parts of Southern India, the passions arose due to the atrocities committed upon them and several parts of the country witnessed communal riots. Communal riots also took place on large and bloody scale in those areas where the immigrants had not reached but which had the past history of communal violence and hatred. Most of the casualties took place in the trains and buses and in inadvertent movements within affected areas. Life became miserable especially for those men and women who could be recognized by their faces or religious apparels or who were obliged to seek livelihood in majority dominated areas due to poverty. Special compartments were provided for Muslims by Indian Railways under police protection with a view to provide safety, security and protection to their lives, honour and properties. Muslims lived in tense atmosphere and made their own arrangements for safety and security. Muslims were certainly at the receiving end for the prevailing atmosphere was surcharged with communal hatred and violence especially by the settlement of the immigrants from Pakistan in nearby Muslim colonies. Many properties were declared as evacuee properties. Even those properties which were occupied by any member of the family were declared evacuee properties due to the migration of one or a few members to Pakistan. In some cases, people were harassed by the goons and on their false reports of migration to Pakistan many Muslims had to undergo litigation to save their skins. Besides, many people were black listed and the fanatics were at liberty to terrorize people. Police was playing its own game of hide and seek with the result that the life had become miserable especially for those Muslims who were poor and helpless. Partition of the country changed the total scenario of India. Muslims in Punjab, Haryana, Himachal Pradesh, Bharatpur, Alwar, Northern Rajasthan and in the areas surrounding Delhi either migrated to Pakistan or left the regions for safer places or got converted to save their skins. Muslims in police department, railways, security forces, education and industry and trade as well as in various other segments became conspicuous by absence. As time elapsed they became poorer and poorer, weaker and weaker and deserted and marginalized.

Jihad Type Situation in the Wake of Hockey and Cricket Matches

Whenever any match was played between India and Pakistan, it looked as if the war was being fought between the two rival countries. Players played on the ground as if they were fighting their bitter enemies and the crowd on both sides supported them as they support their armies in the times of war with enemy. People kept fasts, conducted havans and did everything to win the game. On the victory of India or Pakistan, there were celebrations in India and Pakistan which were worth seen. The heads of states, intellectuals and commoners rejoiced the victory of their teams as if they had conquered the enemy country. We find some such things during our times also but there is one great difference. The present victories are sweet victories, the victories of games, sports and players and not of nations. They represent the bright side of human vigour and dexterity and not revenge and hatred. The victories and defeats in games these days do not create a bitter climate between nations but compel them to do better next time. In post-partition days when games were played they created bad blood. Many communal riots in those days took place due to some Muslims' supporting Pakistani hockey team or cricket team or rejoicing on the defeat of Indian teams at the hands of Pakistani teams. There were primarily three reasons for this type of misadventure on the part of a few irresponsible Indian Muslims. Firstly, the communal atmosphere in the country those days was surcharged with quick frequency of riots as a consequence of which the relations between the two major communities of the country were not cordial. Anything which could become the cause of show down or insult and humiliation to the rival community was rejoiced by the other community. Invariably, the defeat of Indian hockey team and cricket team used to work as moral booster for a few irresponsible segments of

Muslim society both educated and uneducated and a few of them indulged in bursting crackers and the distribution of sweets which naturally used to annoy all sections of Indian society both Muslims and Hindus. In the same way, when the Indian teams won the proactive segments of the majority community in retaliation used to give fitting reply to their rivals by bursting crackers, distributing sweets and taunting Muslims. In both the situations, the ground was prepared for communal riots. The second factor which was the root cause of all malady was the perception in the mind of certain segments of Muslim community that deserving and renowned Muslim players in hockey and cricket were either not given chance or when they were taken in the team they were either dropped or suspected especially when Indian teams played against Pakistan. Certainly, there were a few Muslim players in Indian teams and they were given chance in the national and international tournaments. Some of them such as Nawab of Pataudi and Zafar Iqbal were made captains and they played against Pakistan but despite this the perception that Muslims were discriminated continued for long due to a few incidences in which certain Muslim players were dropped in the World Olympics in the wake of confrontation with Pakistan teams. Admittedly, Muslim players too were partly responsible for this perception for whenever they played against Pakistani teams they could not play their natural games due to unbearable pressure from the side of general public and the team managers were compelled to drop them in the larger interest of the country. The third cause was the soft corner in the heart of the Muslim crowd for Pakistani players since during those days many Muslims used to consider Pakistan as their natural friend as many of their kith and kin were in Pakistan and Pakistan used to speak in favour of them in the wake of riots or any untoward incidence committed by any unruly segment of the majority community against them. Besides, in their heart to heart they were convinced that one day every Muslim would go to Pakistan. Thank God that this situation did not last long. When capable Muslim players emerged on the scene, they were given chance in large number which dented the adverse perception of Muslims about team management. Credit goes to Muslim players for they too maintained their calm and delivered good. Majority community adored them, rewarded them and soon a time came when many Muslims began praying for the victory of Indian teams against Pakistani teams. These days we find that the Jihad type situation is not there between Indian teams and Pakistani teams. Many Pakistani players are loved by Indians and there are innumerable fans of Indian players in Pakistan. We very often find Indian and Pakistani players on television screens meeting and discussing as friends. It has been observed that whenever the Indian or Pakistani teams go to play outside India many people of India and Pakistan origins who are the nationals of those countries support Indian and Pakistan teams even when they play matches against their own teams. It has also been observed that even Pakistani crowd supported Indian teams when they were playing against Pakistani team and Indian crowd reciprocated by supporting Pakistani team at the cost of Indian team. Actually, as the people are becoming matured, sportsman spirit is developing among them on both the side of the border. The sport code says that games should be played in the spirit of game and not to win or lose and players and the teams too should be supported on the basis of merit and not on any other consideration.

Blame Game on Both Sides of the Border

Post-partition days between India and Pakistan were the days of mutual mistrust, acrimony and accusations. The two newly created countries were passing in the gestation period. Neither the Indian rulers had any sound experience of conducting the government affairs nor had their counterparts. The problems faced by the countries were enormous and unprecedented. There were no quick solutions. The world in general was also watching these countries with caution and suspicion. Resources were meager and demands were immense. At this juncture, the existence of Pakistan and India was a boon for both the countries because if anything untoward happened in India which the government of India could not control, it generally imputed the blame upon the foreign hand, which necessarily hinted at Pakistan. Likewise when Pakistan failed to solve its problems it too was usually quick in blaming India for all of its ills. It appeared as if a friendly wrestling contest was being played between the two rival players. Generally, the most sensitive issue on which the Pakistani radio came openly against India was the alleged atrocities committed on Indian Muslims or pleading the case of Kashmiri Muslims. Whenever any riot took place in any corner of India, Pakistan was quick to broadcast it giving full details as if its correspondents were present there. This used to surprise and annoy Indian authorities for the fingers of suspicion were bound to lift at some Muslim organizations or individuals within India. This situation used to create doubts in the minds of the majority community about the integrity and loyalty of Muslims towards the country. Many Muslims used to hear the Radio Pakistan with zeal and enthusiasm because this was the only source for them to know about what happened in India especially in the context of Muslims. The Indian radio used to broadcast only the Indian point of view when Pakistan radio used to announce the distorted version of the situation. Since Indian channels broadcasted only the censured news, it did not appeal to many Muslims. The Government of India also used to expose Pakistan on atrocities committed upon Hindus in Pakistan especially in East Pakistan which is now known as Bangladesh because most of Hindu minority was living in East Pakistan and only a smaller fraction of it was in West Pakistan. These out-placed sympathies neither helped Muslims of India nor Hindus of Pakistan. They helped the unfortunate people on both the sides to the extent that they gave them merely a psychic satisfaction but for this misadventure, they had to pay a heavy price. Such follies on the side of Pakistan and India created bad blood between two countries and communities and could not lessen the burdens and agonies of minorities in both the countries. The most unusual aspect of the broadcasting media was when there was a short war between India and China in 1962. Indians were expecting that Pakistan being their immediate neighbour and brother would side with India in the wake of any war with China or would at least keep mum and neutral. They could never imagine that it would play with India. If Pakistan would have shown patience and statesmanship and showed soft corner towards India the situation in this sub-continent would have been different. Alas! Pakistan missed this opportunity. Ironically, it supported neither India nor physically and openly helped China. It provided merely the moral support to China and exposed India's weaknesses by taunting at the drawbacks of Indian armed forces which annoyed Indian masses and created a deep gulf of mistrust and hatred between the two countries which would take years to bridge. The worst aspect of those days was that those people who mattered in policy making at that time had seen the horrors of partition and their hearts were very bitter for many of them had burnt their fingers. They could not imagine for a moment that till yesterday those who were bitter enemies and thirsty of each others blood would become friends. Pakistan being a smaller country always doubted the Indian moves for most of the Pakistanis were of the opinion that India did not relish the existence of Pakistan and it would always try to undo what was done in 1947. There was a lack of proper response from the side of India too because there were many hard-core rightist in India who were propagating in favour of Akhand Bharat and they were not favourably inclined to give any latitude to Pakistan since they too had their adverse experiences in pre-partition days. Thus, the mutual distrust between the two countries and communities worked as petrol in the fire and led to two painful wars.

Muslims of India were very bitter about the division of the country for they were the worst sufferers. Those Muslims who were living in those areas which later became Pakistan were satisfied since they got what they wanted. Likewise, the Hindus of India who were living where they are living now also got their due. The only people who suffered were the Muslims of India and the Hindus of Pakistan who either left their home lands or are living as minorities in their own countries. They faced turmoil, tortures, taunts and what not. Once upon a time they too were the significant part of the mainstream but in one stroke of pen they became redundant and unwanted due to their meager number. They lost their glamour, grace, comforts and dignity being the so-called uncomfortable segment of the society and being depressed, marginalized and handicapped they became a burden on the ex-chequer. Actually, the proactive Hindus and aggressive Muslims of British India were responsible for dividing the country. The citizens of the Princely States were at the mercy of their kings, nawabs and the rulers. They had no say in the process of dividing the country. They accepted what their rulers decided. Likewise, innumerable people were silent spectators sitting on the fences. They never knew what was going on in the country but it is highly frustrating and painful that they too had to face the consequences of the sin which they had not committed. History will always haunt those who thought of partition of the country without realizing the adverse consequences of dividing people on the basis of religion and not making adequate preparations for future eventualities.

To Stay in India by Muslims was a Sound Decision

Muslims of India thank their parents that they took a right decision and did not go to Pakistan for those Muslims who migrated to Pakistan are mostly in bad shape compared to Muslims in India. It has been rightly said that there is no place like one's sweet home. However, fine and pleasant a place may be but it cannot take the place of one's country. The consolation, contentment and satisfaction which one gets in one's country cannot be obtained from any part of the world. Poets, writers and literary geniuses have written volumes after volumes in praise of their motherlands. Only those can understand and appreciate the beauty and warmth of their fatherlands that have lived away from their homes. Besides, it is said that the one who deserts the motherland is not welcomed anywhere else for no piece of earth accepts him whole-heartedly. Over and above this, living in India has its own charms. India is a vast country with ancient heritage, democratic setup, healthy traditions, rich customs and admirable manners extending twenty-four degrees of latitude north and south and for nearly the same degrees east and west. Various forms of its social, political and ideological institutions as well as the knowledge of mathematics, astronomy and the systems of metaphysics and ethics made the people of India famous far beyond their frontiers. The renowned Indian thinkers and philosophers visited many parts of Europe, Africa and the known world and influenced the mankind with their erudition and geniuses. Distinguished by their eminence, they have done a commendable work yet it must be confessed that the knowledge which we possess about the past is shrouded in mystery. It is not only meager compared with which it is pertinent for us to know but it is also a faint reflection of what happened in time immemorial. One who is born in India is really lucky and feels proud and privileged to be called an Indian for to be an Indian means a dynamic, progressive, forward-looking, tolerant and an enlightened human being. India is one of the oldest civilizations in the world with a kaleidoscopic variety and rich cultural heritage. It is a vast country with 29 states and 6 union territories with more than 1.2 billion population. It covers an area of 32,87,263 sq. km. extending from the snow-covered Himalayan heights to the tropical forests of the south. It lies between latitudes 8.4 and 37.6 north, longitudes 68.7 and 97.25 east and measures about 3,214 km from north to south and 2,933 km from east to west with frontiers of about 15,200 km and coastline of 7,5516.6 km. It is a vast country with immense potentialities. A country where the bones of our forefathers are buried, a country where our children can grow, a country where our youth can prosper, a country where our elders can find shelter, a country where the future of its citizens is safe. A country which is the laboratory of the world where people of all religions live peacefully; where white, brown, black and yellow races exist simultaneously; where there are rivers, lakes, springs and mighty oceans; where there are snowy peaks, sand dunes, sea shores and beautiful valleys; where no one can match the beauty of its maidens, courage of its youths, intelligence of its geniuses and large-hearted tolerance of its elders. Where one can notice mountains, oceans, deserts, plains, glaciers and plateaus; where one can observe summer, winter, autumn, spring and rainy seasons; where all types of minerals, flora and fauna are found in abundance; where people speak several languages and dialects, wear different types of dresses, follow varied customs and traditions. A mighty country where lions, elephants, bears, deers, cows, camels and cuckoos flourish. A great country where refreshing monsoons, dust storms, cool breezes and the moisture-laden winds blow in plenty. Where pines, chinars, neem and christmas trees bloom in abundance. Where we grow wheat, rice, barley, coconut; where all types of flowers, fruits, herbs and medicinal plants grow in plenty and where the people possess enough potentials to lead the world on the path of peace, progress, non-violence and piety. It is country which can boast of its saints, geniuses, intellectuals, artists, humanists and the glorious past. India is a country where people recite Vedas, Gita, Quran, Bible, Old Testament and the Granth Sahib with admiration and devotion. A country where one hears the hymns of the priests, bells of the churches, calls of the moazzins and the gurbani of the gurudwaras. A country where there is synthesis of materialism and spiritualism; a country where people believe in golden mean; a country where there is unity in diversity and diversity in unity. It is a unique country where people have freedom of speech, expression and religion, liberty of movement, residence and conscience, and choice of profession, business vocation and worship. It is a country where people believe in non-violence, large-hearted tolerance and peace and prosperity. It is perhaps the only country which has never remained aggressor, unjust and oppressive, and whose homeostasis is based on unity, love, brotherhood, assimilation and good moral conduct. Despite the fact that the country is passing in a difficult period, it cannot be mortgaged by a few reactionaries for a long time to come. Very soon the clouds of mistrust and misunderstanding would vanish and a sense of fraternity, brotherhood, fellow-feeling and peaceful co-existence would generate amongst its great people. Once again India would be heralded as the champion of non-violence, truth, justice, equity, good moral conducts and humanism throughout the world. It would be known as the Golden Bird and the milk of love, honey of affection and liquor of compassion would flow in the rivers of hearts, lakes of minds and oceans of souls. The people of the world would turn towards it for peace, prosperity, salvation and accomplishment.

India's significance in the context of the world is very special. It is the laboratory of the world which the Lord has designed to guide people to live as the members of a united family. When someone produces a machine, one provides a manual to explain its efficient working. For instance, when we buy a refrigerator, we get a booklet which explains various parts of the machine which tells us how to operate it efficiently. Similarly, when the Lord created the world He gave a working manual to the people in the shape of India. It is a miniature world with all its characteristics. Through India, God wants the people of the world to learn how they can live peacefully in the world along with their differences as the Indians live comfortably as a united nation despite innumerable diversities. Just as the homeostasis of the body maintains the body temperature at 98.4 degree Fahrenheit and when it deviates from the normal, the same process brings to its normal position. Likewise, the climatic forces of each country maintain equilibrium in the atmospheric pressure in the sense that when the pressure goes up or down the fresh winds blow and bring the pressure to its normal position. In the same way, the homeostasis of India maintains equilibrium between its five tatvas or elements such as the earth, water, dust, fire and the sky in the shape of unity, love, brotherhood, assimilation and good moral conduct. When there is any disequilibrium in these forces the health of India is jeopardized but its homeostasis is strong enough to bring it back to its normal position. It is in the blood of Indian people to remain united, to love each other, to live in harmony with their brethren, to adopt and assimilate others and lead a life of good moral conduct. When they temporarily deviate from any one of them, the homeostasis forces act upon them and bring them to their equilibrium position. One can see that whenever there is any riot or disturbance, the whole area is disturbed but soon sanity prevails and it appears as if nothing had happened. Indians cannot tolerate two people quarreling on the road side and try to pacify them. What to talk of human beings they come to the rescue of the dogs fighting in the street. One cannot expect violence from them for long. They stand like rock and bounce like lion when their cherished values are challenged or when someone looks towards their country with evil eye or when they find the weak and downtrodden in miseries and exploitation. Whatever adverse things one finds these days in this beautiful country are mere abrasions. They would soon be the matters of the past.

India Custodian of Moral and Spiritual Values

India is a best place for Muslims since it is a biggest democracy and its people are the custodians of moral and spiritual values. It is a known fact that today the whole world has yielded before the prevailing forces of liberalism. Many countries of the world have legalized many institutions and practices which were considered detrimental to the established principles of culture and civilization. It is India where several religious groups from amongst Hindus, Muslims, Christians, Jews, Jains, Sikhs and others are standing firmly to fight against these evil forces. Indians have been taught since time immemorial that they have been created to do good works and invite others to do good deeds. Besides, they are duty bound to avoid bad deeds and to persuade others from evil practices. Thus, Indians are not supposed to go with winds but they are expected to control the winds in order to bring their boats to the shore. It is India which will ultimately lead the world in the field of material, moral and spiritual development. The world's safety, prosperity and moral and spiritual health lies in the welfare and progress of India.

Indians irrespective of caste, creed, class, gender and religion are not happy with most of the western trends which are drifting their children from their past heritage. They are not happy with the unsavoury gifts of modern education because they are the custodian of moral and spiritual values. One should not forget that Indian art, literature, philosophy, culture and religion thrived at an epoch when most of the civilized world was in the stage of decadence. It was perhaps because of the piety of India that the Holy Prophet of Islam felt cool breeze from the side of India. Muslims of India too are averse with modern trends that are drifting their children from the path of Islam. They too will whole-heartedly support their counterparts in the fight against unacceptable forces. It is irony of fate that in modern system there is an inverse relationship between material development and moral advancement. As man is advancing materially, he is generally decaying morally. India too is marching ahead in the economic field but many Indians are lagging behind in piety and good conduct. As India is becoming bigger, many Indians are becoming smaller as human beings. There are a few people who want to legalize many practices which the Indian society does not relish but they are finding it difficult due to the resistance of the moral, ethical, spiritual and religious forces which are raising their heads in every corner of the country. Indian society believes in the dictum that change is the law of nature but it does not believe that changes should be made in the fundamental structure of the society for once changes are introduced in this area, peripheral changes cease to exist. For instance so long as the inclination in the axis, size and the orbit of the earth and distance of the earth from the sun remain same, the earth witnesses changes in day and night, seasons, vegetation, flora and fauna, etc. but once the size, inclination of the earth and its orbit and its distance from the sun is changed, all the harmonious changes taking place on the surface of the earth would fall flat. Thus, peripheral changes suiting to the culture and heritage of the country should always be accepted so as to remain dynamic, progressive and pragmatic. However, whenever any changes are suggested in the fundamentals sustaining the cultural heritage, they should be resisted to save the society from falling in the ditch. The changes in the relationship between parents and children, affinities between husbands and wives, affections between brothers and sisters, love between younger and elders and sanctity of the moral, social, cultural, esthetical, spiritual and religious time tested principles should not be touched. If man is allowed to accept all changes suiting to his cardinal desires on the pattern of animals, he too would resemble with the animals as cat resembles to cat and tiger with tiger. It is hoped that the good and saner people of India would not only create harmony between material and moral development in the country but would also lead the people on the path of piety and good conduct by providing them justice, equity and prosperity.

The Large-Hearted Tolerance of Indian Society

Indian Muslims are privileged like their counterparts to be called Indians because they live in a country where people are religious minded, tolerant and peace loving. The experience of Indian history and traditions reveals that most of the Indians are decent and considerate people. The silent majority consists of most of the 25% SCs/STs, majority of 35% OBCs, a large section of 20% minorities and considerable portion of the 20% high castes who are simple-minded and straight forward people. They call the spade a spade and do not indulge in flattery, intrigues and cheap tactics.

The large-hearted tolerance of Indian people is reflected by the fact that they have already chosen three distinguished Muslims as the Presidents of Indian Republic. They have also elected President, Prime Minister and the military generals from Sikh, Christian and Parsi communities. The manner in which they show their regard and respect to Srimati Sonia Gandhi is admirable. They are willing to accept any Muslim as Prime Minister of the country provided the Muslim community presents any Barack Hussein Obama before them. India's religious diversity is reflected when we find that among its six of the highest constitutional functionaries presently the President of India is a Hindu, Prime Minister is a Sikh, UPA Chairperson is a Christian, Chief Election Officer is a Muslim, Chief Justice of India is a Parsi and Speaker of Lok Sabha is a Dalit. The tragedy with most of the Muslims of India is that they have neither a leader nor listeners. They are mostly governed by their religious heads. Many of them are inward looking people and do not try to reach other people surrounding their community with a view to inspire others to stand with them. India needs an inspirational Muslim leader who with his charismal personality and healing touchstone may mobilize the dynamic emotions and judgment of the passive Muslim electorate to his advantage to create a magic moment in history. Every democracy needs crowd pullers but Muslims unfortunately are either fence sitters or sit in the middle range. Many Muslim leaders do not come from the grass-root level but reach the top through a nudge hence they have to pay the price for staying in the comfort zone. The community abhors such leaders for their historic silence on all issues of significance though they rejoice to be called the leaders of the community without any sanction. Muslims should realize that the process of change starts from home. They should not blame merely the majority community or the state machinery for all their ills but also look within. If they continue to do so, the majority community and the state apparatus would be affected the least but they would continue to remain in the state in which they are. They should make a new experiment of reaching to the majority community with open hearts and demand their democratic and constitutional rights from the state through peaceful and democratic means. They should not expect that the majority community would reach them especially when they have been surrounded by so many insularities. Actually, one cannot gain by fault finding because the age of alibis is over. There is a need of introspection. So long as the Muslim politicians would depend upon the middle men or artificial inducements, they would not be able to help the community though they would get quid pro quo. The community is directionless because there is no guide. There are preachers or sycophants in the community who are so weak and meek that they can challenge neither the ills of the community nor the governing structure because they are interested merely in their own grace and glory. They feel obliged and grateful and are loyal only to those political parties who raise their status and bring them to limelight despite their no liaison with grass-root level. Mostly their vehicle of progress is Congress or certain regional parties from among the backward castes and Scheduled Castes which use them and throw them according to their needs and necessities. The present situation demands that they should not hesitate even to communicate with any political party including the BJP and organizations such as RSS, Vishva Hindu Parishad, Bajrang Dal, Shive Sena and other national parties despite the fact that they may appear to be against them. They need not surrender before them but tell them their point of view with the sole aim of reaching to a consensus. One should know that there is solution to every problem for we do not find any lock without a key. Many misunderstandings and mistrusts are removed by healthy dialogues. Sooner it is done, better it is. It should be kept in mind that endeavouring for only a political change is not the solution of the problem. The road of peace lies not in being the prisoners of past and unleashing all-consuming fire of violence and hatred nor does it lie in mutual recrimination and in passing stringent laws. Hope for better tomorrow rests in mutual respects, peaceful co-existence and in inspiring confidence in minorities and majorities by adhering to our founding principles of equity and justice and in shading deep-rooted prejudices and conjectures.

The most unfortunate aspect of partition of the country was that it altered the past equations of trust, confidence, brotherhood and mutual respect between various sections of the society and opened the gates for the vested interests to fish in the troubled water. Muslims, Hindus, Sikhs, Jains and Parsis and others were living peacefully as good neighbours. They attended the marriage ceremonies of each others, participated in each others festivals and shared the pains and pleasures of their comrades. Despite differences of wealth, positions, distinctions, classes and castes, there was respect for the elders and love for the younger and concern for the poor and the depressed. They built mosques, temples and gurudwaras, constructed roads, schools, pathshalas and established charitable homes and participated in entertainment activities with vigour and enthusiasm. They believed in their Creator, showed reverence to others belief systems, avoided conflicts and maintained communal harmony and faithfully and sincerely relied in peaceful co-existence. Alas! the good olden days became a dream since the post-partition period wiped out all good memories from the mental canvas of the people of Indian sub-continent.

The Martyrdom of Mahatma Gandhi

During the post-partition period, a few things happened one after another in quick succession such as the assassination of Mahatma Gandhi, police action in Hyderabad, the Zamindari Abolition of 1951, the 1962 War with China and 1965 and 1971 Pakistan and India Wars which affected

Muslims adversely. Since these issues are sensitive, they would be cursorily discussed as it would not be in larger interest to discuss them in detail. When the people of both the countries would rise above petty considerations, they would be in a better position to pass judgment rationally in the light of facts and figures as to what was right and what was wrong. Till then it is advisable to leave these matters to posterity. Likewise, the martyrdom of Mahatma Gandhi too would be briefly explained here as it is shrouded with painful events, episodes and experiences. The Father of the Nation, called Mahatma Gandhi was highly disturbed due to the partition of the country. He had opposed the Congress decision to accept the division of the country into India and Pakistan and called it a Himalayan blunder. He tried his best to suppress Hindu Muslim riots. During 1946, he toured for about four months in 49 villages of East Bengal to quell communal rioting. In 1947, he went to Bihar to lessen Hindu Muslim tensions. He relentlessly fasted and prayed to combat riots in Calcutta. Visited Delhi and other neighbouring areas to stop rioting and consoled the refugees in the refugee camps. From 1946 onward Gandhiji's efforts were mainly concentrated on effecting Hindu Muslim unity. He was pained due to communal riots which were broken out all over India. In 1948, Mahatma Gandhi undertook a fast lasting for five days to bring about communal unity. On January 30, 1948 while holding a prayer meeting at Birla House, Delhi, Gandhiji was shot dead by a fanatic Vinayak N. Godse, who was deadly opposed to Gandhiji's efforts to bring about Hindu-Muslim amity. Thus, came to the end the life of one of the greatest Indians since the Buddha who was the only ray of hope for millions of suffering people in India and Pakistan. The assassination of Mahatma Gandhi was a most difficult period in the history of Muslims of India. After having heard the news of the sudden, painful and sad demise of Mahatma Gandhi, Muslims were shocked. Many of them lamented that their saviour was no more and several of them had suspicions that he was perhaps shot dead by some Muslim fundamentalist. Even Muslims had begun to murmur that something most horrible was to happen. Muslims throughout the country were expecting severe backlash and the hard-core

Hindus were preparing for the onslaught. Thanks to Pandit Jawaharlal Nehru that the adverse situation was promptly avoided. He announced on All India Radio the name of the culprit then and there by saying that Gandhiji was killed by a mad man called V.N. Godse and thus saved Muslims from agonies and embarrassment. Martyrdom of Mahatma Gandhi proved detrimental for Indian Muslims because save a few committed people like Pandit Nehru, Maulana Azad, Sarojni Naidu, Rajaji and a few others there were none to stand as shield in favour of Muslims.

The Merger of Hyderabad, Junagarh and Kashmir with Indian Union

The merger of Jammu and Kashmir in India and the annexation of the state of Hyderabad and Junagarh within Indian territories too are the issues which are sensitive in nature. It is a well-known fact that according to the conditions of the partition of the country announced by Lord Mountbatten who had succeeded Wavell as Viceroy, the British provinces where the Muslims formed the majority were to be constituted into a separate state called Pakistan. Thus, parts of Punjab (West Punjab) and Bengal (East Bengal) and the whole of the provinces of Sind, Baluchistan, and the North West Frontier became Pakistan. The rest of India formed another country called Bharat. Nearly the 565 princely states were free to join India or Pakistan depending upon the sweet will of their rulers but Mountbatten had stated that geographical compulsions meant that most of them must choose India in effect. Those Hindu Rajas and Maharajas and Muslim Nawabs who were far-sighted and could read the writings on the walls peacefully surrendered their majority Hindu states to Government of India and majority Muslim states to Pakistan without going into the legalities of the mergers. Nizam of Hyderabad acted in haste. Indian Government had offered him several sops and Mountbatten was also trying to give him a special status by June 25, 1948. Pandit Jawaharlal Nehru was in favour of avoiding any conflict with Nawab though Sardar Vallabhbhai Patel, the Deputy Prime Minister of India was adamant to take strict action. However, the Nizam of

Hyderabad whose state had no common borders with Pakistan and which had 90% Hindus and the Nawab of Junagarh Mohammed Mahabat Khanji III whose state too had no common borders save sea and had 80% Hindu population and Maharaja of Kashmir Hari Singh where there were majority of Muslims could not read the writings on the walls. Nizam of Hyderabad paid the price and Maharaja Hari Singh too had to suffer at the later stage. Shri Swaminathan S. Anklesaria Aiyar at the time of disturbances in Jammu and Kashmir on the occasion of land acquisition pertaining to Amarnath yatris by the State Government discussed the genesis of Kashmir problem in *Times of India* in much detail. He emphasized that Nizam of Hyderabad and the Nawab of Junagarh expressed their desires to stay in Pakistan which did not suit India for these states were Hindu majority states. Likewise, the Maharaja of Kashmir agreed to merge Jammu and Kashmir in India which Pakistan did not relish for it was a predominately Muslim state. India launched a police action against Hyderabad on September 13, 1948 and within four days the Nawab's forces surrendered and India took the control of the Princely State. Police action caused much agonies and immense losses of lives and properties. Muslims, known as Razakars of Ittihad al-Musalimin were fighting from the side of Nawab of Hyderabad under the command of Kasim Rizvi under the misconception that the State would merge with Pakistan. The manner in which the State of Hyderabad was merged in India created heart burning in the large segment of Muslims of the former Princely State and lowered down the already low morale of Muslims surrounding the state of Hyderabad. Junagarh too was taken by sending Indian military but it did not cause much problem for the Nawab had fled to Pakistan. Nawab of Junagarh too was offered several concessions but he too acted in haste. He did not have the farsight as Nawab of Rampur, Nawab of Bhopal and many Nawabs in the country who had willingly offered to merge their states in India. The two rulers of the states, Mangrolji and Babariawadji who were subject to the suzerainty of Junagarh had already decided to accede to India but the Nawab occupied their territories by force. Besides, in February 1948 the plebiscite was called and the people had voted in favour of India. Over and above this, after the abdication of Nawab to Pakistan the Dewan of Junagarh Sir Shah Nawaz Bhutto, the father of the slain Zulfikhar Ali Bhutto had invited Indian Government to take charge of the state. Thus, Junagarh became part of India until November 1, 1956. Pakistan retaliated and provoked the Qabailis in the last week of October 1947 to attack and take over Kashmir by force. This war is called the Indo-Pak War 1947 or the First War on Kashmir. Maharaja of Kashmir with the help of late Sheikh Abdullah who was a mass leader of Kashmiri people sought India's help and India sent its troops in Kashmir. Many Indian Muslims fought in Kashmir along with Indian forces. Captain Hameed lost his life in protecting his motherland. Indian forces reached Srinagar and saved Kashmir from going to Pakistan. Cease fire was caused by the U.N.O. and the status quo was maintained and the fate of the people of Kashmir was left to the referendum by people whether they wished to go to India or Pakistan. Since much water has flown in the Chenab after that and several democratic elections have taken place in Kashmir, India is not willing to yield Jammu and Kashmir to Pakistan for it believes that the Kashmiri people have already expressed their opinion in favour of India. India believes that plebiscite and the 47 Resolution of UN Security Council passed on 21 April 1948 are not relevant for according to Resolution 47, A-1 a, Pakistan was obliged to vacate the occupied Kashmir and India too was asked to pull its forces save such which were needed for civil administration but Pakistan did not vacate the occupied territories. Besides, India has spent huge amount of money and resources on the development of Jammu and Kashmir and sacrificed thousands of lives for the protection of the state. Over and above this, India is a secular state and the division of the state on religious lines is contrary to the principles of secularism. Furthermore, the division of the state on the basis of religion is likely to cause adverse affects upon India and the people of Jammu and Kashmir are bound to suffer as the Hindus and Muslims suffered in the wake of the division of India on communal lines. Pakistan is still insisting on referendum for which U.N.O. too has shown cold shoulders. However, there is a strong section in the valley which is demanding freedom. India may perhaps agree under very exceptional circumstances to the status quo, treating the Line of Control as the dividing line between the two countries though the Indian Parliament has emphasized its claim that Jammu and Kashmir including the occupied area is an integral part of India. Some people are suggesting the trifurcation of Jammu and Kashmir in such a way that Jammu and Laddakh go to India and the occupied area to Pakistan and valley either remains free or may go to Pakistan. There are a few who want Jammu and Kashmir as an independent state and urge India and Pakistan to leave Jammu and Kashmir to the people of the state. There is no dearth of people who are pleading for a joint control of India and Pakistan on Jammu and Kashmir. Recently, some bold and progressive Indians have come openly to undo the historical wrong but there are few takers of this theory. Currently, the mood is in favour of porous borders between Jammu and Kashmir and giving more autonomy to the people of Jammu and Kashmir. India insists on confidence building measures in the hope that if this is done in earnest ways, the people of India and Pakistan would solve the vex problem in due course of time in accordance to the wishes of the people of India and Pakistan including Kashmiri people. The world is worried due to Kashmir conflict for India and Pakistan have fought four wars on this issue in 1947, 1965, 1971 and 1999. The Obama administration has also shown its willingness to help India and Pakistan to arrive at a just and peaceful solution with a view to stop bloodshed and maintain permanent peace in the region and enhance cooperative endeavours between two nuclear powers. It is irony of fate that whenever India and Pakistan move towards the path of peace and harmony some untoward things happen which derail the process of peace and progress. It is certain that as time goes on things would settle and the misunderstandings would be minimized but one thing is certain that the peace process would be dented for years to come if the present conditions continue to prevail.

The Zamindari Abolition Act, 1951

The Zamindari Abolition Act was the single most important Act which broke the backbone of Hindu and Muslim aristocracy in the country. Muslim and Hindu Zamindars who were gracious, dignified and gorgeous class of the society and who were occupying a prestigious position in the elites and the higher ups of the country and who were responsible in providing fillip to shopkeepers, moneylenders, brothels and law courts, faded in obscurity with one stroke of pen. Most of the big landlords of UP and Bihar were responsible for the creation of Pakistan. Incidentally, the Muslim landlords formed the largest single segment in the League council as out of 500 members, there were nearly 160 landlords who were the significant part of the Muslim League. The bulk of their estates were taken from them and distributed among the cultivators. They were provided 99 years' bonds whose present net worth was negligible. Many of the small and medium landlords sold their bonds at petty prices and came on the road. The Muslim Zamindars were affected most because they were compelled to stay in the rural areas where they had already lost their influence since most of their landed property was distributed among Hindu cultivators. As against this, 70% large landlords from the majority community had migrated to nearby cities between 1947 and 1955 where their urban properties were situated. They sold some of their peripheral properties and invested the proceeds in constructing the shops and markets. However, in comparison to Hindu landlords, the percentage of migration among Muslim landlords was merely 15 due to communal tensions prevailing in the cities and their inability to undertake commercial ventures due to the fear of uncertain future. The biggest Muslim landlords also suffered due to the migration of several members of their joint families to Pakistan because the remaining members had to face litigations and atrocities from the evacuee department. A few big landlords among the Muslims could survive by selling their urban properties, gems, jewels, antiques and the barren orchards at throw away prices to the unscrupulous property sellers and investing them in suitable ventures. However, a large number were squeezed within their decaying palaces surrounded by a retinue of servants, wives, children, eunuchs and sycophants. There were some lucky landlords such as the Kidwais of Masauli, Bare Gaon and Gadia who got the political patronage of the Congress Party and survived with dignity and grace.

The smaller Muslim Zamindars and taluqdars of Awadh, Rampur, Bhopal, Patna, Hyderabad and other princely states were reduced to ashes for most of them were the absentee landlords and depended wholly and solely on the income of their lands. Their palaces and mansions were deserted and they had to eke out a living. Many mosques, makatibs, madaris, imambaras, orphanages and rest houses which were financed by them faced closure and moazzins, imams, madrasa teachers suffered heavily. A large number of artisans, retainers, cooks, barbers, washermen and service providers lost the patronage of the networks of these landlords who provided sustenance and livelihood for them and their extended families. It was painful for these landlords to see their palaces being converted into government offices, schools, hospitals and their ornamental gardens being divided into building plots and colonies for the refugees. With dusty marble statues of the kings and emperors, framed portraits of their ancestors, projected horns of the preys, British crockery and carved tables they faced everything with courage and fortitude. Living in retirement, dignified and aloof, the mighty landlords such as Nawab Mohammad Ismail Khan, Nawab of Rampur, Nawab Muzammilullah Khan, Habibur Rahman Khan Sherwani, Nawab of Chattari, Nawab Jamshed Ali Khan and the Rajas of Salempur, Nanpara, Kotwara, Pirpur and Jahangirabad who could not go to Pakistan, decided to stay in India and most of the time remembered their good olden days.

1962 Sino-India War

As soon as the country came on the track after the shocks of partition, the Government of India launched Five-Year Plans for the growth and development of the country. Sardar Patel with his extraordinary genius and boldness amalgamated almost all the princely states within India without much bloodshed. India's foreign policy was also based on neutrality. India was trying to have good relations with China and other neighbours. Its influence was also spreading in Asia, Africa and many important parts of the world. This was perhaps not taken lightly by China and one fine morning the Indians were taken aback when the Chinese forces intruded within India's boundaries in June 1962 and fighting started with the Republic of China on 20 October 1962. This war is called 1962 Sino-India War or the Sino-India border conflict of 1962. The war ended when China captured the so-called disputed areas and unilaterally declared a ceasefire on 2 November 1962. According to India, China has captured Indian territories in South Xingjian region known as Aksai Chin and China claims that India has captured Arunachal Pradesh which according to China is the part of Tibet. The Sino-India War took Indians by surprise but within the country there was not much bickering. There was no tension among Hindus and Muslims due to this war though Government of India was in shock due to several reasons. Firstly, the good relations between India and China were dented because there was the atmosphere of 'Hindi Cheeni bhai bhai' and this brotherly relationship was betrayed. Secondly, for the first time the lack of preparedness on the part of the country came to light and many weaknesses of Indian Armed Forces were exposed. Lastly, the attitude of Pakistan which should have been of a younger brother at the time of emergency was bordering belligerence. Pandit Nehru was shattered and it is said that at the time of his death in 1964, he was pained due to the wounds of 1962.

The 1965 Indo-Pak War

In 1965, India confronted another war known as 1965 Indo-Pak War. It is also called the Second Kashmir War of 1965. This war was the culmination of a series of skirmishes that occurred between April and September 1965. It started following the failure of Pakistan's operation Gibraltar which was designed to infiltrate Pakistani forces in Jammu and Kashmir to precipitate insurgency. On August 15, 1965, Indian Forces crossed the Line of Control and launched attack on Pakistani forces. However, the actual war started on September 6, 1965 when the Indian Cabinet under the Prime Ministership of Lal Bahadur Shastri took the decision to launch a full-blooded war against Pakistan. Indian forces under General Chaudhri crossed international border and they were defended by Pakistan forces under General Ayub Khan. The fighting ended in stalemate with United Nations mandated ceasefire on September 23, 1965 and the subsequent Tashkent Declaration which took the life of Indian Prime Minister Lal Bahadur Shastri and left several bitter memories between India and Pakistan. This war created hysteria in India and Pakistan. There were fears, suspicions and uncertainty throughout the country. Muslims' patriotism, loyalty and integrity were at stake. At many places bearded Muslims and veiled Muslim women were ill-treated in the name of paratroopers. It has been alleged that even the Government of India under Lal Bahadur Shastri suspected Muslims. Many respectable and innocent Muslims were put behind the bars especially near the bordering states. It had become difficult for Muslims to travel in the trains and buses due to fear of reprisal from the fanatic groups. The tension used to mount in surrounding areas with arrival of the bodies of Indian martyrs to their villages. Thank God that no Muslim acted as a fifth columnist and no Muslim was captured as spy. However, the fact is that Muslims of India did not relish the policy of Congress Government of suspecting Muslims during 1965 War and placing them behind bars with no fault of their own save this that they were Muslims. Admittedly, no self-respecting person would bear the insult of being called traitor and anti-national.

Indo-Pak War 1971

India and Pakistan fought another war in 1971 which is known as Indo-Pak War 1971 or the Third War on Kashmir. The genesis of this war started with 1970 when East Pakistan Awami League under Sheikh Mujibur Rahman had acquired simple majority in 313-seated house by winning 167 of 169 seats in East Pakistan. Sheikh Mujibur Rahman presented his six-point plan which was not accepted by Zulfiqar Ali Bhutto and he did not give the premiership to Sheikh Mujib. General Yahya took control and started reprisal upon East Pakistanis. On 26 March 1971, General Ziaur Rahman under the stewardship of Sheikh Mujib declared independence. On 27 March 1971, India recognized the Government of Bangladesh. Eight to ten million East Pakistan refugees who supported the freedom struggle had to leave East Pakistan after their persecution at the hands of Pakistani forces. They came over to India and it became difficult for the Indian Government to support them. Prime Minister Indira Gandhi supported the Mukti Bahini, a group of Bengalis which was fighting against the atrocities of Pakistani forces. Pakistani army attacked Indian borders to penalize the Mukti Bahini. India declared war against Pakistan, under the over all command of General Manekshaw, provoked by the bombing of Agra Air fields and the surrounding areas by General Yahya Khan. Within two weeks Pakistani forces under General Niazi were defeated and 93000 POWS were captured. Pakistan was bifurcated into Pakistan and Bangladesh and Pakistani army, economy and morale were shattered. This did not create any major tension among Hindus and Muslims for everybody knew that Pakistan was fighting a losing war. The creation of Bangladesh proved a blessing in disguise for Indian Muslims. It woke them from their dogmatic slumber for prior to it they were thinking that one day they would have to go to Pakistan. Virtually, many of the Muslims were living in the state of waiting. They took practically no steps in constructing new houses, starting new ventures and participating in governing structure. Their apathy was reflected in their old and depleted houses, poor economic condition and frustrated mind-set. If one room of the house was damaged, most of them shifted to the other rooms without thinking of repairing the damaged room. When the author got his house constructed in 1968 many of his well wishers advised him not to proceed with the project as one day everybody was destined to proceed to Pakistan. There was a small chunk of people who was not so much desperate but the condition of most of the people especially the uneducated, poor and conservative section of the society was miserable. They were surviving on their hereditable professions and past savings. They were taken aback when they found that Pakistan refused to accept even those Biharis who had migrated to Bangladesh and who had expressed their desires to move to Pakistan.

Having seen all their boats burnt, they tightened their belts and got ready to face the future with confidence, determination and dignity.

Certainly, the Muslims of India owe a token of gratitude to Mahatma Gandhi who not only gave freedom to Indians but also led them as a friend, guide and philosopher on the path of sanity and helped Muslims during the post-partition days through thick and thin. He was the product of good olden days and possessed tremendous resilience and believed in peace, progress, harmony, tolerance and non-violence. He checked the bewildered masses from drifting to the ocean of barbarism and fanaticism. Besides, the reigns of the country were in the hands of a galaxy of excellent people headed by Pandit Jawaharlal Nehru who were above narrow and communal considerations and who had will, determination and power to bring the derailed system on the path of progress and harmony. Though they failed miserably in their initial efforts due to contradictions in the society and the lack of experience of governance, yet ultimately succeeded in pulling the country out of the mess. Thus, after the horrible aftermath of partition which no body could avoid, peace prevailed in the country and things settled down with changed paraphernalia. The author would certainly like to place on record his heart felt gratitude to all those saner Indians from amongst all sections of the society who showed tolerance, magnificence and greatness and despite several odds did not allow the vested interests to sink the glorious heritage of the country in bewilderedness and handed over a peaceful, progressive, dynamic and a resilient India to posterity.

Muslims, however, lament that despite such a nice leadership and several saner people in the country and the wonderful Constitution, they remained where they are. As soon as the country got free, the Constitution of India was adopted by the countrymen on January 26, 1950 declaring the country as a Sovereign Socialist and Democratic Republic with a view to secure to all its citizens, justice and liberty, equality and fraternity. The commendable aspect of the Constitution from the viewpoint of minorities was the right to freedom of religion, conscience and profession. It also allowed people to practice and propagate religion as well as to manage religious affairs, pay taxes for promotion of any particular religion and allowed attendance at religious instructions or religious worship in certain educational institutions. The cultural and educational rights of the minorities too were protected and they were allowed to establish and administer their educational institutions. Article 14 ensures equality before the law and equal protection by the law and Article 15 prohibits discrimination on the grounds of religion, race, caste, sex and place of birth. Similarly, Article 21 states that no person shall be deprived of his life or personal liberty except through the procedure established by law and Article 25 ensures freedom of conscience and the right to freely profess, practice and propagate religion. Likewise, Article 26 ensures right to manage religious institutions, religious affairs, subject to public order, morality and health. In the same way, Article 29 protects minorities' right to conserve their language, script or culture and Article 30 provides for the protection of the interests of minorities by giving them a right to establish and administer educational institutions of their choice. The state is directed not to discriminate against minorities' institutions in granting aid. And Article 350A directs the state to provide facilities for instruction in the mother tongue at the primary stage of education. Besides this, there are number of other directives that safeguard the religious and cultural practices of Muslims. However, there is a sense of despair and suspicion among minorities concerning the lack of necessary will on the part of governing structure and meaningful Indians in matters of affirmative actions for the progress and prosperity of the Muslims and non-implementation of the recommendations of various commissions and committees despite several memorandums. They insist that the mindset of the state and its people needs change in such a way that the problems of Muslims may not be looked upon as the problems of a specific minority but they should be taken up as a major national concern. Unless and until the needful is done much cannot be thought for the betterment of minorities in the country.

3

Stability, Pressure Tactics and Apprehensions

The next phase of transition called the period of stability, pressure tactics and apprehensions started from 1971 when Pakistan was truncated into Pakistan and Bangladesh and lasted up to 1992 when Babri Masjid was demolished by some of the fundamentalist and reactionary groups from majority community. Till Pakistan was not bifurcated most of the Muslims of India were under the impression that one day they would have to migrate to Pakistan. This uncertainty had paralyzed their professions, vocations, business establishments, socio-cultural institutions and behavior patterns. There was lethargy and hopelessness lit large on the foreheads of the elders, frustration breaking the backbone of the youths and economic decadence indicating at the misfortune of the community. It appeared as if the Muslims were in the state of waiting expecting some horrible thing to happen.

The Phase of Stability

As soon as Pakistan was bifurcated, Muslims of India realized that it was futile to think in terms of going to Pakistan for Pakistan was not in a position even to accept its own nationals called Biharis who were trapped in Bangladesh. This worked as an elixir and they started thinking positively. By that time three important developments had taken place. Firstly, the Middle East and Africa had created lucrative demands for the teachers, engineers, medical doctors and other skilled and unskilled labourers hence Muslims especially from the high castes who were ruined due to lack of jobs in government, semi-government and private organizations and who were educated but had no work, took the advantage of this God-given opportunity and improved their financial lot by going to these countries. Many Muslim engineers, medical doctors, MBAs, Commerce graduates, plumbers, fitters, technicians, cooks and laborers migrated from the important Indian cities to Nigeria, Uganda, Somaliya, Sudan, Malaysia, Indonesia, Saudi Arabia, U.A.E., Iran and Afghanistan with the result that the condition of Muslim middle class improved. There was hardly any member from the educated families from Aligarh, Lucknow, Delhi, Jaipur, Hyderabad and many important cities of Kerala, Tamil Nadu, Karnataka, Bihar, West Bengal and several other Indian states who had not gone to these countries. The NRI money helped Muslims in constructing new houses, purchasing consumer durables and investing money in the education of their children. Even today the educated Muslims are moving to these countries in large numbers due to the employment opportunities there. Many young people who have earned enough money from these countries and who have come back have started their own nursing homes, shops, educational institutions and construction work. There is a great demand for multi-storey flats in Muslim localities which has given boost to the works of the builders and others. The NRI money has changed the complex of many Muslim mohallas and localities in most of the cities of India and it is primarily the NRI money which helped people in marrying their sons and daughters, in providing higher education to their children and in obtaining necessities and comforts of life. Several children of Muslim NRIs are getting education in America, England, France, Russia and Australia. Many of them have started their own ventures and several of them have joined national political parties. As a matter of fact Muslims who were ruined by partition of the country got a new lease of life by the NRI money and one can see their economic revival to a large extent. Besides, the industrialization and the urbanization of the country improved the fortunes of the big and small Muslim landlords who had been completely destroyed by Zamindari abolition. Due to industrialization initiated by the Five-Year Plans, industries were being set up in urban areas which enhanced the values of the real estates. The Muslim landlords who had become more or less penniless and who were facing acute financial difficulties got the opportunity to sell some portion of their huge urban properties which were lying at the prime centres of the cities at peak prices and this helped them to improve their financial position. Many zamindars started shopping complexes on their prime lands, several of them constructed multi-storey flats, marriage houses and a few of them entered even in politics. They constructed beautiful houses and provided higher education to their children and thus partly regained their lost glory. In addition to this, the consumerism gave impetus to artisanship. Facts testify that Muslims' role in the growth and development of artisanship had been exemplary. For instance, the lock industry of Aligarh, the silk industry of Benaras, the leather industry of Kanpur, the wood carving industry of Saharanpur, the brass industry of Moradabad, the knife industry of Rampur, the pottery industry of Khurja and in the same many industries in the important cities of the country have been promoted and developed by the Muslim artisans. When the economic conditions of Indians improved people started spending huge money on their dresses, household goods, ornaments and the construction and decoration of their houses. They also spent lavishly on marriages, house warming ceremonies, parties and entertainment. The pomp and show became a way of life of many educated and rich families as a consequence of which the demand for decorated goods, carved utensils, fancy items, attractive dress materials, ladies embroidered clothes and show pieces increased exponentially. Muslims mostly being artisans took the advantage of the new challenges and thus, the various classes of Muslim artisans which were badly affected by partition gradually and gradually moved towards the main-stream. They too constructed pucca houses, sent their children to schools and married their sons and daughters comfortably without incurring any debt. Over and above this, the relatively peaceful communal atmosphere in the country too helped Muslim entrepreneurs to come in the field of business, trade and commerce. Muslim businessmen were mostly afraid of communal riots. They could not dare to open any shop in the mixed areas due to the fear of arson and looting for the experience had shown that mostly the shops of Muslims were looted and destroyed. Besides this, they also hesitated to invest in any business venture due to uncertainty and risk. However, with the peace prevailing in the country Muslims came forward in large numbers and opened their shops in various cities of the country. Several of them also entered in the manufacturing business and trading activities. In addition to it, most of the educated young men took the advantage of the existence of the local markets which had emerged in the Muslim dominated areas due to the persistency of the communal riots. They opened their mobile shops, cafeterias, and luxury shops in these markets. Many of them started their coaching institutes, tuition shops, computer centres and Internet activities. Initially, these local Muslim markets were opened primarily for Muslims because Muslim families were afraid of going to the Hindu dominated areas due to the fear of communal clash. However, over a period of time these centres became cosmopolitan centres. Muslim youths brought cheap and fine material as well as the fancy items from the chosen markets of the country and sold them in these areas which attracted Hindus and Muslims alike. The flip to these markets was provided by the NRIs for whenever they returned to their native cities they purchased dress material and other items from these markets and when they were to go back, they spent substantial amount of money in buying gift items for their friends and acquaintances. One can see many Hindu, Sikh and Christian ladies mostly buying from these markets for the products here are cheaper, quality finer and the behaviour of the traders is also highly cordial and personalized. The businessmen knew that few would come to them if their prices were not low, quality not fine and behaviour not exemplary. These riots proved blessings in disguise. Today, we find clusters of shops practically in every Muslim mohalla which is providing livelihood to millions of people. Experience regarding the business development reveals that many communities in the world developed simply by following the principle of 'buy from your own' on the pattern of 'buy from a Jew' for this provided them the initial push which was needed for every business to take off and finally they became the pioneers. History also testifies that when minorities were rejected in government jobs they entered in the field of business and overshadowed all other communities in the long run because of their hard work, low profit margin, honesty, excellent behaviour and simplistic living. The Jews became world class business magnates and researchers because they were discriminated in government jobs. Most of the Christians were not prepared to see them on their heads as district heads or police officers. Thus, despite their following 'plus one theory' that is raising efficiency level above the rate of discrimination by one per cent so as to be selected in competitive examinations, when they failed, they came in the field of business and research where there was no major opposition for them. They propagated the idea of 'buy from a Jew', which ensured their livelihood at a reasonable level. Finally, they sold their commodities at a lower price, kept the quality top most and behaved nicely which attracted others towards their business and they spread throughout the world as the owners of multinational companies. Similarly, they joined the research centres where nobody objected them while they were engaged in their laboratories in the process of research and investigations. Since they were not visible in the dominant positions, nobody took notice of them. After a few years when they emerged, they were researchers and the scientists of world fame. Likewise, when Gujaratis, Punjabis and Marwaris went to England, Canada, Europe and America and sought jobs in government and private sector and when they failed, they started their own shops selling daily needs. Nobody took notice of it for initially their products were purchased mostly by the Indian origin people or the poor from East European countries. However, with the passage of time they attracted the local population too due to their cheap and fine products and better behaviour pattern. The facts reveal that in most of the cities of America, Canada and Europe, Indians are presently the owners and controllers of various important departmental stores and other business centres. The present trends indicate that since Muslims in India too have been cornered and they are not getting jobs in government, semi-government and private sectors in adequate numbers, they too would move towards research centres and the business units and they are destined to be the future researchers and business magnates and the entrepreneurs in the long run provided they too follow the Jewish and Gujarati models.

The period between 1971 and 1992 was marked by pressure tactics by the fanatics and extremists from a fringe portion of the majority community and apprehensions and frustrations from the side of Muslims. It is stated that many a time the Indian Muslims were kept terrified by several reactionary, wicked and vested groups from among the vocal section of the majority community by their frightening and irritating techniques. Several right minded individuals, groups, organizations and political parties raised controversial issues from time to time harassing Muslims which were painful and annoying. Many ill-founded theories were propounded by the rightist to pressurize Muslims most of which were imaginary and baseless. Muslims too did not react as a matured community and many of their reactionary, extremist and fanatic groups replied in the same coin which resulted in bickering and even bloodshed. There is no dearth of such people in Indian society who relish in creating hatred against one another and indulge in inter-communal conflicts and vitiate the peaceful atmosphere of the country. Some of the thorny and mind boggling matters often raised by various disgruntled elements have been discussed below.

Muslims Being Invaders are Aliens

Sometimes, it was said that Hindustan was for Hindus alone and Muslims had no place in it since they were invaders and the outsiders. This thesis was rejected by the fighters of freedom struggle who were both Hindus and Muslims as well as by the founding fathers of our Constitution who treated all Indians equal in all respects without any difference of caste, creed, class or religion. Indian culture was the product of the synthesis of various cultures and civilizations. It was enriched by all segments of the society and India's actual strength lied in its plural culture, ethnic and religious diversity and peaceful co-existence. Needless to say that all Muslims are not invaders for some of the Muslims have been living in India since long. For instance, Muslims of Kerala and Gujarat came in the seventh century. Several Muslims from Turkey, Iran, Afghanistan and Arab countries came to India as traders, merchants, artisans, masons and made India their home. Even those Muslims who came as invaders also adopted India as their sweet home and fought against the invaders. History is witness to the fact that Ibrahim Lodhi came to India as an invader but he fought a bitter war against Babar to protect India from going under his subjugation. In a sense, many Indians who had their connections with Europe, Central Asia and even Africa came in India as invaders or peaceful citizens and got themselves assimilated in the cultural stream of India. The greatness of the country and its people was that they neither discriminated against them nor discarded them but embraced all of them within their folds and transformed them as equal and worthy citizens. Besides, Muslims assert that the theory of associating some people with some areas and communities does not stand the test of time for almost all the people had originated at a common place and over a period of time they moved from there compelled by the circumstances in search of livelihood and shaped countries, communities and nations.

It was also said by some extremist that all Muslims should go to Pakistan because they had created it for themselves. The history of partition was wrapped in mystery but gradually and gradually many facts have come in open. Many people have begun to believe that Muslims alone were not responsible for the creation of Pakistan. Partition was the culmination of communal politics played by the elites of both communities which was abetted by the British to dent the freedom struggle. The failures of various Round Table Conferences and Coalition Politics convinced both Hindu elites and Muslim elites of those times that they could not co-exist peacefully and it was in the interest of both the communities to part away peacefully. The demand for partition was made by Muslims from various provinces but it was also rejected by the Muslim majority frontier provinces. The Muslims and Hindus of 665 princely states were not at all involved in the creation of Pakistan and India for the merger decisions were taken by the rulers of the princely states. Many poor Muslims and Hindus did not know anything about Pakistan and those who knew something were under delusion. There were Muslim League people and many orthodox, conservative and extremist among Muslims who too wanted a separate state for them since they did not want to live under Hindus as their subjects or under their domination. Similarly, there were several rightist and extremist Hindus who never wanted to work along with Muslims. They could never tolerate their presence in the significant portion of Indian mainstream. They wanted them to be out of the country *en masse* believing them to be the invaders and the aliens. They mostly used to talk in terms of 1000 years Muslim rule as the extreme type of slavery. For them Rana Pratap and Shivaji were the heroes and Aurangzeb and Mehmood Ghazni were the dreaded enemies. In a situation with people with different mindsets, many Indians believe that it was not possible even for the British to keep them tied to one country. Thus, the division of the country, in their opinion, was the inevitable result of the communal hatred between Muslims and Hindus for which no one single section, group or individual can be held responsible.

Singing of Vande Matram

Muslims are often bullied by saying that they should sing Vande Matram which is a National song. They go to the extent of saying that one who wants to live in India shall have to sing Vande Matram else he would be thrown out of the country. Muslims claim that Vande Matram is a poem identified with Hindu nationalism and revivalism. It is essentially a devotional song dedicated to the worship of Mother India and since Muslims do not worship anything including their mothers, Holy Prophet, Holy Qur'an and Holy Ka'bah save God, the singing of the song in the spirit of worshipping Mother India goes against their religious rights which are guaranteed by Indian Constitution. Moreover, if the whole song is translated and rightly interpreted in English one can easily say that historically the song was written in the spirit which did not suit the belief system of Muslims. Even during pre-partition days, the song was objected by most of the Muslims and it had created a great controversy. However, if the Vande Matram is translated as respect to mother or salaam to mother, Muslims have perhaps no reservation and hesitation in singing the song as composed by A.R. Rahman as a mark of respect to India or to pay salaam to Mother India. Indian minorities desire and hope that the people of India shall always be above certain dreaded pragmatism and would never violate the basics of the belief systems of linguistic, ethnic and religious minorities in the name of patriotism, nationalism and similar fervours. Fortunately, we can boast that India is a country where people have freedom to profess their religion in their own ways. For centuries, Indian people have been praised for their liberal approach and tolerance towards other belief systems. Even today Indian people show equal regards to the religion of all people and never discriminate one person from another merely on the basis of religion. Besides, our Constitution too has provided freedom to profess one's religion hence such controversies do not auger well for a country which has pluralistic culture and rich composite heritage and which is moving on the path of peace, progress and glory. It is the irony of fate that the loyalty, sincerity and integrity of Muslims as well as Muslims' respects and regards for the country and its culture, ethos, traditions are tested from such petty issues when they have already proved their mantle by scarifying their lives, persons and possessions in the cause of the nation.

Divergent Views of Muslims

It has also been observed that on many matters such as on the issue of terrorism or relation with Israel or United States of America many extremist elements do not tolerate the divergent views expressed by some of the Muslims. They not only expect similar views from them but also expect proactive reactions from their side. Muslims are free citizens of a free and democratic country. They can have divergent views like other Indians in matters of some of the national and international issues such as the Palestinians right to an independent state, signing of Nuclear Treaty and India's opposition to Iran in the larger interest of the country. Such healthy dissents or constructive moves with good intentions never reflect the Muslims' lack of loyalty or integrity towards the country but they exhibit the vibrancy and dynamism of Indian democracy as well as the recognition of the cherished rights of freedom of speech, expressions and belief systems as enshrined in Indian Constitution. We observe that even among Hindus, Sikhs, Christians, Parsis and many political parties and organizations difference of opinion is found regarding various national and international issues which never mean that all are anti-national. It is well known that on many political issues the Communists differ from the Congress. Likewise, on the issue of Hindi there are differences between the BJP and the DMK. Actually, these irritating issues arise because of past misunderstandings and mistrust between communities. There is a section of Indian society which is demanding Uniform Personal Laws but Muslims are resisting for they consider such a move against their religion and culture. Besides this, there are several matters where many people from the majority community want Muslims to behave as they behave but it is not possible for Muslims to do so due to the constrains of their religion. These constraints and inabilities on the part of Muslims should not be taken otherwise but they should be taken in good spirit in the light of our plural cultural heritage. The heartening aspect is that the younger generation of India is coming on the scene. This generation is liberal, broad-minded and considerate. As time elapses, these minor and irritating issues would become the matters of past and a new climate of trust, confidence and peaceful-coexistence would develop which would take India to the path of grace and glory.

Muslims are Rigid and Conservative

It is emphasized again and again that Muslims are a hurdle in the process of modernization since they abhor change. The irony of fate is that some of the new generation is mostly under the influence of Western culture, Western ways of living and Western type of morality, human rights and democracy. It is moving with the wind without caring for the age old value system, rich heritage and golden mean. Many of them are coming openly in favour of sodomy, lesbianism and permissive ways of living which the Indian society has been discarding since time immemorial. This generation of ours is directionless. Many of our youths are indulging in drugs, alcohol and obscenity. Their behavior in educational campuses is in variance with our age-old culture. The dress code of our boys and girls is frustrating. Their body language, behavior pattern and code of conduct are repelling. No sensible person can approve such misadventures. Our youngsters need not be encouraged in what they are doing but they need to be guided on the path of sanity, piety, peace and progress without undermining the rich heritage and moral base of the country. It is worthwhile to point out that on this issue Muslims and many orthodox and conservative Hindus are on the same platform. It is an open secret that Muslims are duty bound to oppose those things which Holy Qur'an prohibits and which have been prohibited by the Holy Prophet for they cannot accept those things which are against their religion. The Indians should show respect and regard to Muslims' sentiments in matters of their fundamentals for unlike other people they do not have any freedom with respect to the principles of Islam as enshrined in Holy Qur'an and as practiced by Holy Prophet. As long as they remain within the purview of Islam they have to accept them as the pillars of their faith whether they like it or not. Hence, if a Muslim opposes sodomy or nudeness or anything which goes against the age-old value system or fundamentals of his religion, he should not be considered as conservative and an obstacle but his healthy dissent too should be respected and guarded and a space should be provided for his ideology and way of living in a tolerant and democratic and vibrant country like India.

The Cow Slaughter

It is alleged that apart from what has been written above it was propagated silently among a section of people by the vocal section from the hard-core majority segment that Muslims of India did not care for the sensitivities of the majority community and pursued their religious agenda and social and cultural practices without caring for majority sentiments. Very often attempts were made by hard-core Hindu organizations to incite the feelings and emotions of masses on the issue of cow slaughter. For instance, it was told that Hindus worship the cow and the Muslims slaughter it in their own land openly without any regard to the sentiments of Hindus and when the Hindus of India insist on the ban of cow slaughter they oppose it and confront them with all their might. Needless to say that for Muslims cow slaughter is not a significant issue for cow is one of the permissible animals like goats, buffalos and fowls whose meat can be eaten. There is no preference of any kind for beef over mutton or chicken. If they do not eat it there is no religious compulsion upon them. Likewise, it is not obligatory on their part to sacrifice only cows at the time of Eid-al-Adha for there are several other animals which can be sacrificed with equal religious sanction. We know that in almost all the princely states where there were Hindu Rajas there was ban on cow slaughter during British time and Muslims of those states never raised any objection against it though cow was slaughtered in provinces controlled by the British. Hindus worship the cow and consider it as their mother hence cow slaughter is a most sensitive issue worth caring compared to the slaughtering of the swine which Muslims abhor. If Hindus expect from their Muslim brothers that they should show care and concern for their sentiments, their expectations are genuine. Muslims live with their Hindu brothers, it is expected from them that they would show utmost respect and regard for the religious sentiments of the majority community. Since they expect that the Hindus should respect their sentiments, it becomes obligatory on their part too to show utmost concern for the sentiments of their fellow brothers. It is a fact that most of the sensible Muslims of India show due regard to the sentiments of their Hindu brothers and avoid eating beef with all sincerities at their command. Mostly beef is not eaten by Muslims. The poor among them eat buffalo meat instead and most of the well to do and educated people use mutton and chicken. They avoid even buffalo meat. It is not at all a issue before majority of Muslims. Only a select few Muslims who are either poor and ignorant buy beef wherever it is cheaply available or a few of the butchers who are marginalized sections of the society and who are ignorant indulge in slaughtering the cow since a cow can be acquired freely or cheaply because many of the stray cows are roaming in each city and nobody owns them. Besides, there are irresponsible people who either sell their cows at nominal prices after they fail to give milk to the butchers or leave them at the mercy of criminals. Many a time these cows are sold in neighboring countries after collecting them from various parts of the country. Since the cow has lost much of its economic significance, it is vanishing from the scene like the camels. People prefer a buffalo in comparison to cow for milk purposes and the oxen are also not in much demand due to the introduction of tractors and modern techniques of sowing and harvesting. Since cow is a sacred animal in the eyes of majority of the people, it should be made incumbent upon those who buy a cow that they would not leave the cow at the mercy of the criminals after it ceases to give milk but would either care for it or send it to some government or charitable organization for its upkeep. Likewise, the government should also care for the upkeep of the stray cows and oxen as this issue concerns the sentiments of millions of people. The Central Government and some of the governments of the states are hesitating to declare the cow as the national animal or faltering to ban cow slaughter perhaps because it is the staple food for many in Nagaland and its surrounding areas. The Central Government should show courage because whenever some states think of banning cow slaughter many vested interests from among several sections of Indian society raise their heads and the issue is thrown in the cold storage.

Muslims Keep Foreign Names and do not Respect Their Indian Ancestors

Another objection which they generally raised against Muslims was that wherever Muslims went they kept their names according to the prevailing practices of those countries and also included the names of the great men of those countries in their Holy Books and considered the ancestors of those countries as their own. For instance, when Muslims entered the Christian countries they included Jesus Christ in their Holy Book, kept Christian names and after conversion owned the ancestors of the Christians as their own. Likewise, when they confronted the Jews, they included Moses in Holy Qur'an, kept Jewish names and owned the Jewish ancestors in their Holy Books. In the same way, when they went to Egypt and Iran, they kept Arabic and Persian names and accepted their cultures and traditions. However, when they came to India they kept their Persian and Arabic names, did not include Lord Rama, Krishna, Gautama and Mahavira in their Holy Book and did not own their Hindu ancestors. This is a fact that when Islam spread from Saudi Arabia to other countries of Europe, Asia and Africa, it confronted the problem of adjustment and assimilation. People of those countries were gladly willing to accept Islam but they were not ready to accept the simple and nomadic culture of the Arabs at the cost of their own rich cultures, magnificent social customs, time-tested ethos, healthy traditions and distinct individualities and the unique identities. Islam being a God-given religion made no concession in the fundamentals of Islam, however, it allowed people to pursue all those ancestral traditions, cultures and customs which were not against the fundamentals of Islam. For instance, in case of marriages it gave no concession in matters of performing Nikah ceremonies in the presence of witnesses and asked them to perform Nikahs involving the consents of the prospective brides and bridegrooms in lieu of prescribed Mehar amount. Regarding other ceremonies it permitted all those ceremonies which their ancestors were performing and which were not specifically against the fundamentals of Islam. Likewise, in matters of keeping names it allowed them to keep their ancestral names provided they were not derogatory, meaningless and against the spirit of monotheism. Similarly, they allowed all customs, ethos and practices which were not specifically against the fundamentals of Islam such as dress code, cooking and eating habits, birth and death ceremonies, etc. This helped in the spread of Islam and the world knows that in no time Islam spread throughout the known world. It is not right to say that Muslims included the great men of every country where they went within Holy Qur'an for many people do not know that Muslims believe that Holy Qur'an is the Book of God. It is the word of the Lord and it is in its purest form as it was revealed only by God. Nobody has added or deducted anything from it and nobody can do so in future also. Muslims consider Prophet Jesus and Prophet Moses as prophets of God because the Holy Qur'an says so and not to please the Christians or the Jews. Muslims throughout the world believe that Lord sent warners in every country and nation. They were the true messengers of God. They were from among their own people and had brought the message of the Lord in their own languages. They were human beings but were chosen by Lord for special purposes. They took food and moved with people and tried their best to bring people on the path of sanity and righteousness. As we know that the true religion in the eyes of God is one, all messengers of God irrespective of the fact whether they were born in India, Africa, America, Australia, Asia or any part of the globe were all brothers, one people, one nation and one ummat. They brought the same message. It is because of this reason that the moral code of conduct of all people in the world is the same despite the fact that the people were separated from each other in space and time and knew nothing about each other. Muslims of the world or for that matter Muslims of India cannot include any name of any religious head or great man in Holy Qur'an and pronounce him as the prophet of God for Holy Qur'an specifically says that it sent several messengers but told the names of only few. Thus, we can say with certainty that those whose names have been mentioned in Holy Qur'an were the true messengers of God. Regarding those such as Lord Rama, Krishna, Gautama and Mahavira whose names have not been mentioned specifically in Holy Qur'an no one can say that they were or were not the messengers of God. They could be the true messengers of God for Holy Qur'an says that Lord has sent warners in every nation but we cannot say with certainty that they were the messengers of God for Holy Qur'an has not mentioned their names in the list of the declared prophets. Similarly, Muslims specifically say that New Testament, Old Testament and Psalms were the books of God and they were in purest form when they were revealed upon

Jesus, Moses and David. However, regarding other books such as Gita, Ramayana, Mahabharata and others they cannot say whether they were the revealed books or not. They could be the revealed books for the Holy Qur'an says that messengers were raised from several regions of the world and they were given the messages in the languages of the people of those regions. Thus, these books could be the revealed books if the prophets of God brought them but we cannot say with surety that they were the revealed books because the Holy Qur'an has not mentioned these books in the list of revealed books. Guess work and conjecture are dangerous in such situations. Islam categorically directs Muslims to respect the religious heads, religious books and religious places of all people for per chance they might be the prophets of God and the books too might be the revealed books. Indian Muslims give highest respect to all the religious heads and pious people of India and look towards the religious books with respect and reverence.

It is generally said that Muslims do not adore their ancestors despite the fact that they are converts from their Hindu ancestors. In order to understand the presence of large number of Muslims in India, it is imperative to look at the process of conversion in this country. The geographical distribution of the density of Muslim population in Kashmir valley, in the North West Frontiers, Sindh, Bangladesh, Malabar and Assam reveals that the conversions were not affected by the might of the medieval Muslim States over six centuries for these areas fell within the political peripheries of the medieval Muslim states. Kashmir under the influence of Sufis had accepted Islam long before medieval Indian state reached there, West Punjab was the land where the hold of medieval state was always in question, East Bengal was seldom under Delhi or Agra during medieval times and no Muslim ruler had ever reached Malabar. Islam had reached Kerala in the seventh century. The first mosque in India was perhaps built in 629 AD at the behest of Cheraman Perumal in Kodungallur by Malik Bin Deenar Rehmatullah during Holy Prophet's time for Malik Bin Deenar Rehmatullah had reached Kerala during those days along with his 20 companions.

Mappilas were probably first converts to Islam in India due to the magnetic influence of Arab traders. Likewise, Islam had entered Sindh during Umayyad Caliphate in the 8th century. Similarly, Islam in Assam spread due to catholicity of Muslim saints and pirs like Shah Akbar, Ghiyasuddin Aulia, Hazrat Shah Sufi, Shah Kamal and many others. As against this, in the heartland of Muslim empire such as UP, Bihar, Delhi and East Punjab the Muslims never exceeded 15% of the total population. Likewise, Islam spread in Southern India, Sri Lanka, Western Burma, Bangladesh, Southern Thailand, Indonesia, Malaysia, and various parts of Asia and Africa where no Muslim conqueror had ever reached. Interestingly, there is not a single book on the subject of forceful or voluntary conversion in India. The reason is that there is not enough historical evidence to substantiate the conversion of one Muslim in every six inhabitants by religious zealots as the process of conversion was so slow and imperceptible and spread over six centuries that it escaped the attention of medieval historians and literary people, both Hindus and Muslims. If such had been the case, there was no possibility that it could have escaped the attention of Islamic scholars or their opponents for so long.

First of all, one thing should be made clear that all the original ancestors of almost all the religions who accepted another religions after abandoning their original religions were converts since it has been the practice of the Lord that when the pure religions sent by God were polluted and man-made religions were introduced by the vested interests Lord sent new messengers who introduced the purest forms of religions along with religious procedures and practices in the light of the changed circumstances. Many people accepted the new religions after leaving their old ones. Thus, all such persons whether they were Sabians, Jews, Christians, Buddhists, Hindus, Zoroastrians, Chinese or others were converts in the sense in which the word is used in the context of Indian Muslims. According to this interpretation, those Muslims who first embraced Islam were surely the converts whether they lived in Saudi Arabia, Egypt, Iran, India, Africa or any part of the world for Islam came just 1500 years ago. Prior to it generally people were mostly the Jews, Christians, Sabians, Fire Worshippers, and Buddhist, Hindus, aboriginals or others. Wherever Islam went people abandoned their original religions and converted to Islam. The only difference is that some people accepted it earlier and others accepted it at a later stage. When Islam came in India, those non-Muslims who were living in India abandoned their original religions and accepted Islam influenced by the preaching of the saints of Islam like Khwaja Moinuddin Chisthti Ajmeri, Nizamuddin Auliya, Amir Khusro, Outubuddin Bakhtiarkaki, Kalyar Sabri, Bu Ali Shah Qalandar, Hamiduddin Nagauri, Shah Jalal, Shah Alla-Ul-Haq Pandwi, Makhdoom Ashraf Simnani, Waris Shah Sahib, Ahmad Sirhindi and hundreds of Muslim sufis of those days. It is a well-known fact that there is no caste system in Islam in the sense in which the caste system is found in India. However, Indian Muslims always remained the victims of caste system because they had inherited it from their forefathers. It was the caste system of Islam which dented the spread of Islam in India. When the people of India who were the victims of caste system and who could get rid of it by accepting Islam found that the disciples of Islam despite being the followers of religion of equals permitted caste system, they did not accept Islam for they thought that no material difference would come in their situation after accepting Islam. This proved to be true for those poor Muslims of lower castes who had accepted Islam but they remained within the clutches of caste system even after embracing Islam. The teachings of equality and brotherhood which the converted Muslims had received at the hands of Sufi saints and which had prompted them to accept Islam proved deceptive. They got highly frustrated for in real practice the adherents of Islam were not different from other people of the country. Muslims of the so-called high castes or high positions not only allowed the caste system to flourish but encouraged it which checked the spread of Islam in India during the Muslim rulers. Whatever good work the Muslim saints had done was made useless by the Muslim rulers and the elites of the society. Ironically, the caste structure which is found today among Muslims was present during the days of

Muslim rulers too. The water carriers, weavers, masons, oil crushers, artisans and tillers are the relics of old days. Many a time those who are not well versed with the conditions of Muslims during the days of Muslim rulers emphasize that Muslims of India enjoyed princely life during the days of Islamic rulers and inflicted heavy causalities upon the Hindus of those days. This perception is baseless for there had never been Islamic rule in India. There were Muslim dynasties who were ruling in the same way as the other Hindu dynasties were ruling and considered all people under their domination as their subjects and did not make any discrimination between people and people. They even did not bother about their own relatives and well wishers. They killed and punished even their near and dear when they came in their ways. Aurangzeb rightly said that kingship knows no kinship. They helped and supported those sections of the society irrespective of their castes, colours, creeds and religions who came to their rescue and penalized those who created hurdles for them. History testifies that most of the time of the Muslim rulers was passed in fighting and suppressing the revolts of Muslim rebellions rather than fighting Hindu Rajas and Maharajas. During Mughal periods, the Kayasth from Hindus were the important functionaries of the courts, Hindu Seths and Sahukars were the treasurers and Rajputs of Rajputana were the commanders. Only those Muslims who were good fighters, commanders, courtiers, darbaris or men of etiquettes were honoured and graced in Muslim darbars. The poor Muslims were treated like other poor of other communities. It is unimaginable that these miserable Muslims at any stage ever harmed the Hindus of those days for being in miserable stage, they were powerless. They could get some psychic satisfaction at the time of Muslim festivals save this they were as good or bad as others. If any harm reached to Hindus it must have been from the side of Muslim rulers or those who were in power rather than by the majority of Muslims of those days. The same was true to Hindus during the days of Hindu dynastic rulers. Most of the Hindus were the victims of the caste system in which the areas of operations were clearly marked. They too were treated as subjects. Hindu rulers also helped those who were useful to them and harmed those who opposed them. They too knew no kinship. The poor Hindus too were not privileged in the sense that they could think of becoming the rulers or receive those privileges which were being received by the privileged sections of society. Save some emotional satisfaction at the time of Hindu festival they sailed in the same boat as others. Hindus and Muslims benefited only when there were pious, soft hearted and beneficial and efficient rulers. These rulers due to their piety and large-hearted tolerance helped all their subjects according to their abilities and capacities. However, one cannot say with certainty that in recent past India ever had the rule of Indians of all segments. It is for the first time after centuries that we are having the rule of the Indians by Indians and for Indians where a downtrodden can dream of becoming the Prime Minister or the President of India. We are privileged in the sense that we have been born in such good times. We should utilize this opportunity for the good of all people irrespective of their castes, colours, sexes, creeds, religions and cultures. In this lies our greatness and in this lies our success.

It was also alleged time and again that the entire Muslims living in India are converts from their Indian ancestors. The truth is that the entire Muslims of India are not converts from the Indian ancestors since thousands of Muslims came in India from Iran, Turkey, Afghanistan, Arab countries and the surrounding areas during the days of Muslim rulers and settled in India permanently. Many came as soldiers, innumerable came as traders, some came as artists, scholars and artisans, several came in search of jobs and there was no dearth of people who came as chiefs, ambassadors, officers and friends, guides and philosophers. They came here and settled here permanently and adopted this country as their own. Many of them established towns, localities, roads and charitable institutions in the memory of their home towns and also kept their ancestral names as well as the sub-castes. There are several areas of Muslims which bear the names of similar areas in the neighbouring countries. Luckily, Muslims of India are not refugees as some of the sects of Parsis and Jews of India are who had to leave their countries due to the fear of religious persecution. Most of them are the sons of the soil. Incidentally, Islam gives highest regard to parents and elders but never believes in ancestor worship. Muslims of India too maintained their ancestral traditions, customs, cultures which were not against the fundamentals of Islam even after converting to Islam. Their birth, marriage, death and other ceremonies not only reflect the old culture of their ancestors but also very much resemble with the culture of their counterparts. They have maintained their ancestral castes and names such as Panwars, Bhattis, Pundits, Gurus, Raos, Chaudhris, Lal Khanis, Batliwalas and what not. Thank God that Muslims did not keep two names in India one Persian or Arabic name and the other Hindu name as the Jews and some other persecuted groups of society kept in Iran, Thailand and other places to avoid discrimination. The credit for this goes to Indian society for it seldom happened that in normal times anyone in India was openly discriminated, rejected and punished merely on the basis of name or religion.

Indian Muslims do not Follow Indian Culture in Toto

Many a time it was expected from Muslims that they would follow the Indian culture in toto being Indians. Those who emphasized this forgot that all of us indeed follow India's composite culture. There is nothing wrong in it for we are Indians, Bharti, Hindustani and Hindi as we live in India, Bharat, Hindustan and Hind. We are proud of our Indianness and Indutva. All of us follow the Indian composite and pluralistic culture which reflects unity in diversity and diversity in unity. There was a time when the cultures, customs and traditions of different people, places and regions were different. India was a miniature world with diverse patterns and contrasted differentiations but thanks to the mainstream and international stream that all of us have come more or less within the same cultural milieu. During fifties, one could see the different patterns of cultures, customs, traditions and ethos in different parts of the country within several segments of the society. The architectural patterns of the houses of Muslims and Hindus were distinct. Their drawing rooms, kitchens and even bed rooms were slightly different. One could find the variation in the types of utensils, patterns of apparels, use of language, customs and traditions. Likewise, there was tremendous divergence between one state and the other state, one region and the other region but now all those distinctions have more or less vanished. One can relish some such cultural and architectural differences in the hill stations only. Rest of the cities, towns and villages are more or less the same. The patterns of houses, markets, hawkers, commodities and sign boards everywhere are same. Everywhere one finds flat-roofed concrete buildings or multi-storey houses with modern sofa sets, beautiful dining tables, attractive cutlery and wonderful interior decoration. If the pictures, names or religious paintings and signs are removed from the modern drawing rooms one cannot say whether they belong to the minority community or the majority one. The dress code of the people is more or less the same. Hindus, Muslims, Christians, Sikhs, Jains and all males of all religions wear more or less the same type of clothes mostly pants and shirts, kurtas and pajamas. Their ladies wear both saris and salwars and shirts. Even the language is more or less the same. Some segments of males and females of the society can be identified by the pattern of beards and head coverings but mostly it is difficult to identify a youth just by seeing his face, apparel and behaviour pattern whether he is a Hindu or a Muslim or a Jain. Just as the mainstream of India has absorbed all the minority and regional streams in it, likewise the international mainstream would absorb the India's national mainstream within its fold. People would see big malls, flyovers, vast and smooth roads, food joints, entertainment and recreation clubs, bars, cosmetic stores and fashion shops. Our young and old would wear the branded clothes and would follow western customs. It would be difficult to revive and maintain the older cultural traditions. All things would resemble with the rest of the world as white resembles with white.

In order to secure uniformity in the country some times it is emphasized by a negligible section of the right minded segment of the society that Muslims should call themselves Hindus since all those who live in India are Hindus irrespective of their religions. It is also stressed that Muslims should follow Hindu sanskriti which is the culture of India. It is often stressed that they should not follow any distinctive culture and laws including personal laws and should resemble with other Indians in all respects. They should also keep Hindu names to avoid distinction and should follow their religion and religious practices freely without any restrictions. Just as a Jat keeps his name as Bijendra Singh and follows the Hindu customs and in the column of caste writes Jat. In the same way, a Muslim instead of keeping his name as Abdullah should keep the name Ishwar Das, follow Indian sanskriti in toto and write in the column of caste Muslim. There are few takers of this innovative demand even in majority community because first of all the connotations Hindus and Muslims have been understood for centuries by all the people of the world as the followers of Hinduism and Islam and not as the inhabitants of India and the Hindu sanskriti too has been taken as Hindu culture. Likewise, Hindu names too have always been associated with Hindu religion and Hindu sanskriti rather than India and Indianness. Besides, what to talk of Muslims, as the situation exists today, even Hindus are not following Hindu sanskriti, Hindu traditions and Hindu ways of living. Similarly, Muslims, Jains and Sikhs too are far from their religions, cultures and traditions. They are floating in the international stream. If this practice persists the world would see that Indians too would behave in all respects as the followers of Christianity and they would follow Christian and Western ways of living. The need of the hour, therefore, is not to think in terms of one culture and uniformity in all respects but we should call us one people one nation with diverse, composite and pluralistic cultures backed by different religious groups possessing good moral, ethical and spiritual conducts possessing large-hearted tolerance, progressive and scientific outlook and soft, kind and humanist hearts. In this lies India's success and this alone would take India to great heights. However, if we remained in search of one culture, one mode of living and uniformity in all segments, we will do much harm to the country and its people. There are ample opportunities for India to become a super and strong power worthy of leading the world on the path of peace, progress, harmonious co-existence and non-violence. We should utilize this golden opportunity to our advantage. We should concentrate more on reforming the modern education system which is giving our children merely skill and professional etiquettes but ruining them morally and spiritually. If we faltered in our tasks at this stage the posterity would never forgive us.

Apprehensions of Muslims

The redeeming feature of the post-partition period was that the majority from the minority and majority communities was sensible. However, there were some reactionary forces in both sections which were indulging in inter-communal conflicts. There was a negligible section of minority community which was apprehensive that there were a few reactionary forces in the country which were planning to punish them by inventing various techniques. Generally, this section was believing in the rumours which were floated amongst some sections of Muslims that the reactionaries from the other group had certain models such as the Spain model, Hitler model, Conversion model of the Christian missionaries and the assimilation and the uniformity model of the Russians to demoralize them. Though the majority from both the societies was unaware of these apprehensions, we are discussing these issues simply because there was a small section of Muslims which had taken a serious note of these imaginary and artificial fears.

The Spain Model

Many a time Muslims with weak mindset were often led to believe by a mischievous section of the Indian society that no Muslim in India would be permitted to live here and all of them would be asked to leave the country one fine morning as the Arabs were asked to quit Spain after having ruled it for more than eight hundred years. The Spain model proved to be true because most of the Arabs of Spain were elites, high ups, land owners, important government officials and businessmen and they were well connected with their Arab brothers in Africa. They were the privileged sections of the society and their position was like the floating cream of milk which floats on the surface of the pot and which has no roots. Whenever the pot is shaken slightly, the first thing to fall from the pot is the floating cream. Since these Arabs were not connected with grass-roots they were uprooted at the time of their downfall. In the wake of the defeat of Muslims in Europe, the cream in the shape of elite Muslim Arabs fell on the Northern shores of Africa from the land of Spain since they were rootless. Likewise, the cream of Muslims from India who were high ups, business magnates and important government servants with little connection with grass-root level fell on the land of Pakistan when this part of the sub-continent was disturbed. There was a fundamental difference between the two countries. In Spain, most of the Muslim Arabs were rulers with no connection to the grass-root level hence being the cream of the society they fell on the soil of Africa when Spain was conquered by Christians. Likewise, those Muslims of India who were the cream of Muslim society slipped to Pakistan when India was partitioned. However, most of the Muslims who were the sons of the soil were attached to the grass-root. They were not the cream but the residual of the milk which is clinched with the pot and which does not leave the pot even if the pot is broken. They too clinched firmly to their mother land even after the country was partitioned. They could not go and cannot go because for them there is no alternative save to live and die in their own country. This fact was perhaps not known to those who were frightening the Muslims.

The Genocide Model of Hitler

Another model which was used to frighten the poor Muslims was the genocide model of Hitler who had killed six million Jews during World War II. Muslims were told by certain extremist groups that communal riots on mass scale were hatched in the country simply to wipe out Muslims from India. Many extremists used Gujarat episode and the killing of Christians in Orissa as the genocide models to frighten Muslims and Christians. They forgot that those who tried to cause genocide were wiped out from the face of history whether he was Hitler or Radovan Karadzic. The world in general and the liberal Indian community in particular cannot tolerate any such cleansing on the basis of religion, language or ways of living. Those who dared to move towards harming people on the basis of religion, colour, creed and sex were confronted by the world governments as well as human right activists rigorously. Besides, it should not be forgotten that Indian Muslims are a significant force in themselves. They are minority only in the context of Hindu majority but in themselves they are the second largest Muslim majority in the world. No sensible person can ever imagine that any fool would ever think of destroying them *en masse*. Over and above this, India is a great country with its wonderful Constitution which gives equal rights to all its citizens. It also gives special privileges to the minorities. Moreover, the people of India are by and large religious minded and broad-minded and large-hearted. They have appointed three Muslims as President of Indian Republic and many from minority communities as Prime Minister, Chief Ministers, Commanders, Supreme Court Judges and Chief Justices. The alert media is in the hands of young and dynamic Indians who do not hesitate to expose anyone irrespective to his religion, political affiliation and position in the country who dares to go against any segment of the society. So long as the democracy prevails in the country and so long as the sanity and piety rule the minds and souls of Indian people there is no danger to any minority in this country. India is a big country in which minor episodes involving minorities, SCs/STs and others cannot be avoided but one thing is certain that the state machinery and the human right group as well as the saner Indians do not condone these events. The time has shown that with the passing of every moment zero tolerance is developing against such things and it is hoped that communal riots, communal violence and communal hatred would soon become the matters of past.

The Conversion Model of Christian Missionaries

The third model which was used by stray fanatics to terrify Muslims was the conversion model of the Christian missionaries. It was told to the Muslims that rightist organizations were trying to convert Muslims through their Shuddhi Movements. By giving money, jobs or temptations and convincing them that their forefathers were Hindus and they were forcefully or tactfully converted to Islam, they were converting the poor and ignorant masses of Muslims to Hinduism. Certainly, a few organizations tried this approach and merely succeeded here and there but this was an exception and not the rule. Besides, it was also heard that a few Hindus had also converted to Islam. India is a free and liberal country where many Dalits are converting from Hinduism to Buddhism and nobody is stopping them. Many tribals and poor Hindus are converting to Christianity in many parts of India. No community can tolerate that its people get converted to other religions by force and they become minority in their own country. If the Hindus of India resist forceful conversion, they are not wrong but credit goes to the Hindu organizations for they are not agitating against free, fair and will full conversion as such but they are resisting only the conversion by force or temptations, or undue influence or by exploiting the sentiments of the weak and downtrodden people. A community whose people themselves are converting to other religions with their own free will would think several times to convert others within its fold. They would at most try to stop their own people from converting due to certain malpractices to other religions or try to bring those back within their fold who had been forcefully or tactfully converted to other religions in recent past. If they peacefully and constitutionally endeavour to do so there is no harm in it. It was also told to Muslims that certain rightist historians were trying to convert the Muslim historical buildings to Hindu monuments by emphasizing that they were not built by Muslims but by Hindu Rajas and Maharajas. Admittedly, a few pro-active rightist historians tried to convince people that most of the historical buildings in India were not built by Muslim rulers but by the Indian kings, princes and nobles. They even pleaded for their restoration to their original shapes. Few even went to the extent of emphasizing that all the prominent mosques, forts and monuments presently existing on the important locations were built by fanatic Muslim rulers after destroying Hindu temples, forts and monuments. It is heartening to say that this misadventure failed miserably for the Hindu historians did not buy this idea and forcefully stood in support of the historical heritage of India. The credit must go to the leftist historians for the work they have done to dent the misadventure of the rightist historians. They left no stone unturned in exposing the truth in favour of authenticated and well established historical facts.

The Assimilation Model of Russian Type

The last thing which was very often told to Muslims was that the rightists neither wanted to throw them out nor kill them *en masse* nor convert them to Hinduism for these probabilities, in their opinion, did not exist but they wanted Muslims to live in India but not with their distinct religious, cultural and historical identities. They want to assimilate them and impose upon them not by force but by persuasion the uniform culture on the pattern of the Russian culture which USSR had imposed upon Muslim Republics during its rule after assimilating them within communist ideology. Those who know something about Islam or who have read Islam must be certain that no real and devoted Muslim can ever think of leaving his Islamic identity under normal or abnormal circumstances. Even in USSR despite the despotic Communist rule for about seventy years Muslims preserved their culture, religion and identities with dexterity and genius. Islam asks Muslims to accept Islam in toto and not in parts. Thus, those who have accepted Islam have to accept Islam as it was revealed and communicated to them by their Holy Prophet. They cannot coin anything from their side and are constrained to follow the commandments of Holy Qur'an and the pious sayings of the Holy Prophet. They are free to do anything which does not clash with the fundamentals of their religion, however, if they are asked to do anything which is against the very dictates of Islam no sensible Muslim would yield to it. Certainly, there are Muslims who call themselves Muslims but do not believe in Islamic principles. There are others who do not mind making compromises. Such Muslims can say anything and do anything but they represent neither Islam nor Muslims. It appears that such allegations and hunches as explained above were the creations of some perverted minds or they were mere hunches and apprehensions of Muslims for such matters never became public and they were never discussed in the groups of saner people. Only God knows who circulated or propounded such ideas but this is certain that those who harboured such feelings either do not know India or are unaware about mindset of Indian people. The models, techniques and tactics as mentioned above could be the brain child of a few disgruntled and perverted section of the society. India is a forward looking country where such petty-mindedness is ignored as an abrasion. Tomorrow's vibrant India would not be a merely economic super power but it would also be an embodiment of moral and spiritual values and herald the dignity of man along with their social, religious, cultural, ethical and aesthetical differentiations.

The only solution for achieving lasting peace amongst various communities, caste groups and religious denominations is to respect and trust one another, have faith in fellow beings without fear and hatred and consider all of them as the members of a large family. Admittedly, Muslims are not much different from others. They are as good or bad as others are. There are very good people among Muslims and also very bad ones too. Similarly, Hindus, Sikhs, Christians, Buddhists and Jains too have nice people and there are a few ugly ones also among them. One does not become good merely by being born in a particular religion. One becomes excellent or rogue by his training, education and the company he keeps. The statistics show that in all matters Muslims resemble with Hindus as gold resembles with gold and silver with silver. The educated Muslims have smaller families with two to three children like the educated Hindus. They do not marry more than one wife like their counterparts. In the same way, the illiterate, ignorant and economically backward Hindus are found to have bigger families and the glimpses of polygamy too are found in them here and there. Likewise, the poor, uneducated and uncultivated Muslims too have larger families and a few of them practice polygamy. Besides, their dresses, addresses, behaviour patterns, problems, agonies and joys too are similar in nature. Nobody should grudge Muslim's cultural and religious distinctiveness for they are bound by their religious code to cover their bodies up to a definite point. Just as the Sikhs despite having been distinct culturally and religiously remained part of the Hindu society, similarly the Muslims too have been the part of Indian society for centuries along with their distinct cultural and religious identities. What matters is not the sameness in dress, language and habits or uniformity in culture, customs and ethos and oneness in religion, belief system and ideology because many European countries despite these identities have shed the blood of their own fellow beings. What actually matters is the love, commitment and devotion towards one's country; infatuation, fellow feeling and concern towards one's countrymen and pride; admiration and exaltation for country's composite and rich heritage; compassion, tenderness and passion for humanity and zeal, enthusiasm and yearning for truth, justice, and peaceful co-existence.

It is heartening to know that the former RSS Sanchalak Sudarshan ji initiated a dialogue with a fragment of Muslim community to allay their fears. In India nobody could ever imagine that RSS which was painted as a hard-core Hindu communal organization by some segment of the society would ever think of inviting Muslims of India for peaceful and constructive dialogue in the larger interest of the country. There was a microscopic minority of Muslims which was earnestly feeling the necessity of such a meet for heart to heart they knew that an organization which was doing yeoman's service to Hindu community could not be so bad. Fingers could be raised at some of its pro-active members but the whole organization which was sincerely committed for the social and cultural development of majority community and which was headed by educated and enlightened people could not be so bad. Similarly, many Hindus too were thinking that some Muslims could be bad but all Muslims could not be as bad as depicted. There was a need for such meetings but nobody was coming forward. It is a fact that many Hindus and many Muslims fear each other and in this mutual incrimination both are partly true and partly wrong. However, when both the groups would sit on the common table many fears and misunderstandings would be removed. Actually, this work should have been taken by the people of India much earlier for it was the need of the time but thanks to the genius, large-hearted tolerance and far-sightedness of Sudarshan ji that he has taken the lead. Let us hope that such a move would be encouraged and praised by the general masses as it possesses enough potential to create a climate of goodwill, fellow-feeling and peaceful co-existence among Hindus and Muslims which every Indian wants from the core of his heart.

It will not be out of place to mention here that the recent poor showing by various right wing extremist parties in the 2009 elections has compelled their leaderships to ponder over the future strategies of the parties. Many people are raising their fingers at some of the hateful and anti-Muslim speeches and aggressive anti-minority postures as well as the minority bashing by these parties as the contributing factors in causing their debacle. The new generation of the people does not like hate campaign and victimization against any individual or group. Each one wants constructive work in the field of health, education, economic empowerment and social harmony for all the people of the country. Every one abhors religious discords, caste conflicts and cleavage between people and people on the basis of religion, caste and parochial considerations. It is because of this reason that today nobody talks in terms of Mandir and Masjid. Everybody desires pure water, all-weather roads, uninterrupted electric supply, good educational and health centres and jobs for the unemployed youths. This can be achieved only when the right wing extremist parties shed their extremism and adopt a new avatar in the shape of a centrist party with rightist leaning. There is much scope for centrist right leaning conservative party both from the side of Muslims and Hindus. There are innumerable people who want the right wing parties with their moderate approach to fight for the preservation of social, cultural and religious values of the people of India. Several want them to inculcate a brotherly feeling among people of different faiths with nationalistic zeal. Many of them desire that they should fight for the poor, minorities, dalits and downtrodden sections of the society without playing vote politics. There is no dearth of people who want them to pursue a dignified and independent foreign policy without tilting towards influential foreign countries. There is a large section which feels that these are the only parties which can solve many disputed and controversial matters boldly both at the national as well as international level provided they adopt a liberal and all-pervasive approach. Over and above this, there is a significant section which wants that these parties in their new shapes should encourage privatization in various fields so that the economy may become competitive but side by side they should provide the social security, unemployment insurance, sickness benefits and pragmatic plans for the weak and the needy. There is much scope for a nationalist, liberal and right wing party with indigenous outlook, value-oriented approach, humanistic fervour, peaceful co-existence, bold and independent foreign policy, aggressive economic policy together with safety measures for the downtrodden and corruption free image. It is hoped that the rightist and extremist parties would read the messages written on the walls and grab the opportunity in the shape of progressive, dynamic and a competitive parties for the betterment of the country.

4

Strain and Stress Exerted by the Right-Wing Extremist Parties

The period between 1971 and 1992 was very critical and painful for Muslims as the right wing and extremist national and regional parties of the country were highly bitter and aggressive towards the problems of Muslims. They were thriving mostly on the hate campaign against the minorities especially the Muslims and the Christians and left no opportunity to dent their progress and development. They were complaining of the appeasement of the Muslims by the Congress Government and demanding uniform personal law, abrogation of Article 370 of the Indian Constitution in Jammu and Kashmir and construction of a grand Ram Temple where the Babri Masjid existed.

Appeasement of Muslims

Muslims were under a great stress and strain from the charge of appeasement leveled upon them by the right wing extremist parties. They new well that they were the most deplorable lot but nobody was willing to accept their plea. A concerted attempt in repeated form was made by these organizations and parties that there was appeasement of Muslims by the ruling Congress Government. The dictionary meaning of appeasement is to pacify, placate or satisfy by making or effecting concessions, i.e. giving to someone more than what is due to him to please him due to his strong and favourable position. This meant that Muslims were getting more government jobs in civil services, police, judiciary and public sector undertakings than their percentage and they were securing more bank loans at cheaper rates compared to their numerical strength and the infrastructure was far superior in content and magnitude within Muslim segments in contrast to Hindu areas. It also meant that Muslims were given proportionately more admissions in medical, engineering, management, computer and other professional courses in comparison to their brothers of majority community and their share in State Assemblies and Parliament at ministerial levels and others far exceeded their strength and they were getting preferential treatment in matters of granting licenses, government contracts and quotas. This blatant lie was repeated thousand times so tactfully that the artificial lie artfully created became truth even in the eyes of those enlightened and broad-minded non-Muslims who knew Muslims' conditions more than the lines of their palms. In every election, in every speech and in every paper, it was forcefully emphasized that thanks to the Congress' appeasement policy of Muslims that the Muslims were the 'First Class Citizens' and the Hindus were 'Second Class Citizens' in their own country. They cited several examples such as that the Muslims along with Christians were running their own educational institutions for themselves without any public accountability. They were allowed to marry four wives and did not follow family planning with the result that they would one day surpass Hindus. The government was afraid of them and did not want to annoy them due to their voting power. Likewise, Rajiv Gandhi banned Salman Rushdie's *The Satanic Verses* and brought the Muslim Women Protection of Rights on Divorce Act, 1986 and his successor V.P. Singh declared Prophet's birthday a national holiday merely to appease Muslims. These things rose passions especially among younger generation of Hindus and they moved vehemently towards right wing parties to redress their grievances. Surprisingly, the Congress Government did not refute such baseless charges with utmost force knowing it fully well that Muslims were languishing in poverty, ignorance, diseases and frustration perhaps because either it lacked the necessary will or considered it as a blessing in disguise. It appeared as if it put the implied seal of approval to the alleged allegation in order to show its soft corner towards Muslims to secure their votes. Muslims tolerated everything since they had neither means nor resources to refute the lie through words of mouths or media. In Ghalib's words, it amounted to saying that if we utter 'ah' we are nick named and when they kill there is no talk.

Thanks to Prime Minister of India Dr. Man Mohan Singh and the Congress President Shrimati Sonia Gandhi that the Sachar Committee opened the eyes of all the Indians pertaining to the miserable conditions of Muslims practically in every field. According to many Muslims, the Sachar Committee Report was a double-edged weapon. On the one hand, it exposed the BJP and the similar parties and organization for propagating that Muslims were the most privileged section during the Congress regime and on the other hand, it also exposed the Congress for it was during the period of Congress rule at the Centre and the States that the Muslims became what they were now. Besides, the manner in which the Congress Party and the UPA Government reacted after the publication of the Report and practically did nothing or very little, frustrated several Muslims and alienated many of them from the Congress party. The election results concluded in UP, Bihar, Orissa and Karnataka, etc. revealed that they did not vote for Congress enthusistically where they had some choice. However, wherever any choice was available, the Congress was not perhaps the first choice of Muslims. The Indians realized for the first time that Muslims are highly backward in all fields including education, seeking jobs in government and organized and unorganized sectors, getting benefits from banks, carrying business, vocation, industry, trade and seeking health care and in getting infrastructural facilities. In the field of education, they had fallen below SCs and STs in many spheres. The literacy rate among Muslims in 2001 was 59.1% which was far below the national average of 65.1%. The literates as proportion of population in the age groups of 6-13, 14-15 and 16-17 were below that of SCs/STs which is revealed by Table 4.1.

Table 4.1: Literates as Proportion of Population by Age Group, 2004-05

Age Groups	Hindus			Muslims	Other
	Gen.	OBC	SCs/STs		Minorities
6-13	90.2	80.8	74.7	74.6	88.5
14-15	95.7	87.5	80.0	79.5	91.9
16-17	95.0	85.2	78.6	75.5	91.3
18-22	91.4	76.9	65.0	70.5	85.8
23 Years and above	74.0	50.6	36.5	46.1	67.0
Total	**80.5**	**63.4**	**52.7**	**59.9**	**75.2**

Source: Sachar Committee Report, Table 4.1

The above figures show that in literacy as proportion by age group between 6-13 and 23 years and above, Muslims were far behind General Hindus and OBCs. Besides, they faired very poorly compared to other minorities. Over and above this, the enrolment position of children currently studying too was not sound which is revealed from Table 4.2.

Table 4.2: Children Currently Studying as a Proportion of Population by Age Group, 2004-05

Age Groups	Hindus			Muslims	Other
	Gen.	OBC	SCs/STs		Minorities
6-13 years	19.1(17.3)	6.1(35.5)	25.7(27.4)	14.0(15.1)	5.1(4.8)
14-15 years	24.3(19.9)	36.1(35.2)	21.4(25.2)	12.2(14.5)	6.0(5.3)
16-17 years	28.9(21.1)	33.7(35.0)	20.2(24.7)	10.7(14.0)	6.3(5.1)
18-22 years	34.0(20.8)	30.5(34.4)	17.7(25.5)	10.2(13.9)	7.6(5.5)
23 years and above	35.6(23.9)	29.2(35.1)	18.3(24.1)	7.4(10.9)	9.5(5.9)

Note: Figures in parentheses report the share of each socio-religious group in the total population of that age group.

Source: Sachar Committee Report, Table 4.4

The above statistics reveal that the share of children currently studying as a proportion of population by age group was highly in favour of the General Hindus and the OBCs for General Hindus were getting education more than their share in the population and the OBCs were getting education more or less in proportion to their share in the respective population group. Likewise, other minorities too were getting the benefit of education more than their share in population. Similarly, the percentage wise representation of SCs/STs was also better than that of Muslims though they too were not getting education commensurate to their population ratio. Certainly, Muslims fared badly in all the segments because they were getting the benefit of educational facilities less than the share of their population. If we look at the increase in enrolment in 2004-05 we find that compared to 95% for SCs/STs in 1999-2000 it was merely 65% for Muslims. Nearly 25 per cent of Muslim children in the age group of 6-14 years had either dropped out or never attended the schools. The drop-out rates among Muslims too were highest at the level of primary, middle and higher secondary compared to all socio-religious communities. According to Census data 2001, while nearly 7 per cent of the population aged 20 years and above are graduates or hold diplomas, this proportion is less than 4 per cent among Muslims. Likewise, those having technical education among Muslims are as low as 1 per cent. In the same way, graduates as proportion of population among Muslims in age groups of 20-30, 30-40, 40-50 and 51 and above are 4.5, 3.3, 2.8, 2.1 and 3.4 respectively compared to 11.6, 9.2, 8.1, 5.7 and 8.9 for all other minorities. Needless to say that only one out of the 25 under-graduate students and one out of the 50 post-graduate students is a Muslim in premier colleges. Not only this, the incidence of graduation and those pursuing post-graduation studies among poor and non-poor households in the age group 20-30 during 2004-05 was quite unfavorable for Muslims, compared to other segments of the society which is revealed by Table 4.3.

Table 4.3: Incidence of Graduation and Those Pursuing Post-Graduate Studies among Poor and Non-Poor Households According to SRCs; 20-30 Age Group, 2004-05

SRCs		20-30 years old persons		Graduates		Attending PG courses		
		Percentage population	Distribution across SRCs	Percent-age of population in the age groups	Distribut-ion across (SRCs)	Percent-age of graduates in the SRCs	Distribut-ion across SRCs (% age)	Unem-ployment rate among graduates
Non-Poor	SCs/STs	66.3	21.8	3.8	10.1	21.5	8.9	19.1
	H-OBCs	78.5	35.1	6.2	26.6	22.1	24.2	23.8
	H-General	89.2	25.5	15.7	48.9	26.6	53.4	20.5
	Muslims	71.2	11.4	4.9	6.8	22.9	8.4	25.6
	All Minorities	86.1	6.2	10.1	7.6	22.4	7.2	25.3
	Total	77.3	100	8.2	100	24.4	100	21.4

Poor	SCs/STs	33.7	37.7	0.8	17.4	27.6	19.6	9.8
	H-OBCs	21.5	32.7	1.7	30.8	23.0	29.0	16.2
	H-General	10.8	10.5	5.8	34.9	29.3	41.9	14.4
	Muslims	28.8	15.7	1.2	10.5	16.3	7.0	16.7
	All Minorities	13.9	3.4	3.4	6.4	9.5	2.5	17.4
	Total	22.7	100	1.8	100	24.4	100	12.7

Source: Sachar Committee Report, Table 4.5

Table 4.3 shows that the graduates and post-graduates among non-poor Muslims during 2004-05 were 6.8% and 8.4% compared to 10.1% and 8.9% among SCs/STs. Likewise, the graduates and post-graduates among poor during 2004-05 were 10.5% and 7.0% as contrasted to 17.4% and 19.6% respectively among the SCs/STs. Moreover, the unemployment rate among Muslim graduates for non-poor was 25.6% compared to 19.1% among non-poor SCs/STs and 16.7% in poor Muslims compared to 9.8% among poor SCs/STs Muslims have benefited least from Jawahar Navodaya Vidyalayas in rural areas. The changes in the pattern of education across socio-religious communities indicate that SCs and STs have reaped the advantages of targeted government and private efforts compared to Muslims.

Likewise, they do not stand anywhere in the area of seeking government jobs. All communities are far better compared to them. The Civil Services examinations of 2006 show that 3% Muslims were selected in the IAS, 1.8% in the IFS and 4% in the IPS. Muslim community has a share of only 4.5% in Indian Railways out of which almost 98.7% of them are lower grade people. As against this about 11% of group A jobs have been occupied by minorities other than Muslims. Ironically, the share of Muslims in security agencies is around 4% and that too mostly at the lower cadres. Representation of Muslims in the education sector is merely 6.5% and in the home department it is 7.3%. The total share of Muslim constables is 6%. The presence of Muslims in health departments is just 4.4% and in the transport department merely 6.5%. The overall representation of Muslims in judiciary is about 7.8% compared to 23% for OBCs, 20% for SCs and STSs and the general category is over represented for its share is almost twice its share in the population. In no state, the representation of Muslims in the government departments matches their population share. The share of Muslims recruited through State Public Services Commissions during the last five years shows the following picture as per Table 4.4.

Table 4.4: Share of Muslims Recruited through State Public Service Commissions during the Last 5 Years (Recommended/Selected for recruitment: 63,402)

Category	All	Hindus				Muslims	Other Minorities
		All Hindus	SCs/ STs	OBCs	Upper Castes		
Higher Positions	25.4	88.8	20.9	22.7	45.3	3.2(20.7)	8.0
Lower Positions	74.6	98.0	35.2	29.0	33.9	1.6(10.4)	0.3
Group 'A'	3.8	82.2	10.3	23.7	39.2	7.5(48.6)	10.3
Group 'B'	12.4	86.4	19.8	21.2	45.3	2.2(14.3)	11.5
Group 'C'	21.1	95.8	12.6	20.8	62.4	3.0(19.4)	1.2
Group 'D'	53.4	98.9	44.1	32.2	22.6	1.1(7.1)	0.0

Note: Figures in parentheses are ratios of Muslim share to their population share in per cent terms.

Source: Sachar Committee Report, Table 9.7

The above figures show that all Hindus share was 88.8% on higher positions compared to 3.2% for Muslims and 8.0% for other minorities. The shares of SCs/STs, OBCs and upper castes were 20.9%, 22.7% and 45.3% respectively. Likewise, on lower positions the share of Muslims was merely 1.6% compared to 98.0% for all Hindus and 0.3% for other minorities. However, compared to Muslims' share of 1.6% in such positions the shares of SCs/STs, OBCs and upper castes were 35.2%, 29.0% and 33.9% respectively. If we now look towards group 'A' services we find that the share of Muslims was 7.5% compared 82.2% for all Hindus, 10.3% for SCs/STs, 23.7% for OBCs, 39.2% for upper castes and 10.3% for other minorities. Likewise, for group 'B' the representation of Muslims was 2.2% in comparison to 86.4% for all Hindus, 19.8% for SCs/STs, 21.2% for OBCs, 45.3% for upper castes and 11.5% for other minorities. Similarly, the proportion of Muslims in group 'C' was 3.0% as contrasted to 95.8% for all Hindus, 12.6% for SCs/STs, 20.8% for OBCs, 62.4% for upper castes and 1.2% for other minorities. In the same way, the Muslim share in group 'D' was merely 1.1% as against 98.9% for all Hindus, 44.1% for SCs/STs, 32.2% for OBCs, 22.6% for upper castes and 0.0% for other minorities. Muslims participation in the elected bodies at all levels is meager. Out of the 543 members in the previous Lok Sabha only 36 were Muslims and in the current Lok Sabha their number is merely 29. In Bihar Assembly where Muslims constitute 16.5% of the total population their share in the Assembly had been 19 in 1995, 20 in 2000, 16 in 2005 and 19 in 2010 out of 243 when their number should have been around 40. The same is the more or less the condition of other states. Thus, it is abundantly clear that the participation of Muslims in governance as well as political processes is negligible.

If we now analyze the infrastructural, educational, medical and other facilities in Muslims mohallas and localities at all-India level we find that they are miserable. Tables 4.5, 4.6, 4.7, 4.8 and 4.9 show the percentage of villages having educational institutions, medical facilities, post and telegraph facilities, bus stop, approach to village and pacca approach road to village, 2001 Census.

Table 4.5: Percentage of Villages Having Educational Institutions Within Village, 2001 (Census)

States	% of Villages Having Facility				No. of Villages not Having Facility			
	Within Muslim Population Share of							
	All	< 9%	10-39%	40%+	All	< 9%	10-39%	40% +
	Small (Less than 1000 Population)							
India	80.4	81.6	71.7	69.4	53458	44542	4676	4240
	Medium (1000-2000) Population							
	95.4	96.4	92.4	90.3	5931	3667	1186	1078
	Large (More than 2000 Population)							
	98.3	98.7	97.8	96.8	1711	906	423	382

Source: Sachar Committee Report, Appendix Table 7.2

Table 4.6: Percentage of Villages Having Medical Facilities Within Village, 2001 (Census)

States	% of Villages Having Facility				No. of Villages not Having Facility			
	Within Muslim Population Share of							
	All	< 9%	10-39%	40%+	All	< 9%	10-39%	40% +
India	Small (Less than 1000 Population)							
	20.2	20.2	21.0	19.1	217884	193640	13051	11193
	Medium (1000-2000) Population							
	43.5	44.9	39.7	36.0	73378	56813	9345	7130
	Large (More than 2000 Population)							
	70.7	73.5	67.2	60.2	29052	18181	6191	4680

Source: Sachar Committee Report, Appendix Table 7.3

Table 4.7: Percentage of Villages Having Post and Telegraph Facilities Within Village, 2001 (Census)

States	% of Villages Having Facility				No. of Villages not Having Facility			
	Within Muslim Population Share of							
	All	<9%	10-39%	40%+	All	< 9%	10-39%	40% +
India	Small (Less than 1000 Population)							
	30.1	30.7	29.4	20.4	190771	168088	11670	11013
	Medium (1000-2000) Population							
	54.7	57.5	49.1	36.2	58908	43838	7959	7111
	Large (More than 2000 Population)							
	79.8	83.7	76.7	62.2	20040	11194	4398	4448

Source: Sachar Committee Report, Appendix Table 7.4

Table 4.8: Percentage of Villages Having Bus Stop Within Village, 2001 (Census)

States	% of Villages Having Facility				No. of Villages not Having Facility			
	Within Muslim Population Share of							
	All	< 9%	10-39%	40%+	All	< 9%	10-39%	40% +
India	Small (Less than 1000 Population)							
	28.5	29.1	24.9	23.8	195005	172048	12410	10547
	Medium (1000-2000) Population							
	45.0	48.4	33.9	29.2	71433	53199	10336	7898
	Large (More than 2000 Population)							
	61.6	67.1	53.1	42.9	38095	22519	8859	6717

Source: Sachar Committee Report, Appendix Table 7.5

Table 4.9: Percentage of Villages Having Pucca Approach Road to Village, 2001 (Census)

States	% of Villages Having Facility				No. of Villages not Having Facility			
	Within Muslim Population Share of							
	All	< 9%	10-39%	40%+	All	< 9%	10-39%	40% +
India	Small (Less than 1000 Population)							
	45.2	45.1	48.6	42.8	149469	133063	8496	7910
	Medium (1000-2000) Population							
	65.5	66.9	63.3	55.4	44843	34124	5749	4970
	Large (More than 2000 Population)							
	82.1	84.5	80.7	70.2	17773	10627	3644	3502

Source: Sachar Committee Report, Appendix Table 7.6

The above tables reveal that according to 2001 Census the statistics show that educational, medical, post and telegraph, bus stop, approach road and pucca approach road facilities in almost all the small, medium and large villages with less than 9% Muslim population were better than all types of villages with 10 to 39% and 40%+ Muslim population. It is irony of fate that the infrastructural facilities decline with the increase in Muslim population. The larger their share, the lesser the facilities.

Likewise, the share of Muslims in industry, trade, commerce, business, professions and vocations is also highly unsatisfactory. They are nowhere in seeking bank loans, government contracts, licenses and quotas. They are mostly living in slum areas and depleted conditions with no roads, adequate sanitary conditions and proper water and electric supply. Many Muslims who were landless labourers or petty artisans or who were unemployed took to rikshas in cities and adopted the profession of the Scheduled Castes since such castes had moved vertically upward and had left the vacuum which was filled by the poor and destitute Muslims. One can see many Muslim cobblers in every city who were conspicuous by absence before pre-partition days. Likewise many professions, businesses establishments, trades and vocations which were previously carried on by the Scheduled Castes and Scheduled Tribes have now been adopted by poor Muslims merely to satisfy their hunger. Many Muslims were rendered homeless and helpless due to the closing of various professions due to the introduction of new techniques and technologies. For instance, the professions of bhistis, nutts, animal charmers, kalals, madaris, nalbands, mirasis, oil crushers, cotton carders, utensil polishers, mimics, fur cleaners, which were mostly carried by the Muslims were faded in obscurity due to the advent of industrial era as a consequence of which Muslims became jobless. They had neither means nor training hence they found no alternative but to fall back to those professions and vocations which were vacated by the Scheduled Castes and which needed no training and money. Governments and political parties which boasted of being the friends of Muslims were exposed after the revelations of the Sachar Committee. The adversaries of Muslims too have begun to yield that Muslims need help and assistance. Even those Muslims who were complacent and in dark with respect to the economic conditions of Muslims realized for the first time that they were in the dock and many of them are now thinking of affirmative actions on the part of the government and the political parties to come out of the rut. However, the irony of fate is that no party, no group and no caste is willing to give any concession to Muslims because they fear that such a step would in the long run affect their interests. Even Scheduled Castes know that there are Muslim Scheduled Castes such as Halalkhor, Lalbegi, Abdal, Bediya, Bhangis, Mehtars, Chamars and Doms who are depressed ones and who should be given the same concession as given to them but not at their own costs. Likewise, the backward castes too confess that there are Muslim Backward castes such as Faqirs, Julaha, Itrafrosh, Gadaria, Nanbai, Kalal, Panfrosh, Madari, Gawli, Darweshi, Nalband, Atishbaz and many more who need help but not at the cost of the share of the existing backward castes. The higher castes too feel the necessity of helping the Muslims but they are not willing to exceed the fifty per cent quota. Thus, Muslims despite being declared backward and downtrodden find no friend in any party, caste and class. The Congress Government is making false promises and save cosmetic help it is not willing to do anything for Muslims due to fear of adverse reaction from the right wing majority parties. So far Muslims have lived in dogmatic slumber. They were mostly dependent on Congress and on their few well wishers from backward classes who save lip services have done nothing. A cursory look at the findings of the Sachar Committee Report would reveal that the charge of appeasement of Muslims was a cruel joke because Muslims are a deplorable and a miserable lot and not a privileged one.

The Demand for Common Personal Law

Another factor which caused considerable stress upon the Muslim community was the demand for a common personal law. An agitation was launched by the right wing parties with vigour pertaining to the question of Common Civil Code after Shah Bano case. Shah Bano a divorced housewife of Indore from the State of Madhya Pradesh approached the judicial magistrate in 1978 for a maintenance allowance of ₹ 400 per month from her former husband Ahmad Khan. The magistrate ordered Ahmad Khan to pay ₹ 25 which he later increased to ₹ 179 and 20 paise despite the fact that Ahmad Khan had told the magistrate that he was not obliged under Sharia Law to pay maintenance to her divorced wife as he had already given her three talaqs. Ahmad Khan challenged the decision of the judicial magistrate in the Supreme Court on the plea that under Islamic Law he was not obliged to pay maintenance to his former wife since his liability was confined to iddat period lasting for three months only which he had already paid. The Supreme Court did not agree and upheld the maintenance order under Section 125 which agitated the Muslims. Under the pressure of Muslims, the Rajiv Gandhi Government passed the Muslim Women (Protection of Rights on Divorce) Act 1986 and annulled the order of the Supreme Court. This agitated the Hindus throughout the country. Many enlightened Hindus and the progressive and pro-active educated Muslims tried their best to impress upon the Muslims that there was an urgent need to bring significant changes in Muslim Personal Law as if the Personal Law was the only obstacle in the progress of Muslims and the development of the country. They studied vehemently the Personal Laws of various Muslim countries and tried to convince the Indian Muslims that it was the need of the hour to change their Personal Law. They formed organizations of like-minded Muslim men and women and tried to change Nikah-nama or marriage contract but with no results. There was hue and cry about injustice to Muslim women. Many advocates especially the learned judges from amongst the majority community stood up in support of family planning, gender equality, giving maintenance allowance to divorcees and providing modern education to Muslim women. There was no dearth of people who were deadly against triple talaq, polygamy, veil system and segregation of Muslim women. Several advocated for registration of marriages. Muslims were astonished and surprised because those who were supporting these wonderful ideas in support of Muslim women were Muslims as well as non-Muslims, many of whom were not so active when the injustices were done to the unfortunate Hindu women. Incidentally, many of them remained docile when several young, beautiful and educated brides were being burnt for not fulfilling dowry demands. Several of them did nothing to see many children marrying in their infant stages. There were hardly a few who pleaded the cause of the marriages of the widows. A large magnitude from amongst them kept mum when the girls were denied their appropriate rights in inheritance. Hardly any section came forward when girls were supposed to be linked with their husbands for all times to come with no power to leave their husbands even in the wake of extreme adversity. Nobody doubted their sincerity but there were a few Muslims who were apprehensive for they contended that why these meaningful personalities did not come to the rescue of Muslim women when they were raped, molested and dishonoured during communal riots? Why many of them kept silent when the kith and kin of these unfortunate women were killed and their dwellings were looted and places of worship gutted and they were suffocating within the grip of poverty, hunger, ignorance and diseases? Hardly anyone spoke when they became wretched widows and their children languished in unemployment, misery and persecution. There was a general consensus among most of the Muslims that almost all the well wishers of the Muslim women from majority and minority community who were supporting the cause of Muslim women were those who were more interested in replacing the Muslim Personal Law by a Common Personal Law rather than in fighting the cause of Muslim women. They were under the illusion that Muslim population in the country was rising rapidly due to polygamy and the instrument that supported the polygamy was the Muslim Personal Law. They were convinced that if the Muslims' Personal Law was not amended or modified, Muslims would surpass Hindus in due course of time which was not too far. They put the whole blame to Muslim Personal Law for they believed that polygamy, triple talaq, lack of family planning, absence of maintenance allowance and gender inequality which were increasing Muslim population exponentially were the by-product of Muslim Personal Law. They thought that once Personal Law was changed, Muslims would not be able to marry more than one wife. Besides, they would not be able to get rid of their women at will by giving them triple talaq due to the fear of maintenance allowance in the wake of divorce. In addition to it, the gender equality and freedom to Muslim women would help reduce Muslim population within reasonable limits. Actually, it was a mere propaganda because Muslim population was not rising so rapidly as suggested. First of all large-scale polygamy amongst Muslims was a myth for it is a universal phenomenon that in each and every country or community the ratio between males and females is around fifty-fifty. Among Muslim the child sex ratio was 986 girls for 1000 boys in 1989-99 and the sex ratio according to 2001 Census was 936 compared to 931 for Hindus and 933 for national average. This shows that there is not even one woman per man leave aside four women for every man within Muslim society. Besides, a report on the status of women in India prepared in 1975 showed that the number of polygamous marriages among Hindus was 5.06% compared to 4.3% among Muslims. Moreover, if a large number of Muslims have four wives, majority of Muslims would remain without wives for there would be no wives left for them. In such a situation their population should decline faster for what twenty-five per cent husband can produce with four wives would be far less than what hundred per cent would generate with one wife each. Everybody can verify that educated Muslims seldom marry more than one wife and they do not produce more than two or three children. The same is the case with educated Hindus. They too abhor polygamy and believe in family planning. However, poor and illiterate Muslims certainly produce more children compared to the educated and middle class Muslims. The condition of the poor and illiterate Hindus too is exactly the same as that of poor Muslims. They resemble with each other in totality.

It has been generally observed that in the absence of any adequate social security network such as unemployment benefits, old age pension, health care, the poor and the marginalized people mostly depend upon their children. The children of the poor in under-developed countries supplement the incomes of their parents by working as child labourers. They serve as their supporters during their old ages and come to their rescue during the turbulent days. In addition to it, sex is the only source of enjoyment for the poor for they cannot afford other costly means of entertainment and pleasure, hence their children increase in number compared to the rich and the resourceful persons. Since the proportion of poor among Muslims is more than that of Hindus, their marginal increase compared to Hindus is understandable. The myth of Muslims overtaking Hindus has been prevailing for the last sixty years but the fact is that their share in population has increased only marginally. For instance, in 1961, the Hindus accounted for 83.5% and Muslims 10.7%. By 2001 the share of Hindus has fallen to 80.5% and that of Muslims has risen to 13.4%, the rise of 2.7%. It is no more than a joke to assume that the 13.4 per cent minority would surpass 80.5 per cent majority. It is true that in the recent past the growth of Muslim population has been higher than the average. The annual growth rate has averaged 2.7% over the period 1961-2001, well above the national average of 2.1%. However, the record of the Indian population during the last decade has shown the reversal in the growth of India's population from 23.9% during 1981-91 to 21.5% during 1991-2001. Incidentally, the Muslims population too has fallen from 32.9% to 29.5% or 3.4 percentage points during the same period. The projections show that the Muslim population during the decade of 2030's would rise somewhat, to just below 19% and stabilize at around 320 million in total population of 1.7 billion.

Table 4.10 shows projected Muslim population as the percentage of total population under the most favourable alternative for Muslims of India ranging from 2011 to 2101.

Table 4.10: Projected Non-Muslims and Muslim Population under Various Alternatives India, 2011-2101

Projection Year	Total Population (in thousands)	Percentage increase in Muslim population projected under most favourable alternative
2011	1197671	14.27
2021	1358930	15.25
2031	1480067	16.03
2041	1585806	16.83
2051	1659311	17.63
2061	1707381	18.41
2071	1736136	19.19
2081	1748499	19.92
2091	1768150	20.52
2101	1783308	20.98

Source: Sachar Committee Report, Appendix Table 3.14

The above figures reveal that the Muslim population would never come near fifty per cent but hover around 18% and 19%. Muslim population in the past increased due to several reasons, the important amongst them were: mortality, fertility, poverty, illiteracy and migration. The 1981 and 1991 Census shows that infant and childhood mortality among Muslims is slightly lower than the average. It could perhaps be due to the fact that Muslims are more urbane, they constituted 35.7% in 2001 compared to 27.8% of the overall populations and we know that due to several facilities in the cities the urban population has lower than average child mortality. Incidentally, the infant mortality rate among socio-religious communities, SCs/STs, and other backward sections is much higher. In South, the infant mortality rate among Muslims is 29 per 1000 live births compared to 61 among SCs/STs and 52 among other Hindus. The results also indicate that the decline in infant and under five year mortality has been faster among Muslims than among others save Madhya Pradesh and Rajasthan where child mortality among Muslims has worsened both absolutely and relatively. Likewise, the total fertility rate among Muslims is higher than average by 0.7 to one point. For instance, the crude birth rate among Muslims is 30.8 against 24.9 for Hindus and 25.9 for the total population. The fertility among Muslims in Kerala, Andhra Pradesh, Tamil Nadu, Karnataka and Jammu and Kashmir ranges between 2.5 to 2.8. Besides, Muslims do not have a lower age at marriage than average and the proportion of women married in reproductive age-group was relatively higher because of widow marriages. The facts do not support the perception that Muslims dislike family planning. Various research studies show that contraception and several other methods are widely prevalent among Muslims but to a lesser degree. Certainly, Muslims rose against the coercive practices of Sanjay Gandhiji during emergency but by and large they do not abhor birth controls. Another cause of the increase in their population growth is their poverty, ignorance and illiteracy. Migration is not a very significant factor save in bordering states of Bangladesh, the statistics of which is not available. With the spread of education, female literacy and progressive outlook, the rate of growth of population among Muslims is bound to converge to the national average. We know that educated Muslims practice family planning but poor Muslims cannot afford that luxury. However, if their financial position is improved, they are educated and their women too become literates, family planning is bound to become part and parcel of Muslims. Thus, the myth of increase in population has nothing to do with Personal Law. Marriage in Islam is a sacred contract sanctioned by God. Islam hates talaq. However, when it becomes inevitable, it asks the couples first to try to adjust with each other by following reconciliatory methods but when it becomes impossible, it allows them to separate peacefully and harmoniously without creating bad blood and bestowing the wives with gifts and presents commensurate to one's status. Triple talaq cannot be banned because it is to be used under exceptional circumstances. For instance, if the husband has seen his wife in a hopeless and compromising position with other male with his own eyes, it would be too much to expect from him that he would wait for two to three months and reconcile with her. In that case, the best course of action for both of them would be to separate without creating bloodshed. Thus, the myth of increase in Muslim population has nothing to do with Muslim Personal Law. The pro-active moves and the propaganda of the rightist parties targeting Muslim Personal Law considering it against the interest of Muslim women and national interest seem to be merely the political ploys and parts of their well thought out game plans to harass the minorities. They have nothing to do with the realities in the context of Indian conditions.

Abrogation of Article 370 of the Indian Constitution in Jammu and Kashmir

Another issue which was highlighted by the BJP and other Hindu organizations was the abrogation of Article 370 of the Indian Constitution in Jammu and Kashmir and the complete integration of Jammu and Kashmir within Indian territory. Under Article 370, the State of Jammu and Kashmir enjoys special status and privileges. The Government of India cannot enforce any law connected with Jammu and Kashmir without the approval and concurrence of the State Government. Article 356 dismissing the State Government cannot be directly applied upon J&K. Likewise, the financial emergency under Article 360 too cannot be enforced in Jammu and Kashmir. The State has its own Constitution, Flag and Symbol. On Government buildings the Flag of J&K and Government of India fly simultaneously. Similarly, the Urban Land Act, 1976 is not applicable in Jammu and Kashmir. In the same way, the Government of India cannot implement International Agreements and Accords under Article 253 of the Constitution in the State and it can neither increase nor decrease the borders of the State. Over and above this there is dual citizenship, one of the State and the other of the country. An Indian who is an ordinary resident of Jammu and Kashmir is not allowed to construct or buy house in the State and also he is not allowed to contest election there. Incidentally, the provision that non-Kashmiris cannot buy land in Kashmir, regardless of religion was introduced by Hindu Dogra Rulers in 1928. Similar provisions also exist in Hindu majority states like Himachal Pradesh as well as some North-Eastern states. There is Article 371-A for Nagaland, 371-B for Assam, 371-C for Manipur, 371-D for Andhra Pradesh, 371-F for Sikkim, 371-G for Mizoram, 371-H for Arunachal Pradesh and 371-I for Goa. All these Articles grant special rights and privileges to those states depending upon their cultural ethos, social bindings and historical backgrounds. If an ordinary Indian resident marries a Kashmiri, Jammu or Laddakhi girl, she loses her rights in Jammu and Kashmir. Many Constitutional experts feel that this article is unnecessary and it should be abrogated. There are others who claim that this Article has created separatism and anti-India feelings among the residents of the Valley. Besides, due to this Article the poverty in the State is perpetuating for land and other reforms cannot be applied in the State. There is no dearth of people who believe that this Article is a hurdle in the complete integration of the State in Indian Union and hence it should be abrogated as early as possible. Some of the safeguards to protect the local populations are found in a few hill states like Himachal Pradesh, Nagaland and the Eastern states but not on such a comprehensive scale. However, the position of Jammu and Kashmir is slightly different. Maharaja Hari Singh agreed to the accession of Jammu and Kashmir to India on October 26, 1947 and empowered the Union of India to have absolute jurisdiction in respect of three subjects, namely defence, foreign affairs and communications. At the time of accession, the people of Jammu, Kashmir and Laddakh were assured by Pandit Jawaharlal and the Indian Parliament that they would be accorded a special status. Hence, many people feel that abrogation of the Article would tantamount to betrayal to the people of the state. Admittedly, on the issue of Special Status of Jammu and Kashmir, the people of Kashmir are very particular and sensitive. They would resist any attempt towards the abrogation of Article 370 for they fear that they would become minority in the Valley. Their number is not highly significant both in Jammu and Laddakh and if they lose their majority in the Valley they would be nowhere. The fear of being reduced to minority is bound to agitate the people of Jammu and Kashmir in the wake of abrogation of Article 370. The experience shows that in many hill areas the businessmen from the Indo Gangetic Plain have migrated in large number and have captured the markets of the hilly areas. They have not only controlled the local segments but have also changed the culture of those areas. The locals have been pushed to the background and they have emerged as the dominant class. The local residents were obliged to sell their properties to these business magnets and had to move either in the interiors or were forced to work under their subjugation as labourers and petty attendants. The Kashmiris are not willing to yield to the demand of the BJP and other rightist parties. There was a hue and cry in the valley and people had come on the roads in the wake of giving a piece of land for the use of Amarnath yatris. What to talk of abrogation of Article 370, the people and even the political parties are not willing to surrender their autonomy to Indian Union. The National Conference and the PDF had fought elections not for seeking independence or merging the State in Pakistan but to remain in India within the clout of Indian Constitution but side by side their demand was to acquire more autonomy or as much autonomy as it was available to them before 1953. Needless to say that most of the political parties of India and several segments of the country including the Muslims are in favour of keeping Article 370 as promised to the people of Jammu and Kashmir. Although Article 370 did provide a special status for Kashmir due to historical reasons, yet all the provisions which gave it greater autonomy than other states ceased to operate in 1954. Since then Kashmir has been under the direct control of the Central Government and many of the democratic rights have been curtailed there due to prevailing conditions. Many meaningful Indians agree that Jammu and Kashmir is the integral part of India but they are also convinced that it is a disputed matter in which Indians, Pakistanis and the people of Kashmir are involved in one way or the other. The need of the hour, therefore, is not to touch such sensitive issues when the general political climate in this region is not conducive to peace. It is hoped that through confidence building measures, proximity between the occupied Kashmir and Jammu and Kashmir and good neighbourly relations between India and Pakistan, the issue of Jammu and Kashmir would be solved so as to satisfy all the stakeholders and then there would be no need of the abrogation of Article 370. Actually, the need of the hour is a dialogue between Pakistan and India which unfortunately is not happening because as soon as there is a talk of any dialogue some untoward things happen in the country which derails the whole process. The dialogue should emphasize on confidence building measures and porous borders and trade relations and educational and cultural exchanges between the two countries. These measures are bound to generate a healthy climate for the solution of the vex problems between India and Pakistan including the dispute of Jammu and Kashmir.

The Demand for the Construction of Ram Temple at Babri Masjid

The fourth factor that created problems for Muslims was the Babri Masjid issue. The hard-core section from the majority community believed that Babri Masjid was built by Mir Baqi, the Governor of Faizabad in 1528 after destroying an old Hindu temple in Ayodha so that on his arrival Emperor Baber could perform Namaz. They also contend that Mahant Raghuwar Das sought permission from the British in 1885 to construct a temple at the place of the mosque but the permission was rejected. At some later stage a wall was erected between the mosque and a place known as Ram Chabutra but the same was demolished in 1934 but later on the British Government rebuilt it. Muslims, however, contend that nothing like this happened. There lied a vacant place on which rightfully a mosque was erected during the days of Baber which became famous by the name of Babri Masjid. They sight legal documents in support of their arguments. However, as most of the Muslims from Ayodhya had migrated to Pakistan certain hard-core right-minded fanatics placed Hindu idols in the mosque on the night of 21-22 December 1949. Pandit Nehru knew that the conduct of Faizabad district officer K.K.K. Nayar was not above board. He also knew that the influential Congressmen like Baba Raghavdas and Vishambar

Dayal Tripathi were fomenting trouble. He was also in know of the facts that Pandit Govind Ballabh Pant, the Chief Minister of UP having dissuaded him from visiting Ayodhya, refrained from taking any positive action. Pandit Pant anyhow agreed to lock the door of the mosque on the advice of Pandit Nehru. The mosque was locked on December 29, 1949. The matter remained silent for many years because a few Muslims used to go to the mosque for prayers. However, to appease the rightist forces that were not happy with the enactment of Muslim Marriages Act, the locks of Babri Masjid were opened by Congress Government on the 1 May 1986. Actually, the Supreme Court had decided in favour of maintenance allowance for a Muslim divorcee in the context of Shah Bano case which had agitated Muslims of India since it was against the Personal Law of the Muslims. They came on the roads against it and persuaded the Central Government to annul it by bringing new legislation. In order to appease Muslims, Rajiv Gandhi yielded to Muslims' demand and Muslim Marriages Act, namely Muslim Women (Protection of Rights on Divorce) Act, 1986 was passed in the Parliament on 6 May 1986 overruling the Supreme Court Judgment. This action of the government was considered as the appeasement of Muslims of the highest order for behind the thinking of the hard-core sections of the majority community was the fact that this act would strengthen the Muslim Personal Law which in turn would lead to Muslims overtaking Hindus in the long run. There was a hue and cry in the country and even sensible people among Hindu society came out openly against the government and media became vocal. Since the Congress Government at that time was confined merely to the Northern India, Congress Government could not afford to annoy the majority community since it had lost its hold over South India and was depending upon Hindi speaking people for its votes. Hence, it tried to please the majority community by laying Shila Niyas just as it had pacified the minority community by bringing Muslim Marriage Act. This appeasement policy of the government with a view to please the Hindus and Muslims pleased none and litigations and agitations started which spoiled the peaceful climate of the country. Hindu organizations took the issue of construction of Ram Temple at Ayodhya to their hearts and made it a national and international issue due to the adverse policies of the government and the irresponsible utterances of Muslim and Hindu leadership of those days. Muslim leadership could avoid confrontation by its peaceful and polite approach but it became volatile which annoyed even those right thinking Hindus who were aloof from the whole scene. Majority of Hindus throughout the country became emotional and a climate of hate and disgust arose against the minorities. Seeing the situation going out of the control of the State and Central Governments, the Congress Government thought of pacifying the Hindus and Muslims by proposing to erect a mighty Hindu temple in Ayodhya near the Mosque avoiding the disputed area. The foundation stone was laid within the disputed area during the regime of the Congress Government both at the levels of State and the Centre misleading Muslims by saying that the foundation-laying was done out of the disputed area. This step of the Congress Government embolden the advocates of temple construction and as time elapsed even the eminent saints and the heads of Hindu religious organizations entered the scene and the situation went out of the control of the government. Since Mulayam Singh Government was in control of Uttar Pradesh on the support of Muslims, he came in support of Muslims openly. Lal Krishan Advani started his journey in support of the Ram Temple from Somnath to Ayodhaya through many states of the country. His Rath Yatra spread the communal virus in the country and polarized people on communal lines. Nobody dared to stop him from his misadventure. It was Lalu Prashad Yadav in Bihar who dared to check him. Mulayam Singh ordered the police to disperse the crowds of sadhus in 1990 at Ayodhya which resulted in the violence and death of several kar sevaks and this misadventure paid rich dividend to the BJP. Riots started on large scale in the country and the climate of the whole country deteriorated. The Rath Yatra proved boon to RSS and BJP. The RSS membership increased immensely and BJP made effective inroads in UP, Himachal Pradesh, Rajasthan and Madhya Pradesh. The heart-touching episode on Ramayan by Ramanand Sagar, glorifying

Ram, Laxman and Sita extended over several serials was broadcasted which arouse love for these deities among the hearts of Hindus and involved the masses in the issue of Babri Masjid. Thousands of religious dignitaries including sadhu sants spread throughout the length and the breadth of the country and influenced the millions of people living in five lakh villages of the country. Besides, huge financial support came from NRIs and expatriates from United States of America, Gulf countries, UK and Europe. Thus, the issue of the Babri Masjid was internationalized very effectively. When the next election came Mulayam Singh was defeated by the Hindus due to his anti-temple policies and BJP Government came in power in many Hindi speaking states including the State of Uttar Pradesh. From then onward the agitation took a very curious turn. Plans were perhaps made to demolish the mosque secretly and people were trained for this purpose. Volunteers were sent in all the villages to mobilize support in favour of the construction of the temple. Kalyan Singh, the Chief Minister of Uttar Pardesh assured the Supreme Court regarding the protection of Babri Masjid but to the surprise of many the 430 years old Babri Mosque was demolished on 6 December 1992 by a group of fanatics in the presence of armed forces and the paramilitary units under the allegations that it was built on the birth place of Hindu deity Rama. Narasimha Rao was the Prime Minster of the Congress Government at the Centre. He kept mum till the Mosque was razed to the ground and the bricks of the Mosques taken away by the mob and the temporary Ram Temple was erected on the mosque. When the needful was completed, the government forces moved and dispersed the mob without harming any one.

The demolition of Babri Masjid on 6 December 1992 is the significant event which has left deep scars on the country's fragile Muslim community. The physical collapse of Babri Masjid was symbolized not only as the moral collapse of India's so-called liberal majority community but it was also seen as the collapse of centuries old Indian heritage and a massive assault on the very foundations of Indian culture and civilization. It exited religious passions, caused widespread violence, polarized life along antagonistic lines and created anguish and fear among Indian Muslims. Property worth crores was destroyed during eighteen days after demolition. Industrial houses suffered huge trading loss and the loss of gross value of output of goods and services exceeded ₹ 1000 crores. The loss of exports touched approx. ₹ 1,900 crores and state suffered the revenue loss of ₹ 200 crores. The ensuing loss of lives coupled with the humiliation of womenfolk, persecutions of the innocents and harassment of young and old by police and painful litigations in the law courts torn Muslims to pieces. It struck at the very roots of democratic, secular and pluralistic consensus envisaged by the founding fathers of Indian Constitution. It dented India's tryst with destiny, eroded pluralist, democratic and secular spaces and negated the framework of ideas that seek to strengthen the very base and fabric of the modern state. Some called it as the Hindu backlash against Muslim appeasement and the dogged refusal of Muslims to join mainstream. Others termed it as cultural nationalism and Hindu awakening and an attempt to erase a hated symbol of Muslim rule. Many believed that it was a movement for Hindu self-assertion and nationhood to rewrite the nation's agenda through the medium of Hindutva to impose a Hindu Rashtra upon it with a view to weaken the secular forces and reduce minorities to the status of second-class citizens. There was no dearth of people who believed that it was the triumph of repressive and regressive forces of hatred and vandalism to intimidate their adversaries in full view of state machinery The Congress which professed to de-link the state and religion and encourage inter-community relationship came on the back foot. The leftist and centrist forces lost their moral and intellectual fiber. The regional parties were marginalized and thrown in the peripheries. Only the Hindu parties triumphed on the political spectrum. The holocaust in Mumbai, Surat and Bhopal proved the hollowness of cosmopolitan life of Indian cities, the violence, vandalism and the alleged connivance by the police and security forces exposed the governing structure and radical Muslims started collecting arms for protection. From north to south and east to west, a section of radical Muslim youths was agitated. Inspired by the extremist ideology, as a means to solve the problems of the community, some of the hard-core Muslims were talking in terms of raising Adam Sena, defence leagues and other similar organizations. The bomb blast at Mumbai on 12 March 1993 was perhaps the culmination of the hatred that was nourishing among some misguided radical Muslim elements since long.

Muslims of India were shocked as they could not do anything since they had to confront the paramilitary forces which were already on the roads. Communal riots started in the country on a large-scale. The worst riots were in Mumbai and Surat which cannot be expressed in words for many Muslims lost lives, many properties were destroyed and the humiliation they suffered at the hands of majority community as well as the paramilitary and police forces is beyond description. Muslims blamed the BJP Government for the demolition of the Mosque but they never forgave Narasimha Rao for erecting Ram Temple on the spot of Babri Masjid. The Congress Government shed crocodile tears and removed BJP Governments from various states and assured Muslims to erect the Mosque at the same place. Cases were registered against prominent BJP leaders including Lal Krishna Advani, Murli Manohar Joshi and Uma Bharti and others but till now no action has been taken against anybody. The cases are pending in the courts and it is hoped that it would take years to decide the cases. Jayendra Sarswati Shankracharyaji of Kanchi wanted to solve the problem by allowing Hindus and Muslims to erect both Mosque and Temple side by side as temples and the mosques stand in Mathura and Banaras but many Muslim organization such as Babri Masjid Action Committee, Jamiat Ulema-e-Hind, All India milli Council, Khanqa Ahmad Raza Khan Barelvi, Shahi Imam Sayed Ahmed Bukhari, Jama Masjid Delhi, All India Imam Organization, Tanzimul Maktab Lucknow, Muslim Khanqa Rehmania, Jamiat Ahle Hadees and others did not agree. Likewise, the RSS, Bajrang Dal, Vishwa Hindu Parishad, Shiv Sena and many more Hindu organizations and country's many prominent saints were averse to it. The situation has become more complicated because the hard-core Hindus contend that there are thirty thousand mosques in India which were erected after destroying Hindu temples. They demand all such mosques under their control for reconverting them into the original temples. They are, however, willing to give latitude to Muslims provided they handover them three mosques one at Ayodhya, the other at Mathura and the third at Banaras. It will not be out of place to mention here that the Parliament of India has passed a law according to which the status quo of all the religious places as they were existing on August 15, 1947 would be maintained excluding Babri Masjid but hard-core Hindu organizations are not happy. They want two more mosques one at Banaras and the other at Mathura to be excluded from the list.

One thing is certain that the demolition of Babri Masjid has led to the aggression and militancy among a few sections of the majority community. The Akhil Bhartiya Pratinidhi Sabha of the RSS, the Dharma Sansad and the BJP's think tank idolized the Hindutva and cultural nationalism and sants, swamis and acharyas threatened to liberate the temples at Mathura and Varanasi amid chanting of Vedic hymns and ringing of temple bells. The RSS Chief Rajendra Singh warned that his organization would not sit idle till the three most sacred places were returned to them. The Communists, Mulayam Singh, Lalu Prasad and Ram Vilas Paswan and a few more were trying to check the belligerence of the majority community but it seems that there were several hidden forces in the regional parties of the country which provide moral and material support to the pro-active forces. It appeared that even many liberals and the so-called secularist from the majority community too are heart-to-heart sympathetic to some of the rightist and extremist forces for they criticized them openly but support them secretly.

The demolition of Babri Masjid can be considered as one of the greatest events of the country after partition. It was a unique event of its kind because the Mosque was not demolished during turbulent and extraordinary situations, it was destroyed during peace times when the legally constituted, properly elected and the powerful governments stood both at the level of Centre and State. Muslims know that many mosques and temples have been demolished in the past during the days of fanaticism. Even today many mosques are in the possession of the Hindus and Sikhs in Punjab, Haryana and Rajasthan and many temples and gurduwaras are in the hands of Muslims in various provinces in Pakistan but it seldom happened that such things occurred during peace times in the presence of the government forces. This event was a most frustrating event for Muslims as it shattered their confidence in the government machinery and the majority community. Nearly, a year later the BJP suffered heavily in the November 1993 assembly elections in Himachal Pradesh, UP, and Madhya Pradesh. In UP, Muslims, Yadavs and Harijans tilted the balance against the BJP. The physical fall of Babri Masjid was taken by the people as the moral fall of BJP's Hindu Nationalism. Especially after the bomb blasts in Mumbai on 12 March 1993, the mood of people changed drastically. The business community in Varanasi came in support of the Gyanvapi mosque, the Kashi Vyapar Mandal organized peace march and Hindus and Muslims organized rallies and pledged to shun violence. Many Muslims appreciated the large-hearted tolerance of the Hindu community in defeating BJP in many states and calling it a communal party. Even the BJP stalwarts condemned the event as a black spot on the face of the country. Nevertheless, the spirit of revenge and retaliation seems to be there in one form or the other on both sides and only God knows when unity, love, brotherhood, peace and harmony would prevail which is the chief feature of this great country.

The question of Babri Masjid is very perplexed. Muslims want the reconstruction of the mosque in its original place whereas the Hindus want to construct the magnificent temple on the original sight of the mosque. Both the parties have gone to the courts and courts are sitting on the files and it appears that it would take years to the courts to decide the case. The Babri Masjid dispute is so ticklish that it appears to have no solution save the decision reached through consensus by both the communities for if one party wins the other would go to the higher courts for appeals and the case would linger for long. Over and above this, the defeated party whoever it may be shall never accept court verdict. The Vishwa Hindu Parishad has already expressed its sentiments by emphasizing that since it is the matter of faith, the court order if goes against its belief system would never be accepted by Hindu masses. Similar sentiments too have been expressed by the Muslims for they too believe that all proofs are in their favour and in the presence of solid documentary evidence no court can ever give judgment against them. Muslims are not happy due to the presence of the make-shift temple at the sight of Babri Masjid and Hindus are unhappy for they have not been able to construct the temple of their choice. BJP wishes to assure the voters that in case it comes in full power, it would construct the temple by consensus or by bringing a new act in the Parliament. However, if it came in a fractured form it would find it difficult due to the constraints of coalition politics as it could not do when it ruled for six years. No party is willing to convert the place in a public utility or national monument or an object of common concern for both. Likewise, no party is ready to forgo its claim in favour of other party. In the same way, the efforts of many saints and clergies, to create mosque and temple adjacent to each other on the spot of Babri Masjid as the mosques and temples are found on the controversial places in Mathura and Banaras, have failed.

That was the history. Now the current situation is that the Lucknow bench of Allahabad High Court consisting of Justice S.U. Khan, Justice Sudhir Agarwal and Justice D.V. Sharma ruled on the sensitive 60 year-old title dispute on Ram Janmabhoomi-Babri Masjid structure judgment on September 30, 2010 by a majority verdict that "the disputed area to be split into three equal portions to be given to Hindus (Ram Lalla), the Nirmohi Akhara and Muslims. All the three parties, i.e. Muslims, Hindus and Nirmohi Akhara were declared joint title-holders of the property/premises to the extent of 1/3 share each for using and managing the same for worshipping. The area covered by the central dome to be part of the area given to Hindus. The area covered by Ram Chabutra, Sita Rasoi and Bhandar to form part of the share of the Nirmohi Akhara. Muslims to get not less than one-third of the total area of the premises (2.77 acres) and if need be they may be given a part of the outer courtyard (which was earlier with Hindus) or compensated from the land acquired by the Centre in 1993 (67 acres) Centre's land should be made available so that all the three parties may utilize the area to which they are entitled, by having separate entry for egress and ingress of people without disturbing each other's rights. For this purpose, the parties concerned may approach the Centre which shall act accordingly in terms of Supreme Court verdict of 1994. The parties can file suggestions for actual partition of the property to the high court and status quo shall meanwhile be maintained for three months." The minority view of Justice D.V. Sharma, who retired as the high court judge the next day of delivering the judgment, was that "the entire disputed area belongs to Hindus (Ram Lalla and his representatives). Entire premise to be given to Hindus. All other parties to the dispute permanently restrained from interfering with, or raising any objection to, or placing any obstruction in the construction of the temple at Ram Janam Bhumi Ayodhya at the site. "It is heartening to know that the majority verdict delivered by Justice S.U. Khan and Justice Sudhir Agarwal was hailed by all parties and all countrymen as a whole with certain reservations. Though the Centre, the State Governments and the general public were apprehensive of the fall out of the judgment, yet to the surprise of all there was not a single case of any untoward incident in the country, the credit for which goes to the religious heads of various Muslim and Hindu groups, the heads of the political parties, the Central and State Governments and the general public. The Central Government under Congress and its allies and Mayawati Government at the level of Uttar Pradesh deserve praise and appreciation from every section of the society for their nice implementation of law and order in the country especially in the State of Uttar Pradesh and the surrounding sensitive areas. Muslims were certainly shocked for in their opinion the judgment was given keeping in mind the faith and belief system of the majority community rather than facts, witnesses, evidences and legal issues. They are afraid that the judgment may be used as precedence in several other cases involving the belief system of the majority community such as the disputed shrines at Mathura and Kashi and several issues pending in the courts pertaining to the faith and belief of the people. Moreover, the people who are involved in the demolition of Babri Masjid may be exonerated taking the advantage of faith. It is also highly commendable that the reaction of RSS Chief Mohan Rao Bhagwat was praiseworthy so also the reaction of BJP, Congress, CPM, BSP and others. There are some people who are trying to play politics but the climate of the country is such that nobody would be allowed to play the dirty game in the name of Mandir and Masjid. The youths of the country and the majority of the people from among the Muslims and Hindus are in favour of out of court settlement or settlement with the help of Supreme Court in such a way that neither Muslims feel humiliated and defeated nor do Hindus feel the same. They want that just as two disputed shrines are existing near each other in Mathura and Kashi, similarly the mosque and the Ram Mandir should exist near each other as the symbols of India's brotherhood, harmony, peaceful coexistence and large-hearted tolerance. All indications lead to the trend that meaningful people from both sides would try to find out the peaceful solution to the vex problem out of the court failing which the disputed parties would go to the Supreme Court. This judgment and its healthy reaction have once more shown that India is really a great and mighty country with its old value system and marvelous and healthy traditions. Its people can falter but they cannot go astray. They believe in rule of law, fellow feeling and truth, justice and good conscience. The bright side of the picture is that the country has come out of the rut and it is hoped that all outstanding issues including the Mandir-Masjid problem and all pending controversial issues would be solved during a meaningful time horizon peacefully and amicably. Let us hope and believe with confidence and conviction that a new beginning has been made for a prosperous, mighty, peaceful and grand India which would heal the wounds of Muslims which they got during and after the demolition of Babri Masjid and this new resurgence would prove boon for the people of the world in general and for Indian masses in particular.

5

The Contemporary Phase of Assertion, Depression and Contemplation

The third phase from 1992 till date may be called the phase of 'assertion, depression and contemplation'. The experience of the demolition of Babri Masjid was an eye opener for the Muslims especially those who believed in rule of law, civilized behavior and respect for commitments. Muslims believed in the assurances given by the State of Uttar Pradesh as well as the Centre but when the time to protect the Mosque arose nobody came to their rescue. Their leaders and well wishers made loud noises but practically did nothing when the situation demanded, due to the reasons best known to them. Most of the Muslims lost confidence in Babri Masjid Action Committee and many of them raised fingers of doubt, suspicion and mistrust at few of them. Various political parties befooled them in the name of helping them. For the first time Indian Muslims realized that perhaps they had practically no friends in the country and they made a mistake in believing people. Instead of depending upon pseudo leaders, it would have been better for them to have fought their own case in the peaceful and constitutional manner as rightful claimants taking the saner elements of the majority community along with them. The demolition of Babri Masjid was frightful and ghastly for the post-partition born Muslims who were without any guilt since they were born in free India where they saw Pakistan in the same way as they saw other countries on the world map.

When they witnessed hooligans riding on the roof of the mosque chanting slogans, demolishing the holy structure brick by brick in broad day light in full view of multitude of people and thousands of paramilitary forces, they were shocked and bewildered. Alas! They found themselves helpless and frustrated in their own country at the hands of their own people and the governing structure and they were convinced that all was not well in the country. They felt that they need not be over optimist and complacent for the future was not so much smooth and bright for them. It was bumpy, thorny and full of obstacles and challenges. They realized that problems would come from various quarters, their many genuine demands would not be met, they would be discriminated but they have to face all the odds and difficulties with courage and fortitude and find their own way even against the stream. They felt the need of their presence especially in the governing structure of the country for they thought that in a democracy one could achieve one's objectives only through the power of ballets rather than the bullets.

Various Models to Rule the Country

Muslims are convinced that there is enough space for them in Indian politics despite the fact that Indian politics has become the victim of caste, religion, region and language groups. They too have been used as vote bank by various political parties with disastrous consequences. Nevertheless, they are by and large convinced that so long as the political game plan of the country is played on caste, communal, regional and other such divisive cards they too should play their game safely and should not become the part of any vote bank politics but carve out their place on the basis of their strength and dexterity and long run interest. They must become part and parcel of various models for governance keeping in mind the interest of the community as well as the nation in mind. As we know that in the wake of divisive environment, there are basically several models to form government at the centre as well as the states. Firstly, by taking the support of 20.8% upper castes, 19.6% minorities and 16.4% SCs and 8.5% STs, one can rule over the whole country conveniently because the combined voting power of these segments comes to 65.3% which is enough for obtaining comfortable majority. Besides, these castes and classes are natural allies of one another and there is no conflict of interest among them since they are complementary rather than competitive in nature. The second model to form a majority government at the Centre and States is to take the help of the 34.6% OBCs and 19.6% minorities for their combined strength would provide them 54.2% voting power which would help them to form government easily and conveniently. These two constituents too are complementary and not competitive and can form good allies being the backward segments of the society. Since both these segments have been neglected for too long, they can form a harmonious combination provided they care for each others' interests. The third possibility is to rule the country by uniting 34.6% OBCs and 24.9% SCs/STs for their combined strength comes to 59.5%. This combination appears to be functional but it seldom works because there is inherent conflict of interest between them as they are competitive sects rather than complementary one. However, if they tactfully function according to a well thought out strategy being the depressed sections of the society, keeping each others interest in mind, none can check them in forming a viable and stable government both at the Centre and the States. The fourth strategy is to unite various segments of Hindu society with a view to garner their 80.4% votes on the basis of Hindu religion, Hindu culture, Hindu sanskriti and Hindutva in order to minimize the impact of religious minorities and various class and caste groups by creating in them the feeling of religious affinity based on Hinduism. This combination can work in exceptional circumstances when the safety and security of the country is in danger or where the religious places, cultural identities and belief system of the majority are at stake. Save this it cannot work as this combination is composed of various groups having contradictory interests. Besides, there are other methods to form the government where castes and religious groups are not involved such as the fifth one is to rule the country with the help of the working class or through the mechanism of Communism and Socialism which can garner the votes of 64.4% workers in the age group of 15-64 years. This type of model can work well provided it is utilized keeping in mind the various religious, cultural and emotional sensitivities of different segments of the workers and the labourers in mind. This type of model is working in many countries due to the commonality of interest between various stake groups. The sixth model is to acquire the votes of 71% farmers and all those parts of the society which are directly or indirectly related to agricultural and rural activities. This group is also a homogeneous group since the interests of various ingredients of this group are more or less identical. The seventh model is the coalition politics where the dominant party takes the help of the likeminded or willing parties to form the government. This model is effective for in the wake of hung Parliament or hung Assembly, this is an ideal solution. The eighth one is to form a national government by taking elected members from each party in proportion to their strength in the Parliament or Assemblies. This model too is nice in the wake of hung Parliament or hung Assemblies. The ninth method is to have two-party system having left of the centre and right of the centre leaning parties. The parties representing various vocal, religious, cultural and ideological groups and those fighting on the basis of economic criteria, political expediency and social constraints can form the centrist party with rightist leaning and centrist party with leftist leaning to rule the country. This type of model is suited to modern democracies and India too should strive to move towards this pattern. There are indications that in the long run the Congress would tilt towards left of the centre and the BJP would shift towards right to the centre. Tenth strategy is a kind of indirect democracy choosing people at grass-root level such as Pardhans and Mayors at Panchayats and Municipal Corporations' level directly and giving them power to elect heads at Zila Parishad level so that they may form government at the level of assemblies by electing MLAs. The Parliament is to be formed by the MPs elected through the MLAs. This type of indirect democracy can also survive if there are well-established Zirgas, caste or class groups and clans. The eleventh strategy is to rule the country by one party dictatorship as the Communist Parties of Soviet Union and China did or which the Congress Party could do after obtaining freedom. The thirteenth mode is to rule by forming all women party. This is possible for the women constitute nearly 50 per cent of the population and they are a homogeneous and complementary group. They can form their own party and rule the country and the states with a view to protect their interests. This type of government can prove to be compassionate, pragmatic and constructive. The fourteenth method is giving representation to various castes, religious, regional and linguistic groups in proportion to their numerical strength. In the age of reservation, this method would surely find many takers. The fifteenth method is ruling the country by qualitative mode such as allowing the people to elect only those men and women who command respect among people due to their honesty, integrity, genius and good moral conduct and who have shown their worth in the field of betterment of mankind and who are capable of running the governments. Such people should be persuaded to fight elections in order to take the responsibilities as MLAs and MPs in the larger interest of the country as a mark of respect for their sincerity, loyalty, efficiency, honesty and competence without any quid pro quo. The sixteenth model is through declaring emergency or President Rule in the country which was done by Indira Gandhi but which people of the country did not relish. The seventeenth mode is ruling through military rule which is also found in many countries but which is highly improbable in India. The eighteenth one is rule by the middle class or urbanites if they happen to be in significant numbers crossing the limit of 50%. There are various other models which are prevalent in many countries but we as Indians do not approve them such as the kingship model and dictatorship models, etc.

The Congress Strategy

The Congress Government ruled the country by seeking the support of the higher castes, minorities and the Scheduled Castes and the Scheduled Tribes. Most of the Brahmins, Rajputs and Thakurs, Dalits and the Muslims supported whole-heartedly the Congress Party for many years. The

Congress Government could get the support of the Scheduled Castes and the Scheduled Tribes easily due to the reservation which it provided to them in the Constitution. The minorities were compelled to support the Congress because of their compulsions due to their helplessness after the partition of the country and due to the fear of the rightist parties as well as due to the lack of any viable alternative. The higher castes supported the Congress for they were the main beneficiaries since most of the government jobs were captured by them due to their competence in judiciary, media, civil departments and defence establishments and industry, trade and commerce despite the fact that numerically they were insignificant. Besides, these communities were the natural allies. There was no clash of interest between them because SCs/STs were at the lowest ebb and they had no clash of interest neither with the Hindu upper castes nor minorities for they were not the competitors but were complementary to them. Similarly, Muslims too were not averse to higher castes for they had lived with Hindu upper castes for centuries as equals and the SCs/STs too had no complaints with Muslims since they had also lived with them comfortably. Congress Government's secular and socialist policies, Five-Year Plans and an independent foreign policy together with law and order in the country won many hearts. Muslims were impressed due to its non-communal approach, sympathy towards Muslims and its good neighbourly policies with the Muslim countries of the Middle East and the Far-East especially its support for the people of Palestine.

It will not be out of place to mention here that Muslims were not happy heart-to-heart with Congress for it did practically nothing for them in matters of providing government jobs to Muslims even at the levels of clerks and peons and also it failed to do anything concrete in the fields of business, professions and vocations as well as during communal clashes and thereafter. They were satisfied up to some extent for its policy of keeping Muslims in adequate numbers in the State Assemblies and Parliament and appointing Muslim Ministers, Governors, Ambassadors and

Judges and even Presidents and the Vice-Presidents of the country. Keeping Muslims on the higher positions not only raised the secular image of the Congress Party, Congress Government and the country in the eyes of the countries of the world especially the Muslim nations, it also raised the standard of Muslims in the eyes of the masses and it worked as deterrent for the anti-social elements. Undoubtedly, the Congress Party during the days of Pandit Jawaharlal Nehru had a soft corner for Muslims and it wanted to do something for them but it was helpless due to the anti-Muslim attitude of various right wing parties and the unfavorable circumstances prevailing in the country just after partition as well as due to the coloured approach of the petty government officials and biased attitude of the lower-level Congressmen and the bias of the executives who were working at grass-root level. Over and above this, many communal elements had entered the Congress Party by back doors pretending to be the secularists who behind the scenes helped rightist and reactionary forces at the cost of Muslims. This fact came in the open when BJP Party formed the government at the Centre under Atal Bihari Vajpayee when many staunch Congressmen, film personalities, business magnets and others having secular image deserted the Congress and joined the BJP. Despite the fact that the Congress Government during the times of Pandit Jawaharlal Nehru sincerely wanted to control the communal riots with strong hands, it could not succeed for the total machinery which was the implementing and executing authority had misleading notions about Muslims. The Muslims of India put the whole blame of riots upon the shoulders of Congress Government though the initiators and the perpetuators of the riots were mainly the extremists and the anti-social elements supported by some of the local people, political parties including many Congressmen and a few biased administrators. Muslims believe that the maximum number of riots took place during the Congress regime and maximum loss of life, property honour occurred during that period and the party did nothing for the rehabilitation, compensation, punishment of the culprits and redresser of Muslims' grievances.

One cannot deny that the Congress Government created a conducive climate for the safety and security of Muslims and opened indirectly various avenues for their growth and development through the process of planning. It adopted mixed economy as a means to development and followed the Mahalanobis model which emphasized capital goods vis-à-vis consumer goods. Since there was food shortage in the country specially after the partition of the country, the government gave more emphasis on agriculture in the First Five-Year Plan. The First Five-Year Plan (1951-56) showed tremendous success. The country which was passing in the stage of food shortages, controls and rationings came out of the crisis successfully. Unfortunately, it had to face food crisis and foreign exchange problem during the Second Five-Year Plan (1956-61) due to its heavy emphasis on industries. Since the First Five-Year Plan had solved the food problem, the planners thought that it would be better to embark upon the industrial growth. However, later on it was realized that the food problem of the country was not solved for ever. It was temporarily solved due to the favourable monsoon resulting in the bumper food crop and the exemplary efforts of Rafi Ahmed Kidwai, the then the Food Minister. He with his sheer genius solved the food problem during First Five-Year Plan. Indian Government was able to establish heavy industries, power projects, public sector undertakings and maintain peace, progress and harmony in the country and could face international challenges in the fields of defence, foreign policy and international relations. The Fourth (1969-74), Fifth (1974-79), Sixth (1980-85), Seventh (1985-90), Eighth (1992-97), Ninth (1997-2002) and Tenth (2003-2008) Five-Year Plans provided employment opportunities to millions of people though they also created inequalities at sectoral, regional and individual levels. The major planning flaw of the Government of India was that it thought mostly in terms of fulfilling targets without bothering about end result of income creation. As the business class was already in the business since time immemorial, it provided most of the resources for the plans and thus major portion of the income from the plans went to this class which became rich and prosperous. No efforts were made to create new beneficiaries. Moreover, the controls, quotas, building and infrastructure contracts, license raj and corruption in government offices created a new class of rich people from amongst the traders, politicians and government servants who lived the life of rajas and maharajas. Even Rajiv Gandhi, the Prime Minister of India admitted that "Out of every 100 crore allocated to an anti-poverty project, I know that only about ₹ 15 crore reach the people. The remainder is gobbled up by middlemen, power brokers, contractors, and the corrupt." Presently, the condition is worst. The country is facing scams after scams in which many unscrupulous politicians, government officials and business magnates are involved. Besides, the excessive tax rates in those days crossing even the 90% limit at the higher levels created black money in the economy which led to smuggling, extravagance and transfer of money from India to secret Swiss bank accounts. Nearly, ₹ 37,000 crore or about 1.5 to 2 per cent of the GDP surfaced as part of the Voluntary Disclosure Scheme in 1977 alone. The soft attitude towards black money by the government prompted some of the big industrialists and film industry people to buy big pieces of agricultural lands with a view to convert their black money into white by showing their income as agriculture income which was free from income tax from the big farms which were seldom cultivated. The same pieces of land became pieces of gold for them since they were used as industrial plots later on. Consequently, during the lengthy planning period a rich trading, political and bureaucratic class had emerged on the Indian scene which possessed resources next to government. They owned industries, business enterprises, properties, mansions and luxury cars. Their children got higher education in the premier institutes of the world and they had more than their share in government jobs. It is only they who participated with the foreigners in industrial undertakings, it is they who had command over education and health sectors and who owned the press and media. It were they who controlled the share market of the country and it were they who had hold over the gems, jewels and gold of the country. It were they without whose concurrence no fiscal, monetary, export, import and balance of payment policies could be decided and it was this rich and famous business and influential community which was destined to be the future rulers of the country. In the days of globalization and free economy, they are the largest employers and the income providers in the country and hence they are bound to have their command over the votes of their employees. Mahatma Gandhi's prophecy would prove correct one day when these brown Indian haves would rule the country in place of the white goras. If we look at the current scene we would find that these mighty businessmen are emerging on the scene and overshadowing even the regional leaders. Soon a time may come when they may become taller than the national leaders.

Likewise, the other community which gained most from the partition of the country and the Five Year Plans was Brahmins who had the privilege of being on the highest ladder of the society since time immemorial. They had been king makers, teachers and the advisors of the kings in the past because of their calibre and genius. Thus, when opportunity came to them they took its full advantage and recaptured their lost glory. They became IAS, IFS, IPS officers and PCSs in large number and captured the important positions as DMs, Commissioners, Secretaries and Chief Secretaries. They were ideally situated as they were highly educated and occupied the highest positions in the hierarchy of the society. Besides, they got the advantage of Pandit Jawaharlal Nehru and many of the eminent Brahmin freedom fighters. Consequently, most of the Prime Ministers, Chief Ministers, Ministers and important dignitaries came from them. It is because of their genius that whatever government comes in power they are there. They are practically kings and the king makers. Since they are in each and every field starting from the lowest to the highest levels, they are able to influence the policies of the country. They have become so powerful and so nicely entrenched in the system that others cannot ignore them in years to come. They are like the lotus flower which always remain above water, however, shallow or deep the water may be.

Similarly, the police departments, the defence establishments, the paramilitary forces, the jail departments and other security agencies have been dominated by the Rajputs and Thakurs because of their capabilities, valour and historical past. History is witness to the fact that most of the Rajas and Maharajas and rulers were Rajputs. They ruled the country and died for the country. Thus, they too got the advantage of their historical past and occupied most of the prominent positions in the country which needed valour, courage, sacrifice and dedication and commitment. Generally, many of the major and important posts pertaining to defence, paramilitary organizations, police and security agencies and jails are in their hands and they have their major say in many matters pertaining to safety and security of the country. Thus, the higher castes such as the Brahmins, Rajputs and the businessmen are in dominant positions and prosperous conditions due to their merits, hard work and golden opportunity provided to them by partition and the ensuing developments in the country.

In the same way, the Scheduled Castes and the Scheduled Tribes who were suppressed for centuries are found in abundance in government organizations both in the Centre and at the level of States. They too have become prosperous due to reservations provided to them in government enterprises and educational institutions. They have a large chunk of MLA's, MP's and senior government officials. Their lobby is very powerful and they dictate Indian politics and nobody can dare to go against them. Their participation in business, vocation, profession, industry, trade and commerce is also increasing day by day. Many of them have become efficient and competent. They are competing with their counterparts in the higher castes with success. The only sufferers in the country are perhaps the Muslims because of their lack of patronage and historical past and the farmers, artisans, labourers and supportless backward castes for most of these segments of the society were poor, illiterate and leaderless and they could not get the advantage of the opportunities provided by the planning and globalization due to their weak position, lack of education and paucity of state patronage. The Congress Government or for that matter any segment of the society cannot be held responsible for the miserable condition of some of the segments of Indian society as the policies of the Congress Government were cosmopolitan and they were based on merit where only the able and competent people could find their place. Government apparently showed no favour to the privileged sections. The Brahmins, business class and the Rajputs and Thakurs being highly educated took the advantage of their caliber and competence and naturally went ahead of others.

The country was lucky to have in it sincere and committed persons who had lived with Mahatma Gandhi and who were influenced by the personality of the Father of Nation. Such persons were competent, honest and committed. They used to think in terms of the nation and they used to promote such persons who were honest, efficient and devoted. During their days, the interference in administration and other government agencies was minimal and the system worked fairly well. Over a period of time, interference in government agencies especially the police and bureaucracy increased and the public sector undertakings began to show the signs of sickness because they were manned by the bureaucrats rather than the technocrats. They became the centres for providing jobs to the inefficient people recommended by the higher ups. Since these enterprises were not run on business principles, they became bankrupt due to over employment, inefficient people and poor products. Besides, since during planning period the controls were imposed upon the systems, they created a political class of quota holders, licensees, builders and others which created a horrible demonstration effect upon the people and the whole system got derailed over time. In addition to it, the extremely repressing tax rate compelled people to avoid taxes and the black money was created in the country. The surplus funds were transferred in Swiss banks and a large amount of money is still lying in these banks unnoticed. The parallel economy in the shape of black money gave birth to smuggling, lavish spending, drug trafficking and crimes. Thus, the system which was neatly erected on sound foundations collapsed. Moreover, when some of the adversaries of the Congress Party especially the rightists and the leftists who were craftly realized that it would be difficult for them to capture power at the centre due to the popularity of the Congress and Nehru family for a considerable period of time, they played a dirty politics. They joined the Congress in large numbers, with the result that they occupied important positions and carried out their communal and party agenda by appointing people from their cadre in village schools and government offices especially in the field of education, home, foreign relations and minority affairs. When the undesirable element entered the Congress Party, the Congress ideology was polluted and regional and parochial interests got stimulus as a consequence of which communal atmosphere was vitiated. Urdu was targeted and Muslims were not provided education, jobs and adequate safety and security that drifted the minorities from the Congress. Over and above this, the demolition of the Babri Masjid annoyed Muslims beyond redemption. When the Congress realized its follies, it was too late and the damage had already been done. During Nehru rule, the Congress Party and the government believed in inclusive development, good governance and accountability and welcomed constructive opposition which helped them to rule the country from Kashmir to Kanyakumari and Amritsar to Assam. With the passage of time, it is said that inbreeding, dynastic politics, flattery, group politics, nepotism and regionalism developed in the party which promoted mediocrity, diluted accountability and created complicit environment for corruption. The governing structure failed to set standards for good governance and faltered to take responsibility for missgovernance which drifted the party perhaps towards feudocracy, dictatorship, intolerance towards healthy dissent and constructive criticism. It is claimed by many that today a fawning culture of servitude has developed in the party where there are hardly a few Congressman with independent opinion, and the democratic traditions of the party are compromised by the allegedly nepotic internal structure and its alliance with regional clones merely to keep power with hook or crook. It is heartening to note that Rahul Gandhi is trying to reestablish the past glory of the Congress which was admired by the world as a party with purpose and ideology and which had Congressmen of vision and integrity. He is also positioning the Congressacross rural India as an empathetic party of inclusive development. Despite the fact that he has a sense of political entitlement based on dynasty but he also knows that family-centric parties often put self-interest above public interest, entitlement above accountability, nation above party and party above self. He is aiming at a progressive, dynamic and all-inclusive party with a genuine care for the rural poor and the marginalized sections of the society and he is willing even to sacrifice his government rather than aligning with bankrupt political forces. Rather than relying on family and clan privileges, he is struggling at grass-root level to emerge as a force to reckon with by proving his worth as a mass leader by mingling with people and knowing their problems at grass-root level. He wants to carve out a path for himself by proving his worth for he is sure that privileges political, economic or social have no place in modern India. He is setting a high bar for the party men by bringing competent, honest, dedicated, committed and professionals of integrity at the helm of affairs and stopping criminals, anti-social, sycophants and undeserving people from the political arena of the country. In all probability, he would create three cadres for the party such as the cadre of the seniors based on their past contributions, experience and loyalty, integrity and dedication towards party and the country, the cadre of intellectuals and professionals based on their professional competence, merit, integrity and love for the people of India and the sincerity towards the policies of the Congress Party. Lastly, he is supposed to prepare a cadre of dedicated, committed and sincere youth of the country which may provide efficient and competent persons for governance based on their selfless work at grass-root level, concern and care for the rural poor, love for pluralistic culture and visionary sense of direction. A sound three-tier cadre for the party would go a long way in supplying the type of future leaders the party needs provided the cadre is not corrupted over a period of time by undemocratic and unhealthy traditions. The condition of all other political parties is more or less the same. They too have been affected by the maladies of the Congress Party for most of them knowingly or unknowingly consider it as a leader or trend setter in the political circle. They too should create a sound three-tier cadre if they wish to survive for long as a viable force.

The Congress Party and the Congress Government as well as leaders of other political parties should know that they cannot take most of the Indian Muslims for granted. Several Muslims are more averse with Congress and a few regional parties to whom they voted blindly but got nothing save lip service, hollow promises and false hopes. It appears that the voters of Uttar Pradesh and Bihar have not forgotten these parties especially the Congress. They seldom prefer the Congress Party and those who have ditched them but support them where they have no alternative. The recent experience of Bihar elections is an eye opener for Lalu Prasad's RJD and the Congress Party. The party got merely 4 seats in 243 despite campaigning in six-phase elections by stalwarts like its President Sonia Gandhi and General Secretary Rahul Gandhi. It is said that Muslim voters not only voted actively to Janta Dal (United) under the leadership of Bihar Chief Minster Nitish Kumar helping the party in obtaining 115 seats but they also supported the BJP in many areas which secured 91 seats. They conveyed their displeasure to Lalu Prasad and Ram Vilas Paswan by withdrawing their substantial support consequently RJD-LP could secure merely 25 seats. Nitish Kumar was able to win the confidence of Muslims and other electorate by his secular perception and development-oriented image. People believed in what he said due to his contribution which he made in various spheres of Bihar. He helped Muslims to his utter most and tried to preserve his secular image up to the last phase despite excessive pressure from his alliance partners which paid him good dividend. The political parties of the country seldom know that the educational and religious centres of Muslims shape Muslims' course of action. The opinion is formed in the campuses of Aligarh Muslim University, Jamia Millia Islamia and various minority run educational institutions in the country as well as in the mosques and makatibs run by various important religious centres such as

Nadwa, Deoband, Bareilly and others. Whatever meaningful people feel in these centres, the message is conveyed throughout the country. Mostly, these centres are the benefactors of Muslims and whatever music the Muslims face or the constrain under which these centres work or the difficulties which Muslims in general and these centres in particular confront from the side of the parties and governments, is passed silently to the Muslim masses by words of mouth which in turn is reflected in their vote bank politics. The Congress Government is on the wrong side due to passive response to Sachar Committee Report, Reservation for Muslims, giving minority character to Aligarh Muslim University and Jamia Millia Islamia and police and paramilitary atrocities on innocent Muslim youths and its not so pro-minority image in several matters affecting the well-beings of Muslims. These matters are very often discussed within the four walls of the dwellings, in drawing rooms, on special occasions and in important private gatherings and the gist pass conveniently from one corner to other. Governments seldom consider these institutions and places as vital centres for opinion making because they are led to believe by some Muslim politicians that they are the leaders and the opinion makers when the facts are contrary to what they say.

The Excessive Reliance of Muslims upon Congress

The redeeming feature during the riots for the ruling Congress Government was that Muslims considered the Congress Government as their sole saviour and voted *en bloc* to ensure its victory for more than four decades. They despised the Communist Party as they considered it atheistic and against their religion. They feared Hindu extremist organizations due to their anti-Muslim and anti-Islamic postures and did not rely on the smaller regional parties because of their vulnerability. It is an admitted fact that Muslims initially did not like the Congress Party and looked to those with contempt who joined it but gradually and gradually they accepted the Congress Party as the only political party worth joining due to its secular approach. The presence of Maulana Abul Kalam Azad, Dr. Zakir Husain, Rafi Ahmed Kidwai, Fakhruddin Ali Ahmed and the host of eminent Congress leaders who refused to go over to Muslim League and remained firmly within the fold of Indian national mainstream encouraged many Muslims to join Congress. Many erstwhile Muslim Leaguers who could not migrate to Pakistan and who were disillusioned by the type of Pakistan that was created against their expectations also joined the Congress Party at the initiative of Maulana Azad. Muslims respected Pandit Nehru and other secular Congress leaders with the core of their hearts. They had full faith in Nehru family for this family was a secular and Muslim friendly family. Pandit Nehru and his colleagues had helped Muslims during post-partition days. Actually, it was because of them that they could come out of the rut. Moreover, Pandit Nehru was followed by Shrimati Indira Gandhi and Shri Rajiv Gandhi who were secular and humanists to the core and had soft corners for Muslims and hence Muslims felt no problem at top level during Congress days. However, the irony of fate was that the Congress leaders at grass-root level who mattered most were mostly communal and reactionary. Besides, the Congress Party had become regional and parochial due to several outsiders who had joined the party to bring its downfall and achieve their nefarious ends.

During the days of Pandit Nehru, Indira Gandhi and even Rajiv Gandhi, Muslims generally believed what the Congress said. They did not repose faith in the Communists and others. Many highly educated Muslims especially having conservative religious background but possessing liberal, secular and even un-Islamic outlook who were uncomfortable with Islamic principles and practices had joined the Communist Party. Muslims by and large did not like such ultra liberal and ultra secular Muslims due to their adverse comments on sensitive Muslim issues. It was indeed less cumbersome to govern Muslims those days since they created no problem for the ruling governments as they were passive onlookers with defeatist mentality and devoid of any ambition. They were not sure of their future and hence demanded no concessions, reservations, quotas and privileges save the right to live honourably without fear. Their share in the national wealth and resources was utilized by the ruling governments for the benefit of other sections of the society. Thanks to the fear and the nuisance caused by the extremist parties and the fanatic sections of the majority community that the task of the Congress Party became easy because it utilized the fear psychosis among Muslims to its advantage by frightening those who were already frightened. Muslims mostly kept quite and remained passive, fearful and frightened and supported knowingly those who were not their real friends. They could not launch their own party since it was doomed to failure. Despite having secular, enlightened and Muslim friendly leaders like Shrimati Sonia Gandhi and Dr. Manmohan Singh The Congress Party came in its true colours in the wake of the demolition of the Babri Masjid as well as after 9/11, 2001 when it supported anti-Islamic and anti-Muslim forces such as America under Bush, Britain under Blair and Israel and others simply because many rightist Congressmen were pressing for such a move. It voted against Iran, did not help Saddam who was India's best friend and ignored the interest of Palestinian people and others.

The only distinguished and the eminent person amongst Muslims whose contribution the Indian Muslims would never forget for years to come was Maulana Abul Kalam Azad. He was the staunch believer in United India. No Indian was hurt as much by the partition as Maulana Azad. He took the event as personal defeat. From 1947 to 1958 when he left this world he whole-heartedly worked for the reconstruction of India. He established Sahitya Akademi, the Sangeet Natak Akademi and the Lalit Kala Akademi and various scientific and cultural institution of world fame. He was most suited for the post of Foreign Minister of India due to his versatile personality, dynamism and vision. Despite being practically number two in status, when he accepted the Ministry of Education and Culture in 1951 after the first general election in the country, every one was surprised. Like Pandit Jawaharlal Nehru, he was not interested in trifling matters of the state but wanted to shape the future course of events for the secular, progressive and vibrant India based on empirical inquiry, visionary approach, scientific fervour and cultural and spiritual connotations. He was a wonderful orator, politician, statesman and reformer. His speech to Muslims when they were migrating in large numbers to Pakistan was praiseworthy. He reminded them of their duties and responsibilities towards their past heritage, ancestral affinities and assured them of their bright future. The impact of his heart-touching appeal was marvelous and Muslims adhered to his advice. He persuaded Dr. Zakir Husain who was close to Mahatma Gandhi to accept the Vice-Chancellorship of Aligarh Muslim University, Aligarh. Dr. Zakir Husain agreed to accept the responsibility after much persuasion and hesitation for Aligarh Muslim University was an eye sore to the majority community due to the past association of many of its alumni with Muslim League. The stewardship of such an institution was bound to tarnish the image of a staunch nationalist like Dr. Zakir Husain who was running Jamia Millia Islamia as an ante-dote to Aligarh University. Many people were in favour of changing the name of the University from Muslim University to Sir Syed University or simply to Aligarh University. However, once Dr. Zakir Husain joined Aligarh Muslim University as its Vice-Chancellor all criticism against the University subsided. The second thing which Maulana Abul Kalam Azad did was the promotion of Urdu as a language of instructions for it was the mother tongue of many Indians including Muslims and Hindus. There was much opposition to Urdu in those days for there were many who were in favour of Hindustani, a combination of Hindi and Urdu as the national language of the country rather than Hindi. However, since Hindi was accepted as the national language and Urdu was associated with Muslims, Urdu lost its grace and dignity forever.

The Fear of Backlash Frightened Congress to Help Muslims

Several Muslims claim that the Congress Party and the government talks of Muslims' benefit and even of reservation when it is on the weak turf. However, as soon as it comes in power with comfortable majority it becomes absolutely secular and takes the help of Indian Constitution in matters of providing special privileges to Muslims. Before 2009, Muslims were expecting reservation in the wake of Congress Government coming in power at the Centre on the pattern of Kerala, Karnataka and AP but one fine morning the Minority affairs Minister boldly declared that reservation to Muslims on the basis of religion was not possible. The assertion of Hon'ble Minister was perhaps against Congress manifesto as promulgated during the period of elections. The educationally, socially and economically backward Muslims too can be provided reservation but it seems that the Congress Government appears to be shaky to fix a certain percentage of reservation in the category of reservation for backward castes due to the fear of backlash of backward castes. Likewise, it appears hesitant to increase the quota of the backward castes beyond 27% due to the backlash of the higher castes. As things exist today, it appears that BJP Party is the only party which does not care for any backlash. If it wants it can boldly give reservation to Muslims without bothering for any adverse effect upon its vote bank politics. When Dr. Murli Manohar Joshi was HRD Minister he proposed 50% reservation for Muslims in Jamia Millia Islamia and Hamdard University which the Congress Government could not do despite remaining in power for many years. He was willing to give 50% reservation to Muslims in Aligarh but the Aligarh people did not agree with his proposal. In the same way, when the BJP Party was in power and Atal Bihari Vajpayee was the Prime Minister the people were confident that the Kashmir problem would be solved but it is alleged that the Pakistan military spoiled the whole show.

Muslims seldom believe in the promises and assurances of the Congress because they find wide difference in its saying and doing. The Congress Government surveyed and identified 90 Muslim concentration districts (MCD) in 2007 and an ambitious multi-sectoral development plan (MSDP) was launched to provide better housing, sanitation, education, healthcare, credit facilities, employment opportunities to minority community members. MSDP was designed as the chief vehicle to remove the development deficit among Muslims. Out of the total allocation of ₹ 1,756 crore to the

Ministry of Minority Affairs in 2009-10, the MSDP alone drew ₹ 889.5 crore that is over 56% of the Ministry's funds. However, the picture of implementation of the programme is highly dismal. Out of 90 Muslim concentrated districts, 16 have yet to formulate a plan under MSDP. As of September 2009, project activities worth ₹ 1,562 crore had been sanctioned for the remaining 74 districts but only ₹ 77 crore was utilized. For the 11th Plan (2007-12), a total of ₹ 2,750 has been set aside for the MSDP but after half the period has already gone by the expenditure amounts to just 2.8% of the total. Likewise, as per report of the ministry, covering 44 of the 90 MCDS, expenditure still stood at a shocking 17% of the total funds available with the districts. In most states, funds for 2009-10 were being released in December 2009. For current year just 3,201 houses had been built out of a target of 205, 260 for Muslim families under Indira Awas Yojana, only 1,523 hand pumps had been installed out of the targeted 14,020, only five health centres had been built out of a target of 1,715 and only 20 anganwadi centres had been built out of 18,970. The recent statistics show that only 5% of the total grant allocated for Muslims has been spent. The Central Government has made provision for the Ministry of Minority Affairs in 2009-10 budget to the tune of 2600 crores for the development of minority districts. It has raised the amount by 50% compared to the last budget but its fate too would be terrible for the money would not be spent. The main reasons cited include the lack of trained and adequate staff, the paucity of infrastructure and deficiency of planning at the district and state levels. Muslims complain that wherever the money has been spent, the complaints are being received that it has not been spent mostly on Muslims. Since according to the conditions of the project the money was to be spent in Muslim Concentration Districts, it has been spent in these districts on the constructions of roads and infrastructures which benefitted Muslims as well as others. The real tragedy with Muslims is that it is difficult to benefit Muslims at implementation stage because of narrow parochial interests. There is an adverse perception about Muslims at the lower levels and hence the money sanctioned for the benefit of Muslims is either not spent or spent on collateral heads which dent the sharpness of every scheme. Besides, since Muslims are practically absent in government offices consequently the matter does not come out to the public. The government too has not taken any action against those officers who sabotaged the amount allocated for the minorities nor adopted any strategy to see to it that the money allocated for the poor Muslims reaches to them.

The Equal Opportunity Commission and Wakf Act

The minority affairs ministry is trying to bring the Equal Opportunity Commission in the Parliament to pacify Muslims. First of all, the Equal Opportunity Commission is not meant only for Muslims. It is designed for the benefit of each and every citizen of India for it would provide equal opportunities before law to every citizen irrespective to his caste, colour, religion, sex or place of birth. Besides, it is pertinent to know that without creating abilities through affirmative action, the commission would remain ineffective for the existence of equality of opportunity depends not merely on the absence of disabilities but also on the presence of abilities. The Equal Opportunity Commission would apply only in those cases where there would be discrimination between two people similarly situated in all respects. If a high school pass Muslim student is not appointed in comparison to a Ph.D degree holder Hindu, he cannot complain under the EOC for they are not similarly situated in all respects. Muslims are educationally backward and they are drifting from worse to worst. In such a situation, the Equal Opportunity Commission would prove merely a paper tiger. The Ministry is also trying to satisfy the Muslims by bringing amendment to Wakf Act which too would prove counter productive. First of all the Wakf property is generally meant for a specific purpose for which the Wakf is constituted as such it cannot be used for other purposes. Suppose if someone has donated his property for the upkeep of the mosque, it cannot be used for giving scholarships to needy students. Likewise, the graveyards cannot be used for erecting malls and cinema halls. Secondly, these Wakfs have served a very useful purpose in the shape of keeping Islam alive among Muslims especially in those days when no help was provided by the state to Muslim religious institutions. Many madrasas, maktabs, makbaras, imambaras, khanqahs and mosques are being supported and financed by Wakf properties. If the wakf money is diverted to the financing of modern education in the shape of skill formation and scholarships, etc. it would be at the cost of religious education. Lastly, it would send the wrong signal to Muslims that the government is indirectly throttling the madrasas and religious institutions by transferring the money from wakfs to other uses. The government can certainly use those resources of the wakfs which have been earmarked for the growth and development of modern education and skill formation but not those which have been devoted for religious fervours.

The Backward Castes' Tactics

Another strategy to run the country is to combine backward castes and the minorities for these two castes are also natural allies. The beauty of the minorities is that they can unite with the higher castes considering them socially high and they can also combine with the backward castes treating them economically backward. Besides, the peculiarity with the backward caste is that it can seldom unite with Scheduled Caste and Scheduled Tribes nor it finds itself comfortable with the higher castes for its economic interests clash with both of them. The Scheduled Castes and the Scheduled Tribes cannot combine with the Backward Castes for they always remain at log head at the village level. Since most of the Scheduled Castes and the Scheduled Tribes are landless labourers and socially very low, they are being exploited and despised by the backward castes. The people of the backward castes are not willing to give them equal status in the society hence they will remain at a distance for a considerable period of time. Likewise, there is clash of interest between the higher castes and the backward castes. The backward castes are mostly farmers and rural people and the higher castes are the urbanites and traders and professionals, bureaucrats, technocrats and traders. The agriculturists produce their product and sell it to the urbanites that add values in their products and sell the same back to them at higher prices and thus reap huge profits. The terms of trade always remain in favour of the higher castes. In addition to this, most of the government jobs and the industry and trade, media and health and educational centres are in their hands thus, the backward castes feel a sense of loss and alienation at the hands of the higher castes. However, since the children of the backward castes are getting higher education the national scenario is changing fast. The backward caste fellows too are entering practically in every field due to their political patronage, improvement in their economic conditions and better awareness. It is hoped that they too would compete with higher castes in the long run and share power in proportion to their numerical strength. Their competition would be mostly with the higher castes for they cannot usurp the share of the Scheduled Castes and the Scheduled Tribes due to reservation provided to them by the Constitution. Similarly, they would have no grudge against the minorities for they too have paltry share in government jobs, business enterprises and other ventures of the country. Their direct competition, in the opinion of many, would be with the higher castes for most of the privileges and advantages which could accrue to backward castes in business, profession, vocation, bureaucracy, judiciary, media and top defence and security positions according to their numerical strength have gone to the higher castes due to their better competitive position and historical past. As a matter of fact whatever the backward caste would get it would be mostly at the cost of the higher caste which is likely to cause heart burning between the two important segments of the country. We observe this trend operating in several sectors especially after globalization of Indian economy. Many educated and financially well-off sections from among the Jats and from other backward castes have entered in education and health sector and opened reputed educational and health centres in Aligarh, Meerut, Ghaziabad, Rajasthan, Haryana and various other parts of the country. They have started engineering, management and medical colleges, nursing homes, agency business and are moving towards opening universities and manufacturing and trading centres. Their share in competitive examinations, print media, universities and judiciary and armed forces and security forces is also increasing. The children of the backward castes have better motivation before them due to their meagre economic conditions for they know that they can get a lot in case they succeed in life. Thus, they work hard compared to the children of the higher castes most of whom lead a comfortable and luxurious life. Besides, the backward caste fellows have their maximum strength in the legislatures hence they are exerting pressure in all those spheres where they are underrepresented. The economic and power clash between both these segments many times comes out in the open in the form of demonstrations, agitations and even mass uprising. Since bureaucracy, executive, judiciary, defence and media are in the hands of mostly the upper castes, alternative means are being designed by the saner element to avoid direct conflict but this situation would not last for long. As the stuff of the backward castes would improve, other things remaining the same, the upper castes would mostly be confined to the strength of their population. Thus, the country is poised for a keen competition between the higher castes and the backward castes. Many people from the backward castes claim that the Governments at the Centre and the States are mostly controlled by the urbanites and they do not allow the farmers, who are mostly backwards, to prosper. These governments follow policies which prove detrimental to the backward castes. The government neither increases the prices of agricultural products commensurate to the needs of the times due to the fear of their impact upon the urban poor, nor raises the productivity of agricultural products by introducing innovation in agricultural sector and bringing reforms in agro-sector nor provides cheap inputs and easy credit and better storing facilities with the result that the backward castes are hit hard. Much progress has been made practically in all the sectors but the agriculture sector is in miserable condition. The poverty rate is highest in the villages and so also the illiteracy too is high among backward sections. They lament that their economic condition is so bad that they cannot plan their future, cannot send their children to schools and cannot ponder over their miserable condition and thus fail to compete with the higher castes. This type of mindset for the backward castes is detrimental for the progress of the country. Efforts should be made to satisfy the genuine demands of the backward castes before it that they become restive and hopeless.

The entry of the backward castes in State Assemblies and Parliament in large number has changed the political texture of the country. Since more than sixty per cent Members of Legislative Assemblies and the Members of Parliament come from rural areas, the National Capital and the State Capitals have been dominated by the rural people both from backward castes and the Scheduled Castes and the Scheduled Tribes. Besides, since many of them are either less educated or uneducated, their behaviour pattern is quite different from that of the residents of the established cities and classes who are culturally most advanced. When some of these people occupy positions of power, they seldom care for the niceties of the rules and regulations but insist on doing things according to their sweet will. This has led to unnecessary interference in police, bureaucracy, judiciary and all administrative matters. Besides, some of the criminals from various castes have entered in politics and they have taken the shape of mafia. This mafia is operating in the fields of drug trafficking, building industry, land grabbing, kidnapping, extortions and what not. The money power and the muscle power and tongue and lung power have shook hands and it has become difficult for any sensible fellows to contest elections. Corruption, lawlessness and favouratism, nepotism and scams are very common. Even a few political parties are selling seats of Assemblies and Parliament at exorbitant prices. Money is being taken on transfers and national resources are being drained away by the vested interests on foreign tours, luxury products, on raising the symbols of dignity and on unnecessary entertainment items.

Women's Reservation Bill—A Bone of Contention Between Higher Castes and Backward Castes

The women's bill providing 33 per cent reservation to women was passed by the Rajya Sabha on March 9, 2010. It has become a bone of contention between the backward castes, Scheduled Castes, minorities and the higher castes. The bill was supported by the Congress, BJP, Communists and other like-minded parties such as DMK, JD(U) and NCP that are supposed to represent mostly the higher castes. As against this, the bill was opposed by the SP, RJD, LJP, TC and BSP who are believed to be the champions of the backwards, minorities and the marginalized sections of the society. The pro-Mandal parties believe that the higher castes are in a dominant position in the judiciary, bureaucracy, security and paramilitary forces and media as well as health, education and financial sectors but they are in minority in the legislature. Thus, to enhance their legislative powers in the Parliament and State Assemblies, they have brought this bill to reduce the influence of the backward castes, the Scheduled Castes and the minorities. The opponents of the bill are demanding reservation for the backward castes, Scheduled Castes and minority women within the 33% quota but it is not being agreed by the parties supporting the bill. It is claimed by the opponents of the bill that their demand is genuine because the reservation to the backward segments of the women is the need of the hour. Besides, it is also alleged by these segments that once the bill is passed in its present form invariably the women of higher castes would win the elections due to their educational background, economic backing and political patronage. The past experience also reveals that wherever the political parties gave tickets to their women candidates, generally the women from the higher castes won the elections. Besides, they allege that the manner in which the Bill was introduced in the Parliament by taking into confidence the BJP and the Communists who were sitting in opposition and ignoring SP, RJD, TC, BSP, Ittehadul Muslemeen and others who were supporting the government speaks volumes about the intentions of those who are supporting the bill. Many Muslim MPs and some of the MPs from other parties as well as Mulayam Singh, Lalu Prasad, Sharad Yadav, Ajit Singh, Satish Mishra and Mamata Banerjee pleaded for the quota for backward caste Muslim women within the 33 per cent limit, but it was quite strange that the idea found only a few takers. Many Indian Muslims were shocked and dumbfounded to see the behaviour pattern of the highest legislative body of the country after sixty years of independence. They were astonished that those who used to speak in favour of Muslim women in the wake of any violation of human rights were conspicuous by absence. They were also shocked to see that when the Members of Parliaments—men and women, young and old from across the country met to ponder over the fate of Indian women they did not deem it necessary to think of the interest of Muslim women as if they were non-entity though they knew that they were in bad shape. Every one knew that like women, the share of Muslim women and Muslim men in Parliament and State Assemblies was not commensurate to their population and it had been declining year after year but nobody paid any heed to it. More so, it was after knowing the facts that the Sachar Committee appointed by the Congress Government had pointed out that the condition of Muslims was worse than that of the Scheduled Castes and the Ranganath Misra Commission deputed by the government too had recommended reservation for Muslim Backward Castes and Sonia Gandhi and Dr. Manmohan Singh had promised to adopt affirmative action for the amelioration of Indian Muslims and the Communists and the Congress Government had recommended reservation for the backward Muslims within the 27 per cent quota for backward castes within the states ruled by them. Actually, Mulayam Singh, Lalu Prasad, Sharad Yadav, Ajit Singh, Mayawati and Mamata Banerjee have shown to the Muslims that they are their true friends. Many Muslims believe that Communists who are mostly from higher castes at the top level and who had subjugated Muslims for about 15 years especially in West Bengal are not their real well wisher. Likewise, several of them contend that despite the fact that Congress Government is manned by Sonia Gandhi, Manmohan Singh and Rahul Gandhi who are supposed to be the true benefactors of Muslims, the majority of the Congressmen seem to possess the reactionary mentality. Over and above this, most of the media controlled by the vested interests too blew whistles in support of the bill with utter disregard to the interests of minorities. Many editorials of the prominent dailies considered the bill as a 'milestone moment' and maintained that history was made on March 9, 2010 with the passage of the women's reservation bill in the Rajya Sabha. They considered the policy of reservation to the Scheduled Castes and Scheduled Tribes and other backward classes as the landmark provision or a path-breaking social reform adopted by independent India over the decades since it had changed the complexion of the body politic and power equations in a fundamental manner, paying the path for the establishment of a more egalitarian society. They further held that the transformative potential of reserving seats for women would not only empower women in political, social and economic fields but would also enhance the prospects of women and the growth of the society as a whole. However, when it comes to reservation for Muslim women who have been historically denied social, economic and political opportunities and they are facing discrimination of one sort or the other both in the private and public spheres, they call the move as bogus and against the Constitution as well as against the larger interest of the country.

In the opinion of most of the backward castes and minorities and the dalit sections of the society, this new found development indicates at the polarization of like-minded parties consisting mainly of higher castes like the Congress, BJP, Communists and others on one side and the backward castes, minorities, Scheduled Castes and other marginalized sections of the society on the other. Whatever the outcome of the bill, one thing is certain that most of the Indian Muslims are by and large convinced that save a few political parties and enlightened leaders and individuals no political party would support the cause of their reservation in the Parliament and State Assemblies because the country's political climate is not conducive to them. They have once again witnessed more or less the same situation which prevailed when India's Constitution was being framed in the Constituent Assembly and Muslims were demanding reservation for them but their demand was not adhered to. The message for them is very loud and clear and they have been shown the door. In future, they have to stand on their own feet. It is a fact that many liberals of the country agree that on the whole reservations have done significantly more good than harm and over the years the Scheduled Castes and Scheduled Tribes have substantially benefitted as a result of reservation. The study by Devesh Kapur, CB Prasad, Lant Pritchett and D. Sham Babu entitled, "Rethinking in Equality: Dalits in UP in the Market Reform Era" covering all dalit households in two blocks in UP, one in the relatively prosperous west (Khurja) and one in the backward east (Bilaragang) between 1990 and 2008 reveal interesting results. The dalit share with pucca houses increased from 18.1% to 64.4% in the east and from 38.4% to 94.6% in the west. The ownership of TVs rose from virtually zero to 22.2% and 45% respectively. Likewise, the ownership of cell phones too increased from almost nothing to 36.3% and 32.5% respectively. The proportion eating roti-chutney for lunch has fallen from 82% to just 2% and 9% in two zones. The kids eating previous night's leftovers came down from 96.9% to 16.2% in the east. The proportion eating broken rice fell from 54% to 2.6% in the east and from 22.7% to 1.1% in the west. Likewise, the dalits consuming dal rose from 31% to 90% in the east. 61% dalits in the east and 38% in the west stated that their food and clothing situation was improved. Only 2% said that it was stagnant or worse. The proportion of dalit population migrating from one region to other increased from 14% to 50.5% in east and from 6.15 to 28.6% in the west. The proportion running their own business rose from 4.25 to 11% in the east and from 6% to 36.7% in the west. The proportion of agricultural labourers came down from 76% to 45.6% in the east and from 46.1% to 20.5% in the west. The ownership of bicycle was up from 46.6% to 84.1% in the east and 37.7% to 83.7% in the west. Similarly, the ownership of motorcycles or two-wheelers rose from practically zero to 7.6% and 12.3% respectively. The economic condition of the dalits has shown a remarkable recovery. The proportion that mortgaged jewellery to upper castes dropped from 75.8% to 29.3% in the east and from 64.6% to 21.2% in the west. These two decades in which the dalits have improved a lot can be marked for the meteoric rise of the Bahujan Samaj Party under the stewardship of Mayawati. Not only the reservation has caused their betterment, the entire society as a whole too has gained immensely. However, this affirmative action of reservation which could help Muslims to overcome their backwardness is not found suitable by those who are at the helm of the governing structure in view of the fact that they believe that it impinges on the principle of free and fair competition that all citizens ought by right to lay claim to in a truly democratic society. Time has thus shown that as a mass or as a religious group with distinct Islamic identity there is little space left for them in the governing structure through the door of reservation. If they want any space in the governing structure or legislation as Muslims they shall have to compete with other citizens of the country. Muslims are also critical of the Communal Violence Bill. Their aversion with Congress Government is increasing day by day. All India Muslim Personal Law Board has condemned the Prevention and Rehabilitation of Victims Bill, 2009 and has called it draconian as it would in effect curb the civil rights of the minorities. ALMPLB has asked the government to scrap the bill with immediate effect. The apex body has also berated the harassment and witch-hunting of Muslim youths in the name of counter-terrorist measures. The members of the Board were of the opinion that number of fake cases implicating Muslim youths were growing. There were reported cases where young men from minority community were arrested, tortured and later released by the courts as the charges could not be substantiated. They have asked the government to stop such harassments. The positive aspect of the Indian democracy is that brilliant, liberal, moderate and meritorious individuals from amongst Muslims would always find enough space in political, social, cultural, religious and other segments of the vibrant India at par with the individuals of the majority community but the majority of the marginalized sections would have to face the music.

Mulayam Singh, Lalu Prasad, Mamata Banerjee and Mayawati are likely to receive a temporary boost from the side of Muslims for giving lip service to Muslims community but it is not sure that it would be reflected in their vote share in the coming Assembly and Parliament elections. Muslims have seen many time this type of drama and they are convinced that these parties would hardly take any positive step in support of Muslims such as withdrawing their support from the Congress in view of their personal interests. It appears that these parties are not very serious about quota within quota for Muslim women. Many Muslims believe that they are basically afraid of the idea of rotational method of reservation that would make two-thirds of the Lok Sabha or about 360 members one-term MPs. They would perhaps agree to a reduced quantum of reservation limiting reservation for women to the extent of 20% or 25% without quota within quota or to dual constituency method or to the increased strength of Lok Sabha.

It is a fact that Muslims have become cautious and conscious. They are by and large not happy with the BJP and the Communists as well as many regional parties the manner in which they supported the Women's Reservation Bill. The Congress Government too has paid a lip service. It has not given any assurance to Muslims but merely said that it would look into the problems of Muslims but side by side it has also expressed its resentment by communicating to the parties supporting Muslims' cause that if they are so sincere to Muslims they should nominate Muslim women in their parties. Actually, the empowerment must be the right of all women not just some women. The argument that political parties can always select Muslim women rather than do so under legal compulsion does not hold only for Muslim women. It applies to all women. During the last six decades, no one prevented the Congress, BJP, Communists and others from nominating half their list with women candidates but they have not done so. They knew that without providing legal quota for women, the political empowerment of women was not possible. It is irony of fate that what they consider better for other women, find inappropriate for Muslim women who are least empowered politically, socially and culturally. Those Muslims who know the Congress Party more than the lines of their palm know that the Congress would hardly support the cause of reservation for Muslim women so easily. They know that it did not support the Muslim cause in the Constituent Assembly and it did not give them reservation during the last sixty years. The Congress also knows heart to heart that Muslims are averse to the policies of the Congress Party. The Congress Party cannot take them for granted now as it did in the past. Thus, to cut them to their size and reduce the influence of the backward castes and Scheduled Castes, the Congress Government has perhaps brought this bill with the support of BJP and Communists in the hope that the women in the country would vote Congress across party line. The planners in the Congress Government and Party are perhaps not aware that Indian society is dominated by males. The females in the shape of mothers, sisters, daughters and wives cannot dare to go against the wishes of their male members. The women can defy the age old traditions, customs, ethos and practices only in the ultra modern societies or in broken families or in the individualistic nuclear societies or in those societies which are primarily governed by Western patterns and styles of living. The likelihood of such societies emerging on the Indian scenes in near future is highly remote. The experience of Panchayati Raj or wherever the reservation has been provided to the females is that the females act according to the wishes of their male members. Besides, the rotational system and other complications resulting in the loss of seats to the sitting members and the imminent possibility of women members dominating the Parliament and State Assemblies would force the male members to think twice before voting in favour of the bill.

There is complete polarization concerning the bill in the country. The media is vehemently supporting reservation without quota within quota and practically all intellectuals and the meaningful people from the majority community seem to have given their implied consent by keeping quite. As against this, all Muslim men, women, young, old, intellectuals, thinkers, political workers and religious heads believe that the present bill without any provision for Muslim women is anti-minorities and anti-Muslim. It would not only reduce the number of Muslims in Parliament and State Assemblies but would also kill Muslim leadership and make them second class citizens. Surely and certainly, the women's reservation bill would work as a watershed in the lives of Muslims across the country. It would jolt them and compel them to ponder over their future. As things stand today, it appears that the question of reservation to Muslims including the reservation to Muslim women would not subside but it would come on the centre-stage. Muslim youths would fight peacefully and democratically to acquire their Constitutional rights in a democratic country like India. The young and dynamic youth leader Asaduddin Owaisi, Member of Parliament has got the ball rolling by calling a mammoth meeting in support of reservation in Hyderabad. It is hoped that similar types of demands would also emanate from rest of the country.

The Communal Card

Another method or strategy to rule over the country is through 'Divide and Rule Policy' which the English people followed during the pre-partition period. The British model to divide majority and the minorities can be followed to rule the country by minimizing the importance of minorities in the national mainstream. The idea of a strong Hindu state based on Hindu religion can unite the Hindus on a common platform. Similarly, different segments of the society having contradictory interests can be pitched against one another to seek their votes. Likewise, the role of minorities can be minimized to a large extent by creating a strong feeling among the majority community against the minorities with a view to garner majority votes. It is the only situation where minorities become defunct. BJP was quick to perceive this situation. With the intention best known to the party, it raised a few emotional issues such as the construction of Ram Mandir at Ayodhya, Common Civil Code, abrogation of Article 370 of Indian Constitution in Jammu and Kashmir, appeasement of Muslims, madrasa education, cow-slaughter which were dearest to its electorate. Without doubting the intentions of its functionaries, it can be said that these issues certainly divided the majority community and the minority community into two watertight compartments and benefited the BJP. These issues benefited the higher castes too because by involving the backward castes and Scheduled Castes in religious matters the higher castes were able to dent the inherent power struggle between higher castes and the Backward Castes and Scheduled Castes and the backward castes. These emotional issues united most of the segments of Hindus on a common plane on the issue of construction of Ram Mandir and finally led to the demolition of Babri Mosque and the installation of the BJP Government at the Centre with the help of the like-minded parties. When the BJP Government came in power at the Centre, it openly did nothing against the interests of the Muslims but allegedly tactfully saffronized the whole atmosphere. Many Muslims, Communists and the Congressmen claim that ideological changes were introduced in syllabi, eminent people with specific ideology were appointed on important positions and the Hindutva network was cautiously and craftily spread throughout the country without offending anybody. Muslims were conspicuous by absence in all the important segments of the government especially at the top level such as Ministers, Governors, Chairmen and Vice-chancellors, etc. Demoralization of the Muslims reached to the highest level in the wake of Gujarat riot and Muslims felt helpless and frustrated. They could not approach the BJP Government for they knew that they had not supported the BJP Party and the party had come into power on the basis of its hard-core Hindu votes. Besides, those whom they supported considering them as secular also went within the fold of the BJP due to the charm of becoming Ministers and important dignitaries. Muslims by and large believe that within five to six years Muslims became a rarity in the cabinets at the state levels and the centre. What the Congress Government did in fifty years, the BJP Government apparently demolished within a short period of five years. The communal virus which was perhaps limited to the lower and lower middle level spread probably at all levels and Muslims drifted to their ghettos. One thing, however, remained peculiar and that was the absence of communal riots in the country. The frequency of communal riots certainly decreased but the opponents of the BJP did not give its credit to BJP but blamed the ruling government by saying that those who were committing such riots were in power and hence they were desisting from riots because it was not in their interests. It is a fact that the period of Atal Bihari Vajpai was commendable in many respects. He started the process of dialogue with Pakistan despite provocations from Pakistan and kept the controversial topics under cold storage. The image of the BJP Party too was enhanced during his days. Save Godhra riots Muslims too had no complaint against him as he was presumed to be the enlightened face of the BJP. However, the communal massacre of Muslims during Modi régime tarnished the image of the BJP in India and abroad. It appeared that these post-Godhra riots in which the role of state machinery was supposed to be questionable were perhaps pre-planned and they were perhaps initiated to terrorize Muslims. We would not like to delve upon Gujarat for it is full of horror and agony and possesses enough potential to revive emotions. However, its impact upon Muslims and rest of the enlightened and right-thinking Hindus was terrible. Each and everyone condemned these riots save a select few. These riots awakened Muslims from their dogmatic slumber and they could read the hidden agenda of the rabid communal parties and forces.

It is quite strange that Muslims are at log head with the BJP when the fact is that they are the natural allies. Both believe in morality, value system and spiritualism, both abhor nudity, obscenity and proximity, both value culture, finer elements of life and rich heritage, both are against the cultural invasion, horrible lifestyle of the West and the Western types of human rights, both provide highest dignity to women as mothers, wives, daughters, sisters and colleagues, both believe that the world is passing in worst times and soon a time would come when the truth, justice and piety would prevail and the sinners, criminals and the wicked would be degraded, abolished and ruined. With these commonalties between them, there appears to be no dichotomy between the two important segments of the society. Many Muslims believe that the BJP in its new avtar and new ideology based on economic development, nationalism, brotherhood, communal harmony and peaceful co-existence and enlightened international policy would emerge as a strong political party which would encourage Muslims to join this party in large numbers. There is a much scope for a right of centre party in the country. There is 'aam aadmi' rhetoric in the country, the Indian business is frustrated, the foreign policy is in jeopardy, the urban middle class is looking for new avenues, the urban artisans and the rural poor are desperate and the culture of the country is in danger. It is an opportune time for BJP to show its dynamism and magnanimity. It should not look towards its short-term interests but move on the broader path for the betterment of Indians and the humanity.

The Communist Model

The country can also be ruled by propagating Communist and Socialist ideology by forming a Communist regime where people are not discriminated on the basis of religion, castes and colour. Communist Party is successfully ruling in many states of India but it has failed to seek the permanent support of Muslims due to its atheistic and anti-religious leanings. Muslims find it hard to work with those who abhor religions and who despise cultural ethos and the God-given value system. On the world level also Muslims are nearer to the religion-oriented countries than those who abhor religion. The same is true to Indian masses. They too are basically religious minded and believe in value system. They can accept Communism as a last resort or as a tool to solve their miseries and agonies but they would never feel comfortable and would overthrow it at the slightest opportunity. The irritating tactics, taunts, antipathy and anti-Muslim and anti-Islam policies of communists, especially of those opportunist Muslims who are occupying prominent positions in communist regimes and who are prospering on the hate campaign against Muslims and Islam would always keep Muslims away from communists. Thus, in order to be all-pervasive and cosmopolitan, the Communist parties should read the writings on the walls. They have to see that the old type of Communism is no more. The controlled and socialist economic regimes are matters of the past in the age of globalization. In the same way, there is revivalism of belief system everywhere. These parties should also take lesson from other Communist countries which are opening up and embracing belief system with grace and dignity.

If we look towards Indian profile, we find that these Communist parties in their present forms are not acceptable to many segments of the society. We know that farmers who constitute the largest segment of India are too far from the hold of the Communist for they live near nature and depend upon nature and hence they cannot accept any system which keeps them away from their sustainer. Likewise, the big businessmen, industrialists, traders and affluent artisans do not come nearer the Socialistic system simply because they are religious minded people and they despise communists for their ant-capitalist approach. Only the urban labourers who are mainly linked with industries, public enterprises and big business concerns and those peasants and artisans who find it difficult to meet two ends come within the fold of Communism. On their own, these segments are not powerful enough to establish their own government at the level of the centre. They can form their rules at the level of a few states due to the heterogeneity of political class. However, if the Communists want to rule over whole of India for a longer period of time they shall have to show due regard to the religions, value systems and rich cultural heritages of Indian masses without which they would remain merely a regional force.

The Kisan Model

The farmers too can form their government because they are spread throughout the length and breadth of the country and they are so overburdened by poverty and loans that they can think of forming an all India party. The commonality of interest found among the farmers based on a common profession unites all the farmers on a single platform. Besides, they know that there is none to look after them. All the political parties are exploiting the farmers due to their weak bargaining and political position. Many farmers are committing suicide but hardly the conscience of any party has been shaken compelling it to do something positive for them. The main difficulty with the farmers is that it is difficult for any person to emerge as an all India figure in a situation where the farmers are not only spread widely but they are economically poor and there are cultural, social and religious differences among them. Thus, we see that save a leader here and there no leader from the farming community could emerge who could combine them into a whole and rule the country. Chaudhary Charan Singh, Chaudhary Devilal, Balram Jakhar and Ram Niwas Mirdha emerged as the leaders of the farmers but their influences remained up to their states only.

Sundry Models

In the same way the artisans, labourers and sundry farmers despite commanding a majority cannot form their own governments. The possibility of a national government is there if the public gives a fractured verdict and where no party is in a dominant position to form government. It may happen any day. We are observing a perverted form of the national government in the shape of modern coalition governments which are prospering at the centre as well as states. However, the possibility of a dictator coming in power is very remote for we have seen the emergency and its consequences. Similarly, the chances of military rules are very remote for the civilian authorities have kept such checks and balances that no military general can think of coming into power merely by the help of army. The composition of Indian army is such that all the three wings of army, air force and navy cannot combine together and no military general remains for a longer period of time at the helm of affair. Besides, the socio-cultural system of the country is such that without the help of civil authority the army cannot move an inch. Over and above this, the Indian masses cannot tolerate military dictatorship due to their fervour for freedom and democracy. The chances of honest and efficient people coming in power due to the massive support of the people of India seems next to impossible for unity among like-minded people on such a large scale is very difficult. The possibility of one-party dictatorship system was there when the Congress Government won the freedom. The founding father could rule the country with one party dictatorship as Lenin did in Soviet Union but under present conditions its possibility is absolutely zero. The country can certainly think of two party systems: the left tilting centrist party like Congress and right inclined centrist party like the reformed BJP or the higher caste parties such as the Congress, Communists and the BJP forming the right inclined centrist mode and the backward parties, minorities and the dalits constituting the left-oriented centrist model or all women party after the passage of women reservation bill. The polarizing forces are at work and it is hoped that the country would soon get two-party system based on secularism, pluralistic culture, communal harmony and peace and progress.

The Aristocratic Model

If we look towards the general profile of the country we observe that instead of two parties two segments are emerging in the country. The people of India should cautiously watch certain trends which are taking place at national and state levels which tend to create two classes, the class of the elitists and the class of the ordinary citizens. Due to the process of privatization and globalization, many schools of world fame are being set up in India with the franchise of the foreigners. Likewise, many medical academies, engineering colleges and the institutions of business management and computer science are being set up in the country by billionaires in collaboration of the foreign universities. These institutions would be of world class and produce excellent people. Since they would provide world class teaching and research and other facilities and comforts to the students, the cost structure would be very high. Only a fraction from the high society would be able to enter into such institutes and the poor students from backward sections, SCs/STs and minorities would be left aside due to their weak economic position. These institutes would be able to produce enough civil servants, engineers, doctors, business magnates and IT experts to serve the needs of the government and multinational and blue chip companies. Consequently, the poor and backward sections of the society would be debarred from entering into government and business sectors because they would fail to compete with the world class products produced by premier institutions. We observe that the process has already started in the country. A select band of people belonging to multinational companies, export sector, IT segment, education and health sectors, media and government machinery and rich farmers is emerging on the scene with its costly cars, beautiful mansions, lavish lifestyles and influence in government which is bound to influence the social, cultural and political climate of the country. As against this, the masses are suffering under the heavy pressure of food inflation and poverty. They have no time to think in terms of forming government, cultural values and social and moral norms. If these tendencies continue, there is every likelihood that the aristocrats, the elites and influential government servants, businessmen and meaningful people from various elite segment of the society would dominate the majority of the poor with the help of the emerging middle class as happened in many advanced countries. They would form their government supported by those who would depend upon them. However, if people like Azim Premji, Ratan Tata, N.R. Narayana Murthy, Anil Agarwal and Anand Mahindra become philanthropists and serve the cause of the poor and the downtrodden, there is no fear to the country from the side of such rich businessmen. Recently, Azim Premji pledged $ 2 bn to fund school education especially in the rural areas, Anil Agarwal Foundation announced an endowment of 1 bn to set up Vedanta University, the Tata Group gave $ 50 million to Harvard Business School and Anand Mahindra gave $ 10 million to the Humanities at Harvard University. The policymakers should take note of this trend before it is too late.

Muslims Got Beating from All Political Parties

As things are, the minorities especially the Muslims are the losers. Save lip service, they got nothing. Mulayam Singh ruled Uttar Pradesh as the Chief Minister on the support of Muslims but Muslims allege that he did everything for his Yadava community and practically did nothing for Muslims. Mulayam Singh is certainly a secular and a socialist as well as a meaningful person. He always speaks in favour of Muslims on issues which are dearest to them. He has appointed several Muslims as Ministers, Vice-Chancellors, Chairmen of various

Boards and has provided assistance to Madrasas, recruited security personnel, appointed Urdu teachers, established minority institutions, provided scholarships to Muslim students and has done much for Muslims, however, since Muslims' problems are varied and massive, they want much more from him. They want government jobs, adequate representation in police and paramilitary forces and rehabilitation of people affected by communal riots, better schools and colleges in Muslim areas, all-weather roads, adequate sanitary conditions, pollution free drinking water, houses for slum dwelling and poor Muslims, social security and employment to the unemployed youth and protection to innocent Muslim youths in the wake of police excesses. They also want him to provide infrastructure facilities in Muslim areas such as electricity, health care and clean environment. They also want full assistance for the propagation of Urdu and appointment of Muslim teachers to teach Urdu. In a sense they want him to do everything as suggested by Sachar Committee to salvage the conditions of Muslims in the same spirit as he did for his Yadava community. Muslims supported Mulayam Singh in the last election whole heartedly despite the fact that many of his eminent colleagues like Azam Khan were critical of his association with some prominent business magnets and the film personalities and his tilting towards the Rajputs and those with rightist mentality. They contended that he was trying to balance the interests of the majority community and the minority community and never wanted to do anything special for Muslims which could cause damage to his majority segment. Muslims wanted him either this way or that way for which he was not prepared. Muslims should know that Mulayam Singh is not a saint. He is simply a politician and what he is doing is to serve his political interests and to satisfy his assured Yadava constituency. He knows that Muslims of Uttar Pradesh have no choice. They are allergic to Congress and abhor BJP and the Communists and do not relish BSP. Thus, they are bound to help him in most of the cases. They would support the BSP and Congress in a few situations where they would find them in a winning position to defeat the BJP. Save this situation, they are bound to help his party.

In the recently concluded Parliament elections, the party of Mulayam Singh got beating from the side of Muslims. Muslims were not happy with Mulayam Singh for his supporting the Congress Government on the issue of Nuclear Deal. Besides, he aligned with Kalyan Singh whom Muslims consider as the destroyer of the Babri Masjid. Many of his Muslim heavy weights like Azam Khan deserted him on this issue but he did not care for them for he was sure that the support of Kalyan Singh would compensate the loss of Muslim votes. Muslims did not support his party on priority basis. They penalized him for his pro-Congress and pro-Communist stand. Their support to BSP too was half hearted. They tilted towards the Congress in Uttar Pradesh which resulted in the loss to Mulayam Singh and Mayawati and gain to Congress. Ironically, all the Muslim candidates supported by the Samajwadi Party were defeated for they were not supported by Muslims *en masse*. According to many Muslims, it is openly claimed that Muslims still have a soft corner for Mulayam Singh especially after the rejoining of Azam Khan provided he sees the writings on the wall. Muslims are willing to support him whole-heartedly provided he assures Muslims of his fullest support in getting their due according to their strength in his winning combination of Muslims and the Yadavas. After the humiliating defeat of his daughter-in-law at Firozabad parliamentary election, he has distanced himself from Kalyan Singh and Amar Singh and he is not willing to play the Rajput, Lodha and Yadava cards. Several Muslims are hoping that the prominent Muslims who helped the Samajwadi Party to become a power to reckon with would now return in the party as Azam Khan has come within the fold of the party with honour and dignity in the larger interest of the community but one thing is certain that Muslims cannot be befooled for all times to come. They want their share in power from Mulayam Singh in the same way as he has provided power to his own Yadava community. He should induct in his party those Muslims who have proved their callibre and who are honest, straight forward and men of integrity as well as those persons who have their influence at grass-root level. Just by taking people from this section or that section or supporting the sycophants would not do the trick. It is a fact that in the recently concluded elections, Muslims have supported the Congress but it was not their positive vote but a tactical one. It was merely their strategic move to dent Mayawati and Mulayam Singh Yadav in UP and teach lesson to Lalu Prasad Yadav in Bihar and humiliate the Communists in Bengal and Kerala for befooling them for many years. The Sachar Committee Report opened the eyes of Muslims and they tried their best to penalize those parties who played with them dirty game. Congress Government could take the advantage of Muslim votes simply because Muslims were bent upon defeating the BJP and in this venture they supported the Congress wherever it was in a winning position such as Rajasthan, Andhra Pradesh, Madhya Pradesh, Assam and elsewhere. Despite supporting the Congress Party, Muslims are very bitter. They want quid pro quo. Sooner the Congress Party understands it, better it is for its health and endurance.

It was for the first time that a younger segment of Muslim youths became proactive and in order to get their desired objectives, constituted their own parties in many states but succeeded only partly. Ironically, no Muslim was elected from Maharashtra and from many constituencies for there was polarization against them in the important cities of the country on communal lines because of terrorist attacks in Mumbai and elsewhere. However, they succeeded in bringing the secular parties at the helm of affairs. Muslims should not get disheartened but should form their own secular political parties in those states of the country where they have significant population. They can experiment in Uttar Pradesh which has 18.2% Muslim electorate and they can align with the like-minded parties on the basis of their pre-pole alliance. If they fail to do so, others would decide the game plan. There are many Muslims in the country especially in Uttar Pradesh who have soft corner for Mayawati since she represents the Scheduled Castes and the Scheduled Tribes. Muslims have no difficulty in forming alliance with her for there is no inherent confrontation between the Muslims and the Scheduled Castes and the Scheduled Tribes. They are natural allies of the SCs/STs in the same way as they feel comfortable with SP.

However, many Muslims are not happy with Mayawati for her tilt towards the BJP and her support to Modi during post-Godhra period. It is said that she has expressed openly that Muslims are mostly inclined towards the right wing Maulanas which was not relished by many of them. Several Muslims supported Mayawati in the recently concluded elections as they believed that since she belonged to the depressed section of the society she could understand better their sentiments and the difficulties. She gave tickets to many Muslim candidates according to their share in population. Many of her Muslim candidates won elections. She too has done many good things for Muslims. She has provided scholarships to Muslim students, helped Madrasas and Urdu teachers and appointed many Muslims as ministers, secretaries and on high government positions. The maximum Muslims in UP Assembly are from the BSP. Her administration at the time of declaration of the Allahabad High Court judgment was commendable. She kept strict control and did not allow any communal clash. She also did not allow communal riots to take place for she penalized the officers responsible for showing laxity at the time of communal riots. These things were highly appreciated by the Muslims and they would yield her good dividends. She has a soft corner for Muslims but by and large Muslims are not satisfied for what she did for Muslims during her regimes. Muslims usually do not show political maturity. They generally behave emotionally even in political matters where their reactions must be rational and calculated ones. Mayawati too is not a religious or moral leader. She is a very intelligent and matured political leader and she is surviving merely on the basis of her assured constituency. She would do everything for her community to retain it with her. There is no harm in it. Muslims should learn a lesson from her. She did not hesitate to join with Brahmins despite the fact that her party was anti-Brahmins. However, when she realized their voting power and political strength, she aligned with them and gave them lion's share in the state. Muslims have taken BJP as their permanent enemy and are not willing to mend their fences. Similarly, they are after Congress for the Babri Masjid debacle. They should come out of their shell and have alliances with all those parties who can benefit them for it has rightly been said that in politics there are no permanent friends and no permanent enemies. If there is anything permanent it is the collective interest of Muslim society as well as the interest of the country in general and the interest of Indians in particular. Muslims should keep their doors open for everybody including Mayawati, Mulayam Singh, Lalu Prasad, Ram Vilas Paswan and political parties like the Congress, BJP, Shiv Sena and all those organizations such as the RSS, Vishwa Hindu Parishad, Bajrang Dal and individuals and parties that are willing to help them in their endeavours.

Muslims helped Lalu Prasad Yadav blindly for many years but they allege that they got practically nothing from him. He too is a nice man and a thorough gentleman. He is secularist, socialist and a humanist. He always spoke in favour of Muslims' cause vehemently and has done many things for the good of Muslims. He too appointed many Muslim Ministers, Vice-Chancellors, Chairmen and Urdu teachers and helped Madrasas, provided scholarships to Muslim boys and girls but Muslims are not satisfied from what he did. They found him lacking at the time of dealing with the criminals of Bhagalpur riots. They complain that in the field of providing jobs to Muslims and increasing their representation in police and paramilitary organization he did very little. They are not satisfied for what he did for the spread of Urdu and for the appointment of Urdu teachers, rehabilitation of riot victims and for the growth and development of Muslims in Bihar where they are in a pitiable condition. It is said that he too did everything for his Yadava community and neglected the 16.5% Muslims as a consequence of which Muslims did not support him with the same zeal as they did in the past. It will not be out of place to mention here that as a Railway Minister at the Centre he tried his best to help some of the Muslims. Muslims should appreciate the fact that Lalu Prasad too is a very seasoned political leader. He cannot ignore the interest of his community as well as that of the majority community. He is not a saint. Muslims should not expect too much from him but take lesson from what he did for his community and the constituency. Muslims should form their own secular political party in Bihar too where they constitute 16.5% electorate. If they remain beggars they cannot be choosers. In order to have a decisive say they should come in the field as a political force to be reckoned with rather than the followers of this segment or that. Saner Muslims from the community contend that Muslims should give one more chance to Lalu Prasad for he has probably realized where he faltered provided he assures them of his proactive support in proportion to the strength of Muslims in Bihar. Muslims also appreciated Ram Vilas Paswan for his clear and unambiguous support for Muslims. He wanted a Muslim Chief Minister in Bihar but could not succeed and had to pay a heavy price. Though he had joined the BJP and had gone to Gujarat in support of his party, yet Muslims forgave him due to his secular credentials which he proved by leaving the BJP Government. Muslims have highest respect and regard for him for he too is a thorough gentleman and a committed friend. Muslims could not help him in the recently concluded elections in Bihar in 2010 for they were influenced by Nitish Kumar. Muslims initially supported Nitish Kumar partially for they found him wanting in many areas due to his association with the BJP. However, in the recently concluded elections they came openly due to his gaining confidence of the community. Nitish is a secularist and a thorough gentleman. He seems to have soft corner for Muslims for he rarely speaks against the interests of Muslims. He generally tries to help Muslims but his compulsion of heading a coalition government and his soft corner for Hindutva forces might not allow him to do what he intends to do. The way he came openly in support of women's bill hurt even the backward castes and others. However, his bringing of Bihar on the path of development after serious derailment and his recent tilt towards Muslims and his help to various Muslim organizations and institutions auger well for the Muslims of Bihar.

The real fact is that Muslims of Uttar Pradesh, Bihar, Bengal, Assam and Kerala and at many places do not like the Congress Party by heart since most of them do not consider it as their true friend. They allege that they are in bad shape mostly because of the anti-Muslim policies of some of the communal minded hard-core policymakers both in the Congress Party as well as in Congress Government. Muslims of India have highest respect for Nehru family. They appreciate the services of the Nehru family in the freedom struggle as well as in the transformation of India into a modern and dynamic and vibrant country. The only good point for the Congress is that Muslims are grateful to Pandit Nehru, Indira Gandhi, Rajiv Gandhi and Sonia Gandhi for many good things they did for Indian Muslims. They know for sure that Nehru family is hard-core secularist, humanist, pro-poor and pro-minorities and intends to do good to Muslims but some right wing leaders of Congress who command considerable influence in the party and the government seldom allow the wonderful family to do what it intends to do for Muslims. Muslims allege that some of these crafty and reactionary Congress fellows play with the sentiments of Muslims. They suggest the Congress Government to establish various minorities commissions but without giving them any substantial powers. Likewise, they persuaded the government to open various institutions to help Muslims in the educational, financial and cultural fields but most of them are decoration pieces. Several Muslims strongly feel that these artificial institutions have been artfully created to provide jobs to certain trusted Congressmen and to silence the minority community. Besides, many of them stress that the Congress Government never tried to develop Muslim leadership in the country perhaps due to the fear that it would create problems for the government in the shape of demanding rights for Muslims. Consequently, Muslims are leaderless and there is none to console them, guide them and bring them in the political mainstream. Muslims are suffering and struggling under precarious conditions but unfortunately there is not a single person in the Muslim community who can courageously plead their cases before the government. There are a few liberal and enlightened congressmen who sometimes speak in their favour but they too have their limitations. Another advantage to the Congress Party and the government is that Muslims especially the youth have pinned hope in Rahul Gandhi and

Priyanka Gandhi for they consider them genuine sympathizers of Muslims being hard-core secularists, humanists and pro-poor and pro-depressed and marginalized sections of society. Brother and sister both have soft corner for all minorities and weaker sections of society especially the Muslims since they know that Muslims are passing in a lean phase. They are bound to get whole-hearted support from young Muslims for Muslims are convinced of their glorious credentials. Rahul Gandhi is perhaps the lone figure who has realized the importance of developing Muslim leadership especially among the educated Muslims for he knows that if the Muslim leadership is not allowed to develop at the centres like Aligarh, Jamia and Hamdard, the Muslim leadership would emerge from the conservative and the illiterate and backward sections of Muslims which would cause more harm to Muslims as well as the country. When he visited the Aligarh Muslim University in 2009 he strongly supported the idea of developing Muslim leadership especially among Muslim youths. He is a matured and grass-root politician. Healthy and constructive politics is in his blood and he knows that it is always easy to control the herd when it is under the supervision of a shepherd rather than when it is astray. It is hoped that he would develop Muslim leadership which will not only help the government to understand the problems of the Muslims but would also help Muslims to convey their true feelings before the government. Presently, the position is that several Muslims intend to move towards Congress one step but soon retreat two steps due to its irritating policies. What to talk of the past injustices, many of them feel that it did not lag behind in harming Muslims when it got the opportunity to rule the country after a long period of time. It is the general perception among the Muslims that it was the Congress Government which befriended Bush who was generally averse to Muslims and Islam and who caused havoc in Afghanistan and Iraq and it was none other than the Congress Government which came closest to Israel and distanced itself from some of the Muslim countries in general and Palestinians in particular. It was the Congress Government which provided shelter to those who went against the sentiments of the Muslims despite the resentment of Muslims but kept mum to provide similar support to a few Muslims who had gone against the sentiments of the majority community. Many Muslims are not happy with the Congress in the manner in which it handled the Rushdi and the Cartoon matters. A few did not relish the government policies of not helping Saddam and Iran when they were in trouble despite the fact that they had proved their credentials. Many were surprised the way the Congress Government followed the soft Hindutva policies in Gujarat to attract Hindu votes. Congress Government announced various plans for the betterment of Muslims such as 15-point plan and 20-point programme but the ground reality is that Muslims got practically nothing. Many meaningful Muslims lament that the Congress Government under Dr. Manmohan singh has not implemented the recommendations of the Sachar Committee. The Sachar Committee Report had been placed in the Parliament and it was accepted by the government that Muslims were lagging behind even compared to the Scheduled Castes in practically all fields. Muslims were expecting a respectable amount of budget provision for the betterment of Muslims but when the Finance Minister announced ₹ 750,884 crore so-called the election budget in which he had provided a whopping ₹ 60,000 crore for waiving farm loans, the pea-nut amounting to ₹ 15,000 crore was earmarked for 15% Muslim population of the country. They appreciate the policies of the Congress Government for withdrawing POTA but allege that the government has done nothing for those innocents who are languishing in jails for no fault of their own. They feel pained and grieved to observe that whenever any act of terror takes place in the country whether it is in the mosques, graveyards or in Bhiwandi or Mecca mosque in Hyderabad or in the shrine of Hajrat Khawaja Ajmeri or in Raghunath and Akshardham temples or in markets, railway stations or on festivals only Muslims are targeted and arrested when the fact is that terrorism has become a universal phenomena in which people of many religions and nationalities are involved. Muslims are apprehensive about many encounters during Congress rule and they were reminded of the BJP rule when many young Muslims allegedly faced encounters and several of them were sent behind the bars. They are afraid of the consequences of the recently passed Terrorist Law which is the old wine in new bottle. Actually, Muslims have a Pandora box of complaints against the Congress some of which are genuine and many reflect their conjectures and fears. Despite having known fully well the good intentions of Sonia Gandhi, Rahul Gandhi, Nehru family, Manmohan Singh and many Congress stalwarts they do not expect much from the party due to its coalition nature and internal compulsions. However, one thing is quite probable that in the wake of displeasing 160 million Muslims in the country, the Congress might reduce its voting percentage from 28.55% in 2009 to nearly 22 per cent in 2014 thereby collapsing from 206 Lok Sabha seats to under 120.

Likewise, Muslims have bitter experience of the BJP. It appears that several Muslims are not prepared to support the BJP Government at any cost for the party in their opinion is the lone party which is surviving and prospering merely by creating hatred and ill-will against Muslims. Many of the Muslims consider it against their religion, culture and ways of living and even against their existence in this country. Several Muslims rightly or wrongly believe that the party allegedly glorified the abolition of the Babri mosque, changed several contents of history books, safforonized education to some extent, throttled a few minority institutions, created problems for some of the Madrasas, criticized the Muslim Personal Law, spread the boggy of Muslim appeasement, introduced the draconian laws perhaps to suppress Muslims, caused some doubtful and probably fake encounters, allegedly incited bloodshed in Gujarat, opposed the reservation of Muslims, involved many innocent Muslims in terrorism, doubted the loyalty of a few Muslims, created hurdles in the implementation of the reports of various riot commissions, did not take lightly the Sachar Committee Report, practically closed the doors for Muslims and did not keep quiet in criticizing on issues pertaining to Muslims. Due to above perceptions based on reality or hunches many Muslims fear the BJP Party. Whenever they have to vote, many of them make it sure that BJP is defeated. They allegedly adopt tactical voting to defeat the BJP. Muslims generally support those parties that can defeat the BJP. They mostly prefer supporting those regional parties that are sympathetic to them and avoid even Congress Party. However, in case of a tie between the Congress and BJP, they vote for the Congress candidates if they are convinced that they would defeat BJP candidates. Their main priority is generally to check the BJP from coming in power for they mostly know that once it is in, it would create unthinkable losses both hidden as well as apparent. After the poor showing by the party in many states it appears that the party is in the mood of revising its policies vis-à-vis Muslims especially after obtaining the support of Muslims in large number in the recently concluded elections in Bihar. The party knows that only that party can rule the hearts of all the Indians from Kashmir to Kanyakumari and Amritsar to Kolkata which is secular, liberal and has concern and love for all Indians irrespective of their castes, religions, places of birth and colours. With a hard-core parochial and anti-Muslim and anti-Christian policy every party would find it hard to achieve its objective especially at a time when the new generation of liberal Indians is entering the electoral scene. The role of the BJP leadership especially the role of Lal Krishna Advani and others remained commendable in the wake of Allahabad High Court Judgment. It seems they are genuine in their approach in solving the Ramjanam Bhumi-Babri Masjid problem peacefully to the satisfaction of both the communities for all times to come. If they too do not pay merely lip service to Muslims but help in solving their genuine matters, they surely would not find Muslims lacking in reciprocity.

As things stand today, the indicators show that future trends are changing at national and regional levels. The rightist groups from the majority community and Muslim fundamentalist organizations seem to be coming nearer for both of them being conservative, religious minded and rightists hate perverted practices of modern youths and both of them want religious harmony. Muslims' thinking too is changing for they have been ditched by the national as well as the regional parties. These parties have used them like the napkins and threw them after the use. The regional leaders did for their own communities and electorate and took Muslims for a ride. Many people who are in touch with BJP and RSS leaders are convinced that several of them are not hard-core fanatics but liberals and humanists. They have been painted dark by the vested interests. Many of them are thorough gentlemen and possess enlightened personalities. They really want Muslims' benefit and their genuine growth and development. Likewise, Mohan Bhagwatji and the present President of BJP Nitin Gadkari too are moving towards Muslims to allay their fears. Their present behaviour which sometimes appears to be anti-Muslim is perhaps due to their electoral compulsions. When both the segments would come nearer they would realize that their interests are complementary rather than competitive and they would form a unbreakable alliance which would prove boon to the emerging India both at the national and international levels.

Muslims also have bad experience of the Communist Parties too. They feel that they have been befooled by them also in the same way as others have befooled them. Just as the Muslims do not feel comfortable with BJP similarly they find themselves uncomfortable in the company of some of the Communists. Communism as a matter of fact does not suit many Muslims due to its neutral and unhealthy approach towards belief system. Several Muslim countries especially those which were conservative remained away from the patronage of the Communist regimes. Only those poor countries of Muslims or those countries which were ruled by Muslim dictators came in close touch of the Communist countries because of their similarity of ideas and policies. It is alleged by the Muslims in the light of the Sachar Committee Report that the Communists in West Bengal kept Muslims in miserable conditions despite their long rule. Muslims also did not relish the role of the Communist parties in supporting the Women's Reservation Bill despite the fact that these parties were fully aware of the conditions of Muslim men and women. Many Muslims allege that there are many Communists who appear to be not in favour of providing any special benefits to

Muslims. Muslims also complain that the communist do not hesitate in providing shelter and protection to those anti-Muslim agents who play with the sentiments of Muslims. Some of them especially the ultra liberal and ultra secular Muslims sometimes behave in such a way that Muslim masses are irritated by their actions and utterances. In matters of doing something positively good for Muslims, many Muslims place the Communist Party and the BJP in the same category. This never means that all communists are bad or that communists have not done anything for Muslims. There are several pro-Muslim communists who come to the rescue of several Muslims when they are in trouble. History is witness to the fact that they spoke against communal riots, criticized Modi and condemned the Gujarat riots, stood against Bush, helped Muslims in Babri Masjid case. Besides, the Communist Government at Kerala has done much for Muslims so also the Communist Government at West Bengal has checked riots and done many things which Muslims cherish. Muslims now have become somewhat intelligent. They are thinking of opening their doors for all the parties without any prejudice in the spirit of quid pro quo. Now onward, it is hoped that they would not vote with a single point in mind to defeat the BJP but would vote for those parties who would make them shareholders and stakeholders in the governance of the country.

6

Policy Measures to Tackle Radicalism

It has been very often observed that whenever any segment of the society failed to achieve its objective, which it perceived as rightful through democratic and peaceful means, it did not hesitate to use violence as a last resort. It has been rightly said that those who are severely constrained begin to fight. The world has seen many such groups which after being failed through lawful means participated in violence, militancy, suicide bombing and terrorism harming innocent people, destroying properties and causing chaos in the world. France witnessed the reign of terror from April 1793 to July 1794 when thousands were guillotined. America confronted the terror of the Clu clux clan and Al-Qaeda, Great Britain had to face the brunt from the Irish fighters, Hamas is causing problems for Iran and Palestine, Uighurs are irritating Xingjian, Pakistan is the victim of Al-Qaeda and its own brand of terrorists, India is struggling with Pakistani terrorists, ULFAS, Bodos, Nagas, Maoists, Naxalites, HUJI, LET, and the indigenous rightist Muslim and Hindu fundamentalists. Sri Lanka had been invaded by LTTE, Bangladesh by HUJI and Philippines, Australia and Balkan states are facing their own brands of terrorism. Terrorists belong to no religion. They can be Al-Qaeda, HUJI, the IRA, the Basque Liberation Front, Hamas, Neo-Nazis, SIMI activists, Abhinav Bharat, the LTTE, the Sinhalese Ultra Nationalist or the JVP men. They may come from many countries and many religions. Terrorism is an ideology or strategy to achieve certain ends through violent means. It has nothing to do with any specific belief system. Terrorists generally call themselves freedom fighters but the entire world has rejected them and their strategies and treated them as contrary to world peace and tranquility. It is heartening to know that terrorism has been operating in the world for quite some time but very few Indians were involved in it. It is a well-known fact that most of the Indian Muslims including the Muslim youths distanced themselves from the Kashmiri Muslims who professed that they were the freedom fighters and were fighting to liberate Kashmir. Even on 9/11 or in any Al-Qaeda activity no Indian Muslim was found involved though some fingers were raised upon some educated Muslim youths in Bangalore in connection with some terrorist activities in England and Australia which annoyed the people of India in general and Indian Muslims in particular. Incidentally, the recent serial blasts in Jaipur, Ahmedabad and Delhi exposed the role of some of the activists of SIMI and some right wing Hindu organizations. This indeed was a very serious development especially at that time when the whole world was blaming only Muslims for terrorist activities when the fact was that Muslims, Hindus, Christians, Buddhists, Jews and several others too were involved in this kind or that kind of terrorist activities. The anti-Islamic lobby and the adversaries of Islam were successful in painting Islam and Muslims black. They were talking in terms of war between civilizations and were maintaining that Islam was a danger to world peace and that the Muslims were the enemies of mankind. A section of the perverted media was openly propagating anti-Islam rhetoric just to blame Islam and Muslims and there was none to challenge its nefarious designs because people believed in what it was reporting. The impact of all such Islam maligning campaigns was that it became difficult for Muslim states and Muslim community to save their skin. Just as the Muslims of the entire world were perplexed and terrorized similarly Indian Muslims too were facing different kinds of agonies and tortures because of the adverse world image of Muslims and Islam. However, when the name of SIMI activists came in the context of several bomb blasts in India fingers were raised upon Muslims, their madrasas, mosques, clergies and many of them were forcefully asked to denounce terrorism. The Ulemas came forward and condemned terrorism because they considered it as an un-Islamic act. Despite this, the allegedly fake encounters, discriminations in jobs, police raids upon some Muslim houses, blaming game and aversion from the side of neighbours, intellectuals and government machinery became the talks of the day. It became risky for Muslims with beards and Muslim women with veils to move in odd times. One could see the climate of mistrust and hatred practically in every corner of the country since instead of blaming the terrorists, most of the people were generally blaming the entire Muslim community which was shocking and painful.

The Involvement of Some Hindu Extremists in Terrorist Activities

It is irony of fate that when everything was in flux and the situation was in the process of getting stabilized, Indian society got another unbelievable shock of high intensity in the shape of the declaration of the Anti-Terrorist Squad (ATS) that they had some solid proofs with them regarding the involvement of certain reactionary and rightist fundamentalist organizations from some section of the majority community in Malegaon and Nanded blasts in which several Muslims were killed. The most disturbing news was that some retired and active army officers of Indian Army, which is renowned for its integrity, commitment and impartiality, were allegedly involved in providing trainings and helping hand to the terrorists. Not only this, there appeared to be the connivance of some of the religious sects and their heads in these blasts. Another heart-breaking factor was that it was alleged that one young educated lady who had renounced the world and taken sanyas and declared herself as sadhvi acted as the mastermind. Indian people pay greatest regards and respects to clergies and saints of every religion for these people are supposed to lead them to the path of salvation. What to talk of shedding blood of human beings, these pious people hesitate to harm even the smallest insects. However, when their names are associated with terrorism people are bound to become dumbfounded. Likewise, Army is supposed to guard the borders of the country and protect the life, liberty, property and honour of the people. If the officers of higher ranks are blamed in such heinous activities, the country is bound to take note of it. Admittedly, Muslims of India were claiming for the last so many years that they suspected the hands of certain rightist and aggressive violent Hindu organizations in some of the blasts which took place in Mecca Masjid, Shrine of Khwaja Ajmeri, Shahi Jama Masjid Delhi and in the mosques and grave-yards of Malegaon and Nanded since many hard-core Hindu leaders were openly instigating Hindu youths to raise arms against the indigenous terrorists and create Hindu suicide squads to take revenge from Muslims. Some Hindu activists were found dead and some were caught while handling or manufacturing bombs but police took no notice because nobody could imagine for a moment that Hindus would cause blasts in their own country. The police should have taken lead from Pakistan where Muslims were throwing bombs on their own Muslim brothers even in the mosques while the devotees were performing their prayers. Actually, when one becomes a beast, one does not care for religion, people and the country. One more perplexing thing which was happening in the country was that some rightist political parties and religious and extremist organizations from a minor segment of the majority community were coming openly in favour of the alleged Hindu terrorists. They were blaming the ATS and ruling governments by emphasizing that these agencies were using police force for blaming certain sects of Hindus and saints with a view to take the advantage in the coming elections in some of the states. Many rightist Hindu politicians were openly telling that what happened was to happen for the government of India at the Centre and the State Governments at the state levels had failed to check the terrorists in their nefarious designs. Their morales had gone high and they were taking the majority community for a ride. Under such circumstances those who believed in the religious and cultural sanctities were bound to get disturbed. The only alternative left before the proactive Hindu youths was to blunt the designs of the enemies of the country by taking law in their own hands with a view to give them a fitted reply in their own language. Thus, what happened was in retaliation and hence it was justified. It is said that there were some hard-core activists who had heralded the young lady for taking bold action and pronounced her as the champion of the Hindu cause and a few of them even offered assembly ticket to her in lieu of her heroic act. There was some logic in what was said above but a matured society was supposed not to act in a retaliatory and violent manner even if its cause was genuine. The revenge and counter revenge were the traditions of the days of ignorance and in modern days they were despised by all civilized sections of the society. In modern times, every citizen is supposed to uphold the rule of law. It is the function of the state to provide protection to the people. If the state fails to protect people from the clutches of terrorism, in a democracy like India people should not use bullets but use ballets to change such governments. Whatever happened in the name of terrorism did not auger well for a mighty country like India. All Indians irrespective of caste affiliations, religious identities and political leanings should rise above board and denounce those people from majority, minority or any community who believe in the language of violence, who do not value the dignity of human life and who are the enemies of mankind. We should disown them even if they belong to us. The exemplary punishment should be given to them so that nobody can dare to repeat such acts in future.

Persecution of Innocent Citizens

One warning and caution in connection with the persecution of innocent people is necessary at this stage because it has been alleged from time to time by the Muslims that many innocents were grilled and punished by the police for no fault of their own. The Anglo-Saxon Law allows freeing even nine culprits out of ten to protect the life of one innocent person. It should be ensured by the state agencies and the civil society that no innocent of any community, section, group or religion is punished. Besides, terrorism should be de-linked from caste, creed, colour, religion or place of birth. If a Muslim commits the act of terrorism, the whole Muslim community and Islam should not be blamed. Likewise, if a Hindu terrorist participates in the acts of terrorism, the Hindu religion and

Hindu community should not be associated with terrorism. Shah Rukh Khan and Karan Johar have done tremendous service to Muslims, Indian society and the humanity at large by exposing the fact that terrorists are merely the terrorists. They belong to no religion, caste, creed and they bear no colour. Shah Rukh's assertion in his classic and world fame movie stating that "I am a Khan but not a terrorist" speaks volumes about wrong perception of the world about Muslims, Islam and terrorism. The facts have supported his contention that neither all Muslims are terrorists nor all terrorists are Muslims. The world has seen that the Muslims of the world were blamed for causing terror activities after 9/11, 2001 when allegedly only a few segments of the Muslims were involved in it. The same happened in India after Jaipur, Delhi and Ahmedabad blasts. The whole Muslim community was made ransom and it had become difficult for Muslims to save their skin. Many maulanas like Mahmoodul Hasan Quasmi from Mumbai and many clergies from various parts of the country were tortured and humiliated. Random searches, arbitrary arrests, fake encounters had created fear psychosis amongst Muslims. It had become cumbersome to be a Muslim due to security reasons and the Muslim intelligentsia was highly disturbed the way the Muslim community was treated those days. In the words of poet Faiz Ahmed Faiz, the Muslims of India had started pondering, "Yeh daagh daagh ujala, yeh shabguzida sahar, woh intezar tha jiska, yeh woh sehar to nahi." ("This black-smeared light, this night-ridden morning. This is not the morning we had waited for.") The post-partition like situation seemed to have set in when people were afraid to keep Urdu books with them for the fear of being called the Pakistanis. The guilt conscience which the Muslims of India had shook off after 1971 had begun to haunt them again. It had become difficult for Muslims to buy a house or get a house on rent in a predominantly Hindu locality. Muslim boys and girls were very often denied admissions even in government colleges. The life had become difficult for burqa clad women and men having beards and wearing skull caps. The madrasa students were looked as aliens. It appeared as if the Indian Muslims were under total siege and the communal polity of hard-core rightist organization and the pick and choose approach of some of the media which saw itself as unbiased fourth estate had made things worse. Condemnation of Muslims and the hate campaign unleashed by the extremist organizations were fuelling the fire. Even the liberal space in the majority community was shrinking and many of the liberal sections of the society had started to condone the atrocities committed upon innocent Muslims. At work places or while buying the groceries or standing at bus stop many Muslims felt the sense of being others. Several Muslim youths were facing discrimination in matters of education and jobs. Whenever or wherever any blast took place the police was quick to link it with Muslims of India without going into the details or without considering any possibility of the hard-core indigenous agencies of the majority community. It quickly rounded some of the suspects, issued the sketches of a few criminals and declared the involvement of certain agencies within 24 hours. Instead of capturing the genuine culprits alibis were fed to general public to satisfy their appetite and punishment was awarded to innocent people. The investigating agencies till then had not shown much enthusiasm in booking the culprits where activists from the majority community were allegedly involved. These agencies perhaps showed softness in handling the cases of Bhagulpur in 1987, Mumbai in 1992-93 and Gujarat in 2002, where some of the functionaries from the state machinery were allegedly involved in massacring many Muslims and they also remained soft at Nanded in April 2006 when two Bajrang Dal workers were killed while making crude bombs. A similar situation had arisen in Kanpur in August 2008 but no arrests were made. The new waves of terrorism resulting from the growing alienation of India's minorities due to frustration and mistrust in the words of P. Chidambaram shattered the resilience of the investigating machinery and also the sagacity of the Indian people. The terrorists stroked at will at any moment and venue of their choice. They killed children, aged, women and innocent people who screamed for help and media attention. Consequently, the liberals of the country too lost focus which was quite natural. When the going got tough and the right wing political parties exploded, the investigating agencies became active and for public consumption captured the Muslim youths who were harassed and frozen in suspicion. This proved counter productive. The suspects who were not brought to the book sowed the poison of hatred among Hindu-Muslim seam and exploited the resultant anger among Muslim youths with a view to drift more disgruntled Muslims towards terrorism. However, the general unrest among the majority community and the demand from the side of the right wing political parties to bring draconian laws compelled investigating agencies to book even innocent Muslims to satisfy the hunger of the larger section of the society. Wherever Muslim youths were arrested, it has been found that most of them had documents showing their innocence and genuineness. However, they were arrested, tortured and kept in jails without any prima facie evidence but ultimately released by law courts in the wake of lack of evidence. The police seldom admits its mistake but wherever it admitted, the victims of bias and misjudgments had already engulfed in the doom of uncertainties, job loss and a trauma of being called the terrorists. The Batla House encounter in which two Muslim youths were believed to be killed under suspicious circumstances by the Delhi Police and in which one of the inspectors of Delhi Police too was killed created much resentment among Muslims. Indian Muslims are not completely satisfied though the enquiry conducted by the human rights commission too has confirmed the genuineness of the encounters. Likewise, the Muslims of Azamgarh are highly perturbed for many people have started calling Azamgarh as Atankgarh and several Muslim youths have been arrested from this region and they are languishing in jails.

To win the war against terrorism, it is necessary that we should assure the people that no innocent person would be caught and harassed in the name of terrorism and those police personnel or persons from paramilitary units who would take the innocent lives to get rewards, promotions and distinctions would also be dealt with seriously. As a matter of fact, the state terrorism is as dangerous as the group or individual terrorism. Many a time, some political parties which have no constructive agenda survive merely on emotive issues to get the support of the masses. Several undesirable elements exploit caste, colour, creed, sex and religious sentiments of the people to garner support and there is no dearth of people who even create the climate of hatred and ill-will to get votes. It has also been seen that very often the ruling governments even at international level create fear psychosis in the minds of the people to stay in power. In situations where the seekers of powers are bankrupt socially and morally, they can adopt any means such as money power, muscle power or the power of violence, terror and force to achieve their objectives. It has been observed that a few unscrupulous political parties usually use certain unorthodox techniques to expose the impotency of the ruling parties towards terrorism. They create fear in the minds of general public and present themselves as the protectors and saviours of people with a view to garner peoples' votes.

Dialogue Between Communities a Must

The blame game is harmful for the country. One group calls certain Muslim organizations as communal, fundamentalists and terrorists. The other group retaliates by calling similar Hindu organizations as communal, fanatics and terrorists. As a matter of fact, there is nothing wrong in being called communal, fundamentalist and even inward looking provided these words are used in positive sense. A communal person is a boon to the society for day and night he works for the benefit and welfare of his community without harming others or without any ill-will towards other communities. In this sense, all the great men of the world were communal for they worked for their communities without harming the interests of other communities. Likewise, those Hindus, Muslims, Sikhs, Christians, Jains and other organizations who are working for the betterment of their communities are the useful segment of the society for they are helping in the growth and development of the country without creating hatred, prejudice or ill-will towards any segment of the society. These organizations and religious heads and social thinkers are the conscience of the society. They keep human beings on right path and fight the evils of the society. The government cannot reform society merely by means of legal measures or using the deterrents. It is these organizations that bring social, moral, ethical and religious changes in the society. These organizations and their heads become problematic for the country and people when they merely work for the interest of their communities or organizations and intend to harm the interests of others. In such situations, the dialogue should be opened between them with a view to remove misunderstandings and arrive at a consensus.

These organizations should be reformed rather than banned. It is a fact that both the extreme right and the ultra left wing parties are no more in demand. The left which stood for state control and socio-economic change has fallen back to capitalist incentives and is pleading for a welfare state. The Hindu nationalists called the rightists, the orthodox Muslims known as clergies and hard-core Sikhs with extremist views and political parties having rightist tendencies are tilting towards the liberal right. There are few takers of extremist ideology and the traditional Fabian socialism of political parties with socialistic leanings and Pan-Islamism of the 1920s. Thus, the idealism both at the level of India and the world is vanishing. The history of the 20th century is littered with graves of the ideologies of Lenin, Mao, Hitler and others. People are learning from history and are abandoning the ideologies of hatred and acquiring implementation skills with a view to focus on the needs of the people. Basically, people everywhere want peace of mind and safe place to live; institutions supplying good schools and hospitals; clean air and pure water; uninterrupted electric supply and better roads. They aspire for ample job opportunities and to be able to carry out one's trade without having to bribe; a judge to resolve disputes speedily and a viable state to maintain peace, progress and harmony. The contrasting elaborations between various religions and people too are narrowing down. Since religious cultures, traditions and practices are consciously interacting and new truths and realities are coming open, the ideological speculations too are converging and coming closer. The coming together of the people and the increasing influence of each faith upon every other in an atmosphere of peaceful co-existence is narrowing down the differences. However, it is unfortunate that in our country we have not emerged from the bitter past. We observe that Muslims look towards certain extremist and right wing Hindu organizations with suspicion and consider them against their culture, religion and belief system. In the same way, the Hindu organizations also consider the orthodox, conservative and extremist Muslim organizations detrimental to Hindu community and against their interest. Ironically, many of these types of organizations from among both the communities have common objectives, many of them are sincere in their approaches and several of them believe that they are serving the society selflessly in the name of God. However, they do not realize that somewhere they are faltering because their existence is causing inconvenience to the society and the nation. Thus, the need of the hour is to open communication lines between them. Once they sit on the common table with open mind and good spirit, many problems would be solved. Akbar the Great succeeded in ruling the country for fifty years without creating any ill-will against his empire simply because he opened the communication channels between various religious groups and brought them on a common platform. There is no need of any new Din-i-Ilahi but certainly there is a need of harmony between different religious sects of the country. A religious man is a God's gift. The mankind is safe under his patronage for he believes in one God and thus considers the whole universe as Lord's family. Similarly, a social reformer is a boon to society. He selflessly endeavours for the betterment of the society and he is honest in his perception and his each action is in the interest of his community. Such persons and groups should be respected and encouraged. The tragedy is that the vested interests do not allow these various groups to unite for they benefit by their conflicts, bickering and heartburning. In our country for several years certain political parties have been frightening the Muslims from the very existence of a few rightist organizations from amongst the majority community. They are telling them that if they do not vote for them these extremist groups would strangle them and swallow them. The strategy is working but only to a point. In the same way, a few political parties are befooling certain sections of majority community that rightist Muslims are dangerous for Hindu society, Indian culture and national interest. The mutual fear between communities is keeping them isolated and segmented. Muslims should give due regard to the religious, social and cultural heads of the majority community for they are doing a yeoman's job for their community. There are many selfless, committed and gifted persons in these organizations who are remarkable persons with good conscience and exemplary conduct. They are not as bad as the Brutus has painted them. Likewise, the Hindus should pay respect to the heads of Muslim organizations as many of them are good intentioned people with clean conscience. Many of them are serving their society with their sincerity, integrity and passion. They too are not as ugly and dirty as the biased persons have painted them. Once both the groups start with positive approach, they are bound to solve their problems mutually and amicably. The fundamentalists are also good people for they believe in the fundamental principles of their religions, creeds or ideologies without harming any sects, religious groups or ideological segments of the society. There is nothing wrong if people follow the fundamentals of their religions or sects for the fundamentals of all the religions help people in pursuing the path of God in their own ways. The problem arises when these fundamentalists become parochial and think only in terms of their communities or sects without any regard to other communities or they strive for the benefits of their communities with sole intention of harming other communities. They must be taught to keep the interests of their communities in proper perspectives. So long these fundamentalists follow golden mean and keep the interests of all communities and sects in mind along with the interest of their own community, they prove boon to the society. The moment they begin to pursue the sole interest of their communities at the cost of the interests of other communities, they become an obstacle to the society and their fundamentalism becomes detrimental to the society.

The involvement of certain rightist fundamentalist organizations from the majority community in India in response to the terrorism of certain fanatic Muslim terrorists with a view to take revenge has compelled the Muslims to believe that it is also probable that the enemies of Islam too might have created a terror network of their own through their agents elsewhere in retaliation to terrorism by some hard-core Muslim fundamentalists organization to defame Islam, Muslims and Muslim countries. They also feel that some super powers in order to settle their scores with certain Muslim countries might have started state terrorism as an alibi to punish them with a view to justify their malicious actions in the eyes of the world. The possibility of state terrorism by some unsavioury heads of states to stay in power by creating fear of terror in the minds of the people too cannot be denied. It is not hidden from anybody that from day one Muslims have been maintaining that the manner in which the 9/11, 2001 episode was precisely executed could not be the handy work of the ill-equipped and backward Muslims. What to talk of the Talibans or Al-Qaeda group no Muslim country in the world possesses so much resources and such a technical expertise so as to execute 9/11 type plan. If Muslim terrorists have done this, it is indeed a miracle which cannot be believed so easily. Besides, the way many people of a certain sect absented in large numbers on that day caste doubts on the authenticity of 9/11. Needless to say that doubts have been created even in the minds of American people about the genuineness of 9/11 incidence. The manner in which Iraq was attacked by using the alibi of weapons of mass destruction compels some people to think that it is also possible that 9/11 incidence might have been used by some misguided strategist to invade and destroy Afghanistan. The way in which the world politics has got shaped during last few years speaks volumes of the dirty games the world level politicians have played to achieve their ulterior ends. Since much water has flown in America and there is a regime change it is hoped that American people who are truth lovers would like to go into the details into what happened during the turbulent days when the world at large was looking towards America with suspicion and anger and it is hoped that the truth would come out very soon. Till then all events indicate at the role of Al-Qaeda and Muslim terrorist organizations.

Need to Go to the Root Cause of Terrorism

The most disturbing thing in the context of terrorism is that terrorism is not a new phenomenon. It has existed since time immemorial. It has taken several shapes in the world in which many ancient and modern people of developed and developing countries have been involved. The strange thing is that we have given different names to terrorism suiting to our convenience. Not only this, the same activity is perceived as terrorist activity by one segment while the other heralds it as an admirable act. Everybody in the world hates and condemns terrorism and tries to suppress it by force. But there are a few who try to go behind the factors that compel the youths of several countries to resort to terrorism. One cannot find the cure of the disease unless and until the disease is properly diagnosed. Suman Shekhar has rightly said that the Great Rama beheaded Ravan several times but each time he beheaded him each time he grew many more heads. Having seen this miracle Rama the Great was puzzled. He was finally advised to pierce his naval. When he did this, Ravana fell down as his life force was in his navel and not in his head. Likewise, if we suppress terrorism by using extraordinary, unprecedented and horrible coercive means on some individuals, communities or groups that are innocent, we create an adverse reaction and help in generating more terrorists. It is not hidden from anybody that the Christian world unilaterally decided in 1948 to transfer Jews to Palestine from Europe and other places where they were either in trouble or were creating trouble for them. They asked the Palestinians to make room for them and in return promised them a state of their own. The world knows that Palestinians fought for several years with gun yielding Israeli soldiers with stones in their hands but nobody came to their rescue. Since the super powers were supporting Israel, the rest of the countries of the world remained impotent and save lip service did nothing for the Palestinians. Much time has elapsed yet their problem has not been solved. Admittedly, in a civilized society no sensible man would approve the use of terror as a weapon to achieve ones objectives however genuine one might be. However, it becomes the duty of the conscience holders of the society to see to it that no injustice is done to any segment of the society for as soon as the seeds of injustice and persecution sprout they lead to frustration and even to wars and terrorism. Likewise, there are many people who are fighting for their freedoms in several parts of the world. Their states have been unjustly subjugated by super powers by force during the world wars but nobody is coming to their rescue since many of the super powers themselves are guilty on this count in one form or the other. For such unfortunate people, there is not much choice save to surrender or fight with their might. For the new world order to take its firm roots it is imperative that humanity should rise above narrow parochial considerations and solve the problems of the miserable people irrespective of their colours, creeds and religions so that the menace of ill-will, hatred, prejudice and terrorism may be wiped out from the face of the world. The Lord has provided us an opportunity in the shape of change in world situation where might has been discarded as a means to settle rights. The world at large is tired of the legacy of fighting wars on the pretext of imaginary fears or outrightly supporting Israel or other grabbers of powers. The need of the hour is that wherever and whoever has grabbed others' lands should be asked to vacate and wherever people are suppressed and persecuted should be salvaged irrespective of their backgrounds and political affiliations. There must be zero tolerance in the world with respect to the atrocities and persecution in the world. Only a just and fair world order can create a congenial climate for peace, harmony and a world without fear. However, if we fail in our endeavours due to our personal interests and narrow outlooks we would miserably fail in fighting the menace of terrorism. We would surely succeed in suppressing the menace of terrorism here and there but the malady would raise its ugly head elsewhere and cause immense harm to the humanity in general and world governments in particular.

The people of India and especially the policy planners should be more cautious because for the last so many years we have been facing violent activities in the country in the shape of terrorism, naxalism, maoism, ULFA unrest, kidnapping and several illegal and violent activities involving economic, political and social crimes. We were able to suppress the activities of misguided youths in Punjab and save a select band of few Kashmiri youths, no Indian was ever found involved in any terrorist activities in any part of the world prior to 9/11 incidence. However, for the last few years we have been hearing about the role of some misguided Muslim and Hindu youths in terrorist and violent activities which took place in the country. This is a dangerous trend and it should be checked both by iron hand and reformist and curative acts. First of all, we should go into its very genesis because without finding out the root cause of the malady we would not be able to control it permanently. Broadly speaking, there can be nine major causes for this evil. Firstly, majority of Muslims and several segments of Hindu society come from poverty and below poverty line are by and large uneducated, unemployed and frustrated and as such they become easy prey of the unscrupulous elements of the society. It has been observed in the case of 'the peripheral theory of development' that if people are not given chance to share the benefits of growth in the hard-core sector, they drift towards the core sector and failing which they mark their presence in the periphery. In the same way, depressed and less privileged Muslim and Hindu youths first of all try to get jobs in the hard-core sector where money and dignity go together but when they fail due to their inadequate qualifications, experience, training and background, they move to the core sector which too provides them good livelihood along with respect in the society. There too if they are found lacking, compelled by circumstances, they accept any job good or bad, desirable or undesirable, legal or illegal which is available to them in the periphery. This fact can be verified by the fact that in every jail the number of Muslim and Hindu culprits from the marginalized sections of the society far exceeds their proportions in the national statistics. Muslims constitute 15% of the population but in many Indian jails their number touches nearly 30% mark. Similarly, the depressed sections of majority community too surpass their percentage in almost all the jails of India. Besides, many of them are found involved in smuggling, petty thefts, sharp shooting and dirty jobs. The anti-national and anti-social elements take the advantage of their financial weaknesses, miserable circumstances and involve them in terrorist activities with a promise to pay them handsomely as well as an unfailing support to their families in the case of eventualities. It has been rightly said that a hungry man is an angry man. He has no religion, no caste and no respect for his fellow beings. He has complaint against every section of the society for ignoring him and compelling him to fall in the ditch of poverty, ignorance and crimes. Pressed by circumstances, he is willing to do anything to meet his two ends and help his sagging family. Many Iraqi, Afghani and Indian youths who are involved in terrorist activities are perhaps the victims of poverty, ignorance and frustration. The second factor that may compel them to participate in such dirty activities is the revenge element. Several religious and anti-national and anti-social segments of the society are always in search of such youths who have some miserable past or who are inclined towards religious zeal or who are violent by nature. The anti-social elements from among the Muslims brainwash the young Muslims and convince them that the hard-core Hindus are their enemy number one as they have destroyed Babri Masjid and are in search of demolishing many more of them. They remind them about killing of innocent Muslims in Bhagalpur, Malyana, Mumbai, Surat and Gujarat and blasts at Mecca Masjid, Hyderabad, Jama Masjid, Delhi, Ajmer Sharif, Malegaon and other places and incite them to take revenge from those who are against their religion, culture and the very existence. If they succeed in sprouting the seeds of extreme types of hatred, prejudice and revenge in the hearts and minds of youths especially those who have suffered in these eventualities or who have seen their kith and kin or friends and acquaintances suffering or dying in such incidents, they can easily become their prey. Likewise, the hard-core segments from amongst the Hindu organizations can also exploit the sentiments of Hindu youths by saying that the

Muslims are a curse to the society for they are slaughtering cows, multiplying in numbers, and despite taking Pakistan, are flourishing in India at the cost of Hindus. They arouse their feelings by telling them that the Indian Muslims have caused Mumbai blast and blasts in trains, temples, courts and sacred places and killed several innocent Hindu children, women, young and old. They also incite these elements against the governments at the centre and states by reminding them that they are not taking any action due to the voting powers of Muslims. We observed that after several blasts in recent times especially Delhi, Jaipur and Ahmedabad there was a strong undercurrent amongst various pro-active sections of the majority community. The intellectuals and the saner element from majority community were expecting a majority backlash and thus the militant action of Hindu radicals was not an unexpected development. It was felt that it had only been a matter of time before a violent Hindu reaction manifested itself. It was because of this reason that even many of the saner Hindus did not condemn the Hindu terrorism for they felt that it was for a just cause and those who did it served the cause of Hindu community for they at least succeeded in settling the scores. Hindu militancy was justified by many in the light of the new interpretation of Gita by Bal Gangadhar Tilak stating that it justified the retributive justice. The recent alleged blasts by Hindu rightist organizations were not the handiwork of a few people. There were several others who may not be directly involved but they certainly knew the inclination of the core group. Their call to arms was seen by several as a result of backlash to Jihadi terror. The third factor may be the involvement of foreign agents inimical to India who in order to harm the country and create chaos in the people utilize misguided Muslims, Hindus, Christians and others for terrorist purposes to create division between majority and minority communities on religious or sectarian lines to achieve their ulterior motives. Everybody knows that the strength of any nation lies in the unity of its people. If the unity of any country is shattered the nation becomes susceptible to fifth columnists who generally target the safety and the security of the country. Communalism and sectarianism are contagious in nature. The minority communalism gives birth to the majority communalism and vice versa. They thrive upon each other. Minority communities should desist from communal approach for their communalism encourages majority communalism and compared to their communalism the communalism of majority is more severe and dangerous. It can cause uncalculated harm because the majority community is favourably situated compared to the minority community in all respects. In the same way, the majority community too should not push the minorities back to the wall for a constrained minority too can snatch the sleep of many. Besides, since the minority communities are the integral part of the society, it becomes difficult for any nation to fight with its own people. The involvement of some of the active Muslim, Hindu, Christian and Sikh youths and tribal and depressed segments from the majority and minority communities could be the result of the enemies of India with a view to create division between various segments of the society and weaken the country. The fourth cause is the outburst of anger among youths against the system. We see that so long as the old generation of Muslims was active Muslim or Islamic terrorism in India was absent. Terrorism among Muslim youths increased when the new generation of Muslims especially those who were born in free India came on the scene. When Muslim youths despite being born in free India found themselves constrained in comparison to their counterparts practically in every field, their anger and frustration increased day by day. They observed that their Hindu brothers were mostly better off economically and materially. They had special privileges in several segments due to reservation policy and other favourable factors supporting them but similar concessions and facilities were not available to most of them. Since they were not responsible for the partition of the country, they had no guilt conscience. They did not relish any kind of discrimination against them. In their struggle for equality of opportunity their younger Hindu brothers too were with them for they too could not swallow any kind of discrimination being practiced against their Muslim brothers. The young generation of Muslims struggled for their rights. However, when anything untoward happened to them which targeted them as Muslims despite their being loyal to the country, they felt shocked for they could not reconcile as to why it was happening merely to them. This frustration sometimes took the shape of agitations and violence and sometimes they got themselves involved even in the terrorist activities to vent their anger and disgust. The same is true to those Hindu youths who come from villages or depressed localities from the cities and who have poor background. When they find that their other brothers are favourably situated and they despite being educated, qualified and competent cannot achieve those privileges due to their weak background they get frustrated. Many of them being the first generation candidates find it difficult to compete with their well-situated counterparts. This boils their blood. Their tragedy is that they are rolling stones which gather no moss. They have left their villages and came in the cities from where they can neither go to the villages nor fallback to their ancestral professions. In urban centres, they are outcastes. Such a situation confuses them and disturbs their mental balance. Besides, wherever they go for jobs, they find the operation of the theory of the 'own and known' in the sense that first of all the own people such as the kith and kin, caste fellows and community fellows are appointed by the appointees and later on those are appointed who are known to them. These poor people stand nowhere since neither they have their own nor known. Admittedly, a large army of unemployed youths is standing on the periphery. Some of them have begun to involve in kidnapping, a few in highway robbery, many in crimes and there are a few who do not hesitate even in indulging in terrorist activities to vent their feelings. The state machinery should adopt a firm, tough and a decisive policy against the hard-core terrorists but those impressionable brains which are susceptible to exploitation by the vested interests due to their weak position and poor background should be handled cautiously and carefully. Their grievances should be heard with patience and perseverance and they should be brought within the mainstream as equal citizens with equitable privileges. The fifth cause is to fight for getting freedom or to avenge wrong done in the past. The Punjabi youths were incited by the enemies of India to have an independent Khalistan, the Kashmiri youths have been prompted for the idea of azadi or freedom for Kashmiris. In the same way, the ULFA and Nagas are trying to have a foot-hold for themselves in the shape of their own countries. The LTTE waged war for an independent Tamil Land and Palestinians are fighting for their freedom. Thus, we find that terrorist activities are going on in various countries in the name of freedom struggle. The sixth factor which is responsible for terrorism is the existence of drug and crime mafia and the big criminals who are involved in the smuggling and economic crimes. They try to create unrest in the country where they wish to fish in trouble water. They shake hands with criminals and anti-social elements and finance them in their ventures in order to promote their business. We know that most of the terrorist activities are carried by those who are the drug and arms smugglers and flesh traders. The terrorists in many countries are financed by various hawala transactions by the world mafia only. Most of the terrorism around India is being carried out by drug mafia operating from the soil of some of the neighbouring countries. The seventh factor which leads to terrorism is the zeal, among some of the fanatics to spread their own religion in various parts of the world. There are various segments in the society who consider their religion as the most ideal one and treat other religions as inferior and they want others to accept their religion in order to get contentment in this world and salvation hereafter. In their religious zeal, they propagate their jihadi philosophy by brainwashing and training those youths who are susceptible to their ideas. In this type of terrorist activities many intelligent, rich and professionals of various religions are involved who have special affinity with their belief systems. The eighth alternative is one which is adopted by enemy countries as a means to fight the proxy war. It has been observed that many countries which are at log head with each other use terrorism as a means of proxy war. They send their soldiers or trained personnel in the enemy country to spread terror and devastation. They do not mind in smuggling drugs and fake currencies and weapons to harm their adversaries. The ninth cause generally lead to the state terrorism. The state terrorism too is acquiring prominence these days. Many countries of the world have controlled terrorism by using terrorism as their decisive and firm weapon. Sri Lanka has subdued the members of the LTTE by using disproportionate force and USA and Britain have immobilized Al-Qaeda in Iraq and Afghanistan by using extreme type of terror tactics. What we need is a clear, firm and decisive policy towards terrorism purely in the interest of the nation and the Indian masses.

The Economic Unrest Leads to Frustration and Radicalism

It is an admitted fact that poverty anywhere is a danger everywhere. Those countries which do not aim at regional balances, sectoral equalities and justice to all sections of society usually face the ire of the people. We have been observing this phenomena operating in Middle East and the surrounding countries. India should be cautious and adjust its planning process in such a way that the masses are not sacrificed at the cost of few privileged people. If we look towards the Indian scene we find that we have made enough progress during the last sixty years. We have produced world-class engineers, doctors, scientists, politicians and journalists. We have built lakhs of km of new roads, complexes, dams and bridges and sent satellites and rockets in space. We have multiplied steel production by fifty times and cement production by almost twenty times. Besides, it is generally asserted that since the reforms of 1991 India has made tremendous progress. Our economy is growing at around 9 per cent a year, our hard currency reserves are at an all-time high. They have gone up from US $ 1.5 billion in 1991 to over US $ 220 billion in 2007. India's GDP has increased at an average of 6 per cent a year thus making India a fastest growing country in the world. The poverty level in the country too has fallen from over 36 per cent during 1990 to below 26 per cent in 2003. The IT sector grew from just US $ 100 million revenue in 1992 to more than US $ 40 billion in 2007. Our exports are growing at 20 to 25 per cent a year and they touched an all-time-high figure of US $ 79 billion in 2004. Global trade of India now accounts for nearly 25 per cent of the world's GDP and our stock markets are booming. The FDI in 2007 was nearly US $ 25 billion or five times what it was three years ago. We are adding 9 million phone lines a month and the Internet has grown to reach more than 450 million users. On the basis of purchasing power parity, India is the fourth largest economy in the world next to the USA, China and Japan. It is expected that India would exceed China by 2015, Britain by 2022 and Japan by 2032 to become the second biggest economy after USA. The number of billionaires in India is highest in Asia. By 2020, India would have a surplus of 47 million working people who would prove beneficial since USA will be short of 17 million people of working age, China 10 million, Japan 9 million, and Russia 6 million. There is new-found confidence everywhere and hundreds of new ventures are coming up in every city every day.

The author has immensely benefitted from the remarkable work of N.R. Narayan Murthy entitled *A Better India: A Better World* in which he has provided a useful statistics pertaining to Indian economy. If we now look we find that the poverty rate in India stands at 26 per cent as against 11 per cent in China. In absolute terms, 260 million poor are struggling in the country out of which 193 million live in rural areas and 67 million reside in cities. There are 300 million Indians who are not free from hunger, diseases, ignorance and illiteracy. Besides, 65 per cent Indian population depends upon agriculture and its share in the GDP is merely 22 per cent. This means that 650 million Indians add just ₹ 800,000 crore to the GDP every year or ₹ 13,200 per person per annum which comes to less than ₹ 40 a day. Besides, the situation of the rural areas is miserable for the growth rate of agriculture has gone down from 3.2 per cent in pre-1985 to about 1.9 per cent during the current decade. If we assume that our current growth rate of 8 per cent continues along with 2 per cent or 2.5 per cent agricultural growth for another decade, the rural population would remain where it is for the 2 per cent growth in rural population would swallow the 2 per cent growth in agricultural sector. In addition to this, the contribution of agriculture in GDP would also come down from 26 per cent to 16 per cent after ten years. Thus, in order to get the same per capita GDP from agriculture as the national per capita GDP, at the current 8 per cent growth rate by 2017, we will have to move 25 to 30 million job-seekers every year for ten years in either new jobs or better earning jobs which appear highly improbable. The other solution to absorb larger people is either to create low-tech manufacturing jobs or to invest in 100 per cent export-oriented units by inviting foreign participation on a larger scale which seem difficult in near future. N.R. Narayana Murthy has further remarked that nearly 250 to 300 million Indians are unemployed. The problem becomes more acute when we add 15 to 20 million new job seekers every year, 70 per cent of whom are illiterates aged between eighteen and twenty five. Out of these unemployed people, the country can absorb only 2 to 3 million people every year. Moreover, about 92 per cent jobs are in unorganized sector where the salaries and benefits are low.

The misfortune of majority of Indians is that their purchasing power is low. Rural per capita income is approximately ₹ 11,000 per year or a little over ₹ 30 a day which is barely sufficient to manage two meals a day. Unemployment in India is estimated at around 10 per cent. Twelve per cent of the country's 41 million unemployed have either graduate or post graduate degrees. We have to create jobs at the rate of 10 million a year over the next five years to sustain the present unemployment rate. The fact is that we have been creating less than 1 million new jobs every year. We rank 127th in the world on the Human Development Index. The labour productivity in India is merely 10 per cent of US level and the productivity of a Chinese worker is 30 to 180 per cent higher than that of an Indian worker. Over and above this, about 318 million population in the country does not have access to safe drinking water, more than 24% population in India does not have approach to tap water and the demand for clean water in the cities far exceeds the supply by an average of 30 per cent. It is regrettable that 630 million people are far from acceptable sanitation conditions, 25 per cent people live without sanitation facilities and 250 million Indians do not have access to basic medical care. Around 50 per cent of the population does not have access to essential drugs and about 190 out of 100,000 people are afflicted with malaria. Besides, India's 40% rural areas lack all-weather access roads, 28 per cent Indian villages lack primary school and 54 per cent villages are over 5 km away from the nearest health-care centre. We have 1.5 beds, 0.6 doctors, 0.08 nurses per 1000 people as against 6 to 8 beds, 12 doctors and 2.6 nurses in developing countries. The coverage of health insurance is only 2% and 80% expenses are paid by the individuals. Our adult illiteracy is at 39 per cent, over 25 million children are out of schools and 51 per cent children are undernourished. India spends 1.9 per cent of its GDP on higher education which is the lowest among nations with a GDP higher than US $ 500 billion. India produces PhDs to the extent of one-tenth the size of US pool. India's annual output of PhDs in the Computer Science area is around 25 compared to 88 in the USA and 2,500 in China. About 10 per cent of Indian students with degrees in humanities and 25 per cent in engineering are globally competitive. India has only two universities in the top list of 500 while Japan had thirty four, China eighteen, South Korea seven and Brazil four.

The gap between rural people and urban people had widened as urban economy grew at an average of 7.3 per cent over the last decade compared to 1.9 per cent growth in rural economy. It is expected that by 2015 the population of India's major cities would increase by an average of 25 per cent and by 2030 India would be 72 per cent urbanized. There would be a need of 3.6 million housing units in urban areas every year. The housing shortage in India's towns and cities is to the extent of 22 million when the fact is that about 22 per cent of India's urban population lives in slums and by 2030 about 35 per cent urban population would be forced to live in slums. Likewise, the growth of India's population would require 66,000 new primary schools and 3000 health centres every year. There is tremendous traffic congestion in India's cities which has cut road transport efficiency by 50 per cent as India's vehicle population has increased a hundred-fold from 0.3 million in 1960 to 30 million in 2004, the road network increased merely to just eight times from 0.4 million km to 3.3 million km. Since by 2050 nearly 26 per cent population would retire, the burden of ageing population would increase upon the economy of the country. Merely to provide food we would be needing increase in food production to the tune of 3 per cent per annum. These indicators show that the future is not as bright as it is painted.

We know that the Universal Declaration of Human Rights states that "Everyone has the right to a standard for the health and well-being of himself and his family, including food, clothing, housing and medical care, and necessary social services, and the right to security in the event of unemployment, sickness, disability, widowhood, old age, or other lack of livelihood in circumstances beyond his control." Our planners too had conceived India free of hunger, diseases, ignorance and miseries. Today, we have political freedom but we are far from economic freedom in the sense of the freedom from hunger, diseases and illiteracy. We have failed to fulfill the dream of our Founder Father of wiping the tears from the eyes of every poor and downtrodden child. The main problem with India is that its economy is not in a position to provide the necessary doses of comforts and luxuries to its entire people. Those people who say that India is shining are in illusion for the growth and development that we observe in the country is deceptive. Indian markets are full of imported goods. Indians too feel proud and comfortable in buying imported goods from America, China and other European and Asian countries due to their qualities and prices. Since there is little demand for Indian goods compared to the imported goods, the Indian businessmen have resorted to trading rather than manufacturing. Compared to manufacturing which have several bottlenecks and problems from various segments, the trading is more comfortable and profitable. Indian businessmen have acquired franchise rights from the multinational companies and are dealing in the imported goods after assembling them in India. Thus, the manufacturing process in the country has been dented and country's manufacturers are facing problems in marketing their products.

This has resulted in the retrenchment of working force and the decline in the income of the people and their effective demand. The condition of agriculture is miserable. The electricity charges have been increased practically in all states, supply of electricity is inadequate, diesel prices have gone high, fertilizers are in short supplies, sowing and harvesting costs have become unbearable. It has become difficult for a marginal farmer to meet his two ends. The then Finance Minister of the country Shri P. Chidambaram confessed in the Parliament that country's 73 per cent population is earning twenty rupees per day. Most of the farmers and landless labourers and urban artisans and workers are below poverty line. The country has certainly made progress in some key sectors due to which a significant section of the middle and upper middle class of the country has benefited immensely. According to N.R. Narayana Murthy, the Green Revolution started by Dr. M.S. Swaminathan in 1965 benefitted 400 to 500 million Indians. The White Revolution initiated by Dr. Verghese Kurien helped millions of children who were undernourished. The Economic Reform of 1991 pioneered by P.V. Narasimha Rao, Dr. Manmohan Singh, P. Chidambaram and Dr. Montek Singh Ahluwalia created a healthy climate in the country for the growth and development of the private sector as well as the entry of foreign participants in the Indian economy. Besides, the emergence of world class media and the journalists of world fame like Barkha Dutt, Shekar Gupta, Sucheta Dalal, N. Ram and Rajdeep Sardesai and many others provided grace to the Indian democracy. Likewise, the Telcom Revolution designed by Sam Pitroda linked people and villages, Yash Pal's SITE provided television to millions of people in the cities and the villages, Dr. Homi Bhabha innovated nuclear science research programme and N. Vittal's software technology and the related programmes led to the foundation of the IT industry in the country. Consequently, we find that a specific sector of the Indian economy is flourishing. For instance, the sale of mobile phones has given boost to the market. Besides, practically every household has a mobile phone and each one is spending three to four hundred rupees every month. This huge income is supporting the urban middle and upper classes.

Likewise, the computer sector too has made much progress. Every office and practically every educated middle class has purchased a computer or a laptop, the software and hardware of which are sustaining the upper and middle urban class. In addition to this, in every town private educational centres have been opened which are minting money. Hardly, there is any urban centre left where there is no provision for teaching of the MBA, MCA, B.Ed, BBA, BCA and dental and engineering and medical courses. The teaching and research provided in most of the private institutions is below standard. Most of these centres have been started on business principles by business class to mint money where quality of the faculty is very poor and inadequate and where there are no infrastructural facilities for imparting proper education. Mostly, the ignorant people from the poor and educationally backward classes and minorities who do not know about the consequences of joining a third grade institution generally join these institutions and they repent after getting degrees from such institutions for they are mostly rejected in the job markets. In addition to it, several ignorant people join these institutions under the impression that just by getting degrees in management or engineering or medical or computer sciences, they would be able to get good jobs. These institutions are also surviving due to the fact that there are many people who are already in their business and they need no employment. They simply want degrees to decorate their names without bothering about the quality of education. Besides, there are many rich and spoiled children who join such institutions just to pass their time and enjoy the life of the colleges and universities without bothering about divisions and degrees. There are, however, a few bright students who join these institutions because they fail to get admissions in reputed institutions. They are confident that by sheer hard work they would be able to carve out a good future for themselves. Similarly, there are many people who are running nursing homes or carrying on their private practices in healthcare or legal sphere or similar business, professions and vocations. They send their children to these institutions merely to get degrees so that legally they may continue their ancestral business. Over and above this, there are many people from among the SCs/STs and backward castes and important government functionaries who know that if their children have the necessary degrees, they could be absorbed due to reservation provided to them or due to their influence in government circle. It is because of these factors that many inefficient and incompetent and third grade institutions are surviving in the country despite their practically no contribution in the field of education. As against this, there are certain rich and influential people who are opening world class institutions to cater to the needs of the rich and the powerful class. They have taken franchise from top class institutes of world fame whose product can be sold easily in the world market at very high premium. However, such institutes are meant for the haves and elites only as the poor and backwards cannot think of sending their wards in these institutes due to high fee structure. In the same way, the coaching institutes too are the source of money. These centres are attracting the majority of the students of the established universities for in most of the mediocre or below mediocre universities the teaching standards have fallen. Many of the unscrupulous and irresponsible teachers take less interest in teaching. Mostly, they have either started their own coaching centres or teach at some of these centres to improve their economic standards. In medical colleges too there is no dearth of teachers who despite getting non-practicing allowances have started their own clinics or teach at private medical colleges as part time teachers. The privatization of education has made education a lucrative business in which the capitalists, politicians and influential people have entered and they are using private universities, colleges and the institutes as firms and private limited companies with the sole aim of earning profits. They adopt all business promotional principles ethical or non-ethical to promote their business with scant regards to ideals of education. Likewise, the nursing homes are earning huge money for government hospitals have failed and the masses are bound to revert to them and this money too is going in the hands of urban middle and upper classes. Similarly, the advocates of High Courts, Supreme Courts and legal luminaries in the district and lower courts and the law firms too have minted money due to economic offences. Besides this, the manner in which the salaries of government officials have been increased have made the middle income group comfortable. It is irony of fate that when the worker on the lower ladder in the country is earning just ₹ 1,000 per month, the government is paying a minimum amount of ₹ 10,000 to its lowest cadre along with several other benefits. If he is retrenched he cannot earn more than ₹ 1,000. In the same way, the opportunity cost of other employees whom the government is paying between ₹ 10,000 to ₹ 90,000 is far less. Since the governments at the Centre and States have become weak due to coalition formula or lack of required strength, the bureaucracy which is a permanent agency has taken the advantage of the situation with disastrous consequences to the economy of the country. Moreover, the development money which is supposed to be spent on the development projects through the representatives of the public and government officials is also helping the middle class to become richer for hardly a fraction or 16 per cent of the total is reaching to the grass-root level. Similarly, the governments are dolling out huge amount of money in the shape of social and unemployment schemes which is also going in the pockets of the middle and upper classes. Ironically, the money so dolled out is making the rural generation docile and lethargic. They do not want to earn money by hard work but try to depend upon such easy money. They are indulging in alcohol and gambling. Besides, the Indian economy is being sustained by entertainment industry, media and the remittances which the NRI's are sending to their families. The actors and actresses in film industry and the celebrities in advertising sector charge crores of rupees for appearing on television screens. The owners of fast foods, ready-made garments and children's toys and fashion houses, massage centres, and owners of hotel industry are multiplying money. Likewise, the television serials and media reporting have opened avenues for the urban middle class to become rich. One can count several crorepatis in cities like Delhi, Mumbai, Chennai, Kolkata, Bangalore, Hyderabad and many state capitals whereas the majority of villagers, farmers, and artisans who are living along with them are starving. In addition to it, a smaller section of the farming community which is living near the cosmopolitan cities too has become richer for their agricultural lands have been sold at exorbitant rates. The cumulative impact of the money so generated is that a significant section of the upper class and the middle class in urban areas is buying cars, constructing houses, purchasing consumer durables, going on holiday tours, acquiring gold, shares in blue chip companies which is giving boost to the economy in the shape of growth of iron and steel and cement industries, branded clothes, food joints and the employment to various technical and non-technical workers in service sector and others. Admittedly, a country like India cannot survive merely on the development of a few sectors. It needs multidimensional growth without which one day it would face hurdles due to the lack of effective demand. A mighty country like India needs a sound and solid foundation to bear the load of its super structure. It cannot survive on the weak shoulders of the masses or on the strong might of a few rich and influential persons or on the strength of the corrupt and inefficient government officials or on the power of the professionals who are merely interested in earning money. It needs dedicated, committed and sincere and honest masses with reasonable level of prosperity which is not there. It is a fact that many Indian businessmen are moving out of the country and capturing foreign markets in the shape of opening multinational Indian companies but their benefits too are accruing to a select few. History testifies that many super powers came down when their supporting structure became weak. Indian economy would survive due to subsistence agriculture as well as the employment in construction, cement, iron, steel and service sector and doles provided by the government to the rural and urban poor. When the income of majority of Indians would dwindle due to lack of manufacturing activities in the country and worsening condition of Indian agricultural sector, the demand for imported goods too would decline and the multinational companies which have provided franchise to the Indian businessmen would run away from the country with hard cash and would leave unsold goods at the disposal of the Indian traders. The foreign investors have invested their money mostly in such areas where they may move out in case of emergency without any substantial loss to their stock. They have entered in food sector, cloth segment, consumer durables, soft drinks and luxury items which can be manufactured using Indian labour, raw material and the same can also be sold to Indians in their own markets. Their risk is minimum. They would move out *en masse* as happened in Malaysia, Indonesia and Thailand and their neighbouring countries. At that juncture, it would be difficult for Indian industries to pick up a fresh production process after having faced the closure of many indigenous industries for a considerable period of time. Admittedly, a situation in which masses remain in poverty and a significant section of the Indian middle class, upper middle class and the upper class prospers would not auger well with the health of the country. It would create social, economic and political problems with adverse impact upon the growth and development of the country. There is a need of inclusive development in which each section of the society may be benefited. The purely capitalistic model in a country like India is not suitable. It suits only those countries where there live equals or where the haves have enough funds to pay in the form of taxes to the government out of which the have-nots may be supported through various social security measures. India is inhabited by the societies which have geological layers. They cannot compete with each other. The multi-dimensional poverty index reveals that there are 81.4% poor among Scheduled Tribes, 65.8% in Scheduled Castes, 58.3% in Other Backward Castes and 33.33% in General category. By the new measure, just eight states—Bihar, Chattisgarh, Jharkhand, Madhya Pradesh, Orissa, Rajasthan and West Bengal have more poor people, at 421 million, than the 26 poor poorest African countries combined, at 410 million. India does not have merely the poor quality of life as reflected in its poor human development index, it has also a poor quality of death. It fares badly as progress on providing end-of-life care despite its health-care system as it finished at the bottom of the list, which includes 30 OECD nations and 10 developing countries. Indebtedness is growing in the country and each child born in

Uttar Pradesh comes with a burden of ₹ 10,000. Uttar Pradesh alone is presently indebted to the extent of ₹ 1,80,999 crores which works out to be 45% of state's gross domestic product. The annual interest repayment on this loan comes out to be around 16,000 crores which would be sufficient to take below poverty level families out of poverty and bring them to their per capita income equal to that of state's average of ₹ 18,710 per year. Besides, it is a big country where the masses cannot be supported by the tax collections of Indian companies or direct and indirect taxes paid by the affluent sections of the society. Capitalism is based on the rule of jungle where there is competition for the survival and those survive who are fit and those perish who are weak and downtrodden. The keen competition in the country has taken heavy toll. The prices of almost all the commodities have reached international level but income levels are nowhere near the world level. The medicines which were cheapest in the country prior to globalization, their prices are now rising abnormally and poor people and the lower middle class find it difficult to afford them. The prices of vegetables, meat, eggs, flour and other commodities of daily use are sky rocketing. Government hospitals are in mess and people find it cumbersome to pay the heavy bill of private nursing homes. There is widespread corruption even on highest positions. The law and order position is not satisfactory and divisive forces have been raising their heads everywhere. Besides, there is a pressure on the government to withdraw subsidies from agricultural sectors and from those areas where poor and lower middle sections get benefit. It is fallacious to expect that the poor farmers and the ill-equipped traders of India with all their drawbacks would compete with their counterparts in the technologically developed countries of the world. The economic indicators suggest that the terms of trade in a free economy are always against the weak nations. Likewise, in the internal transactional analysis, the upper and the middle classes gain at the cost of the lower middle and poor classes. Just as the rule of jungle creates class structure dominated by the lion at the top and followed in lower order by others according to their power structures, similarly the capitalist system too creates class structures or varnas in the society. We find that the regional and inter-class and inter-personal inequalities are fast increasing after the globalization in the country. Over and above this, the jerks which the system provides in the form of trade cycles and recessions and booms cause immense harm to the weak and downtrodden. The country should think of reverting to mixed economy because it insulates the poor and weak against the vagaries of the exigencies. However, the public sector undertakings should not be used as the personal jagirs of the government officials and the politicians as they were used in India. They must run on business principles and should be managed by professional and technocrats rather than autocrats. The government should give more importance to the development of agricultural and rural areas and should think of the development of 73 per cent people who are earning merely ₹ 20 per day. The poor find it difficult to travel in the congested trains. They cannot get reservation for the reservations are closed ahead of months. There is no place for them on platforms. They sleep on the grounds while waiting for trains. Buses are over crowded. Government hospitals are without qualified doctors and adequate medicines. Government schools have no teachers and no class rooms. Roads are broken and bumpy. Water is polluted and electricity is conspicuous by absence. Housing, health care, social security are beyond their reach. Unemployment, under employment and the disguised employment are rampant. Poor have no place to sit in the vicinity of the law courts. Law cases have been lingering for years. There is none to look after them in government offices, cultural centres and power gallery. India is shining to the extent of New Delhi, certain posh areas of state capitals and the isolated pockets in the important cities of the country. The gentry in these areas is found purchasing costly goods in malls, enjoying in food joints, relishing at the entertainment centres and building mighty mansions and riding in luxury cars. However, the moment we leave New Delhi, the rikshas, carts and tongas of old Delhi, the crowd of Dadri, the poverty of Sikandrabad and the depressed and miserable faces of people everywhere convince us that all is not well with the mighty India.

Really, the condition of that India which is not shining is not good. Thousands of farmers are committing suicides every year due to illness, bankruptcy and poverty. Nearly 17,060 farmers committed suicides in 2006, 16632 in 2007 and 16196 in 2008. Maharashtra has been a worst state in matters of farmers' suicides over the years. The other states with a history of large number of farmer suicides are Andhra Pradesh, Chattisgarh, and Madhya Pradesh. Corruption has taken heavy toll. Even fingers of mistrust are being raised against many of the Chief Justices of the Supreme Court, High Court judges, Military Generals, Chief Ministers, Governors, Ministers and high government officials. The Indian society in the words of some of the Supreme Court judges has become sick in the sense that no work is done in government offices without greasing the palms and people are burning brides for the sake of dowry. Many of them consider illegal gratification or laxmi earned by graft and bribe as the pious gift of nature irrespective of its source though they consider it as illegal for it has been declared so by the state but not immoral. Besides, whenever any financial or administrative or moral scandal is exposed by the media or any significant section of the society, it is projected on national television channels and in print media as something horrible, anti-social, anti-national and unprecedented. Demonstrations are held, Assemblies and the Parliament are blocked and finally commissions or committees are appointed. The television dramas last for few days and sooner new issues come on the scene and the old ones are forgotten. The commissions and committees continue for years, reports come which are either shelved or placed before appropriate bodies and the end result is nil. Those who gamble with astronomical sum have better chances to get clean chit due to their strong paying capacity but the minor officials involved in the illegal gratifications worth a few hundred or a few thousand of rupees are punished as their capacity is limited. As a consequence of all these bungling, the corruption is increasing in the country day by day with vigour and speed. There are two parallel Indias, one of the rich, progressive and dynamic Indians which is vibrant, full of hope, excitement and confidence. It is marked with many storey abodes several meters above the sea level dominating the skylines of the cities and resembling the Taj Mahal of the 21st century with exquisite ball rooms, lush green terrace gardens, pearl floors, marble canopies, lotus pools, high speed elevators manned by gracious attendants and decorated by the dazzling chandeliers, gigantic stairways, beautiful sculptures as well as ornamented villas, fairy boats, luxury islands and comfort zones tucked away in exotic destinations with retinue of servants and army of luxury cars costing billions of rupees, and the other is that of the poor which is depressing, miserable and pitiable. Unfortunately, Muslims are most sufferer for most of them fall in the category of lower middle, poor and the poorest and for many it is difficult even to meet their two ends. They are living in villages and in congested areas and are the victims of poverty, diseases, ignorance and neglect which does not auger well for the country.

Need for a Reverse Village-Oriented Growth Model to Contain Public Ire

The socio-economic condition of India as depicted above reveals that the country is standing at the crossroad. If the interest of the masses is not taken into account in the process of growth and development, country is bound to suffer. By following urban-oriented growth model, the planners have already commited a blunder. There is a need to reverse the process. It is an admitted fact that from day one the planners faltered in matters of their priorities pertaining to planning process. We developed an urban-oriented growth model based on the models of Western countries which moved people and resources from villages and rural sector to cities and urban areas and not vice versa. We thought of the short run conveniences for the infrastructure was available in urban areas only. In doing this we benefited the 25 per cent urbanites and neglected the interest of the 75 per cent people living in rural areas. This one-sided migration is taking heavy toll. It is expected that within next twenty years nearly 60 per cent population of the country would be living in the cities. We concentrated all the departments of the Central Government and State Governments in Delhi and in state capitals as a consequence of which major development took place within these areas. People, products and resources from various parts of the country reached Delhi and the state capitals which helped in the development of the residents of these areas at the cost of other segments of the society. We should have established only the core and important offices of the Central Government in Delhi and all other offices in various state capitals so that people from different parts of India could move to different state capitals for their day-to-day work. Under the present scenario, if a person has to do something with any matter which falls within the purview of Central Government, he has to move from Kolkata to Delhi, Mumbai to Delhi, Kerala to Delhi and Assam to Delhi while the people of Delhi never visit Kolkata, Mumbai, Kerala and Assam for their official purposes. This one-way flow of wealth and resources proved costly to the entire economy and caused inconveniences to the people of rest of the country and enriched people and areas around Delhi at the cost of other people and regions. In the same way, we concentrated most of the offices of the states in the state capitals rather than at district levels. We should have kept only the core offices at the level of the state capitals and remaining departments should have been disbursed among the districts of the states. This would have facilitated the movement of the people of the state between different districts and helped in the balanced growth of the state. Likewise, we established major offices of the State and Central Governments at the zonal and district levels rather than the towns and villages which compelled people from villages and towns to move to these areas which led to their growth and development. We should have planted the important offices of the states at taluka, tehsil and village levels. This would have led to two-way traffic between cities and tehsils and villages resulting in the simultaneous development of both the sectors. It is quite strange that nobody wants to go to the rural areas. Even rural offices, panchayat offices, revenue offices, agricultural offices, agro-industries offices and all offices pertaining to agriculture and villages have been established in the cities rather than in villages. Consequently, the cities and urban areas attracted the entire resources for development and the villages became barren and neglected. Over a period of time, the situation deteriorated so much in the villages due to lawlessness, lack of educational, health and employment opportunities that people started migrating from villages to the cities because the cities had the required facilities which were absent in villages. India needs a decentralized economic model in which the focus of development must be the urban and rural poor who constitute more than 80 per cent population of the country. The process of growth should be gradually reversed. Initially, model villages with educational, health care and recreational facilities should be built near the important cities. There should be an adequate police force and the backing of a few important government offices together with a fine infrastructure including better roads, stable electric supply, clean water and beautiful layout. If such model are planned, the village people would not like to move from such villages and would prefer to stay in their own dwellings. Besides, these villages would also prompt the city dwellers to go to such villages for fresh village food and healthy climate. Just as new colonies are being built away from the congested old areas of cities well equipped with all modern facilities similarly the model villages too can be built on modern lines away from the old cities or old villages. Such villages should be connected with cities through better transport facilities and means of communications. They should have a few Central and State Government offices so that the city people also may go there and thus the two-way traffic may develop between villages and cities. Once the reverse process of development starts, there would be no end to it. A cluster of beautiful villages would be seen throughout the length and breadth of the country. This would not only solve the housing and other problems pertaining to slums, congestion, law and order but would also open two-way traffic between villages and cities and restore the terms of trade between rural and urban areas in the long run without any tint of exploitation of any segment of the society.

New Cultural Priorities for Enlightenment

Since the beginning of the Planning Era, India emphasized on material parameters such as the growth of GDP, per capita income, regional balance and reduction in inequalities, etc. and ignored the other parameters for health, housing, family planning, social security and human welfare. It was at a very late stage that the indicators affecting human welfare began to be taken into consideration. Much progress took place around these parameters but our misfortune is that several Indians became educated, wealthy and prosperous but they cared least for the ethical and moral aspects of their respective professions, vocations, trades and business establishment. Our school, college and university going children mostly lost the penetration of their culture, ethos and morality and many of them adopted the perverted ways of Western living causing immense harm to their balanced development. The peculiarity of India is that it is a country with a rich heritage of nearly 5000 years with a very sound value system for cordial family life, better neighbourly relations, healthy kinship, respect for the elders, love for the younger, concern for the downtrodden and enlightened attitude towards dissenting opinions, inclination towards harmonious relation, peaceful co-existence and flavour for truth, justice, equity and good conscience. Our people used to give more importance to self respect, honour and human dignity. They considered it as martyrdom for dying for the protection of the women, children and aged. They relished sacrificing their lives for good cause and it was within their blood to preach non-violence, good moral conducts and spiritual way of life. It is an irony of fate that with the material advancement, there appears to be moral decay in the country. Our children are abandoning our age old value system influenced by the value system of those materially advanced countries which had practically no sound value system. Our younger generation is blindly running after material advancement ignoring their past heritage with the result that cracks have begun to appear in family system, divorce rate has increased and parents' respect is at the stake. We would not like to see around us rich families with mighty mansions, luxury cars, retinue of servants and modern gadgets but with no regard for parents, no love for children and no concern for healthy customs and dynamic traditions. Nobody would like to live with rich, prosperous and wealthy neighbours who do not come to the rescue of their neigbours when they are in peril. Hardly anyone would admire the young, healthy and vigourous youths silently watching the honour of a virgin shattered in the broad day light. There would be rarely a sensible man appreciating corrupt people on high positions. Alas, all this has started happening in the country and practically all of us are silently watching our own decay. Instead of fighting the corrupt practices, we are making compromises and giving credence to them. The misfortune in India is that we want to change people by bringing physical and material change and forgot that the material change simply brings change in material circumstances. For deeper changes we need mental revolution and the revolution in the conscience of the people. After independence we have practically done nothing to bring changes in those social, cultural and aesthetic values which are the backbone of our society and which are presently out of tune with modern times. Our children admire the popular celebrities representing entertainment sector, sports segment and media and the well to do section of the society. They follow them in their day-to-day life. They are their ideals. However, they know very little about the reputed scientists, famous innovators, dynamic technocrats, dedicated bureaucrats and eminent social figures simply because their priorities are lopsided. Our misfortune is that we feel that the modern education would set things right. We forget that the education system per se is neither good nor bad. It is not necessary that educated people are always good. Most of the wars were fought by the educated people and the destructive weapons have been invented by the educated lot. Modern economic and big crimes are being committed by the so-called educated people. Education is a double-edged weapon. It has to be blended with moral and spiritual contents so that it may prove effective. The need of the hour is that within our planning priorities we should include the preservation and the enhancement of the value system, protection of the national heritage and revival of our healthy social, cultural, religious, moral and spiritual systems. We should set targets for such values and earmark funds for the development of such institutions and agencies which may strengthen our cultural, spiritual and pluralistic heritage. The sooner we do the better it is.

Muslims Benefitted Least from India Shining

Ironically, most of the Indian Muslims are mainly the artisans, urban workers, landless labourers, petty shopkeepers or farmers. Very few of them are in industry, trade and commerce. They have been marginally benefited through trickle effect from the massive planning of the country and the new creation of incomes in the country since their presence in government sectors, Parliaments and State Assemblies, computer segments, education industry, health care and diagnostic fields, communication channels and NRI's is negligible. If at all they have gained a little they have gained in the service sector where many of them work as technicians or in the small scale industry where they are toiling as artisans. It is the tragedy of the Muslims world over that they remained mostly traders and abhorred manufacturing because of the fear of acquiring money on interest which was strictly prohibited by Islam. The Christians also did not allow usury but the Protestants allowed it so also did the Jews despite the fact that they too were asked not to take and give interest. It is a fact that Muslims were pioneers when the process of development was confined to artisanship. The important world centres testify their mastery in craftsmanship, their architectural marvels speak volumes of their dexterity and expertise and wherever the wheel of growth had moved it was due to their artisanship. Almost all the cities of India which flourished prior to industrial revolution did so due to artisanship of Muslims. Till-date they are renowned for their arts and crafts. However, when industrial revolution knocked at the doors of Muslims they did not utilize the God given opportunities and missed the bus. They could directly jump from their artisanship to the field of manufacturing and mass production. The only factor that deterred them was the taking and giving of interest which Islam strictly prohibited. Since interest was one of the most important ingredients of the industrial revolution because without taking money on interest large-scale production was not possible, Muslims resorted to trading only which made them backward. Not only this, since they could not participate in the process of manufacturing they could not produce better arms and ammunitions and thus lagged behind their enemies and were defeated on the battle fields in world wars due to their poor economic base, obsolete technologies and poor weapons though they were more brave than their enemies. Muslims failed miserably to develop interest-free Islamic banks as well as the mutual funds and they faltered hopelessly in utilizing the potentials of zakat or the tax collected for the poor and other charities for their benefits. Even today many devoted Muslims resort to trading only and avoid manufacturing due to the fear of involving them in the process of giving or taking of interest. Most of the Muslim countries also rely in trading and it is because of this reason that they could not produce deterrents and had to depend upon the mercy of others for their safety and security. Basically, Islamic economic system is based on risk-sharing, rightful earning and permissible spending, moderation, circulation of wealth, equitable distribution of resources and service to the weak and the well-being of the whole society, keeping this world and hereafter in mind and heralding the principles of truth, justice, piety and fair-play. Just as in an undiluted and pure capitalism the ownership of wealth and possessions lie in the hands of individuals, in absolute communism and complete socialism in the state and in mixed economy partly in the state and partly in the individuals. Similarly, according to the blue-print of the Holy Qur'an, the Islamic economic system is based on the principle of trusteeship according to which the ownership of everything lies with God. Man is merely a trustee of the God-given resources. He can use them as per the dictates of Lord as mentioned in Holy Qur'an or as specified by the Holy Prophet. There are marked guidelines for permissible, non-permissible and discretionary items. A man is free to earn, acquire, spend and consume as much as he likes within the permissible and discretionary items through rightful means and within the limits of moderation, piety and state regulations. He is strictly asked not to deal in interest of any kind, desist from hoarding and miserliness. He is duty-bound to pay zakat or poor-due, spend on charity and leave his wealth after death to be distributed amongst the rightful heirs according to the dictates of Lord. He is not permitted to earn from or spend on items like gambling, games of chance, liquor, intoxicants, prostitution, obscenity, lustful entertainments, and all those things which have been prohibited by Holy Qur'an and sayings of the Holy Prophet. Islam also discourages wasteful expenditure, show of wealth, vanity and abhors cheating, frauds, deceits and exploitation of all kinds. Actually, the objective of Islam is not to provide maximum material satisfaction to the individuals merely in this world but to provide maximum welfare and well-being both in this world and hereafter. The criterion of welfare and well-being in Islamic economic model is not confined to the material satisfaction only but it includes material, mental, moral and spiritual satisfaction. Thus, Islamic economic system is a comprehensive, exploitation-free, cooperative and welfare-oriented model which Muslims failed to deliver to the humanity. If they would have succeeded, the world would have accepted it willingly as it accepted the economic model given by Karl Marx and they would have been better off in this world as well as in the hereafter. Muslims also miserably failed to develop their own education system suiting to the modern conditions and the requirements of the Sharia. If they would have developed their own modern value and piety based education system, it would have benefitted them as well as the humanity at large. Though they have lost much, yet still there is enough time and space available for them to build their dynamic institutions for the betterment of Indian Muslims as well as their counterparts. If they accomplish the task within a meaningful time horizon, they can expect a better future for their posterity.

7

The Socio-Religious Structure of Muslim Community

It is an admitted fact that majority of Muslims in India are illiterate and poor. They are not homogeneous in nature but their heterogeneity is reflected in their professions, vocations, trades and behavior pattern. They are not governed by the political parties or socio-cultural organizations. Educated, enlightened and the meaningful Muslims find it difficult to convince them on issues pertaining to Muslims. They blindly follow their religious heads and whole-heartedly believe in what their maulanas and peers tell them and behave accordingly. For their day-to-day matters, family affairs and religious and other problems they approach them. Thus, the role of religious organizations in shaping the destiny of poor Muslims in India is remarkable. It is, therefore, imperative for us to know about the socio-religious structure of various sects of Muslims as well as the nature, pattern and the types of various religious organizations which are ruling the hearts and minds of poor Muslims with a view to see how far they are succeeding in their tasks. The majority community generally considers Muslims of India as a homogeneous lot but like Hindus they too are a heterogeneous group. There is bewildering diversity among Muslims. Their social habits, cultural traits, occupational patterns vary from class to class, from place to place and from region to region. They speak numerous dialects and languages and observe widespread regional customs and local rites. However, in matters of ideologies and values and social and cultural complexities, they are an integral part of a larger Islamic lot. Before the partition of India, the Muslim society too was descent-based and there were social stratifications and hierarchical ordering of social groups, endogamy and hereditary occupations among them. They too were the victims of caste system though they seemed to believe in casteless society. However, after partition of the country, they have become more or less similar in almost all aspects.

The Ashrafs, Ajlafs and Arzals

On the pattern of Hindu high castes, backward castes and Scheduled Castes and Scheduled Tribes, Muslims too had ashrafs, ajlafs and arzals. The ashrafs belonged to two categories: Firstly, those who traced their descent to foreign lands such as Arabia, Persia, Turkistan or Afghanistan and secondly those who traced their origin to the upper caste Hindus who were converted to Islam. In Uttar Pradesh, Bihar and West Bengal, Sayyids, Sheiks, Moghuls and Pathans associated them to foreign lands. As against this, in Kerala the Thangals, traced their descent to Holy Prophet's daughter, Arabs linked them to Arab men and local women and the Malabaris had lost their Arab lineage and followed matrilineal descent. In Andhra Pradesh, Sayyids, Sheiks, Pathans and Labbais claimed their foreign descent. In the second category came those ashrafs who were converted from high caste Hindus such as Raos, Kayam Khanis, Lal Khanis, Panwars, Bhattis and innumerable high caste converts across the country. The ajlafs means the unholy and the degraded middle caste converts whose professions were clean such as carpenters, artisans, painters, grazers, tanners, milkmen, jolahas or weavers, dhunias or cotton carders, telis or oil-crushers, kunjras or vegetable sellers, hajjams or barbers, darzis or tailors and so many others. The nao Muslims in Bihar, nasya in North Bengal, the pusalars and ossans in Kerala and dudekula or cotton cleaners, fakirs and budbudkis in Andhra Pradesh were also included in ajlafs. The arzals fell in the lowest category and they included the converts from the erstwhile untouchable castes such as scavengers, mehtars or sweepers, chamars or tanners, doms. Halalkhor, lalbegi, abdal and bediya. Admittedly after partition of the country many of the caste and class differences have been blurred. They are there but only in name sake. The so-called higher castes among Muslims during 2004-05 constituted 59% of total Muslim population followed by 39.2% Muslim OBCs, 0.8% Muslim SCs and 0.5% Muslim STs. Thus, we find that the caste profile of Muslims too is varied. Economically, the industrialists, merchants, traders, businessmen are comparatively better placed compared to the bulk of the poor who are peasants, landless labourers and self-employed lot. Religiously, one can observe Shia-Sunni conflicts, ceaseless doctrinal controversies among Deobandi and Barelwi schools and assimilation and absorption of various local customs and practices among the Muslim societies of Kashmir, Bengal, Rajasthan and south of Vindhyas. At many places, there is a fusion of Hindu and Muslim cultures.

The Segmentation of Various Castes

Prior to partition of the country, the various caste-groups among Hindus and Muslims were segmented into various areas, localities and mohallas representing different trades and the followers of different vocations and business were known by their respective professions such as tailors, carpenters, water carriers, oil crushers, potters, gardeners, blacksmiths, washer-men, cooks, cotton-spinners, butchers, weavers, masons, chamars, safai walas and the like. There were distinct and marked localities of these caste groups. There used to be even the separate mohallas or localities for the beggars or fakirs who were associated with different segments of the society. Likewise, there were the localities of the criminal tribes too which were situated outside the periphery of the city but near the police stations. The localities or mohallas of various castes and sub-castes were situated in the city according to their importance. Generally, the high ups of the society lived in the central portion of the city followed by the lower serving castes and the lowest groups used to live in the periphery and in the direction of wind depending upon the nature and gravity of their vocations and professions. For instance, the chamars and safai wallas lived at the extreme ends of the city where the direction of wind was not towards the main city. There were watertight compartments between various caste groups. Their customs, ethos, value systems, names, dress codes, eating habits and patterns of living were different from each other. The lower strata could not keep the names of higher ups and many segments could wear only brass and copper ornaments and not silver and gold. Silver and gold were worn by high ups and certain permitted sections from amongst the lower ones. In the same way, many of them could not build pakka houses. They had to live in kaccha houses only. Similarly, many sections could not send their children to schools. The marriages among various caste and class groups used to take place within those caste and class groups only. Even the mosques, grave-yards and charitable homes were known by the names of the community owning them. However, after partition and industrial development and new and dynamic changes and social and economic transformation of the country, many things have become the matter of the past. Since many professions have been replaced by modern machines, new techniques and innovative means, the castes and classes associated with those professions and vocations too have vanished. Besides, many professions and vocations have now been de-linked with castes. Even the people of higher castes are pursuing them due to high margin of profit. For instance, export of meat, the business of washing and dying, oil crushing, hotel business and restaurant business and so many others have been taken over by high castes due to their viability. Anyone who wants to become a carpenter or tailor or washerman can do so without being the member of the old professional groups. One can live in any locality, build any type of house, send the children to any school and can do what others do. Despite this, there are certain reservations at least in matters of social mingling and marriage customs. Mostly, people do not want to marry in the social group which was looked down yesterday. Such things are more marked and distinct in villages and small cities compared to the big cities. The big cities have become cosmopolitan. Nobody knows anything about others. Many dalits and the lowest castes from majority and minority communities have migrated to the big cities and they are working shoulder to shoulder as equals because they have hidden their identities from others. The urbanization has brought a tremendous change in bringing caste and class equalities in the country. If the process continues as it is, we would soon see that the caste distinctions or varna system would vanish and there would be economic varnas in place of caste varnas. We would find hardly any dalit or weaker caste fellow for being hard workers they would be absorbed in the industrial society. As the traditional professions and traditional arts are disappearing, the concerned people are moving to service sector and a new and cosmopolitan class is emerging. Many of us go to the hotels and restaurant and take our food but never ask the bearer or cook his caste. In all probability, he might be a fellow from the lowest caste which was considered untouchable till yesterday. These people are preferred by the owners since they are cheap, efficient and devoted compared to the hot-headed fellows of the higher caste. Among Muslims the two major caste segments such as butchers and weavers are surviving as Quraishis and Ansaris for these professions are in much demand even during our times. The rest of the professions have become cosmopolitan and interchangeable.

Cultural and Social Mobility Among Various Sections

After Mandal Commission, the backward sections from Muslim community too tried their best to create the boggy of backward Muslims but there were few takers of this ideology. During election times, the Quraishis and Ansaris have been generally found voting *en masse* wherever they are in majority and live in chunks but the rest of the Muslims usually vote depending upon their political affiliations or ideological segments to which they belong. It is because of this reason that all Muslims votes are seldom cast in favour of a particular party or group. Their fragmented votes cause more harm to them because if they combine together they can mark their presence on the political scene of the country. Efforts are now being made by Muslim OBCs to form a political party of their own. If it is done, it would be a new development among Muslims. Muslims have failed to extract any substantial concession from the government in their favour. By forming a viable secular, nationalistic and cosmopolitical party, they would be able to get their due by forcing the government to take affirmative actions in their favour. The dalits are merely 25% of the total population of the country but they have carved out their place in the polity of the country but Muslims are merely the rolling stones which gather no moss. Muslims do unite but in the wake of danger to their religion, culture and identity or when anything untoward is said or done against their religious leaders, belief system and cultural and religious practices. When they got angry *en masse* from Congress for not checking the demolition of Babri Masjid, they did not vote the party wherever they were in a position to cause harm to the party. Presently, they are against BJP for they feel that it is an anti-Islam, anti-Muslim and anti-Islamic country party having the negative policies. The party wants to build Ram Mandir on the place of Babri Masjid, it is against their Personal Law and it wants to destroy their culture and religious identities. One of its constituents had caused Gujarat massacre and the party always takes a line which is invariably against the interests of Muslims such as constructing Hajj Houses, giving Hajj subsidies and providing them reservations. Thus, they *en bloc* try to defeat the party without consulting anybody. It has been seen that minorities are strongly united in comparison to majority community for they always pass under fear psychosis. Any move of the majority community which they perceive to be detrimental to their religion, culture or identity compels them to unite. Many a time several issues such as hijabs or coverings of the heads if left alone would have been solved automatically in the long run but the Muslim girls became more particular and adamant about the veil and clinched it to their hearts simply because the majority community criticized their hijabs and strived to abolish them. The general rule is that smaller the minority, the strongly united it is and the larger the minority, the loosely united it is. Actually, there is an inverse relationship between the size of the minority and its power to unite. Muslims in India are more united compared to Hindus of India and Shias are strongly united in comparison to Sunnis. Likewise, amongst the sects of Shias, the Khojas are more strongly united in contrast to general Shias. The redeeming feature is that in post-partition period the Sunnis and Shias are more united now than they were previously. The constructive role played by saint, philosopher and reformer Imam Ayatollah Khomeini and the role played by adversaries of Islam and Islam blaming forces world over brought both the sects of Muslims nearer to each other. The pre-partition segmentation and isolation between the two communities is no more in Muslim society. Inter-caste marriages between various Sunni-Shia segments of Muslims are very common. There is social and culture mobility across various sections of the society. Shia, Sunni, Ansari, Siddiqui, Quraishi, Farooqui, Sayyed and Pathan marriages are very common. For the last few years, an un-Islamic trend too has been observed among certain so-called liberal sections of Muslim society where the Muslim girls have either married a Hindu boy or a Hindu boy has married a Muslim girl. This is certainly not liked and approved by a large section of Muslim and Hindu society. Mostly, it has happened in such places where the Muslim parents live either among the predominantly majority sector and have their day-to-day or professional dealings with majority community or where the boy and girl study together or work together or have the opportunities of interacting together. When this type of situation happens many parents on both the sides do not relish it but yield due to compulsions of the situation for invariably they are convinced that stopping their children at that stage would either lead to their suicides or compel them to run away from the house without the permission of the parents. The community fellows from both the communities do not appreciate the actions of the boys and girls as well as those of parents on both sides. Mostly, such marriages fail for the power of love and lust never lasts too long and soon comes a time when negatives of both the parties overshadow their positives and cracks begin to appear openly and violently. Nevertheless, there are certain marriages which are successfully surviving. However, as old age approaches, religion begins to show its colour and cracks begin to appear in the minds and the souls of the couples but by that time it had become too late. Besides, the children always remain in dilemma for they can neither adopt the religion of father nor mother for they love their father and mother equally. This trend is very common in the celebrities especially in the entertainment and cultural sector. Many actors, film heroes, superstars have married Hindu girls and many Muslim actresses, heroines and top stars have married Hindu boys and most of such marriages are flourishing because the atmosphere of film industry is congenial for such transactions. It is believed that many Muslim gentlemen have occupied higher positions in judiciary, army, legislature and bureaucracy due to their caliber but it is generally said that the contributory factor was their Hindu wives. In the good olden days, there was a practice amongst Muslim actors and actresses to keep Hindu names instead of the original Muslim names perhaps to avoid discrimination or seek attention of the audiences or just for fun sake. Many prominent Muslim actors and actresses were known by their Hindu names than their original Muslim names such as Dilip Kumar, Madhu Bala and Meena Kumari, etc. However, this practice is seldom followed by new Muslim actors in the Bollywood. There was a time just after the partition of the country when a few liberal Muslims had abandoned their Muslim names and had adopted Hindu names due to the reasons best known to them but that practice too is no more prevalent now, though we hear some composite names half Muslim and half Hindus here and there. Many innovative and liberal parents keep common names for their children such as for boys Shan, Aman, Iqbal and Sameer and for girls Seema, Neelam, Neha and Aisha to avoid discrimination or with the objective in mind that they may be pronounced easily by all segments of the society or because of their special likings for such names. Just as some Muslims keep complex Arabic and Persian names for their houses, villas and bungalows such as Bab-e-Rehmat and Aiwane Masarrat similarly, some of them keep Hindi and Sanskrit names such as Kalpana, Manmandir and Kuteer. Likewise, the Hindus also keep Muslim names for their villas and bungalows such as Afsana, Tarana and Jannat.

The heterogeneity of Indian Muslims is reflected in every sector such as business, professions, vocations, trade, dress code, languages and eating habits. The dresses, eating habits and languages of the Muslims of Assam, Bengal, Kerala and Uttar Pradesh differ immensely from each other, so also their marriage customs, social ceremonies and cultural festivals. In the same way, there is a commonality between Hindus and Muslims in matters of business, trade, professions and vocations. One can see Hindus and Muslim carpenters, tailors and blacksmiths working together at the same work place without observing any kind of distinction. Likewise, one can see the difference between the ethical and moral codes of different economic segments of Muslim community. One cannot say that if one is a Muslim one would necessarily follow this profession or that profession, wear this dress or that or eat this or that. Certainly, there is a broad commonality amongst most of them as far as their fundamental social, cultural and religious norms are concerned. However, they are supposed not to take pork, liquor and are believed to perform circumcision, nikah ceremony and burry their dead in the graveyards. Muslims of India are disturbed that their children too are becoming the victims of Western ways of living which will remove them from their religion and culture. The modern education devoid of moral and spiritual values is prompting the well to do Muslim children to follow Western culture, European norms of morality and Christian code of conduct consequently they are behaving in matters of dresses, food habits and behaviour patterns in the same way as the affluent sections of Hindu, Sikh, Christian, Jain and Parsi societies are behaving. This commonality on the basis of Western culture, permissive ways of living and obscenity would ruin them beyond redemption. The same is more or less true for elite Muslim men and women. Most of them are drifting towards Western culture and Western ways of living which are not approved by a large section of Muslim community.

Various Religious Shades Among Indian Muslims

There are several sub-religious sects among Muslims such as Sunnis, Shias, Hanafi, Shafei, Ahl-e-Hadith, Ithna Ashari, Ismailis, Deobandis and Barelvis and many others. All these sects follow the fundamentals of Islam but differ in peripheral matters. For instance, the major difference between the Shias and Sunnis is in matters of Khilafat. Shias believe that Hazrat Ali being the first paternal cousin and son-in-law and nearest to Holy Prophet should have been the First Khalifa of Islam in place of Hazrat Abu Bakr and not as the Fourth Khalifa. As against this, the Sunnis do not believe in blood or family succession but believe in the rule by consultations and consensus and consider the choice of Hazrat Abu Bakr as the First Khalifa in conformity to the wishes of Holy Prophet. Shias consider Hazrat Ali as the Wasi (regent) or First Imam. The other differences are of minor nature. For all practical purposes Shias and Sunnis are brothers in faith. They are the two most important pillars of Islam. Sunnis give highest respect and regard to Shia Ulemas and care for the sentiments and sensitivities of their brothers. Likewise, Shias too place Sunni Ulemas on the high pedestals and do not try to antagonize their brothers in faith. They follow many common practices, customs and codes of conduct. Their social, cultural and religious ceremonies are more or less similar. There are several sub-sects among Shias such as Zaidis, Ismailis and Ithna Asharis or Jafris. The Jafris are further divided into Akbaris and Usulis and the Ismailis into Nizris and Mustalis. Likewise, the Khojas and Bohras are the part of Ismailis. Most of the Sunnis in India are the followers of Abu Hanifa and thus called Hanafi. There are practically no Malikis, the followers of Imam Malik and Hanbalis the follower of Imam Hanbal among Sunni Muslims of India, though many Muslims in South and West follow Shafei School. In the same way, there are very few Zaidis amongst Shias in India. As against this, there are so many sub-sects among Sunnis such as Wahabis, Deobandis, Barelvis, Ahl-e-Hadith, Jamiat Ulema-e-Hind, Jamate Islami, Tablighi jamat and others.

Wahabis and Bareillvis

Wahabis, known after Abdul Wahab of the Hanbali School belong to famous seminary Darul Uloom Deoband of U.P. though in the strict sense they are not Hanbalis and Deobandis. They believe in purest form of Islam as enunciated by Holy Qur'an and preached and practiced by Holy Prophet. They follow puritan ideology and abhor veneration of graves and pursuing certain objectionable customs at the time of marriages and other family functions as well as observing certain rituals at religious places and Khanqahs and Dargahs. They are very strict in their principles and approach and do not deviate from the fundamentals. They believe not only in pursuing the Islamic principles but also insist on keeping and maintaining the Islamic identity. They believe that by dress, address, gestures, postures, body language and code of conduct a true Muslim should leave the impression of a good Muslim and a good human being upon his counterparts. They want each and every Muslim to pursue what is good and persuade others to follow the good and avoid what is bad and check others from following the bad. The Jamiat Ulema-e-Hind is one of the most important representatives of Deoband School. They have millions of followers in the country. The important dignitaries of the organization took active part in the freedom struggle. Many of them were sent and tortured in Andaman and Nicobar Islands by the British. They were against the partition of the country. They supported the Khilafat Movement and cooperated with Mahatma Gandhi. After partition of the country, most of them stayed in the country along with Maulana Azad. They are playing a key role in propagating Islam and keeping Muslims on the path of religion by opening madrasas and mosques, guarding graveyards and protecting Wakf properties. Many ignorant people sometimes associate several terrorists with Deobandi or Wahabi ideology when the fact is that hundreds of Deoband Ulemas under the leadership of Maulana Mehmood Madni have unanimously denounced terrorism by giving a Fatwa to the effect that terrorism is against Islam as Islam does not allow anybody to kill an innocent being.

Basically, Jamiat Ulema-e-Hind is a religious organization composed of devoted Muslims but when they feel that Muslims' interest is at stake, they participate in country's politics too. Having seen Islam and Muslims at the receiving end at the hands of adversaries of Islam many Muslim religious organizations including Jamiat Ulema-e-Hind have come openly in support of Muslims and Islam. In this process they have been perhaps influenced by Hindu religious organizations that have formed various political wings at national and international levels for the protection of Hindu rights. Wahabis treat Bareillvis, the followers of the Bareilly School of thought after their esteemed Imam Ahmed Raza Khan of Bareilly in U.P., as the practitioners of innovations and consider many of their acts as Bidats or unauthorized versions of true Islam. As against this, the Barelvis believe in reverence and honouring the saints of yesteryears and believe that these saints are alive at other end of the corridor. They have simply gone behind the veil and possess the same spiritual powers which they had while they were alive. They behave with the saints of the graves as if they are very much alive and visit Dargahs and Khanqahs for taking their blessings. They believe in nazar and niyaz or offerings, that is giving money, clothing or food to the poor and needy or reading the verses of Holy Qur'an, with a view to convey their rewards to their dead ancestors with the consent of the Lord and the blessings of the revered saints. They also celebrate the birthday of the Holy Prophet with grace and glory and pay tribute to him. They are ritualistic and organize several religious functions at the time of births, marriages, festivals, deaths and other social and cultural ceremonies both in their homes as well as in Dargahs and Khanqahs. Those who sit and attend the graves of Sufi saints and Dargahs and Khanqahs are revered by general public. The Mujawars or Muttawallis and the descendants of the saints live like saints. Incidentally, many of the practices of these functionaries resemble with those of the Pujaris, Mahants and the Acharyas of Hindu holy places. They allow Sufi music and ascetic dance near the graves of the Sufi saints. There are four broad classes of Sufis such as Naqshbandi, Qadiriyya, Suharwardi and Chishtiya who are found in various parts of the country. There are minor differences amongst them for all of them arose from the same source and all of them have a common goal of reaching to the Lord through the route of Sufi type spiritualism. The mazars or graves of various schools of sufis are found in every part of the country and innumerable people from all communities and nationalities visit them to take the blessings of these saints. The majority community feels comfortable with the Bareillvis School of thought for most of their practices reflect their past Indian heritage which the Sufi saints allowed to the extent that they were not against the fundamentals of Islam. Bareillvis are liberal in their religious approach since they come in contact with various religious groups and nationalities daily in their day-to-day dealings. The Sajjada Nasheens or who serve and control the affairs of Dargahs and Khanqahs are contributing much in propagating Hindu-Muslim unity in the country through their cosmopolitan Sufi approach. They seldom participate in the active politics of the country and wish to remain neutral for important dignitaries of various religions and belief systems come to them for their blessings. However, when the adversaries of Islam began to link Islam with terrorism they too came out openly in support of Muslims and Islam and denounced terrorism as antithesis to Islam and Islamic ideology. They are acceptable to many hard core Hindu organizations due to their liberal and traditional approach. India is mostly inhabited by Deobandi and Barelvi Muslims. In almost all the states of India, they are in majority save a few areas in South and West where one can confront Shafei in large numbers. It is irony of fate that these two religious schools of thought often confront each other. It has been seen that many a time some of their hard core and proactive groups do not hesitate in calling each other as transgressors. It is quite strange that their elders did not differ as much as their younger ones do now. Many meaningful people from both sides have started the process of reconciliation in the larger interest of the community and Islam. It is hoped that sense would prevail upon different warring groups and they would sit on the table to sort out their differences peacefully and amicably. There are various other religious organizations which are serving the Muslim community in their own ways such as Ahl al-Hadith, Tablighi Jamaat, Jamaat-e-Islami, Jamiat Ulema-e-Hind and the organizations of Imams and Muezzins which have been briefly discussed below.

Ahl-e-Hadith

The name Ahl al-Hadith arose from Imam Bukhari, Imam Muslim and many other transmitters of Hadith who called themselves as Ahl al-Hadith literally meaning 'people of Hadith'. The term Ahl-e-Hadith is very often used interchangeably with Salafi dawah. Ahl-e-Hadith are found in Middle East, South Asia and Pakistan and India. They are not bound by taqlid and consider themselves free to seek guidance in matters of religious faith and traditions from the authentic traditions and Holy Qur'an. They also do not consider themselves bound by any particular School of Law and rely directly on Sunna of the Holy Prophet. Essentially, they are the followers of true Prophetic Narrations. They give emphasis to Tawheed or Unity of God and deny the knowledge of the Unseen to any being other than God. They follow the true and authentic Narrations of Holy Prophet and possess enthusiasm for Jihad and are committed to the total submission before the commandments of the Lord. They believe in taking decisions on the basis of the Holy Qur'an and Hadith and do not rely in applying methodology or qiyas or analogy. They reject the miraculous powers of the saints and abhor the exaggerated reverence to them. They are against bida or non-Islamic systems and attack all those social and cultural practices of pre-Islamic origin which were absorbed by Muslims of Bengal, Kashmir, Punjab, UP, Bihar and many parts of the country. The muftis of Ahl-e-Hadith believe that the popular practice of pronouncing talaq thrice in one sitting was un-Islamic. Their movement is basically a puritanical one and they want to revive Islam on the basis of the fundamental principles.

Tablighi Jamaat

Tablighi Jamaat is the culmination of a wonderful religious project which was originally piloted by Maulana Mohammad Ismail, a descendant of Shah Waliullah in 1920. Later on, Maulana Mohammad Ilyas, a pious and righteous man who used to lead the prayers at Banglewali Masjid close to the dargah of Nizamuddin Aulliya gave it the shape of Tablighi Jamaat. His son Maulana Mohammad Yusuf extended the Jamaat to many parts of India and the world. Maulana Mohammad Ilyas was moved by the Khilafat and Non-Cooperation Movements and had seen the aftermath of partition. He did not participate in active politics but felt that the main cause of the downfall of Muslims was that their hearts were devoid of pure spirit of Islam. They needed cleansing, moral upliftment and regeneration. After returning from Mecca and Medina in 1925, he targeted the Meos community which had lost much of its Islamic glamour and was half Hindu and half Muslim. They knew nothing about Deoband, Nadwa, Bareilly or Ahl-e-Hadith. He asked them to return to the fold of Islam by performing namaz, practicing tabligh and involving themselves in self-reformation and service to Allah. He started a massive and elaborate mass contact programme to spread the meaning of Holy Qur'an and Sunna and cultivate Islamic spirit among Muslims. He raised Jamaats under the leaderships of eminent and pious Muslims and disciplined the preaching groups of pious and simple people who were willing to travel far and wide at their own expenses for imparting Islam and inviting people within the fold of Islam. Whoever saw the tabligh parties traveling on foot, with luggage on their shoulders, Zikr or remembrance of God on their tongues, marks of prostration on their heads and signs of night vigil in their eyes were reminded of the companions of the Holy Prophet. The impact of the great revolution was such that those Meos who were far from Islam became the dedicated and true disciples of Islam and the spirit of Tabligh attracted all segments of Muslims towards Allah and His Messengers irrespective of their sectarian differences. Support came from ulemas of Deoband, Nadwa and Mazahirul Uloom in Saharanpur. Thousands of mosques, maktabs and madaris were established in Mewat where there were none. Hindu customs were abandoned, beards were grown, lewd and profane habits were discarded and the climate of faith and piety was created merely within a decade or so.

Tablighi Jamaat is essentially a voluntary organization of people of all shades such as rich and poor, young and old, businessmen and labourers who endeavour to reform themselves by self-search and move in groups under a leader and mix with people at their dwellings and in mosques. They are not preachers but truth seekers and invite others to seek the truth. The Tablighi Jamaat got added stimulus at the hands of

Shaykhul Hadith Maulana Zakarya after the partition of the country. He was camping at Nizamuddin in Delhi and when he saw the condition of Mewatis in the nearby areas of Delhi, Rajasthan and Haryana, he was moved immensely. During partition, many Mewati Muslims suffered heavily in communal riots allegedly sponsored by men in power. Several of them migrated to Pakistan and during their journey and elsewhere they suffered a lot. Those who had remained behind either converted themselves to Hinduism or changed their names to avoid discrimination and danger to their lives, honour and possessions. They knew nothing about Islam save it that they were aware of the fact that they were Muslims by names. In the same way, when he looked at the conditions of other Muslims who were illiterate and ignorant he found that they too had gone too far from Islam and were in very bad shape. They too knew nothing about Islam and Islamic practices and principles. Moved by the pathetic conditions of Muslims of India in and around Delhi he started the work of self-purification, self-searching and self-learning while being in a Jamaat or group on the pattern of Makki days of Holy Prophet and his pious companions. He told the people to purify themselves rather than reforming others. He guided them to sit in groups or Jamaats and learn about the religion and practice it in order to reform and purify themselves. He advised them to leave their homes and work places in groups under the guidance of guides voluntarily at their own expenses to reform themselves by meeting others who do not know Islam and its principles and prompt them to purify themselves by self-search and self-learning in groups. His main contribution was that he introduced the concept of learners and truth-seekers in place of preachers which encouraged millions of people who were poor and knew very little about Islam to leave their homes voluntarily which transformed their lives in no time. Many devoted Muslims move in jamaat in their areas once a weak and contact people and invite them to come to the mosques to learn and purify and meet the Jamaats from other areas. Likewise, for three days or forty days or even for a few months depending upon once circumstances they find out the time to meet people of other areas, cities and even countries at their own expenses. There they meet in large numbers and purify and increase their knowledge about Islam and learn from others. In the same way, they meet every year at some place and benefit from the combined genius of the jamaat. The good thing in this organization is that it is composed of simple-minded people most of whom are generally poor and illiterate. Moreover, it is claimed by the Tablighi people that their organization is not a political organization because they do not discuss politics and seek no state help and assistance. They do not collect money but believe in self-financing. They discuss peacefully the religious matters only and spend from their own pockets because they believe that it is they who benefit from jamaat activities and not others for they are merely truth-seekers and not preachers. By removing the concept of preacher and introducing the notion of self-reformers, the founder has introduced the element of meekness, humbleness and piety in the task of learning and conveying the message of Islam to others. Besides, being truth-seekers rather than preachers, they do not try to convert others for they meet their own people and try to reform them and themselves by sitting in their companies. They never try to meet other communities with a view to convert them but concentrate upon themselves and their community for they feel that what to talk of converting others they themselves do not know fully their own religion. The Jamaat gatherings everywhere have attracted the attention of the people due to their simplicities, pious and peaceful atmosphere. Even the meaningful people of majority community are not against these people for save a few exceptions here and there, by and large they have not found these people in any destructive activities.

The influence of Jamaat has grown immensely since independence and many professionals and intellectuals from big cities like Delhi, Aligarh, Mumbai, Bhopal, Hyderabad, Kolkata and Bangalore have joined the movement. Nobody knows their actual number but their presence can be felt in every mosque of the country. They can be spotted on railway stations, bus stops and airports. The beauty of this organization is that it is surviving on the basis of self-help and does not believe in charities and donations. Besides, a large section of Muslims including the intellectuals believe that it is purely a non-political party devoid of donation politics and its spirit of self-purification without caring for the worldly favours is good in transforming the sagging personality of Indian Muslims. It will not be out of place to mention here that Tablighi Jamaat is generally not looked with suspicion even by governments of several countries including the Government of India since they ask people to serve their Lord and be satisfied with what Allah has given them. They do not incite people to fight for their constitutional rights or jobs and reservation but tell them to improve their hereafter. Even during 1975-77 emergency when the Jamaat-e-Islami was under severe strains, India's tablighi workers were provided exist visas and foreign exchange. Tablighi Jamaat normally does not enter into any religious controversy but sometimes it finds itself entangled with Jamaat-e-Islami on certain doctrinal issues or it does not get well with Bareillvis ulemas who follow and practice the popular and sufi-oriented Islam. By and large Jamaat is heralded as a good omen for inviting Muslim towards its puritanical and reformist orientation. However, a liberal and ultra secular section of Muslims tilted towards communist ideology doubts some of their credentials. They believe that Tablighi Jamaat involves itself in inter-sect controversies and its puritanical version of Islam is insulating Muslims from the legitimate political processes and it is isolating them from cultural, intellectual and religious currents of modern times. However, Muslims in general believe that it is a non-political organization of simple minded people whose main object is neither to convert people nor to preach Islam to Muslims but make them good Muslims by sitting with Jamaat or moving with it in search of knowledge. Basically, this organization gives more emphasis on Huqooqul Allah or Rights of God compared to Huqooqul Ibad or Rights of People. For a true Muslim it is necessary that he should fulfill his obligations towards his Lord as well as the people with whom he comes in contact. Both these rights are equally important. The rights of men are more important in the sense that every man would have to confront all those people whom he had harmed one way or the other on the Day of Judgment and God would not interfere between them till the sufferers themselves would forgive them. As against this, in matters of the Rights of God, since the Lord is merciful and kind. He may forgive many sins of men. Besides, by patronising the rights of men not only discipline, dedication and goodwill are generated in the society, the society is also reformed and the personality of the individuals is sharpened which benefit humanity immensely. Essentially, Islam spread in the world due to following both rights. When the non-Muslims saw a Muslim behaving honestly and sincerely for the cause of humanity and when they found that he was reliable, trustworthy and a good friend, neighbor and colleague, they were highly impressed and they tried to know about him and his religion. This very factor attracted them towards Islam which helped to a large extent in the spread of Islam and its ideology.

Jamaat-e-Islami

Jamaat-e-Islami was established by Maulana Syed Abul Ala Maududi in 1941 with a supreme purpose of creating a righteous group based on Holy Qur'an and Hadith to establish the sovereignty of God on earth by means of a truly Islamic state. Many educated Muslims of India welcomed it and became its members. However, Indian Government never relished the activities of Jamaat-e-Islami people for their opposing secularism and establishing a pan-Islamic state and many a time its active workers were placed behind bars. The party was bracketed with some extremist Hindu organisations which too wanted to establish Hindu Rashtra. Maulana Maududi, a Hyderabadi Indian in origin, migrated to Pakistan and his mantle in India was inherited by Maulana Abul Lais Islahi. The party believes in ijtehad and in investigating the maladies among Muslims with a view to revive Islamic order and reorienting Islam to its rightful pre-eminent position. The vague concepts like enemies of Islam and Islamic Order and revival of Golden Age were interpreted as abhorrence for secular and democratic forces and non-participation in political processes by some, negation of territorial nationalism and reconciling Islam to universalism by others and moral purity, military conquest and technical superiority and cultural advancement by many. For about two decades their followers remained involved within their naïve and mistaken assumptions and hardly any Muslim country accepted their retrograde ideas. Jamaat-e-Islami failed miserably in Pakistan and there is hardly any taker of its pan-Islamic concept of governance.

Having seen the debacle of Jamaat-e-Islami in political field its Indian counterpart was quick to change itself in the light of the changing conditions in India. They took a fresh look at the ideas and the legacy of Maulana Maududi and came to the conclusion that secularism and democracy were better form of government compared to totalitarian and fascist modes. The recent pronouncements of the party reveal that it is not averse to take part in the mainstream political process of the country. It appears that they are in favour of forming a united Muslim political front to bridge the gulf between Hindus and Muslims and taking part in the election process by backing candidates with principles and good conduct. After 25/26 November 2008, they have become active and are taking part in removing misunderstandings from the minds of non-Muslims about Jihad and Islam and the so-called violent posture of Islam. They are meeting people of various faiths and trying to convey them that Islam is a peaceful and harmonious religion. It abhors violence and bloodshed. It is deadly against terrorism and inter-faith conflicts and disharmony and believes in love, compassion and peaceful co-existence. People are appreciating their new role of Peace Brokers. Their presence can be felt in Aligarh Muslim University, Jamia Millia Islamia, Kashmir University, Hamdard University and various Muslim educational centres of the country. They influence the activities of students by trying to highlight the alternative Islamic model before them. However, the participation of certain hard-core SIMI workers in the recent terrorist activities has dented their activities.

Many people claim that Jamaat-e-Islami is primarily the party of educated Muslims sporting beards, adoring sherwanis and having religious tendencies. They believe that these activists mostly come from Madrasa background. Between 1975 and 1990 they were in much demand in Saudi Arabia, Egypt, UAE, Malaysia, Indonesia and many Muslim countries. They had occupied prominent positions in educational and cultural institutions of world fame. It is stated that they had convinced the Muslim Ummat that they had economic, social and political models based on Sharia for solving the ills of Muslim community. People were impressed by the alleged blend of Sharia and modern education among them and believed in them and opened educational and cultural institutions as desired by them and paid them lavishly. However, it is claimed that within two decades their hollow promises were exposed and they lost their glamour. Jamaat people are believed to be progressive, liberal and dynamic and worldly. Many of their children get education in America and Western countries. They too live a pragmatic life and mingle with all types of people including Communists, non-Muslims and hard-core Hindu elements. They hold conferences and seminars and invite all segments of society and firmly discuss religious issues with open mind. Their popularity can be judged by the fact that just from nearly 240 members in 1947 they had crossed the number of about 2900 members with about 37000 sympathizers in 1983. They had established more than 500 libraries, 400 reading rooms and 250 study circles. They sponsored the publication of more than 500 books in Urdu, 70 in Hindi and 80 in English on Holy Qur'an and Hadith. Their official organs Dawat in Urdu and Radiance in English commented on wide variety of issues affecting Muslims. Their student wing the Students Islamic Moment (SIMI) was born when Students' Islamic Organization (SIO) in West Bengal, Bihar and Tamil Naidu was merged in the Ideal Students League in South India. Jamaat is helping in financing the buildings for mosques, establishing schools, publishing Islamic literature and providing assistance to teachers and scholarship to students out of its funds collected as charitable grants from various sources. The present Jamaat-e-Islami has learnt much from the debacle of the original party. They have transformed them into a new and dynamic force suiting to the conditions of India for they feel that India is best suited for them due to its secular credentials, democracy and large-hearted tolerance compared to other dictatorial and oppressive regimes. They are in search of political legitimacy, social acceptance and cultural relevance in the context of India's plural, liberal and secular identity. The ultra-secularist sections of Muslim do not relish them. They consider them as a retrograde force. They believe that their world-view to Islamize the state and the society is against the emancipation of women, modernizing processes in education and social reforms. They contend that despite certain cosmetic changes they have not transformed themselves into a modern movement. They are part and parcel of the militant Sunni Islam and they help in sectarian conflicts and dent secular fabrics. However, Muslims in general believe that India's wing of Jamaat-e-Islami is a reformed organization. Its members are relentlessly working along with the non-Muslims for the betterment of the country and are trying to remove misgivings from their minds about, Islam, Jihad, rights of women and triple talaq, etc. They have been organizing conferences, seminars and discussion groups for the spread of Islam and Islamic ideology. Their role in establishing Islamic Banks and Baitul Maal is commendable.

Jamiat Ulema-e-Hind

Jamiat Ulema-e-Hind is the brain child of some influential ulemas from Deoband who founded this organization in 1919 to defend the Khilafat and Holy Places of Islam. Actually, the organization is the result of the movements of Shah Waliullah, Shah Abdul Aziz, Syed Ahmad Barelwi, Haji Imadullah, Maulvi Fazl-I Haq Khairabadi and the founders of Deoband, namely Maulana Mohammad Qasim Nanotawi and Rashid Ahmad Gangohi. Jamiat Ulema-e-Hind has functioned as a quasi-political body for the freedom of the country along with Congress under the leadership of Mahatma Gandhi. It participated in joint mass demonstrations along with Gandhiji and during 1930 its 20,000 members were imprisoned for different political offences. The organization also opposed the two nation theory in 1940s and championed the cause for a secular and democratic united India. Maulana Husain Ahmad Madani the sole leader of the organization propagated the idea of mutahida-qaumiyat or composite nationalism and cited the Covenant at Medina as a justification for supporting India's movement for acquiring freedom from the clutches of the British.

After partition there was no change in party's attitude towards democracy and secularism. Jamiat chalked out a programme for the reconstruction of Muslims with a view to bring prosperity not in isolation but marching shoulder to shoulder with members of other communities. It resolved to move with Congress step by step. It appreciated the role of the Constituent Assembly for framing a democratic and secular constitution and treated Indian Constitution as a social contract similar to that concluded by the Holy Prophet of Islam with Jews of Medina. The Constitution was considered as an ideal document since secularism based on democratic traditions and liberal thoughts did not negate or reject religion but on the other hand it fortified religion and cultural freedom. However, the organization was shattered by what happened after partition and temporarily decided to refrain from pro-Congress activities and severed its obligatory ties with Congress. It decided to fight for the creation of non-sectarian atmosphere in the country which was bleeding in communal rights. As time elapsed they found themselves marginalized especially after the death of Maulana Azad. Having seen them in the position of extreme neglect within the political arena, the Jamiat decided temporarily to concentrate on religious affairs only but soon the activists like Maulana Madni, Maulana Ahmad Sayeed and Maulana Hifzur Rahman realized that it was not advisable to keep away from the political power for the Muslim community needed them most to represent their cause before the government. It was felt that the access to Congress politicians was necessary for getting grants for building schools, colleges, mosques, madaris as well as to secure jobs, obtain concessions and licenses and get exemptions from taxes for religious institutions.

Jamiat's history is indeed full of struggle. It has fought for communal harmony, economic reconstruction, social uplift, dissemination of religious education, safeguarding Muslim

Personal Law, supporting language issues and protection of Auqafs. After independence, it shed its pan-Islamic identity and concentrated towards the multifarious problems of Indian Muslims. Since independence, it has passed into various ups and down. When Jamiat's honeymoon with Congress was over during 1970s due to the lack of secular consensus in the country and the spurt of communal riots, it chalked a course for unity and solidarity among Muslims along with striving for prosperity along with protecting identity. Since it had failed earlier in creating a Muslim front during 1953, 1961 and 1962, it adopted a pragmatic approach. The Hyderabad's gathering of the Maulanas of Jamiat under Maulana Mehmood Madni was historical. They unanimously condemned terrorism and declared all terrorist activities against Islam. They highlighted the real spirit of Islam in various forums and tried to show that Islam is truly a peaceful, non-violent and harmonious religion. Their functionaries are helping in Hajj Committees, Wakf Boards, and legislative assemblies. They are running madrasas, maktabs, schools, religious institutions and reforming people by publishing books on Islam and disseminating news through print media and their mouth pieces.

Darul-Uloom Nadwatul Ulama Lucknow

Darul-Uloom Nadwatul Ulama Lucknow is the Islamic Institution situated at Lucknow. It is one of the principal centres of Islamic learning in the North. It ranks next to Darul Uloom Deoband. It was founded in Kanpur in 1894 by Allama Shibli Nomani, Maulana Mohammad Ali Mongiri, Maulana Ashraf Ali Thanvi and Maulana Mehmudul Hasan with the idea of countering the adverse effects of Western education. The founders aimed at providing capable scholars who could project a true image of Islam before the modern world in an effective way. It is a modified version of Deoband and is primarily aimed at bringing harmony between various sects of Muslims and to reaching the middle path between modernity and classical Islam. Maulana Syed Mohammad Ali became the first Nazim of Nadwatul Uloom. The institution serves as a bridge between the old and new without compromising the fundamental principles of Islam and helps in bringing educational reforms and progress within the Muslim community. It aims at producing an educated class of Muslims well-versed in traditional teaching and yet actively involved with ruling power. Arabic both modern and classical is given a place of pride in teaching and research especially with a view to develop strong links with the Arabic speaking countries of West Asia. The institute has a vast and a rich library with 125000 titles including about 3000 handwritten books mostly in Arabic, Persian, Urdu and English. It has a research and a publication department. Its students are spread throughout the country and are mostly found as Moazzins, Imams, Quazis and Madrasa teachers. The Nadwa is indebted to Maulana Abul-Hasan Ali Nadwi known as Ali Mian who was responsible to bring the Institute on the world map. He was the distinguished scholar of world fame and was known for his scholarship, integrity and piety. He had been the Nazim, that is, the Rector of the Institute since 1961 till his death. Needless to say that there are so many other important religious institutes spread throughout the country like Jamia Islamia Darul Uloom Deoband Saharanpur and Jamia Mazher Sadat Gujarat and the organization of Imams and Moazzins which are serving the religious cause of Muslims of India and which are famous in Muslim world.

The misfortune of Muslims is that they have failed to maintain proper balance between modernism and Islam. There are several schools of thoughts with different perceptions and ideologies. Some believe in strict adherence of the classical ideas of the orthodox Islam. Others contend that Qur'anic injunctions and the narrations of the Holy Prophet should be confined to the period of the Holy Prophet and his Holy Companions only and they should not be considered as eternal. In their opinion changes should be introduced in the Islamic principles and practices according to the demands of the time. There are a few who claim that we should concentrate only on Holy Qur'an and the true narrations of the Holy Prophet and should not get ourselves involved in consensus and ijtihad. Majority of the Muslims, however, believe that Muslims should follow strictly the fundamentals of Islam as enunciated in Holy Qur'an and as practiced by the Holy Prophet and as interpreted and accepted by the learned Ulemas after consensus in the light of Holy Qur'an and Sunna and they should introduce necessary changes in the customs, traditions, ethos and social and cultural practices in the light of modern changes to the extent that they are not contrary to Islamic principles.

8

The Economic Deprivation of Muslims

It appears that many sections of Muslims of India are presently in a miserable state of shock, suspicion, anger and disgust. Their frustration is reflected in their drawing rooms and grass-root level discussions. It is mirrored in the Urdu poetry of the contemporary poets and the large number of Mushairas that are held throughout the country in which the younger and budding poets vent the feelings of the community sarcastically in a manner enjoyed by the large audiences. The main reason for their anguish is their perceived deprivation both in the governance structure from grass roots to national political structures and their inadequate participation in development process from panchayat and municipal corporations to states and central levels. Several Muslims feel that during the last sixty years they have occupied scarcely any substantial public spaces in the mainstream. Save a few oasis in film world, arts, sports, games and industry, they are living in barren areas. In the democratic process of India which is based on universal adult franchise, they find themselves marginalized due to their lower numerical strength. Their chances of getting elected in proportion to their strength or their getting benefits in accordance to their share in the total population of the country too are far fetched for they cannot influence the electoral matrix of different political parties since they are scattered throughout the country. Being religious minority and allegedly patronized by the Congress Party and linked with the creation of Pakistan and certain segments of the radical

Muslims, they carry a double burden of being called anti-national as well as pampered. They are more or less convinced that they cannot survive with dignity, grace and honour without state patronage and the help of the civil society which unfortunately they feel are not forthcoming. They are thus finding it difficult to survive and co-exist with respect, grace and contentment in modern Indian society along with their individuality, identity, culture and faith. Many Muslims strongly emphasize that due to ignorance and lack of contact with Muslim community several people in the majority community have misleading notions about Muslims, Islam and Islamic principles and practices. There are myths, misconceptions, suspicions, hostilities and even outright incomprehensions. Some of the rightist organizations from the majority community see Islam as a violent, fanatical and intolerant religion. Some intellectuals of the majority community perceive Muslims as fundamentalists, obscurantists and fanatics and several narrow minded officials and functionaries from the governing structure treat them as more or less second class citizens. Muslims are unable to react as they have neither the capacity nor will. They are educationally backward, economically shallow, politically divided and socially isolated. Battered by economic miseries, insecure by the attacks of some of the sections of biased media, rendered helpless by hate campaigns and suspected of lack of loyalty, they find themselves incompetent to bridge the widening divide between them and the rest of the countrymen. It appears that many sections of Muslim society have lost hope in government initiatives for they are wary of them since they consider them as mere mental gymnastics to provide balm on the aching community. Their main problems include the preservation of their social customs, cultural practices, religious institutions and distinct identities with grace, honour and dignity; providing them safety, security and protection to their lives, honour, possessions and properties through due process of law; giving them equal and comparable economic and growth-oriented opportunities as given to other similarly situated societies in the country in matters of securing jobs in government and private sectors; getting admissions in technical, medical, management and other public and private institutions of higher learning; securing reservations in schools, colleges and universities and technical institutions as well as in panchayats, zila parishads and legislative assemblies; obtaining contracts, licenses, loans, concessions and other benefits; getting infrastructure and social facilities such as all-weather roads, regular electric supply, clean drinking water and health and recreation centres and participation in business, professions, vocations, industry, trade and commerce and lastly, securing all the conveniences, comforts and luxuries transparently and faithfully as minorities according to the provisions of Indian Constitution and commensurate to the norms applied for other sections of majority community.

It is highly painful to note that the thinking of some of the Muslims on these counts is frustrating and disappointing. It is true that all of their allegations may not be true but there seems to be some truth in them. Many complain that several times they feel the sense of being others mainly when they confront the perverted people from the majority community in national mainstream. Since the presence of Muslims in government offices is negligible, many Muslims perceive them usually unwanted and they generally find it difficult to get the work done save by usually greasing the palms of the officials. It is generally told by several sections of Muslims that for the Muslims with identifiable marks the problem becomes more difficult in the wake of surcharged communal atmosphere for they are easily recognized by their external signs. It is also stressed that many a time the poor Muslims with their shabby postures have to stand for hours in pitiable states in government offices especially when they confront the communal and narrow-minded petty officials. The lack of presence of substantial number of Muslims in security services and government offices generally shakes the confidence of many Muslims in the functioning of many officials as well as various segments of the government machinery. Few even claim that any inadvertent misadventure from the side of Muslims in government offices is promptly dealt with by iron hand. More or less the same is the situation in the private sector. Muslim businessmen mostly feel that they are generally considered as rivals and unwanted and they are very often not given that much latitude in matters of discounts, credit margins, commissions and other facilities and concessions which are given to the fellows of majority communities. A significant number from Muslim women allege that they too are treated impolitely several times in public realm while conducting their day-to-day functions. They contend that conservative Muslim women are generally the target of the obsessive focus of some of the proactive media for wrong reasons. Several Muslims very often assert that a large section of the national media seldom highlights their plights in matters of poverty, unemployment, undernourishment and atrocities committed to them and their families during communal riots but it gives a Muslim slant at slightest opportunity to cases of perceived injustice to Muslim women like pardah, triple talaq, inheritance problems and marriage discourses with a view to blame Muslim community for their deprivation. They do not hesitate in painting Islam as the sole cause of gender injustice. The excessive and misdirected focus on the conditions and hopelessness of Muslim women, have shattered them and looking at them with suspicion and disgust have compelled them to seek shelter in their homes. Having seen the community's identity under siege, the Muslim women have become conscious of their special place in Muslim community and are avoiding unsafe places like public hospitals, bus stands, railway stations, market places, police stations and government offices. Besides, Muslims by and large believe that they are lagging behind in all sectors and neither the 'India Shining' has improved their fortunes nor the Indian development plans have contributed in their upliftment. A cursory exposure of Muslims' miserable profile has already been highlighted in the introductory part of this venture. In this portion, efforts have been made to bring certain bare facts before the governing structure as well as the civil society with a view to highlight the fact that most of the Muslims indeed are in deep water and there is an urgent need of a massive rescue operation on an emergency scale to save them from further fall. Even many intellectuals from the Indian society strongly feel that the

Muslim community is already under siege due to lack of education, shrinking political space, division and sub-division, discrimination and deprivation and deliberate pauperization and being pushed into becoming a new class of super dalits to fill the vacuum created by the upward movement of the Scheduled Castes, Scheduled Tribes and the lower classes. Many Muslim families and individuals are convinced that the beginning of the end of their fortunes, identities and existence has set in and if efforts are not made to reverse it, the posterity would never forgive the civil society, the Muslim intellectuals and the well wishers of the community as well as the planners of the country and those who are at the helm of governing structure. A depressing profile of Muslims economic conditions as stated under would reveal that a large chunk of Muslims is in a miserable condition and it needs immediate attention.

The Poverty Among Muslims

For the healthy, sustained, harmonious and conflict-free development in a pluralistic country, the balanced, equitable and perceptible development of all the sections, sectors and regions of the country, is a must. In a multi-culture, multi-ethnic and multi-religious country, if a few stake holders lag behind in the race of progress, the economy becomes handicapped and it affects other sections of the society adversely. The poverty has its own spread affects. Poverty in any segment affects all the segments surely and silently. The planners in India tried their best since the day one to achieve the task of regional, inter-personal and inter-communal balances. They succeeded to a large extent but there are still several areas where affirmative action is needed. Unfortunately, Muslims partly due to historical reasons, partly due to the after-affects of partition and partly due to their on siege mentality could not benefit as much as they should have. The analysis of differentials in poverty across socio-religious communities in India shows that Muslims face fairly high level of poverty. The poverty among Muslims in the urban areas is the highest compared to general Hindus, OBCs, SCs/STs and other minorities. This can be reflected in their depressing dress code, pitiable living conditions and pathetic behaviour pattern.

The state-wise urban and rural poverty incidences across SRCs during 2004-05 are revealed by Tables 8.1 and 8.2.

Table 8.1: State-wise Urban Poverty Incidence across SRCs in 2004-05

State Urban	All	Hindu				Muslims	Other Minorities
		All	SCs/STs	OBCs	Gen.		
Total	22.8	20.4	36.4	25.1	8.3	38.4	12.2
West Bengal	12.0	10.0	22.0	13.0	6.0	27.0	1.0
Uttar Pradesh	31.0	24.0	42.0	28.0	11.0	44.0	6.0
Assam	3.0	3.0	4.0	5.0	1.0	5.0	0.0
Jammu & Kashmir	9.0	4.0	9.0	5.0	2.0	12.0	2.0
Maharashtra	26.0	20.0	33.0	25.0	12.0	49.0	27.0
Gujarat	11.0	10.0	17.0	18.0	3.0	24.0	0.0
Chattisgarh	38.0	38.0	48.0	47.0	13.0	61.0	10.0
All Other States	5.0	6.0	14.0	6.0	3.0	9.0	1.0

Source: Sachar Committee Report, Table 8.3

Table 8.1 shows that nearly 38.4% Muslims were poor compared to 22.8% in the whole country and 20.4% among all Hindus, 36.4% in SCs/STs, 25.1% in OBCs and 12.2% in other minorities. Incidentally, the urban poverty is most pervasive both in Muslims and the SCs/STs. The urban poverty position is bad practically among all states save Assam, Tamil Nadu, Orissa, Himachal Pradesh and Punjab. The head count ratio of Muslims is higher than the state average in Madhya Pradesh, Chhattisgarh, Uttar Pradesh, Bihar, West Bengal, Jharkhand, Rajasthan, Maharashtra, Karnataka, and Andhra Pradesh. In the urban areas of Maharashtra, Gujarat, West Bengal, Chhattisgarh and Uttar Pradesh, poverty among Muslims is higher than that in SCs/STs. At all India level the poverty among Muslims among all states is slightly lower than SCs/STs but considerably higher than OBCs, other minorities and the General Category. Muslims face relatively higher rate of deprivation in urban areas compared to the rural sectors. It is disheartening to note that over a period of time the development projects and globalization and liberalization have not benefited Muslims in the urban areas as much as they have benefited other socio-religious communities. It is strange coincidence that the poverty among Muslims in urban areas is inversely related to the size of the cities. The incidences of poverty are higher in towns with population below 50,000, followed by 50,000 to 2 lakh population. In rural areas, the situation is slightly better but here also the Muslims are worse off compared to all other socio-religious communities except SCs/STs. The state-wise rural poverty position across various socio-religious communities during 2004-05 is revealed by Table 8.2.

Table 8.2: State-wise Rural Poverty Incidence Across SRCs in 2004-05

State Rural	All	Hindu				Muslims	Other Minorities
		All	SCs/STs	OBCs	Gen.		
Total	22.7	22.6	34.8	19.5	9.0	26.9	14.3
West Bengal	25.0	21.0	27.0	16.0	14.0	33.0	32.0
Assam	18.0	12.0	14.0	16.0	7.0	27.0	20.0
Haryana	9.0	9.0	21.0	7.0	2.0	24.0	6.0
All Other States	5.0	6.0	14.0	6.0	3.0	9.0	1.0

Source: Sachar Committee Report, Table 8.4

Table 8.2 shows that 26.9% Muslims in the rural areas were poor compared to 22.7% at all India level and 34.8% for SCs/STs, 19.5% for OBCs, 14.3% for other minorities and 9.0% for General Category. Likewise, state-wise they stood at the level of 22 compared to 12 for all states and 12 for Hindu OBCs, 10 Hindu General, 18 for all Hindus and 3 for all other minorities. In states like West Bengal, Assam and Haryana the poverty level among Muslims in the rural areas is higher than that of SCs and STs.

Income wise, Muslims are far below the all India average for low income group which stands at 22.9%. Table 8.3 reveals the income distribution between various Socio-Religious Categories as under:

Table 8.3

SRC	Urban			Rural			Total		
	Low Income	Middle Income	High Income	Low Income	Middle Income	High Income	Low Income	Middle Income	High Income
H-Gen	8.3	58.4	33.3	9.3	84.1	6.6	8.9	73.9	17.2
H-SC/ST	44.8	32.2	23.1	25.6	71.3	3.1	28.6	65.1	6.3
H-OBC	21.1	74.6	4.3	27.2	72.1	0.7	25.9	72.6	1.5
Muslims	38.6	53.1	8.3	26.9	70.8	2.2	30.8	65.0	4.2
M-Gen	35.7	54.2	10.1	26.1	72.3	1.6	29.3	66.2	4.4
M-OBC	42.6	52.1	5.3	28.0	68.8	3.2	32.7	63.5	3.8
All others	11.8	53.7	34.5	13.8	74.7	11.5	13.2	68.6	18.2
Total	22.9	57.7	19.4	22.9	73.9	3.2	22.9	69.8	7.3

Source: Sachar Committee Report, Table 10.4

Table 8.3 shows that 29.3% General Muslims and 32.7% Muslim OBCs fall within low income group compared to 8.9% Hindu General category and 28.6% Hindu SCs/STs, 25.9% Hindu OBCs and 13.2% all others. In the same way, 66.2% Muslims from General class and 63.5% from Muslim OBCs fall within the middle income group compared to 73.9% for Hindu General and 65.1% for Hindu SCs/STs and 68.6% for all others. Incidentally, Muslim OBCs are worse than Hindu OBCs and Hindu SCs/STs for their percentage is 32.7% compared to 28.6% for Hindu SCs/STs and 25.9% Hindu OBCs. Similarly, Muslims lag behind the all India average of 7.3% for high income since 4.4% Muslims General and 3.8% Muslim OBCs fall within the high income group compared to 17.2% Hindu General and 6.3% Hindu SCs/STs, 1.5% Hindu OBCs and 18.2% all others. Even in matters of High income, Muslim General and Muslim OBCs lag behind Hindu SCs/STs for 6.3% people from this category are in high income group as against 4.4% for Muslims General and 3.8% from Muslim OBCs. The poverty level among Muslims at the urban level in the lower income sector too is bad as 38.6% Muslims and 42.6% Muslim OBCs are below poverty line compared to the national average of 22.9%, and 8.3% for Hindu higher castes, 21.1% Hindu OBCs and 44.8%% Hindu SCS/STs and 11.8% all others. As against this, their percentage in middle income in the urban areas is, Muslim General 54.2%, Muslim OBCs 52.1% as compared to 58.4% Hindu General and 74.6% Hindu OBCs, 32.2% Hindu SCS/STs and 53.7% all others. If we look towards the Higher income group side in the urban areas we would find that only 8.3% Muslims and 5.3% Muslim OBCs fall under high income group compared to 33.3% Hindu higher castes and 23.1% Hindu SCs/STs, 4.3% Hindu OBCs and 34.5% all others. In rural areas, 26.9% Muslims and 28.0%Muslim OBCs come under the category of the low income group compared to all India figure of 22.9% and 9.3% for Hindu General and 25.6% for Hindu SCs/STs, 27.2% for Hindu OBCs and 13.8% for all others. In middle income group, in rural areas, 70.8% Muslims and 68.8% Muslim OBCs fall in the middle income group compared to 84.1% for Hindu General and 71.3% for Hindu SCs/STs,

72.1% Hindu OBCs and 74.7% all others. In high income group, there are only 2.2% Muslims, 3.2% Muslim OBCs compared to all India figure of 3.2% and 6.6% for Hindu General and 3.1% for Hindu SCs/STs, 0.7% Hindu OBCs and 11.5% all others. The condition of Muslim higher income group is worse than Hindu high income group and Hindu SCs/STs for General Muslims are merely 1.6% in the category of high income in the rural areas compared to 6.6% Hindu higher castes and 3.1% for Hindu SCs/STs and 11.5% all others. There are several contributory factors for the poverty among Muslims. One of them is that there are many younger males and females among Muslims compared to other segments of the society as a consequence of which the worker population ratio of Muslims in age-group 15-64 is lower than all India figure and secondly, the participation rate among Muslim female workers from the general category in the labour force is lower than Hindu SCs/STs, Hindu OBCs and others. Nearly 55.6% Muslims in General category and 53.9% in Muslim OBCs constitute the working force compared to 64.4% all India average and 67.3% for Hindu OBCs. Likewise, in the urban and rural areas their percentages are 51.4% and 50.6% compared to 52.7% and 56.4% for all people and Hindu OBCs respectively. Similarly, only 2.4% Muslim women from general category participate in labour force compared to 43.6% in the country as a whole and 48.3% for the OBCs.

The poverty of Muslims is reflected in their comparatively lower mean per capita expenditure. During 2004-05, the MPCE among Muslims was ₹ 635 compared to ₹ 712 for the whole country, ₹ 1023 for General Hindus, ₹ 646 for the OBCs and ₹ 520 for SCs/STs. The average MPCE varied from ₹ 1469 for General Hindu category to ₹ 800 for Muslims and the SCs/STs. The 80% higher mean per capita expenditure for the higher classes compared to that of Muslims and the SCs/STs is a matter of concern. Needless to say that the condition of the Muslims and the SCs/STs in urban areas is more or less the same for the aggregate all India level and the level of consumption of Muslims is more or less the same as that of SCs/STs. The MPCE for Muslims is slightly lower than that of SCs/STs in smaller town across the country. Their deprivation in terms of consumption expenditure is higher in urban areas and smaller towns with population less than 50,000 and 50,000 to 2 lakh. In urban areas, the largest population falls in the range of ₹ 400 to ₹ 500 and about half of the population is in the range of ₹ 300 to ₹ 600. The conditions of High categories OBCs, other minorities and the SCs/STs are better than that of Muslims. Only 20% Muslims spend equal to or slightly higher than the national average but the conditions of OBCs and SCs/STs are slightly better. As against this, the General Category spends more than 50% above national average. In rural areas, Muslims are at par with OBCs. A significant number of Muslims and the SCs/STs in urban areas fall within the expenditure bracket of ₹ 500. The share of high income households above ₹ 1000 among Muslims is negligible. Muslim household have a good number of the middle income house hold between ₹ 500 to ₹ 1000. The higher bracket is widespread among the General Category. If we now look towards the state-level urban mean per capita expenditure during 2004-05 at current prices which is shown by Table 8.4, we find that it is far from being satisfactory.

Table 8.4: State level Urban MPCE According to SRCs 2004-05 (Current Prices)

States	All	Hindus				Muslims	All-Others
		All	SCs/ Hindus	OBCs STs/	General		
All India	1105	1139	793	955	1469	804	1485
Assam	1131	1113	888	994	1265	1199	1198
Jammu & Kashmir	1115	1323	949	943	1489	991	1572
Delhi	1419	1423	879	985	1788	1051	1924
Haryana	1183	1155	744	896	1420	1105	2151
Chhattisgarh	963	956	754	813	1396	590	1545
All Other States	1309	1294	908	994	1676	1112	1395

Source: Sachar Committee Report, Appendix Table 8.2

We find that at all India level Muslims spent ₹ 804 compared to ₹ 793 by SCs/STs, ₹ 955 by OBCs, ₹ 1469 by General Category and ₹ 1485 by others. At All Other States' they spent ₹ 1112 in contrast to ₹ 908 by SCs/STs, ₹ 994 by

OBCs, ₹ 1676 by General Category and ₹ 1395 by others. Their slightly higher average at states level can be assigned to their better expenditure in Assam, Jammu and Kashmir, Delhi, Haryana and Chhattisgarh. Likewise, their state-level rural MPCE during 2004-05 according to current prices is depicted by Table 8.5.

Table 8.5: State Level Rural MPCE According to SRCs 2004-05 (Current Prices)

States	All	Hindus				Muslims	All-Others
		All Hindus	SCs/ STs	OBCs	General		
All India	579	568	468	567	739	553	823
Kerala	1031	970	722	986	1165	968	128
Delhi	1056	1023	796	781	1146	1696	1960
Andhra Pradesh	604	604	490	593	786	610	572
Gujarat	645	644	527	594	932	668	600
Himachal Pradesh	836	834	672	776	949	798	997
All Other States	707	650	535	684	774	621	782

Source: Sachar Committee Report, Appendix Table 8.3

Table 8.5 exhibits that the state level rural MPCE during 2004-05 according to current prices for Muslims was ₹ 553 compared to ₹ 468 for SCs/STs, ₹ 567 for OBCs, and ₹ 739 for General Category and ₹ 823 for all others. At All Other States, level, it was ₹ 621 as against ₹ 535 for SCs/STs and ₹ 684 for OBCs, ₹ 774 for General Category and ₹ 782 for All Others. The slightly higher expenditure at states level was due to slightly higher expenditure by Muslims in Kerala, Delhi, Andhra Pradesh, Gujarat, and Himachal Pradesh. Incidentally, the position of other minorities such as Sikhs, Christians and Jains was much better both at the urban and rural levels. They spent even more than the General Category of Hindus. One of the reasons for low expenditure level of Muslims in rural areas is due to low land ownership. Almost 94% rural households own land and among which more than 87% own more than one acre. As against this, only 83% Muslims own land and their average size is lower than those of the other socio-religious classes. It is heartening to know that poverty over a period of time has declined among all sections of the society but in case of Muslims the incidence of decline of poverty is not very significant. Tables 8.6 and 8.7 show poverty incidences compared over time in urban and rural areas during 1983-2004-05.

Table 8.6: Poverty Incidence Compared Over Time 1983-2004-05, Urban

States Urban	Total			Hindus									Muslims			All-Others		
				All Hindus			SCs/STs			Other Hindus								
	04-05	93-94	87-88	04-05	93-97	87-88	04-05	93-94	87-88	04-05	93-94	87-88	04-05	93-94	87-88	04-05	93-94	87-88
All India	29	33	38	27	31	36	46	51	55	22	26	32	44	47	53	16	23	27
Delhi	21	16	16	21	15	16	46	47	44	10	5	8	29	30	21	2	6	5
Maharashtra	33	35	35	28	32	33	43	57	61	24	28	28	55	50	48	30	32	34
Madhya Pradesh	48	48	43	45	47	42	69	65	67	37	40	35	70	60	52	7	31	39
All Other States	10	13	19	11	14	21	21	15	38	9	14	19	19	15	24	4	9	11

Source: Sachar Committee Report, Appendix Table 8.5

Table 8.7: Poverty Incidence Compared Over Time 1983 to 2004-05, Rural

States Rural	Total			Hindus									Muslims			All-Others		
				All Hindus			SCs/ STs/			Other Hindus								
	04-05	93-94	87-88	04-05	93-94	87-88	04-05	93-94	87-88	04-05	93-94	87-88	04-05	93-94	87-88	04-05	93-94	87-88
All India	28	37	39	28	36	40	41	50	54	21	29	33	33	45	43	18	27	25
All Other States	15	21	21	23	20	20	36	32	32	15	15	16	28	28	22	5	21	23

Source: Sachar Committee Report, Appendix Table 8.6

If we now look towards poverty incidences compared over time period 1987 to 2004-05 in urban rural areas, we find that among Muslims the poverty level decreased from 53 in 1987-88 to 44 in 2004-05 or by 16.98% and among SCs/STs it declined from 55 to 46 or by 16.36%, in other Hindus it came down from 32 to 22 or by 31.25%, and in all others it was reduced from 27 to 16 or by 40.74%, and the all India level was decreased from 38 to 29 or by 23.68% respectively. In rural areas, the poverty among Muslims declined from 43 in 1987-88 to 33 in 2004-05 or by 23.25% and in SCs/STs it decreased from 54 to 41 or by 24.07%, in other Hindus from 33 to 21 or by 36.36% in all others from 25 to 18 or by 28%

and in all India it came down from 39 to 28 or by 28.20% respectively. Thus, Muslims benefited less compared to others. Likewise, among all the states of the country the poverty incidence in urban areas among Muslims decreased from 24 in 1987-88 to 19 in 2004-05 or by 20.83% compared to 44.73% or from 38 to 21 decrease among SCs/STs and 52.63% decrease or from 19 to 9 for other Hindus, 63.63% decrease or from 11 to 4 in all others and 47.36% decrease or from 19 to 10 in all states taken together respectively. Similarly, the poverty level among Muslims in rural areas among all the states of the country increased by 27.27% from 22 to 28 from 1987-88 to 2004-05 compared to 12.5% increase or from 32 to 36 for SCs/STs and 6.25% decrease or from 16 to 15 for other Hindus and 78.26% decrease or from 23 to 5 for all others and 28.57% decrease or from 21 to 15 for all India respectively. Incidentally, the poverty incidences in most of the states in rural areas have decreased among Muslims but such incidences in urban Delhi, Maharashtra and Madhya Pradesh have increased. Thus, Muslims' position in rural and urban areas remained less favourable compared to the rest. Those who would read the figures provided by the government agencies to the Sachar Committee would be convinced that all is not well with the community. Frustration, anger, fear and suspicion is natural in a community which till yesterday was in mainstream but over a period of sixty years it has drifted towards degradation. Over and above this, the irony of fate is that despite knowing their fate nobody is coming to their rescue. The State and Central Governments are showing them dreams which will probably take years to materialize. Most of the Muslims of India have reached such a stage that by themselves perhaps they cannot develop economically to a reasonable level within a meaningful time horizon without a proactive and inclusive development plan. In a vibrant and democratic setup like India, the feeling of discrimination and neglect among a large section of Muslims is detrimental for the health of the country. Over and above this, the perception of lack of equality of opportunity has paralyzed various segments of the community as a consequence of which they have reverted back to isolation since most of them are convinced that they are not the intrinsic part of the socio-cultural mosaic of India.

Low Participation of Muslims in Government Jobs

Ironically, the fate of Muslims in government jobs too is miserable. They are mostly conspicuous by absence. For justice, equity and good conscience, fair and reasonable participation of all segments of the society should be on the top priority of all the democratic and peoples' governments. Government jobs have a special role in the democratic transformation and equitable development. They are lifetime or permanent jobs and provide long run regular and assured incomes along with retirement benefits and social security. Besides, they provide status and dignity in the society and provide ample opportunities to participate in decision-making at various levels and enable them to come in the mass contact and serve all sections of the society justly and transparently. Moreover, in a democracy these jobs ensure equal opportunities to all ethnic and religious groups for equal participation in the participatory governance. If any section is not represented in various segments of the government, the chances of its exploitation increase exponentially. The bureaucracy begins to take them lightly, media rides over them, judiciary becomes indifferent and the legislature plays with their sentiments with disastrous consequences. It is irony of fate that Muslims' representation in these jobs after nearly sixty years is highly dismal. Muslims who constitute more than 14% of the total national population do not get more than 5% share in any all-India services cadres. Similarly, the participation of Muslims in security and defence related activities which are vital for the health of the community are dismal. The share of Muslims in such activities is merely 6% compared to 23% for SCs/STs, 23% for Hindu OBCs, and 42% for Hindu upper castes. At the states level, they are not better off either. Their share is just 7% compared to 21% for SCs/STs, 26% for Hindu OBCs and 37% for Hindu upper castes. The analysis of Muslim employees in government sector employment is revealed by Table 8.8.

Table 8.8: Muslim Employees in Government Sector Employment

Departments/ Institutions Reporting	Reported No. of Employees	Reported Number of Muslim Employees	Muslims as Percentage to Reported Employees
State Level Departments	4452851	278385	6.3
Railways	1418747	64066	4.5
Banks and RBI	680833	15030	2.2
Security Agencies	1879134	60517	3.2
Postal Service	275841	13759	5.0
Universities	137263	6416	4.7
All Reported Government Employees (Excludes PSUs)	8844669	438173	4.9
Central PSUs	687512	22387	3.3
State PSUs	745271	80661	10.8
All PSUs	1432783	103048	7.2

Source: Sachar Committee Report, Table 9.1

Table 8.8 shows the disgusting picture. It is frustrating to note that out of 8844669 government employees Muslims were merely 438173 or just 4.9%. Similarly, in all public sector undertakings their number was 103048 out of 1432783 or only 7.2%. Department wise, at state level departments they were 278385 out of 4452851 or 6.3%. In Railways, they were 64066 out of 1418747 or 4.5% and in Banks and in RBI their number was merely 15030 or 2.2% out of the total 680833. Similarly, in Security Agency which has direct impact upon their safety and security they were 60517 or 3.2% out of 1879134. In Postal Services and the 129 Universities and 84 colleges, their number was 13759 or 5.0% and 6416 or 4.7% out of 275841 and 137263 respectively. In the same way, their participation in central public sector undertakings was 3.3% as they were only 22387 out of 687512 and in state public sector undertakings they were 10.8% or 80661 out of 745271. If we now look at the share of Muslims in All Indian Civil Service-2006 as per Sachar Committee Report, we find that out of the all civil service officers including IAS, IFS and IPS which were 8827, the number of Muslims was 285 or just 3.2 %. In Indian Administrative Services, 142 Muslims or 3.0% out of 4790 and in Indian Foreign Service 15 or 1.8% out of 828 and in Indian Police Service 128 or 4.0% out of 3209 were selected. As against this, only 155 Muslims or merely 2.4% could succeed out of 6460 in direct recruitment through competitive examination. Only 130 Muslim officers or 5.5% were promoted out of 2367 from the state service. The fault in matters of the competitive examinations at the level of central service partly lies at the side of Muslims for apart from being comparatively less equipped due to their financial conditions, they do not appear at these examinations in large numbers due to fear of discrimination which is perhaps not there. In 2003-04, the percentage of Muslim candidates who appeared for Main Written Civil Service Exams was 4.9% out of which 4.8% were selected for interview and 4.8 were finally recommended. Though Muslims appeared in less number, yet their success rate was about the same as of others.

Table 8.9 shows the following Employment Data Provided by State Government.

Table 8.9

States	Muslim Population (%)	Total Number of Employee	Share of Muslims in State Employment (%)	Education Deptt.	Health, Women and Child Welfare Deptt.	Home Deptt.	Transport Deptt.	Other Deptt.
West Bengal	25.2	134972	2.1	....	1.0	7.1	...	2.4
Kerala	24.7	268733	10.4	12.3	10.5	10.7	9.2	10.2
Uttar Pradesh	18.5	134053	5.3	..	5.6	9.8	4.2	5.0
Bihar	16.5	78114	7.6	12.3	2.6	6.9	10.9	7.6
Assam	30.9	81261	11.2	..	10.8	11.3	11.8	11.7
Jharkhand	13.8	15374	6.7	..	3.4	7.4	...	7.0
Karnataka	12.2	528401	8.5	11.9	5.0	4.2	7.5	7.0
Delhi	11.7	135877	3.2	7.2	1.7	2.2	2 1.1	0.9
Maharashtra	10.6	915645	4.4	4.7	2.8	4.2	..	3.8
Andhra Pradesh	9.2	876291	8.8	7.9	6.4	14.6	10.0	8.9
Gujarat	9.1	754533	5.4	4.5	1.5	5.6	16.3	5.3
Tamil Nadu	5.6	529597	3.2	5.5	3.5	2.5	2.4	2.2
Sum of States	15.4	4452851	6.3	6.5	4.4	7.3	6.5	6.0

Source: Sachar Committee Report, Table 9.4

The analysis of employment data provided by the State Governments for West Bengal, Kerala, Uttar Pradesh, Bihar, Assam, Jharkhand, Karnataka, Delhi, Maharashtra, Andhra Pradesh, Gujarat and Tamil Nadu where the average Muslim population is 15.4% and where the total state employees are 4452851, the Muslims shared merely 6.3% jobs in various government departments. In Education, Health and Women Welfare, Home, Transport and other departments of these states, 15.4% Muslims shared 6.5%, 4.4%, 7.3%, 6.5% and 6.0 respectively. In various categories of Education department in the States of Kerala, Bihar, Karnataka, Delhi, Maharashtra, Gujarat and Tamil Nadu where average Muslim population stood at 12.3%, the share of Muslims as per appendix Table 9.5 in Group 'A', Group 'B', Group 'C' and Group 'D' and others was 5.6%, 5.7%, 6.2%, 6.0% and 4.7% respectively. Likewise, in the Home departments of West Bengal, Kerala, Uttar Pradesh, Bihar, Assam, Jharkhand, Karnataka, Delhi, Maharashtra, Gujarat, Tamil Nadu where Muslim population constituted 14.8%, its share as per appendix Table 9.6 in the above categories was 8.0%, 8.7%, 5.7%, 4.05, and 5.7% respectively. The situation in Health department of West Bengal, Kerala, Uttar Pradesh, Bihar, Assam, Jharkhand, Karnataka, Delhi, Maharashtra, Gujarat and Tamil Nadu where Muslims constitute 16.0% of the total population, their share as per appendix Table 9.7 was merely 3.7% in Group A, 5.1% in Group B, 3.4% in Group C, 3.0% in Group D and 5.0% in others. In the same way, in the Transport department of Kerala, Uttar Pradesh, Bihar, Assam, Karnataka, Delhi, Gujarat and Tamil Nadu where Muslims are 15.7%, their shares are as per appendix Table 9.8 just 5.0% in Group A, 1.4% in Group B, 2.8% in Group C, 12.7% in Group D and 11.5% in others. With their 16.6% share in the population in the states of West Bengal, Kerala, Uttar Pradesh, Bihar, Assam, Jharkhand, Karnataka, Delhi, their percentages in all other departments of Group A, Group B, Group C, Group D and others as per appendix Table 9.9 were merely 5.4%, 5.6%, 5.6%, 5.15 and 2.8% respectively. The situation of Muslims in various segments of Judiciary as per appendix Table 9.10 in West Bengal, Kerala, Uttar Pradesh, Assam, Karnataka, Jharkhand, Delhi, Maharashtra, Andhra Pradesh, Orissa and Chhattisgarh was found pitiable. The share of Muslims employed in these states was merely 7.8% and Advocate Generals were 3.5%, District Session Judges 2.7%, Additional District and Session Judges, 5.5%, Chief Judicial Magistrates, 5.2%, Prl. Judges, 4.45% Munsifs 5.8%, Public Prosecutors, 6.3% Group A Officers 6.8%, Group B Officers 7.1%, Group

C and group D employees, 7.7% and 9.0% respectively. The figures for the share of Muslim employees in State Public Sector Undertakings in West Bengal, Kerala, Uttar Pradesh, Bihar, Karnataka, Delhi, Maharashtra, Gujarat and Tamil Nadu show that their share as per appendix Table 9.11 in Higher positions was 7.4% and lower positions, 9.9% and in Group A it was 7.2%, Group B 7.5%, Group C 10.9% and in others 8.3%. The cross section data both at the level of the Central and State Governments show that the representation of Muslims in government sector is dismal. A comparison of the representation of Hindu OBCs, General Muslims and Muslim OBCs in selected Public Sector Undertakings is revealed from Table 8.10.

Table 8.10: Representation in Public Sector Employment

Categories	Hindu-OBCs	Muslim-Gen.	Muslim-OBCs
	Central Security Agencies		
Higher Positions	4.6	0.4	3.2
Lower Positions	11.7	1.0	3.6
Grade A	5.4	0.3	2.8
Grade B	4.1	0.5	3.4
Grade C	11.8	1.0	3.6
Grade D	10.0	1.1	3.2
Others	1.8	0.3	3.0
Total	11.4	1.0	3.6
	Railways		
Higher Positions	2.8	2.8	0.2
Lower Positions	9.4	4.5	0.4
Grade A	3.5	2.3	0.2
Grade B	2.0	3.3	0.1
Grade C	8.7	4.6	0.3
Grade D	10.5	4.5	0.5
Total	9.3	4.5	0.4
	Public Sector Undertakings: Central		
Managerial-I	5.3	1.9	0.3
Managerial-II	10.4	2.6	0.2
Workers	9.2	3.1	0.8
Total	8.3	2.7	0.6
	State Public Services Commission: Interview		
Higher Positions	21.0	5.4	1.9
Lower Positions	20.5	2.6	0.7
Grade A	17.5	10.4	3.0

Grade B	23.2	2.1	1.6
Grade C	20.0	1.8	0.7
Grade D	31.7	17.1	0.8
Total	20.9	4.8	1.6
State Public Services Commission: Recommended/Selected			
Higher Positions	21.0	1.9	1.2
Lower Positions	29.1	0.6	0.8
Grade A	18.8	6.1	1.3
Grade B	20.0	0.6	1.4
Grade C	19.6	1.4	0.9
Grade D	32.2	0.3	0.8
Total	27.0	0.9	0.9

Source: Sachar Committee Report, Table 10.3

Table 8.10 reveals the miserable condition of Muslims. The shares of the general Muslims in the higher and lower positions as well as in Grades A, B, C, D, other categories and in the total in central security agencies in percentage terms were: 0.4%, 1.0%, 0.3%, 0.5%, 1.0%, 1.1%, 0.3%, 1.0% compared to 3.2%, 3.6%, 2.8%, 3.4%, 3.6%, 3.2%, 3.0%, 3.6% for Muslim OBCs and 4.6%, 11.7%, 5.4%, 4.1%, 11.8%, 10.0%, 1.8% and 11.4% for Hindu OBCs respectively. Likewise, in Railways they were: 2.8%, 4.5%, 2.3%, 3.3%, 4.6%, 4.5%, 4.5% for General Muslims and 0.2%, 0.4%, 0.2%, 0.1% 0.3% 0.5% and 0.4% for Muslim OBCs compared to 2.8%, 9.4%, 3.5%, 2.0%, 8.7%, 10.5% and 9.3% for Hindu OBCs respectively. Similarly, in Central Public Sector Undertakings the shares were: 1.9%, 2.6%, 3.1%, 2.7% for General Muslims and 0.3%, 0.2%, 0.8% and 0.6% for Muslim OBCs compared to 5.3%, 10.4%, 9.2% and 8.3% for Hindu OBCs respectively. In the same way, only 1.9%, 0.6%, 6.1%, 0.6%, 1.4%, 0.3% and 0.9% Muslims from the General Category and 1.2%, 0.8%, 1.3%, 1.4%, 0.9%, 0.8% and 0.9 Muslim from Muslim OBCs were recommended/selected by State Services Commission compared to 21.0%, 29.1%, 18.8%, 20.0%, 19.6%, 32.2% and 27.0% Hindu OBCs in higher and lower positions, as well as Groups A, B, C, D and total categories respectively.

The above figures are certainly frightening for just as after 1857 War of Independence the descendents of the Mughal emperors had become horse-cart drivers and paupers similarly within sixty years after independence Indian Muslims had virtually become worse than OBCs and the SCs/STs. Muslims contend that their miserable condition created inferiority complex in their minds and they felt unwanted and humiliated. Over and above this, many unscrupulous people started demanding from them the proofs of their loyalties and integrity. Many openly opposed their genuine demands and there was no dearth of people who relished in taunting and harassing them. Having seen the adverse climate against them they fell back to their ghettos for safety and security which created a vicious circle of doubts and suspicions. Even after six decades, most of the Muslims find themselves helpless and dejected. They are mostly not welcomed in mainstream and they have to struggle harder in comparison to other segments of society to get their work done. They generally do not get proper information through various government agencies about those schemes which are instituted for them. The resources allocated for minorities are often lapsed or misused. The governments at the Centre as well as at State levels fail to get adequate feedback from Muslims due to their meager representation in the government sector. If the governments continued to follow the same methodology and debarred Muslims from their genuine and just and constitutional rights, they would become paupers and non-entity. Under such circumstances there remains only one alternative for them for the redresser of their grievances and that is, their actual condition should be placed before the liberal, secular, conscientious and meaningful people as well as the governing structure of the country. Actually, many people are not aware of the real conditions of Muslims. Most of them have been told that Muslims were far better compared to the rest of the people due to their unique position. The people of India who are renowned for their fair play would have surely and certainly reacted much earlier were they not kept under dark about the miserable conditions of Muslims. Had they knew that Muslims who till yesterday were respectable and significant part of the society had fallen even below the Scheduled Castes and Scheduled Tribes merely due to the apathy of the government and the people, they would have compelled the government to take corrective actions. Muslims have no grievances against Scheduled Castes and Scheduled Tribes and the Backward Castes. They are happy that Scheduled Castes and Scheduled Tribes which were suppressed and oppressed for centuries and the Backward Castes which were deprived of their rightful share could be brought within the mainstream through affirmative action. They are grieved that instead of progressing along with others they have fallen in the vacuum created by these castes. They are also alarmed that the role of several political parties with reference to the affirmative actions for the growth and development of Muslims remained dubious. A few opposed such devices openly while others remained silent and there was no dearth of people who did little save lip service. There were certain hard-core rightists who due to reasons best known to them deliberately mislead people and artfully kept Indian people in dark for sixty years through sustained propaganda by forcefully repeating and emphasizing that there was an appeasement of Muslims to such an extent that they had become the first class citizens and the Hindus had become the second grade citizens in their own land. This naturally annoyed and perturbed the majority community especially the younger people and they closed their eyes. It is hoped that these new statistics provided by the Central and State Governments to Sachar Committee would prompt them to take affirmative action for the benefit of Muslims in the larger interest of the country at various government and non-government levels.

Meagre Representation of Muslims in Industry, Trade and Commerce

A cursory look at the statistics pertaining to the engagement and the participation of Muslims in industry, trade, commerce, business, professions and vocations would reveal that they are a non-entity in most of the sectors. They are engaged in very few professions, vocations and business. Their share in worker population is also comparatively less.

During 2004-05, the average worker population rate of Muslims in the States of Andhra Pradesh, Assam, Bihar, Delhi,

Gujarat, Haryana, Himachal Pradesh, Jammu and Kashmir, Karnataka, Kerala, Madhya Pradesh, Maharashtra, Orissa, Punjab, Rajasthan, Tamil Nadu, Uttar Pradesh and West Bengal was 54.9 compared to 64.5 for All India and 65.8 for

Table 8.11 exhibits Worker Population Rates in each state by SRCs, All workers, 2004-05 as under.

Table 8.11: Worker Population Rates in Each State by SRCs, All Workers, 2004-05

State	All	All Hindus	Hindus			Muslims			Other Minorities
			SCs/ STs	OBCs	UC	All Muslims	OBCs	General	
All India	64.4	65.8	71.4	67.3	57.4	54.9	53.9	55.6	64.5
AP	72.5	73.7	79.3	75.5	64.9	59.4	55.3	60.3	69.8
Assam	59.8	61.4	63.3	66.0	55.9	56.2	54.3	56.3	61.7
Bihar	54.2	55.3	63.7	54.9	41.2	47.1	48.2	45.3	44.8
Delhi	47.9	48.1	50.8	54.9	45.5	52.0	50.5	52.4	40.4
Gujarat	70.0	71.2	80.1	74.5	59.8	61.1	62.3	60.6	56.4
Haryana	62.4	62.3	64.6	63.8	60.1	68.0	72.0	52.9	61.0
HP	76.1	76.1	75.6	78.5	75.8	84.0	87.4	82.7	66
J&K	57.0	65.7	66.9	57.7	66.6	53.2	58.0	55.2	45.0
Karnataka	69.9	71.7	77.8	71.8	66.3	59.4	60.4	58.3	55.1
Kerala	55.0	59.1	64.1	58.1	57.0	40.4	40.4	44.0	60.1
MP	69.8	71.0	79.9	71.0	54.0	57.7	58.8	56.8	55.4
Maharashtra	68.4	69.6	72.2	71.5	66.6	56.0	59.0	55.6	66.2
Orissa	64.8	64.7	75.6	60.9	50.9	51.9	48.5	52.3	73.1
Punjab	61.9	55.4	59.0	61.4	50.7	71.3	70.0	72.8	65.5
Rajasthan	71.1	71.9	76.2	74.5	58.5	56.5	59.1	53.1	78.2
Tamil Nadu	68.6	70.3	73.4	70.4	51.3	45.2	45.1	46.4	59.6
Uttar Pradesh	60.6	61.6	67.9	63.1	50.2	56.5	57.8	54.5	47.6
West Bengal	55.9	55.7	59.6	55.2	52.7	55.8	55.6	55.8	64.8

Source: Sachar Committee Report, Appendix Table 5.5

All Hindus, 71.4 for SCs/ST and 67.3 for OBCs, 57.4 for upper castes and 64.5 for other minorities. The Muslim OBCs were 53.9% compared to 67.3% Hindu OBCs and the General Category of Muslims was 55.6% as against 57.4% for the upper caste Hindus. Mostly Muslims were engaged in manufacturing sector, trade and self-employment which are revealed from Table 8.12.

The average percentage of Muslim workers employed in manufacturing sector during 2004-05 in the States of Andhra Pradesh, Assam, Bihar, Delhi, Gujarat, Haryana, Himachal Pradesh, Jammu and Kashmir, Karnataka, Kerala, Pradesh,

Table 8.12: Percentage of Workers Employed in Manufacturing Sector in each State by SRcs, 2004-05

State	All	All Hindus	Hindus			Muslims			Other Minorities
			SCs/ STs	OBCs	UC	All Muslims	OBCs	General	
All India	11.8	11.0	8.7	11.9	12.4	20.5	21.7	19.7	9.0
Andhra Pradesh	10.8	10.1	4.8	13.8	7.9	19.6	15.8	20.5	13.3
Assam	3.6	3.8	3.8	2.7	4.6	2.9	0.7	2.9	7.9
Bihar	6.2	5.3	4.4	6.2	3.1	13.2	14.4	11.2	10.6
Delhi	25.1	21.9	25.9	28.5	18.3	57.9	68.1	55.5	18.7
Gujarat	16.0	16.3	10.6	14.8	24.9	13.3	9.8	15.0	11.3
Haryana	13.2	13.8	10.4	16.2	14.0	5.6	4.4	11.9	6.3
Himachal Pradesh	5.8	5.8	7.0	4.1	5.5	6.7	5.3	7.3	6.7
Jammu & Kashmir	12.3	6.4	7.9	13.3	4.4	16.2	12.8	16.9	9.3
Karnataka	10.1	8.9	8.2	9.4	9.0	20.3	18.4	22.5	11.3
Kerala	14.9	18.0	12.0	22.1	14.3	9.2	9.2	12.5	10.1
Madhya Pradesh	7.8	6.6	5.7	7.5	6.5	28.3	37.4	20.1	7.6
Maharashtra	12.2	11.1	10.5	10.1	12.4	24.8	25.4	24.7	11.6
Orissa	11.3	11.4	11.6	12.0	9.1	18.0	6.0	19.3	7.3
Punjab	12.9	23.3	23.0	29.6	21.4	19.0	10.7	28.8	7.6
Rajasthan	8.9	7.8	7.6	7.4	9.6	25.3	25.9	24.5	11.9
Tamil Nadu	19.7	19.2	12.0	21.6	19.0	29.8	30.5	20.7	22.1
Uttar Pradesh	12.5	9.5	9.0	9.4	10.4	28.1	29.2	26.2	6.0
West Bengal	16.8	15.8	11.5	17.4	19.4	20.6	26.0	20.5	6.0

Source: Sachar Committee Report, Appendix Table 5.6

Maharashtra, Orissa, Punjab, Rajasthan, Tamil Nadu, Uttar Pradesh and West Bengal was 20.5 compared 11.8 all India figure and 11.0 for all Hindus, 8.7 for Hindu SCs/STs and 11.9 for Hindu OBCs, 12.4 for Hindu upper castes and 9.0 for other minorities. Likewise, the Muslim OBCs and General Category were 21.7% and 19.17% compared to 11.9% and 12.4% for Hindu SCs/STs and the Hindu upper castes respectively. If we look at the engagement of the Muslims in trade, we find that the average percentage of workers engaged in trade as per appendix Table 5.7 in the above states was 16.8 compared to 9.1 for all India and 8.1 for all Hindus, 4.7 for

Hindu SCs/STs and 7.7 for Hindu OBCs, 13.4 for Hindu upper castes and 9.7 for other minorities. The OBCs of Muslims and the General Category from among Muslims too were mostly engaged in trade. Their percentages were 18.2 and 15.9 compared to 7.7 Hindu OBCs and 13.4 Hindu upper castes. In the same way, major portion of Muslims as per appendix Table 5.8 was engaged in self-employment. The average percentage of self-employed workers in the above states was 57.4 compared 44.6 for all India and 42.6 for all Hindus and 33.4 for Hindu SCs/STs and for 46.1 for Hindu OBCs and 41.2 for all other minorities. However, 62.8% Muslim OBCs and 53.9% of Muslim General Category were engaged in self-employment.

Muslims' representation in two-digit industrial groups during 2004-05 for males as well as females in urban and rural areas too was quite unsatisfactory. Table 8.13 shows distribution of workers by two Digit Industrial groups.

Table 8.13: Distribution of All (Principal & Subsidiary) Workers (age15-64) by Two Digit Industrial Group fro each SRCs, 2004-05

Industrial Group	All	Hindus				Muslims	Other Minorities
		All Hindus	SCs/ STs	OBCs	UC		
		URBAN					
Agriculture, Hunting & Related Service Activities	8	8.6	10.3	11.7	4.7	5.3	6.6
Manufacturing & Textiles	4.8	4.4	3.5	6.1	3.3	7.9	2.2
Manufacture of Wearing Apparel, Dressing & Dyeing of Fur	3.8	3.4	3.3	4.2	2.7	6.8	2.4
Construction	8.2	8.2	13.4	9.2	4.7	7.6	8.6
Retail Trade, Except of Motor Vehicles & Motor Cycles, Repair of personal Household goods	17.0	15.6	11.3	14.9	18.0	21.3	17.5
Land Transport, Transport via Pipelines	7.2	6.9	9.0	6.7	6.0	9.4	6.1
		RURAL					
Agriculture, Hunting & Related Service Activities	71.0	73.0	74.5	73.1	70.0	55.2	71.5
Construction	5.1	4.9	7.1	4.2	2.5	6.4	5.3
Retail Trade except of Motor Vehicles & Motorcycles, Repair of personal & Household goods	4.7	4.3	2.7	4.6	6.8	9.1	4.1
		MALE					

Agriculture & Related Service Activities	49	51	57.6	53.3	40	35.6	46.5
Construction	7.7	7.6	11.1	7.1	4.2	8.5	8.8
Retail Trade, Repair of Personal & Household goods	9.7	8.8	5.2	8.4	14	15.4	9.9
Land Transport, Transport via Pipelines	5.1	4.7	4.7	4.4	5.1	7.7	5.4
FEMALE							
Agriculture, Hunting & Related Service Activities	73.0	75.2	79.0	76.5	65.0	50.7	71.1
Manufacture of Tobacco products	2.3	1.7	1.4	2.0	1.4	11.9	1.0
Manufacture of Textiles	2.5	1.9	1.2	2.4	2.1	9.9	1.8
Retail Trade, Repair of Personal & Household goods	2.9	2.7	1.7	3.0	3.8	5.1	3.1

Source: Sachar Committee Report, Appendix Table 5.3

If we analyze the distribution of all principal and subsidiary urban workers in the age group of 15-64 at 58 two-digit industrial groups for various socio-religious communities during 2004-05, we find that in 10 groups or 17.4% sectors Muslims' participation was nil, in 28 groups or 48.3% sector it was less than 1%, in 14 groups or 24.1% it varied between 1 to 4% and in merely 6 groups or 10.2% sectors it was more than 5%. In agricultural, hunting and related activities, it was 5.3% compared 10.3% for SCs/STs and 11.7% for OBCs. In the same way, in manufacture of textiles it was slightly better at 7.9% compared to 3.5% for SCs/STs and 6.1% for OBCs. Similarly, in manufacture of wearing apparels, dressing and dyeing of fur it was 6.8% compared 3.3% for SCs/STs and 4.2% for OBCs. In construction, it was 7.6% compared to 13.4% for SCs/STs and 9.2% for OBCs. In retail trade and household goods, it was slightly better at 21.3% compared to 11.3% for SCs/STs and 18% upper caste Hindus. Likewise, in land transport it was 9.4% compared to 9.0% SCs/STs and 6.7% OBCs. The other urban minorities too had their considerable share in agriculture, construction, retail trade and wholesale trade and transport business. Over and above this, they were present in substantial numbers in public administration, defence, education, health and social work. The upper caste in urban areas was present in all creamy industrial groups like manufacturing of textiles, manufacturing of wearing apparels, construction, retail trade, land transport, public administration, defence, education, health and social security. Muslims' presence in creamy enterprises was negligible. In the rural areas, the participation of other minorities in agriculture and related activities was quite high though they were present in large numbers in construction, retail trade and land transport too. The upper castes were also far better in agriculture, manufacture of food products, construction, retail trade, land transport, public administration, defence, social security and education. The situation in the rural sector for Muslims was not good. In 36.37% groups, Muslim rural workers were practically not visible while in 45.0% segments their share was less than 1.0%, in 13.3% portions between 1 to 4% and in 5.0% areas more than 5%. Only in agriculture and hunting, it was slightly better at 55.2%, however, it was less than that of the SCs/STs which was 74.5% and OBCs which was 73.1%. In construction, it was 6.4% and in retail and home trade 9.1% compared to 7.1% and 2, 7% for SCs/STs respectively. Besides, nearly 20% males were conspicuous by absence in 12 groups and their participation in 31 groups or in 51.6% segment was less than 1.0% and in 13 groups or 21.7% sector it was between 1 to 4% and in merely 4 groups or 6.7% it was more than 5%. They were 35.6% in agriculture and hunting compared to 57.6% SCs/STs and 53.3% OBCs. In construction, they were 8.5% as against 11.0% SCs/STs and 7.1% OBCs. In retail and home trade and land transport, their share was slightly higher than that of SCs/STs and OBCs. It was 15.4% and 7.7% compared to 5.2% and 4.7% for SCs/STs and 8.4% and 5.1% for OBCs respectively. The upper caste males were absorbed in agriculture, manufacture of food products and textiles, construction, wholesale trade, hotels and restaurants, land transport, insurance, post and telecommunication, administration and education. The participation of Muslim females was also not up to the mark. Out of 60 groups, in 48.3% segment or in 29 groups it was nil. In 31.6% portion or in 19 groups, it was less than 1.0%, in 15.3% or 8 groups it was 6.6% and in 9.8% or 4 groups it was above 5%. In agriculture and hunting, 50.7% females were engaged compared to 79.0% SCs/STs and 76.5%

OBCs. Likewise, in manufacturing of tobacco products and manufacture of textiles and in retail and home trade 11.9%, 9.9% and 5.1% were engaged compared to 1.4%, 1.2% and 1.7% SCs/STs and 2.0%, 2.4% and 3.0% OBCs respectively. The females of other minorities were engaged mostly in agriculture, education, health and social work and as private households with employed persons. However, Upper Caste females were engaged in agriculture, retail trade, hotels and restaurants, public administration, education, health and social work. Thus, the overall condition of Muslims in industrial groups too is precarious.

If we look into the occupational groups we find that the percentage distribution of all principal and subsidiary urban Muslim workers by two-digit occupational groups during 2004-05 was marginal. Table 8.14 shows the percentage distribution of workers by two digit occupational groups.

Table 8.14: Percentage Distribution of All (Principal & Subsidiary) Workers by Two Digit Occupational Groups for each SRCs, 2004-05

Industrial Group	All	Hindus				Muslims	Other Minorities
		All Hindus	SCs/ STs	OBCs	UC		
URBAN WORKERS							
Merchants & Shopkeepers, Wholesale & Retail Trade	8.9	8.3	4.1	7.3	11.5	10.8	11.8
Salesmen, Shop Assistants & Related Workers	6.6	6.3	5.9	6.8	6.0	9.7	3.7
Tailors, Dress Makers, Sewers, Upholsters & Related Workers	4.6	4.0	3.9	4.6	3.4	8.8	3.2
Transport Equipment Operators	5.6	5.3	7.2	5.4	4.1	7.7	4.4
RURAL WORKERS							
Merchants & Shop Keepers & Retail Trade	3.1	2.9	1.6	3.0	5.0	6.1	2.4
Cultivators	38.4	39.9	30.8	43.1	49.2	28.3	32.3
Farmers & Other Cultivators	6.3	5.8	3.8	6.5	7.8	5.1	16.8
Agricultural Laborers	25.1	26.0	38.4	22.2	12.2	20.4	19.7
MALE WORKERS							
Merchants & Shop Keepers & Retail Trade	5.7	5.2	2.4	4.8	9.1	9.0	6.4

Salesmen, Shop Assistants & Related Workers	3.8	3.0	2.2	3.0	4.0	6.1	2.2
Cultivators	28.7	30.2	24.5	34.2	30.5	18.8	26.2
Agricultural Laborers	17.2	17.9	30.4	15.6	6.8	14.2	14.4
Bricklayers & Other Construction Workers	4.7	4.6	6.7	4.6	2.1	5.3	4.6
Transport Equipment Operators	3.9	3.5	3.6	3.4	3.6	6.3	4.1
FEMALE WORKERS							
Cultivators	34.4	36.1	30.9	39.4	38.0	23.5	22.9
Farmers & Other Cultivators	12.2	11.0	7.3	12.2	15.2	12.2	28.7
Agricultural Labourers	25.4	27.0	39.3	24.0	11.4	13.9	16.5
Spinners, Weavers, Knitters & Dyers	1.5	1.3	0.7	1.9	0.9	5.3	0.9
Tobacco Preparers & Tobacco Product Makers	2.3	1.7	1.4	2.0	1.3	11.8	1.1
Tailors, Dress Makers, Sewer & Upholsterers	2.6	2.1	1.3	2.0	3.6	6.9	3.0

Source: Sachar Committee Report, Appendix Table 5.4

Out of 95 occupational groups they were unrepresented, in 22.1% segment or nearly 21 groups. Likewise, in 52.6% segment or 50 groups their representation was less than 1.0%, in 21.1% sector or 20 groups they were between 1 to 4% and in merely 4.2% portion or simply in 4 groups their representation was above 5%. In retail trade, as shop assistants and salesmen, tailors, dress makers and transport operators they were: 10.8%, 9.7%, 8.8% and 7.7% compared to 4.4%, 5.9%, 3.9%, and 7.2% SCs/STs and 7.3%, 6.8%, 4.6% and 5.4% OBCs respectively. As against this, other minorities were engaged in nursing, teaching, transport and as proprietors, directors, clerks, supervisors, merchants, salesmen and bricklayers. The upper castes were engaged as teachers, managers, clerks and supervisors, merchants, salesmen and transport operators. The participation of Muslims in rural areas was negligible. Out of 95 occupational groups in 41.1% segment or 39 groups they were conspicuous by absence, in 44.2% sector or 42 groups their representation was below 1.0%, in 10.5% portion or in 10 groups they were between 1 to 4% and only in 4.2% area or 4 groups their percentage was more than 5%. In retail trade, as cultivators, and farmers and agricultural labourers their share was 6.1%, 33.4% and 20.4% compared to 1.6%, 6.34% and 38.4% SCs/STs and 3.0%, 49.6% and 22.2% OBCs. The other rural minorities were mainly engaged as cultivators and farmers, transport operators, agricultural labourers, plantation workers, and teachers. As against this, the rural upper castes were involved as merchants, salesmen, cultivators and farmers, agricultural labourers, transporters, tailors and teachers. As far as Muslim males are concerned, out of the 95 occupations in 23.2% segment or in 22 occupations they were absent, in 56.8% or 54 occupations their participation was less than 1%, in 13.7% sector or 13 occupations their share varied from 1 to 4% and only to the extent to 6.3% or in 6 occupations their participation was above 5%. The share of male workers engaged as merchants and shopkeepers was 9.0%, salesmen and shop assistants 6.1%, cultivators 18.8%, agricultural labourers 14.2%, bricklayers and construction workers 5.3%, transport equipment operators 6.3% compared to 2.4%, 2.2%, 24.5%, 30.4%, 6.7% and 3.6% SCs/STs and 4.8%, 3.0%, 34.2%, 15.6%, 4.6% and 3.4% OBCs. The males from other minorities were mostly engaged in retail trade, cultivation, administration, transportation, bricklaying, and material handling operations. The upper caste males were involved as teachers, proprietors and managers, merchants, salesmen, cultivators, agricultural labourers, construction workers and transport operators. The condition of Muslim female workers was worse compared to the female workers in other segments. Out of 93 occupations in 51.6% segment or in 48 occupations their participation was nil, in 33.3% or 31 occupations it was below 1% and in 8.6% or 8 occupations it was between 1 to 4% and merely in 6.5% segment or 6 occupations it was above 5%. Likewise, 23.5% were engaged as cultivators, 12.2% as farm related works, 13.9% as plantation workers 5.3% as spinners, weavers, knitters and dyers, 11.8% tobacco preparers and 8.9% as tailors, dress makers and sewers compared to 30.9%, 7.3%, 39.3%, 0.7%, 1.4% and 1.3% SCs/STs and 39.4%, 12.2%, 24.0%, 1.9%, 2.0% and 2.0% OBCs. The females from other minorities were engaged generally in cultivation and farming, as well as farm and agricultural labourers, plantation workers, teachers and maids. As against this, the upper caste females were involved mostly as merchants, cultivators and farmers, plantation workers, tailors and dress makers and maids. Thus, among occupations too Muslim males and females both in the urban and rural areas are handicapped compared to other socio-religious castes.

A flying glance at the worker population ratio among Muslims in age group 15-64 is revealed by Table 8.15.

Table 8.15: Worker Population Ratio by Socio-religious Categories, 2004-05 (Principal and Subsidiary Status, 15-64 years)

Social Group		Urban	Rural	Male	Female	Total
Hindus	All Hindus	53.1	70.3	84.9	46.1	65.8
	SCS/STs	56.3	74.5	87.3	54.9	71.4
	OBCs	56.4	70.5	85.8	48.3	67.3
	UC	49.0	63.5	80.8	33.1	57.4
Muslims		51.1	57.0	84.6	25.2	54.9
Other Minorities		51.6	70.2	81.8	47.2	64.5
All		52.7	68.9	84.6	43.6	64.4

Source: Sachar Committee Report, Table 5.1

The above figures exhibit that the worker population ratio for Muslims was merely 54.9 compared to 71.4 for SCs/STs and 67.3 for Hindu OBCs and 57.4 for Hindu upper castes and 64.4 for all-India and 64.5 for other minorities. Likewise, it was 51.1% and 57.0% for Muslims in urban and rural areas compared to 56.3% and 74.5% for SCs/STs respectively. Similarly, for Muslim males it was 84.6 and 25.2 for Muslim females compared to 87.3 and 54.9 for SCs/STs males and females and 85.8 and 48.3 for OBCs males and females respectively. The participation of Muslim females in urban and rural areas is lowest among all the segments of the society. In the same way, the share of Muslims in urban and rural areas too is lowest among all sections of the society save the Hindu upper castes. In the total also their participation is lowest among all socio-religious groups. As per Sachar Committee Report during 2004-05, only 23.7% Muslims were engaged in regular salaried wages as non-agricultural workers in government and 6.5% in public and large private sectors compared to 35.3% and 13.9% for all Hindus, 39.4% and

17.1% for Hindu upper castes and 35.8% and 12.8% for other minorities and 34.2% and 13.1 for all-India. Only 23.0% and 6.5% Muslim males and 24.9% and 6.8% Muslim females were employed in government and private sector in contrast to 41.3% and 9.4% SCs/STs males and 32.4% and 9.9% SCs/STs females respectively. In urban and rural areas too they were far behind SCs/STs for only 19.4% and 7.4% Muslims in government and private sectors in urban area and 33.3% and 4.8% in rural area were employed compared to 36.7% and 8.7% SCs/STs in urban segment and 42.9% and 10.5% SCs/STs in rural sector respectively. Muslims were far behind Hindu OBCs, Hindu upper castes and other minorities as well as below the national average. If we look at the cross section data we find that merely 27% Muslim workers were engaged in urban areas in regular jobs compared to 40.0% SCs/STs, 36.0% OBCs and 49.0% upper castes. Likewise, only 24.0% Muslim worker were engaged in regular jobs in the public sector enterprises or government concerns in comparison to 39.0% SCs/STs, 30.0% OBCs and 37.0% upper castes. Unfortunately, Muslims participation in regular and salaried jobs in private and corporate sectors, public enterprises, formal segments and government jobs is less than the national average for most of them are engaged in self-employed activities, proprietary businesses, non-manufacturing segment, informal wholesale trade, and as shopkeepers, casual labourers, sales persons, bidi workers, tailors, dress makers, spinners, weavers, knitters, dyers, transport operators and merchants. Nearly 34.0% Muslim workers are engaged in production related activities and transport operations compared to 9.0% Hindu and 21.0% all workers. More than 16.0% Muslim workers are engaged as sales workers as against 9.0% Hindu workers and 10.0% national average. As many as 22.0% Muslim workers were employed in non-manufacturing sector, wholesale, and commission business and retail trade. As a matter of fact, the participation of Muslim male workers in government and public sector undertakings is less than that of OBCs and SCs/STs as only less than 6.0% of them have been engaged in these enterprises in comparison to 10.0% Hindu OBCs and 13.0% SCs/STs male workers respectively. In the same way, less than 8.0% Muslim workers in urban areas are engaged in formal sector as against the national average of 21.0% and 22.0% for SCs/STs and 18.0 for OBCs. Muslim workers are highly vulnerable as more than 12.0% Muslim male workers are engaged in street vending compared to the national average of less than 8.0%. Larger number of SCs/STs and OBCs are engaged in agriculture compared to less than 40.0% Muslims. It is most unfortunate that due to lack of education and the necessary skills, Muslim workers get lower daily wages in private as well as public sectors. About 73.0% Muslims work under no contract condition compared to 63.0% each for SCs/STs and the OBCs and 52.0% for upper castes. Almost 71.0% Muslim workers have no social security compared to average of 55.0%. A large proportion of Muslim workers is on piece-rate system and on inferior jobs. The condition of Muslim women workers is terrible since most of them are worse than SCs/STs women folk in almost all fields save women-owned, proprietary enterprises, home-based activities and sub-contracting jobs. We can thus conclude that the general condition of Muslim workers is pathetic. As a rule one can say that, other things remaining the same, the probability of a Muslim worker getting regular job in industrial structure in urban areas is the lowest while that for the SCs/STs, it is highest.

Scanty Role of Financial Institutions in Promoting the Growth of Muslims

The data from various public sector and private sector banks and the one obtained from SIDBI, NABARD and under 15 Point Programme reveal that the flow of credit to Muslims in priority sectors in the form of advances by commercial banks has been highly disappointing. Not only the access of Muslims to bank credit is inadequate, the average size of credit compared to other socio-religious communities is low in public sector as well as private sector banks and in the specialized agencies. The percentages of Muslims availing banking facilities especially in the Muslim-dominated villages are much lower because either these areas have been marked as the negative zones or banking facilities are conspicuous by absence. Likewise, the flow of credit by specialized banking institutions, like the Small Industries Development Bank of India which provides assistance to small and medium enterprises and the National Bank for Agriculture and Rural Development which helps marginal borrowers and the weaker sections of the society, too has been meager. Mostly, Muslims are not aware of banking facilities and their miserable condition is not reported transparently. Admittedly, there is a dearth of various government agencies to display any information among minorities about various schemes that have been specially designed for them as well as there are a few NGOs amongst Muslims or Muslim organizations that can provide consultancy to various sections of Muslim society about various government plans and policies. Minority Affairs Ministry can serve this purpose provided it takes up this matter on war footings. Besides, the share of Muslims in the deposits of these banks has not only been minimal, the amount outstanding too is low compared to other minorities. Muslims are not averse to banking because they are mostly self-employed people and carry on home-based trade. They need credit badly. Their womenfolk who are mostly engaged in their own business are being exploited by the middlemen due to the paucity of funds. It has been found that Muslims are very talented people. They are hard working and capable of doing wonders but their main problem is that they do not have resources to finance their projects. They mostly rely on moneylenders or remain jobless and workless due to the lack of money. The moneylenders exploit them by charging abnormally high rates. These poor Muslims mostly take loans from these moneylenders at the time of sickness, misery or marriages which they fail to repay till their life time. Mostly, the contractors give sub-contracts to Muslim men and women at very low rates. After working for the whole day, the family is merely able to meet two ends. It has been seen that the material which is sold finally in Mumbai, Kolkata, Delhi or any metropolitan city at more than rupees two lakh hardly costs rupees ten thousand at grass-root level. The profit is snatched by various middlemen. Muslim men and women work hard the whole day and in the evening get merely ten to twenty rupees. If they can get cheap and adequate reliable credit at their door steps by government agencies, they can come out of the rut and they would never need any dolls from the government. As we know the micro credit and Grameen Banks have brought revolution in Bangladesh where poor people were being exploited by the moneylenders and the sub-contractors. The same can be done in India.

Table 8.16 shows priority sector advances extended to SRCs by type of banks in India and 44 selected minority concentration districts (Average of 5 Years ending 31 March 2001 to 31 March 2005).

Table 8.16

Parameter	Public Sector Banks			Private Sector Banks		
	Muslims	Other Minorities	Others	Muslims	Other Minorities	Others
No. of Accounts (% of Total)	12.2	8.1	79.7	11.3	10.5	78.2
Amount Outstanding (% of Total)	4.6	6.3	89.1	6.6	7.9	85.5
Amount outstanding per Account (Rs/account)	19837	40686	59055	111634	201840	274911
% Share in Population	13.4	5.6	80.9			
No. of Accounts (% of Total)	21.3	5.0	73.7	20.7	14.9	64.4
Amount Outstanding (% of Total)	7.9	3.7	88.4	9.9	7.7	82.4
Amount Outstanding per Account (Rs/account)	20343	40203	64665	108435	114971	330103
% Share in Population	32.8	2.0	65.2			

Source: Sachar Committee Report, Table 6.1

A glance at the advances extended by public sector and private sector banks between 31 March 2001 to 31 March 2005 in priority sectors shows that Muslims had 12.2% accounts in public sector and 11.3% in private sector banks which was close to their share in population. However, in comparison to other minorities it was low for other minority shared 8.1% accounts for their 5.6% population. As against this, their shares in amounts outstanding were as low as 4.6% in PuSBs and 6.6% in PrSBs compared to 6.3%, 7.9% for other minorities and 89.1% and 85.5 for others respectively. Likewise, the amount outstanding per account too was merely ₹ 19837 in PuSBs and ₹ 111634 in PrSBs compared to ₹ 40686 and ₹ 201840 for other minorities and ₹ 59055 and ₹ 274911 for others respectively. In the same way, the position of priority sector advances in the Muslim dominated and in areas with relatively lesser population was not different. In districts with more than 40%+ Muslim population the number of accounts were 31.6%, amounts outstanding were 12.9% and rupees outstanding per account were 19700 in PuSBs and number of accounts, amounts outstanding and rupees outstanding per account were 31.8%, 13.2% and ₹ 104895 in PrSBs respectively compared to 5.3%, 3.4% and ₹ 31132 in PuSBs and 7.9%, 4.8% and ₹ 154208 in PrSBs for other minorities and 63.1%, 83.7% and ₹ 64317 in PuSBs and 60.3%, 81.9% and ₹ 342882 in PrSBs for others respectively. These figures in districts with 26-40% Muslim population were 13.7%, 6.3% and ₹ 14749 in PuSBs and 4.7%, 2.0% and ₹ 169600 in PrSBs respectively. Likewise, in district with below 22% Muslim population these figures were 11.6%, 3.6% and ₹ 39834 in PuSBs and 10.0%, 2.1% and ₹ 138519 in PrSBs respectively. Thus, the share of Muslims in number of accounts and amounts outstanding both percentage wise and in terms of rupees tend to be significantly below their population share and also less than other minorities and the remaining segments of the society.

If we analyze in absolute terms we find that Muslims' accounts in priority sector were 4559 thousands compared to 3050 thousands for other minorities and 29867 thousands for all others. Similarly, ₹ 10394 crores were advanced to Muslims compared to ₹ 14820 crores to other minorities and ₹ 201005 crores for others during 2001 to 2005. In the same way, the annual average amounts outstanding per account of all scheduled commercial banks were ₹ 22542 for Muslims, ₹ 47546 for other minorities and ₹ 66304 for all others. Likewise, priority sector advances granted to Muslims covered 1139 thousand accounts and ₹ 2495 crore compared to 275 thousand accounts and ₹ 1208 crore for other minorities and 3971 thousand accounts and ₹ 27856 crore for others. Muslims' share extended to 1120 thousand accounts and ₹ 2287 crore in PuSBs and 19 thousand and ₹ 208 crore in PrSBs compared to 262 thousand and ₹ 1049 crore in PuBSs and 14 thousand and

₹ 159 crore in PrSBs for other minorities and 3903 thousand accounts and ₹ 25434 crore in PuSBs and 68 thousand and ₹ 2423 crore in PrSBs for others. The shares of Muslims in number of accounts and amounts in percentages terms were 20.6% and 8.0% compared to 5.0% and 3.8% for other minorities and 74.4% and 88.3% for others respectively. Similarly, the percentage share of Muslims in priority sector advances by scheduled commercial banks on annual average for three years ending 31 March 2002-05 in terms of number of accounts and amount outstanding were 8.3% and 5.2% in Agriculture, 11.3% and 5.2% in Small Scale Industries and 10.1% and 5.9% in other priority sectors respectively. In the same way, the percentage share of Muslims in individual deposit in scheduled commercial banks on annual average base for three years ending 31 March 2002-05 was 7.6% in matters of number of accounts and 7.4% in matters of amounts. The individual deposits per account in scheduled commercial banks were ₹ 29369 for all states as annual average for three years compared to ₹ 28829 for Muslims. Muslims got very little benefit from programmes implemented by SIDBI for during 2000-01 to 2000-06 Muslims had 2865 accounts out of 191178 and they were sanctioned ₹ 179.54 crores out of 31805.29 crore and only ₹ 124.12 crore were distributed out of ₹ 26592.58 crore, i.e. their share in actual number of accounts was merely 1.5% and they were sanctioned merely 0.56% and disbursed just 0.46%. More or less the same was the position with reference to the share of Muslims in NABARD that is in refinance of production credit and investment credit. Out of 9167.65 crore invested by NABARD refinance in production and 8485.48 crore in investment credit on annual average basis for 2004-5 and 2005-06, Muslims got 290.83 crore or merely 3.2% as production credit and 333.41 crore or just 3.9% as investment credit.

The Failure of State Sponsored Beneficiary Programmes in Reaching the Muslims

There are more than 200 programmes for the benefit of the marginalized sections of the society but data reveals that Muslims have been benefited the least. Though 38% Muslims in urban areas and 27% in rural areas are below poverty line, yet their share as beneficiaries in such programmes has been dismal. Muslims in Kerala constitute nearly 30.7% of the poor but save Cooperative Credit, National Tuberculosis Control and National Programme for Blindness where their shares are 25%, 28% and 21.0% respectively, their share under other programmes varies from 5% to 18%. The share of government programmes in Uttar Pradesh where they constitute 23.6% of the poor ranges between 3% and 14%. In schemes implemented by Agriculture and Cooperative Societies, their share is less than 10%. In Swarna Jayanti Shari Rozgar Yojna and Small Scale Industries, their share fluctuates around 16%. The same is more or less the fate in other schemes. For instance, in Yeshasvini Health Care Scheme implemented by Karnataka till the end of March, nearly 60% Muslims in the urban areas and 80% in rural areas failed to get the benefit during 2005-06. Only 0.17 lakh or merely 1.0% persons out of 17.01 lakh availed the benefit from the Scheme. Muslim women in the urban areas and rural areas fail to take the benefit of government institutions for 60% deliveries in urban areas take place in privately run institutions and 80% in rural areas take place in homes with the help of untrained staffs. Muslim children have benefited the least from Integrated Child Development Services, 2004-05. An analysis of the use of ICDS shows that less than 8% Muslim children have somewhat benefited from this programme. In Kerala, slightly more than 9%, in West Bengal 14% Muslim children have been benefited but in the remaining states its coverage has been poor. As far as the Mid-day-Meal scheme-2004-05 for children aged 6-16 is concerned only 7.6% Muslim children got benefit at the national level compared to 10.2% SCs/STs, 12.5% OBCs and 13.5% other minorities and at the states level 12.4% benefited compared to 16.8% OBCs and 32.4% other minorities. Likewise, the Maulana Azad Education Foundation which was established to help weaker sections in minorities failed miserably due to ineffectiveness of the meager corpus. It could help as low as 0.1% of eligible girls from below poverty level from among Muslim community. In the same way, the Madrasa Modernization and Infrastructure Development Programme could not take off effectively for in the four years from April 2002 to March 2006, it was provided with only ₹ 106 crore which were highly insufficient. During this period only 4694 madrasas could be provided some help and merely ₹ 27 crore could be spent on infrastructure development which showed no visible results. The State Backward Classes and Minorities Corporations which were meant for the development of backward classes and minorities have provided some benefit to minorities during 2002-03 to 2004-05. West Bengal got ₹ 64 crore and benefited 17618 persons most of whom were Muslims. In Kerala where Muslims constitute 57% of the total minority, their share was to the extent of 22% in the total share of ₹ 141 crore. In Karnataka also Muslims' share out of ₹ 56 crore was 71%. In Uttar Pradesh, Muslims had a large share of 98% out of ₹ 539 crore due to the payment of salaries and payment of pre-matriculation scholarship to students by the Minority Department. The National Minorities Development and Finance Corporation were designed in 1994 to provide special focus on the economic development of Muslims, Christians, Sikhs, Buddhists and Parsis. The Corporation has given ₹ 803 crore to about 2.87 lakh beneficiaries and the cumulative flow of funds covered under the term loan scheme for 2002-03 to 2005-06 was to the extent of ₹ 400 crore of which 73% were Muslims. During this period, nearly 1.15 Lakh people were provided assistance out of which 77% were Muslims. In twenty states where the share of Muslim population in minority population was 70.5% during April 2002 to March 2006, the Corporation distributed ₹ 40009 lakh out of which Muslims got ₹ 29173 lakh or 72.9% of the total disbursement. Out of beneficiaries assisted, the share of Muslims was 76.7% for 88025 Muslims were benefited out of the total number extending to 114709. National Backward Classes Finance and Development Corporation has not done justice to Muslims for it has distributed merely ₹ 23 crore among backward Muslims out of ₹ 247 crore when Muslims constitute a significant portion of the backward classes. There are several reasons for Muslims deprivation in the various beneficiary schemes such as their lack of knowledge, lethargy, and non-cooperation on the part of the disbursement authorities but most significant among them is the lack or low participation of Muslims in decision-making bodies. Their participation in adequate numbers in political process and governance is bound to tilt the scale in their favour.

The Unsatisfactory Condition of the Muslim OBCs

Muslim OBCs constitutes 40.7% of the total Muslim population and 15.7% of the total OBC population of the country. B.P. Mandal Commission report 1980, has clubbed nearly 82 backward castes of Muslim community with about 3743 backward castes and extended the benefit of reservation to Muslims along with backward groups from other religions. Generally, there is a misconception especially in the majority community that Muslims are a monolith community and hence the descent-based social stratification among Muslims is absent but it is not true. As late as 1901 the Census of India listed 133 social groups which were wholly or partially Muslims. Admittedly, Muslims are a differentiated group in the sense that sociologically they are somewhat different from similar segments though there are several caste groups such as Rajputs, Kumhars, Mochis, Malis, Kurmis, Koris, Darzis, Halwais, carpenters, tanners, milkmen and others who are common among both Hindus and Muslims. It is because of their distinctive nature that several backward Muslim groups could not be included in the list of Mandal Commission when they were struggling in pitiable conditions and were worse than others. The presence of Muslim OBCs is felt throughout the country, however, in the states of Kerala, Tamil Nadu, and Haryana the Muslim OBCs constitute their entire Muslim population. Likewise, in Uttar Pradesh, Bihar, Rajasthan, Madhya Pradesh and Jharkhand majority of Muslims have been listed as backward castes. Their presence in West Bengal and Assam is miniscule. The regional analysis of the 14 out of the 20 states reveals that the share of Muslim OBCs from 1999 to 2005 has increased by 32 percentage points in Rajasthan followed by 23 by Bihar, and 18 by Uttar Pradesh when their share has declined in West Bengal, Assam, Jammu and Kashmir, Karnataka, Delhi and Himachal Pradesh. Besides, the facts and figures show that Muslim OBCs have secured very little benefit under the reservation scheme because they have to compete with other backward sections who are educationally better than them and who have their supporters in various interview boards and selection committees. The need of the hour, therefore, is an affirmative action in the shape of at least a 9% separate quota within the quota for Muslim OBCs so that justice may be done to them. Incidentally, the Havanur Commission 1972 had recommended the creation of a distinct category of minority group within the broader larger group with reservation not exceeding 6%. Unfortunately, the Muslim OBCs lagged behind in all fields. Like many upper caste Muslims the deprivation level at schools among OBC children is very high for a large portion of OBC children do not attend schools. Their literacy level too is lower than that of Hindu OBCs. In matters of acquiring higher education they are inferior to Hindu OBCs as well as Muslim high castes. The literacy level among Muslim OBC children aged 6 and above is 61.9% compared to 65.7% Hindu OBCs, 66.0% Muslim General and 67.3% all India average. In urban and rural areas, it was 70.1% in urban and 57.8% in rural areas compared to 80.8% urban and 61.7% rural for Hindu OBCs and 75.6% urban and 61.2% rural for Muslim general and 82.6% urban and 61.9% rural at all India level respectively. Almost 56% Muslim OBC children aged 12 years or less does not attend schools compared to 55% for Muslim general and 49% for Hindu OBCs. In the same way, the level of education among Muslim OBCs is lower in practically all segments. Table 8.17 shows the distribution of persons (aged 6+ years) in each SRC by levels of education.

Table 8.17: Distribution of Persons (aged 6 years+) by Levels of Education (2004-05)

Educational Level	H-OBCs	M-Gen	M-OBCs	Total
Illiterate	33.4	33.3	37.4	31.6
Just Literate	1.2	2.2	2.9	1.4
Below Primary	0.8	1.7	1.5	1.0
Primary	15.9	18.0	17.5	15.4
Middle	16.0	18.6	16.0	15.7
Secondary	15.0	12.6	13.1	14.2
Higher Secondary	7.4	5.9	5.1	7.8
Diploma /Certificate	3.9	2.8	2.5	4.4
Graduate and above	3.2	2.4	1.9	4.3

Source: Sachar Committee Report, Table 10.5

The above figures reveal that the illiteracy rate among the Muslim OBCs during 2004-05 was 37.4% compared to 33.4% Hindu OBCs and 33.3% for Muslim General. Their 1.5% children were below Primary, 17.5% were in Primary and 16.0% in Middle, 13.1% in Secondary and 5.1% in Higher Secondary compared to 0.8%, 15.9%, 16.0%, 15.0% and 7.4% for Hindu OBCs and 1.7%, 18.0%, 18.6%, 12.6% and 5.9% for Muslim general respectively. In matters of diplomas, certificates and degrees their share in Diploma/Certificates was 2.5% and in graduate and above 1.9% compared to 3.9% and 3.2% for Hindu OBCs and 2.8% and 2.4% Muslim General. If we look at the proportion of persons aged 20+ with higher education as per Table 10.6 we find that Muslim OBCs were 2.3% as General graduates, 0.1% as technical graduates, 1.7% with technical diplomas and certificates and 4.1% with higher education compared to 3.7%, 0.2%, 2.3%, and 6.2% for Hindu OBCs and 3.5%, 0.2%, 1.4% and 5.2% for Muslim general. Likewise, in matter of work participation ratio as per the observations of Sachar Committee Report they lagged behind Hindu OBCs. With reference to unemployment rates they were worse than Hindu OBCs as well as Muslim upper castes. The work participation among 15-64 age group in Muslim OBCs was 55% compared to 67% for Hindu OBCs. However, the difference between Muslim OBCs and Muslim General was just marginal. The unemployment among Muslim OBCs was also high as 9.2% of Muslim OBCs of all ages were unemployed in 2004-05 as against 7.5% for Hindu OBCs and 7.7% for Muslim General. Besides, their presence in formal sector is much less than that of Hindu OBCs and in matters of the employment of males and urban workers they lagged even behind the upper caste Muslims. Only 3.5% Muslim OBCs were employed in former sectors in urban areas compared to 11.3% Hindu OBCs and 7% Muslim General. Similarly, in rural areas their share was 3.4% compared to 7.2% for Hindu OBCs and 5.8% for Muslim General. The proportion of Muslim OBCs in salaried jobs in urban areas was also just 20.4% compared to 36.4% for Hindu OBCs and 32.2% for Muslim General. Male Muslim OBCs are mainly concentrated in employer's enterprises when the female Muslim OBC workers are more in own dwellings. The nature of job of Muslim OBC is revealed by Table 8.18.

Table 8.18: Distribution of Male Workers by Place of Work for Each SRCs (2004-05)

Location of Work	Hindu-OBCs	M-Gen	M-OBCs	All
No fixed place	8.5	9.6	5	8.3
Own Dwelling	14.7	13.8	10.2	12.3
Own Enterprise	17.5	21.9	24.9	18.5
Employer's Dwellings	2.6	3.5	2.9	3.0
Employer's Enterprise	34.3	25.5	43.2	35.0
Street-Fixed Location	3.4	4.3	2.4	3.3
Street-No Fixed Location	4.2	8.0	2.8	4.6
Construction Sites	10.8	9.7	4.8	11.0
Others	4.0	3.9	4.0	4.2

Source: Sachar Committee Report, Table 10.8

Generally, a relatively larger proportion of Muslim OBCs was absorbed in employer's enterprises as 43.2% Muslim OBCs were working in employer's enterprises compared to 34.3% Hindu OBCs and 25.5% Muslim General. Similarly, 24.9% were absorbed in own enterprise compared to 17.5% Hindu OBCs and 21.9% Muslim general. In the same way, 10.2% were employed in Own Dwelling compared to 2.4%, 2.8%, 4.8% and 4% who were working in Street-Fixed location, Street-No-Fixed location, Construction sites and others respectively. The major portion of the Muslim OBCs' female workers, that is, to the tune of 73.6% was engaged in own dwellings compared to 52.1% Hindu OBC females and 66.8% Muslim General females. Though in matters of receiving wages they are somewhat better compared with Hindu OBCs and Muslim upper castes, yet in matters of receiving salaries they get lower than both. The average daily wages for casual Muslim OBC workers as per appendix Table 10.7 were ₹ 49 compared to ₹ 39 for Hindu OBCs and ₹ 43 for Muslim General. Likewise, their males and females were relatively better as the male Muslim OBCs got ₹ 52 and females ₹ 32 compared to ₹ 45 to Hindu OBC males, ₹ 27 to Hindu OBC females and ₹ 46 to Muslim General males and ₹ 27 to Muslim General females. However, as far as the salary for regular workers in public enterprises was concerned they were paid ₹ 176 compared to ₹ 190 for Hindu OBCs and ₹ 196 for Muslim General. In the same way their males and females also got less. The Muslim OBC males received ₹ 177 and the Muslim OBC females got ₹ 173 compared to ₹ 199 to Hindu OBC males and ₹ 138 to Hindu OBC females and ₹ 199 to Muslim general males and ₹ 164 to Muslim general females. Likewise, their rewards in the private sector too were low. The Muslim OBCs got ₹ 79 compared to ₹ 85 for Hindu OBC and ₹ 87 for Muslim General. Similarly, their males got ₹ 83 and females got ₹ 39 compared to ₹ 92 for Hindu OBC males and ₹ 48 Hindu OBC females and ₹ 87 for Muslim General males and ₹ 57 Muslim General females. In Central and State employment agencies, all of them are under represented but deprivation of Muslim OBCs is more than that of Hindu OBCs. Hindu OBCs are well represented in teaching though their proportion in non-teaching jobs is lower but Muslims both OBCs and high castes are far inferior to Hindu OBCs in these areas. The representation of Muslim OBCs in public employment too is far from satisfactory. Table 8.19 reveals the representation of Hindu OBCs, Muslim General and Muslim OBCs in public employment.

Table 8.19: Representation in Public Employment

Department/Undertaking/Institution	H-OBCs	M-Gen	M-OBCs
Central Security Agencies	11.4(33)	1.0(15)	3.6(82)
Railways	9.3(27)	0.9(13)	0.9(20)
Central PSU	8.3(24)	2.7(40)	0.6(14)
SPSC-Recommendation for Selection	27.0(77)	0.9(13)	0.9(20)
University Faculty	17.6(50)	3.9(57)	1.4(32)
University Non-Teaching	24.9(71)	3.0(44)	1.7(39)

Note: Figures in parentheses represent relative deprivation.

Source: Sachar Committee Report, Table 10.10

The above table exhibits that the share of Muslim OBCs in Central security agencies was 3.6%, in Railways it was 0.9% and in General PSU it was 0.6%. The SPSC-Recommended for selection 0.9% and the University Faculty absorbed 1.4% and their share in University-Non-Teaching was 1.7% compared to 11.4%, 9.3%, 8.3%, 17.6%, and 24.9 for Hindu OBCs and

1.0%, 0.9%, 2.7%, 0.9%, 3.9% and 3.0% for Muslim General respectively. Thus, there was a tremendous short fall for both Muslim OBCs and Muslim general compared to Hindu OBCs. The land holdings of Muslim OBCs as well as the Muslim high castes are nearly fifty per cent of that of Hindu OBCs. Actually, the average land holding of Hindu OBCs amounting to 1.9 acres are higher than the national average of 1.7 acres. Muslim OBCs and Muslim General share only 1.0 and 0.7 acres respectively. Thus, Hindu OBCs are superior to Muslim OBCs and spend more compared to Muslim OBCs in urban area. The inequality level among both is higher among Muslim OBCs than Hindu OBCs both in rural and urban areas. The share of Muslim General and Muslim OBCs is higher in low income group and within Muslim community the Muslim OBCs fall within the low income group. Very few Muslims come under high income group and the condition of the Muslim OBC is bad since very few of them are found in the high income group among Muslim community. The incidence of poverty is highest that is, 38% among Muslim OBCs are poor followed by 35% for Muslim General and 27% for Hindu OBCs and 28% national average. This inequality is found both in the urban and rural areas but its incidence is higher in urban areas for the poorer persons among Muslim OBCs and Muslim general are 14 percentages and 9 percentages points higher than that of Hindu OBCs. The weak position of the Muslim OBCs is reflected from their monthly per capita expenditure which has been shown by Table 8.20.

Table 8.20: Average Monthly Per Capita Expenditure by Place of Residence and SRCs

Sector	H-OBCs	M-Gen	M-OBCs	Total
Total	620	633	605	684
Urban	901	833	689	1052
Rural	548	532	566	559

Source: Sachar Committee Report, Table 10.11

The monthly per capita expenditure among Muslim General and Muslim OBCs as revealed by the above table is lower compared to the Hindu OBCs and the national average.

Muslim OBCs spend ₹ 605 compared to national average of ₹ 684, and ₹ 620 for Hindu OBCs, and ₹ 633 for Muslim General. In urban and rural areas, they spend ₹ 689 and ₹ 566 compared to national average of ₹ 1052 and ₹ 559 and for Hindu OBCs ₹ 901 and ₹ 548 and for Muslim General ₹ 833 and ₹ 532 respectively. Thus, we find that while the Hindu OBCs continue to be relatively deprived compared to Hindu General and the national average, the condition of Muslims is worst. They are inferior even to the Hindu OBCs and compared to Muslim General the Muslim OBCs are far more inferior. Kerala and Karnataka have considered the entire Muslim population as backward and have provided reservation to Muslims excluding creamy layer. In Kerala presently out of 40% reservation for backward castes, Muslims, share is 12%. The Karnataka Government has included all Muslims earning less than ₹ 2 lakh per annum under one of the categories of backward castes and has reserved 4% seats for them in government services and has earmarked seats in various courses as a consequence of which substantial number of students could qualify for medical, dental, engineering, management courses. The Tamil Naidu Government has done away with religious reservation but has included nearly 95% Muslims within the reserved category. In Bihar, backward Muslims have been included in the OBC or MBC list depending upon their poverty levels. Looking to the conditions of Muslim OBCs one can safely conclude that without affirmative action these classes cannot come out of the rut for they are miserably placed and over a period of sixty years their condition has fallen from bad to worst.

The Misuse and Mismanagement of the Wakf Properties

Fortunately, Muslims have a tradition to pay charities, Zakat, Fitras, skins of the sacrificial animals to the destitute and the needy and for the sake of God as well as they bequeath large and valuable properties to meet the exclusive needs of the poor and for the perpetual maintenance of the wakf properties. Unfortunately, they pay these charities to beggars and wayfarers, however, if the same is collected properly it can be effectively utilized for establishing and managing universities, colleges, health centres, destitute homes and convention halls. Similarly, the voluntary charities, fitras and the value of sacrificial animals reaching in crores can also be fruitfully utilized for running madrasas, mosques and managing graveyards. Muslims have donated properties worth billions of rupees in the name of Allah for the sake of Muslims' benefits, a glimpse of which is revealed from Table 8.21.

Table 8.21: Properties Gazzetted as Wakfs in Indian States (2005-06)

State	Area (Acre)	No. of Properties	Book Value in Lakh	Total Current Income of All the Properties	7% Share of Wakf Board
West Bengal	59090	148200	16000	457	32
Uttar Pradesh	15000	122639	15200	1214	85
Kerala	22410	36500	135586	803	56
Andhra Pradesh	145512	35703	8135	388	326
Karnataka	18033	28731	..	1288	90
Maharashtra	92207	23566	4185	443	31
Gujarat	8792	22485	600	381	27
Rajasthan	153180	195443	196755	8314	5
Madhya Pradesh	..	15000	..	...	..
Haryana	20895	11929	1125	500	500
Punjab	1778	11243	1589	596	596
Tamil Nadu	34388	7057	165072	1385	97
Bihar	...	2459	2000	33	2
Uttaranchal	...	2032	285	268	19
Delhi	152	1977	...	67	5
Pondicherry	425	589	179	118	8
Assam	190	168	110	35	2
Total	572052	490021	546821	16290	1934

Source: Sachar Committee Report, Table 11.1

The above table shows that there are 490021 properties declared as wakfs in Indian states covering an area of 572052 acres at the book value of ₹ 546821 lakhs yielding ₹ 16290 lakh per annum out of which ₹ 1934 lakhs are paid to wakf boards to carry on the day-to-day activities of wakf properties. The book values of these wakf properties are highly under valued. Whatever standard we follow they cannot be less than 1.2 lakh crores or 1,200 billion in any case and can yield about ₹ 12000 crore per annum at the minimum return of 10%. Presently, they are earning merely 2.98% return on these wakf properties when the experience has shown that where the wakf properties have been efficiently utilized they have yielded 20%

return. The above figures exhibit that the book value of the properties falling in Rajasthan, Tamil Nadu, Kerala and Uttar Pradesh are highest constituting nearly ₹ 512613 lakhs which is nearly 93.7% of the total value of all wakfs taken together. Likewise, the total current income from Rajasthan, Tamil Nadu, Karnataka and Uttar Pradesh is nearly ₹ 12201 lakh which are 74.9% of the total income from all the properties. As against this, the earning from the wakf properties in Punjab, Haryana and Andhra Pradesh is highest for in Punjab, Haryana and Andhra Pradesh nearly the total earning from the wakf properties has been given to the wakfs. The share of wakfs in West Bengal, Uttar Pradesh, Kerala, Bihar and Assam is meager despite the fact that the proportion of Muslim population in these states is very high. The condition of wakfs is hopeless because the return to investment in wakf properties in India is miserable which is revealed by the following table.

Table 8.22

State	Loan given (₹ in lakhs)	Annual Return before Development (₹ in '000)	Annual Return after Development (₹ in '000)	Increase in Return after Development (%)	Rate of Return to Loan
Kerala	49.8	96	877.7	814	15.7
Bihar	23.8	5.8	459	7,814	19.0
Karnataka	633.7	1,087.8	12,001	1,003	17.2
Maharashtra	41	9.7	590	5,988	14.2
Andhra Pradesh	58.7	30.7	1,160	3,681	19.2
Rajasthan	3.2	..	106	...	32.9
Madhya Pradesh	75.4	85	2,512	2,855	32.2
Tamil Nadu	191.4	720.3	3,747	420	15.8
Orissa	188.1	60.4	4,232	6,907	22.2
Punjab	17.6	...	666	...	37.9
INDIA	1241.6	2,086	25,760.7	1,1351	9.1

Source: Sachar Committee Report, Table 11.2

The above statistics show that annual return of wakf properties before development was merely ₹ 20,86,000 which increased to ₹ 25,76, 61,000 after development or in terms of percentages it increased to the tune of 1,135. Besides, the total loan given to wakfs was ₹ 12,42,000 and its rate of return to loan was nearly 9.1%. This shows that the wakfs can earn a significant amount if the income from the wakf properties is properly utilized. The rate of return to loan in Punjab has been to the extent of 37.9% followed by Rajasthan to the tune of 32.9%, Madhya Pradesh to the magnitude of 32.2% and Orissa to the range of 22.2% which is remarkable by all standards. Recent trends show that in the states of Kerala, Bihar, Karnataka, Maharashtra, Andhra Pradesh, Rajasthan, Madhya Pradesh, Tamil Nadu, Orissa, and Punjab the wakfs could earn 19.1% return after making proper development. In a secular country, it becomes difficult for the state to fund the religious organizations purely on the basis of religion. Thus, for establishing and maintenance of the mosques, madrasas, dargahs, khanqahs, Maqbaras, Takias, Eidgahas, Imambaras, graveyards and Anjumans and for paying salaries to the Imams, Muezzin the community has to make its own arrangement. Besides, the community also needs its own resources for the marriages of indigent girls, helping the widows, maintenance of the divorced women, supporting physically handicapped persons, aiding the victims of communal riots and construction of community and marriage halls. Over and above this, since there is considerable amount of deficits in the number of socio-economic development schemes for the community and the state help seems to be far fetched, the Muslims too should come forward on the pattern of NGOs and collect funds from the Muslims for establishing schools, colleges, universities, hospitals, health centres, libraries, playing grounds and for paying scholarships to the needy and promotion of Urdu as well as for the enrichment of culture and the rich heritage of the Muslim community. The irony of fate is that despite the fact that Muslims have sound source in the shape of the wakfs but these are in bad shape. During 2005-06 nearly 316 properties of Delhi Wakf Board, 60 of Rajasthan, 42 of Karnataka, 53 of Madhya Pradesh, 60 of Uttar Pradesh and 53 of Orissa were under illegal and unauthorized possessions. The condition of other states was not much different. Besides, many states have huge amounts that are outstanding against them and they are not willing to pay them. For instance, the Maharashtra Government alone has to pay ₹ 81,68,285. In addition to this, the tenants are paying insignificant rents for the properties which have been located in prime areas. Several litigation cases are there in various law courts of the country. There are some Wakf Boards such as Punjab Wakf Board where nearly there are 11,000 wakf properties but there is no one to take the advantage. Over and above this, the records of the wakf properties are in bad shape and many irresponsible Mutawallis have played havoc. They have illegally gifted, transferred, mortgaged and leased many properties to private parties. Since most of them consider the wakf properties as their own properties, they are not transparent in their dealings with reference to the income and the expenditure of such properties. Moreover, the administration of the wakf is more political in nature rather than professional and commercial in contents.

The best that the community can do is to pressurize government to improve the maintenance and administration of wakfs by bringing appropriate legislations so that wakf properties which are in the adverse possession of private as well as government departments and local bodies may be vacated and handed over to the concerned wakfs and these properties may be exempted from Rent Control, Land Reforms, Agricultural Ceiling, Registration of Properties, Tenancy, Stamp Duty, Court Fee, Income Tax and Private Forest Vesting and Assignment Acts. There is a need of empowerment of the State Wakf Boards and the Central Wakf Council by according them high legislative, administrative and judicial powers. A separate cadre for the wakfs with officers having knowledge of Islamic Law should be created in order to streamline the management of the wakf on scientific lines. The board should consist of professionals, technocrats, bureaucrats, legislatures and the eminent persons from the civil society. The record should be digitized and National Wakf Development Corporation should be constituted by the Central Government with a corpus of at least 1000 crore for financing and supporting various Muslim institutions and spreading knowledge, removing ignorance and for the betterment of the community. The failure on the parts of State Governments and the Central Government to stop the practice of acquiring the wakf properties and safeguarding the wakf properties has certainly disturbed the Muslim community in the country. It is hoped that the government at the Centre would provide proper institutional support for the optimum use of the wakf properties and strictly monitor the management of the wakf boards in the light of the Sachar Committee Report as well as the recommendations given by various Parliamentary Committees.

The Remedial Measures

The above facts are the eye opener for the states and the Central Government as well as the larger civil society and the well-wishers of minority community. They convincingly lead to the conclusion that all is perhaps not well with Muslims of India as they seem to be the miserable lot and need affirmative and positive steps to redress their grievances and solution of their problems. It clearly appears that during the last sixty years they probably could not reap the benefits of development vis-à-vis others and they appear to be grappling with several social, economic, political and cultural issues affecting their identity, security, livelihood, status, dignity and honour. Due to the perceived lack of equity and equality of opportunity and transparency as well as the absence of inclusive approach they could not be brought within the pluralistic mainstream of the country. If they are left with chance or at the hands of competitive forces, the merciless global competition and the world economy would ruin them beyond redemption for in the laissez-faire only those survive who are fit and those perish who are weak and meek. The sooner their problems are attended the better it is for much water has already flown in the Ganges. For the affirmative action there is a prime need of a strong will on the part of the governing structure and the civil society for a big push in the form of reservation to the backward Muslims followed by the establishment of a National Data Bank, as suggested by Sachar Committee to diagnose the ills of the socio-cultural communities including the Muslims as well as there is a need of an autonomous assessment and monitoring authority to evaluate development benefits to various segments of the society. There is a need of strengthening of the legal provisions to eliminate discrimination and empowerment of the National Human Rights Commission, National Commission on Minorities and Other minority related bodies for it would at least help in removing some of the perceptions of discrimination, neglect and injustice from the mind of the minorities. Besides, a separate reservation quota of at least 9 to 10% for Muslims within the 27% limit even exceeding the over all limit of 50% would go a long way in helping some of the marginalized segments of Muslims. In addition to it, reservation for Muslim backward castes on the pattern of the Scheduled Castes, Scheduled Tribes and Backward Castes in Panchayats, Municipal Corporations, State Assemblies and Parliament would work as a balm on the wounds of the community for without a bold policy decision they cannot be brought at par with other backward sections of the society. It is very pity that Muslims were not employed in sufficient numbers as peons, daftaries, chaukidars, drivers, malis, gate keepers and the forth grade employees when there was no dearth of such competent persons. Likewise, they were not absorbed in substantial numbers as clerks and clerical assistants when educated Muslims were available in large numbers among Muslim community. Even the doors of police departments were probably not wide open for them so also the portals of military and security agencies with the result that they remained away from the governing structure as well as suffered the extreme pains of unemployment and during communal riots they became the victims of those ranks and files that were communal. Besides, being educationally backward they could not compete at state and central levels with the result that they are conspicuous by absence on higher positions in government. The same is the condition of Muslims at the levels of the Governors, Ambassadors and Ministers, Chairmen and Presidents of various commissions and corporations and Vice-Chancellors of the universities. To ensure the inclusiveness of Muslims in government departments, public utilities and corporations and in the process of development and governing process, they should be provided special facilities on the pattern of SCs/STs and backward castes at all levels. The history shows that merely by reservations these classes became heroes from zeroes. Over and above this, to ensure transparency and create confidence among Muslims, the eminent experts from Muslim community should be nominated through a transparent nomination procedure on various selection committees and interview boards. It should be ensured that the ultra-secular Muslims or those Muslims who are more loyal than the king should not be placed on interview boards for they would dent the chances of Muslims to prove their secular credentials. Besides, the deficit, wherever it is should be filled on priority basis and their representation in various elected and nominated bodies should be increased to such an extent that it may be visible. Without a positive and affirmative action, it would be perhaps difficult for the community to come out of the vicious circle of frustration and siege mentality.

In order to ensure the fair and free participation of Muslims their voting lists should not be tempered with but it should be made up to date regularly ensuring the fact that all able-bodied adults find their names and they are issued identity cards without much hindrance. Their voting booths too should be at convenient places and free from fear. Besides, the constituencies where they are in substantial numbers should not be reserved to SCs/STs, backward castes and women. Muslim haters and those creating communal feelings at the time of elections to create polarization with a view to defeat Muslim candidates should be dealt with firmly. Those political parties that spread hatred among people on the basis of castes, classes, religions or regions or those who use force and create fear and terror among voters should be disqualified from voting process. There should be a provision of recall or disqualification for any elected member from grassroot to Parliament inciting communal, regional, caste and other parochial feelings or doing or saying anything derogatory or acting or behaving against public security and national interests. There should be a provision against the misuse of civil servants, government employees, public assets and public property and government machinery and other civil and security agencies for or against any person, group or political party or religious organization by the ruling governments at the states and central level. The people generally allege that the manner in which the government staff and the government property were used for personal ends and the way in which some big wigs were booked and left free by using CBI and other agencies have shattered the confidence of the people in democracy. It has been observed that political leaders are generally tolerated so long as they are not uncomfortable to the governing structure. When they begin to create any problem, their old cases are mostly revived by taking the help of CBI or other central investigating agencies to silence them and when they are subdued, the cases are often dropped.

For Muslims' participation in political process in adequate number, all political parties should encourage the participation of Muslims within their influence zones. Muslims should be fielded preferably from such areas where they are in negligible numbers and Non-Muslim candidates should be fielded from Muslim dominated areas to create a climate of mutual good will and to reduce the chances of polarization at the time of elections. Despite their comparatively lesser number in the Assemblies and Parliaments they should be included in substantial numbers in cabinet formation to instill confidence among minority community and dent the perverted mentalities of the communal ranks and files. Their presence in sufficient numbers in the cadre of police constables and at the level of SHOs is a must to check and manage communal riots and instill confidence among the poor Muslims so also their entry in the Army, Navy and Air Force at the grassroot as well as high level is must with a view to create in them the sense of participation and inclusiveness.

In matters of education, all children up to the age of 14 including the minority children should be provided free and compulsory education in their mother tongue as guaranteed by the Constitution of India. There should be standard Urdu schools in Muslim dominated areas with well-equipped qualified and efficient and well-trained Urdu teachers both males and females and with quality textbooks in Urdu. Offensive and distorted historical material should be deleted from the textbooks and teachers and students inciting communal or caste or regional hatred should be dealt with firmly. Those institutions which try to mould the culture of

Muslim students by imposing their culture upon them in the form of compelling them to touch feet or put tilak mark on their foreheads or forcing them to wear certain dress, etc. in variance to Islamic principles should be black listed. Cooperation and coordination never mean surrender to ones' belief system. Muslims should participate with their fellow brothers whole heartedly while preserving their socio-cultural and religious identities. Poor Muslim children should be given scholarships, mid-day meals, cheap hostel and free tuition facilities. In matters of admission, the poverty and illiteracy factors too should be given weight along with merit. Besides, those schools, colleges, institutions and universities that admit minority students and students from the marginalized sections of the society in greater number and who are sympathetic to their cause should be given special aid packages. Since poor Muslim children have no space and no facilities within their ghettoized houses for study, the coaching and study centres should be constructed in minority dominated areas with adequate infrastructure where such children may study and complete their class assignment with the help of their guides. Coaching facilities for competitive examinations too should be provided in Muslim mohallas along with proper infrastructure ranging from fresh drinking water, all weather roads as well as continuous electric supply and health facilities. The coaching centres opened for Muslims by the government should not be left with the discretion of the management but there should be a supervisory agency as to check the misuse of money, manpower and resources by the reckless persons. The schools should be established preferably near the minority dominated areas to avoid the fear of backlash of communal riots. Schools for girls especially at the primary level should be opened separately and female teachers should be appointed in large number in such institutions looking to the sensitivity of Muslim parents for they hesitate to send their daughters in co-educational institutions and in areas which are communally sensitive. Muslim students should be provided cheap credit for pursuing higher education along with merit cum means scholarships. The IITs, IIMs and the universities and other technical and super-specialty institutes should be asked to ensure the entry of the Muslim students as per their quota strength. In order to remove the fear psychosis from the minds of Muslim parents, it should be ensured that competent Muslim students find their places in the campus selections as well as in other interview boards and selection committees. It has been observed that many parents have withdrawn their children from schools and engaged them in their own professions or employed them as petty mechanics or shop attendants because they feared that after acquiring degrees they would not get any jobs. We have seen that most of the Muslims are either cultivators or engaged in their own professions, vocations or business or are artisans, petty mechanics and transport and construction workers. They need skill enhancement and new techniques to sharpen their trades. Thus, the educational institutions should open polytechnics, training centres, vocational courses and information and guidance centres for such people. Besides, their drop outs in high schools or higher secondary schools too should be equipped with technical and vocational training so that they may not become burden on the families and the country. Muslims should be provided consultancy service in matters of various facilities provided by the government and they should have access to banks for loans on reasonable rates of interest. The poor and destitute Muslims and widows, divorcees and women in distress should be looked after on compassionate ground and the poor girls with marriageable age should be financed by the government. In short, the government should look after their multi-dimensional aspects with a view to take them out of the rut.

Up till now we have been simply hinting merely at the government agencies and civil society and have practically said nothing about the Muslims themselves. Holy Qur'an says that God never changes the condition of any community till it shows its readiness to change. It has been rightly said that one can take the horse to the water but cannot compel the horse to drink. Unless and until the community has vision and mission for development, progress and prosperity nobody can do anything to salvage the community from dejection and frustration. Wherever the societies, communities and nations have developed they have done so on the basis of their own strength, efforts and merit. Others have merely assisted them but never provided them cruches. The writings on the wall are loud and clear that there are no cruches for Muslims. In the struggle for self-sufficiency the Muslim community should not look merely towards the state or civil society or towards any miracle to happen but come forward and help the community through thick and thin. History is witness to the fact that the Agarwals, Varshenies, Guptas and Arya Samajis and many sections of Indian society in West Bengal, Assam, Southern India and elsewhere have done tremendous spade work for the development and advancement of their communities during the last sixty years while Muslims remained in their ghettos with siege mentality. Even the minorities like Sikhs, Jains, Parsis and Christians are far ahead of Muslims in almost all fields merely due to their advancement in the field of education, science and technology. Muslims have surely missed the bus, yet there is still time. They should learn from the dynamic communities of India and try to come out of the malice which is partly the creation of their own. It is unfortunate that Muslims have forgotten the charitable works and social projects in the way of God which are integral parts of Islam. They should revive their healthy traditions and move forward with conviction that they are capable of doing all those things which the other dynamic communities of the country have done. In this lies their success and in this lies their salvation. Muslims should sincerely and seriously ponder over the matter as to why they have drifted to the lowest of the low. How have they created so many adversaries within so little time in the country that nobody is actively coming forward for the cause of their affirmative development? Where are their distinctive characteristics, unique identities and differential marks which distinguished them prominently from rest of the communities? What has happened to their entrepreneurial abilities, adventurism, piety and good moral conduct for which they were renowned? Who has snatched from them their elitist habits, cultural charms, social dynamism and political will? Do they see the light on the other side of the tunnel or are they dumbfounded? Are they confident that their future in a democratic, secular and vibrant India is safe, secure and bright? Have the Muslims realized that the major fault for being called by different names by the adversities lies at their doorstep? Are the people willing to believe in what they say? Can the Muslim community say with confidence that the worst days of Muslims are over? These are some of the questions which need to be answered with grace and dignity by Muslims of India themselves. Once they start the process of looking at their faults, follies and omissions and commissions patiently, rationally and scientifically, they are bound to come out of the malice with courage and confidence.

What has been stated above should not be construed that the role of Muslims in the national reconstruction has been dismal or behind other segments of the society. It simply meant that despite their doing the best certainly they could not play their historical role for which they were renowned during pre-partition days. Admittedly, the Muslim community has not remained behind any other community in matters of contribution to national reconstruction. It has produced some great leaders in every field after 1947 such as Maulana Abul Kalam Azad, Rafi Ahmed Kidwai and Sheikh Abdullah who have shined in political field; Dr. Zakir Husain, Dr. Fakhruddin Ali Ahmed, and Dr. A.P.J. Abdul Kalam who have served as the Presidents of India; Hidayatullah and Mohammad Hamid Ansari who have graced the dignified chair of the Vice-President of India and Justice A.M. Ahmadi and Mohammad Hidayatullah who have served as jurists of fame. Likewise, among actors Dilip Kumar and Shah Rukh Khan are marvelous. In the field of music, Allah Rakha Khan, Bade Ghulam Ali Khan, Ustad Bismillah Khan, Begum Akhtar, Rafi Ahmed and Talat Ahmed are rated high. In the list of producers and directors, the names of Mehboob and Kardar can be mentioned. In sports, Syed Mushtaq Ali, Nawab of Pataudi and Azharuddin can be sighted. In industry, Yusuf Hamied, Azim Premji and Mirza Tanners have done commendable work. In religious field, Ali Miyan and Sayyedna Tahir Saifuddin are respected as great seminaries. In the field of art, Maqbool Fida Hussain and as an ornithologist Salim Ali have no match. In literature, Maulvi Abdul Haque and Ali Sardar Jafri have done well. Barkatulla Khan, Abdul Gafoor, A.R Antulay, Sheikh Abdullah, Dr. Farooq Abdullah, Omar Abdullah and M.O.H. Farook have served as Chief Ministers of Rajasthan, Bihar, Maharashtra, Jammu and Kashmir and Union Territory of Pondicherry respectively. G.M. Banatwala and P.M. Sayeed have graced Indian Parliament many times. Muslims have several prominent educational institutions such Aligarh Muslim University, Aligarh, Jamia Millia Islamia, Hamdard University, Darul Uloom Deoband and Darul-Uloom Nadwatul Ulema. Needles to say that there are many dignified, bright and dynamic Muslims who have contributed as Ministers, Governors, Ambassadors, Vice-Chancellors, freedom fighters, politicians and statesmen, chairmen of various assemblies and commissions and bodies. Likewise, there are several graceful and competent Muslims who have served as educationists, geographers, historians, scientists, poets and journalists, performing artists, jurists, athletes, sportsmen, administrators and technocrats and there are several known and unknown figures who are contributing in multidimensional activities of the country but their names could not be cited due to lack of space. What to mention the national heroes, there is no dearth of dynamic Muslims in every city. For example, in Agra having Muslim population around 325,000, there are 160 lawyers, 15 chartered accountants, 20 architects and civil engineers, 150-odd medical practitioners, 30, media persons, 75 poets, 20 Urdu and a dozen Hindi writers, more than a dozen prominent artists, around 300 government officials and 80 plus computer experts. However, looking to the number and the potentialities of Muslims in the country their progress in various fields is practically zero.

It will not be out of place to mention here that Muslims have special affinity with Urdu and madrasas. The single most important factor that has perturbed Muslims after their economic depravities is the step-brotherly treatment meted out to Urdu. It is most unfortunate that Urdu which was the language of all segments of the society has been the victim of discrimination and prejudice merely because it has been linked with Muslims. Since most of the religious and cultural literature of Muslims was in Urdu and their children knew no Urdu, they drifted from Muslim culture and Islam to other cultures with disastrous consequences. The continuance of Urdu as a medium of instruction in Urdu schools up to higher secondary schools and Urdu as an optional subject at graduate level and the provision for getting masters and PhD degrees at post-graduate levels in almost all the states where Urdu is the second official language or where Muslims are in large numbers is the need of the honour. It is also imperative on the parts of the Central Government and the States to use Urdu on important sign boards and issue advertisement and information brochures in Urdu so that the Urdu speaking people may know about various state policies and programmes. Likewise, the condition of Urdu books, magazines, news papers and periodicals is hopeless. There are very few people who read such materials. Besides, it is stated that such papers do not get advertisements from government machinery in adequate quantity which hampers their development. Muslims should also buy Urdu books, magazines, periodicals and other material in Urdu in large number to encourage their sale with a view to increase the popularity of Urdu for this is the surest way to spread the use of Urdu in the country.

Another critical point is the existence of Madrasas. Many people from majority community perhaps believe that most of the Muslim children study in Madrasas which are the centres of terrorism as these Madrasas give the training of suicide bombing, jihad and destruction of non-Muslims. Actually, no more than 3 to 4% Muslim students go to madrasas and madrasas are mostly free from such malice. Since there is no provision of religious education in government and private schools and it is obligatory on the part of every Muslim to read and know Qur'an, Muslim parents send their children to madrasas. Actually, madrasas are not the substitutes of the schools. They are meant to teach Holy Qur'an, the sayings of the Holy Prophet and Islamic law and jurisprudence. They produce Imams, Moazzins and madrasa teachers, Muftis, Qazis and religious preachers and they would continue to do so and would not deviate from their path. They teach what they have received over fifteen hundred years and try to convey to the posterity in the purest form what they have received through their peers. Thus, the talk of modernization of madrasas is a misnomer. Muslims largely do not approve the idea of introducing the content of modern education in madrasas. They want them to remain pure from inadvertent adventurism. Maktabs are certainly complementary to schools as they are different from Madrsas in many ways. They teach religious as well as secular education and a large number from poor families go to such Maktabs since they are cheapest, situated near their vicinities and provide elementary and primary education in Urdu. When we talk of modernization of madrasas, we should mean the modernization of the maktab education for modernization of these maktabs is essential. These maktabs should be linked with school and college education. Their certificates and degrees should also be recognized and wherever possible these maktabs should be upgraded into colleges and universities. Maktab students should also be allowed to appear at the various competitive examinations such as banks, defence and civil services since they have proper background to serve as efficient and honest officers.

We have also seen that Muslims are negligible in the field of industry, trade and commerce. Moreover, many doors for government and private sector are closed for them. They should not consider it as a bad omen or a bad luck but consider it as a golden opportunity. Lord has given them the chance to become entrepreneurs, traders and businessmen. If they start their own shops or trades, they can come out with flying colours. Muslims possess tremendous potentialities but their misfortune is that they are short of funds. They can show miracles if the government of India comes to their rescue and asks banks, lending institutions and development agencies to advance loans to them at concessional rates. Muslims lag behind in matters of number of accounts as well as in getting credits and loans with the result that they have been reduced to artisans, hawkers and petty labourers. The need of the hour is that since most of the Muslims are engaged in their own enterprises, they should be provided credit facilities at cheap rates and on easy conditions. Besides, the Muslim women are mostly engaged as sub-contractors at pitiable return within their own premises. They should be bestowed with financial assistance and loan facilities so that their artisanship may shine and they too may get rid of the exploiters. The Grameen Banks can help them in the field of micro credit as they did in Bangladesh. Over and above this, the Muslim petty shop keepers, mechanics, transport operators too should be given cheap and convenient financial packages so that they too may survive in the competitive markets. Actually, there is an urgent need of providing financial and other supports and initiatives in Muslim dominated areas especially in those professions and vocations which are growth-oriented. Fortunately, the country is passing through a phase of accelerated development and it is proper time to help and assist the under-privileged, marginalized and backward minorities through skill formation, education and financial help so that they may utilize this God given opportunity for their advancement and development.

In the end, we can conclude that instead of lamenting for their ills, Muslims should analyze patiently what they have gained and what they have lost during the last sixty years. Basically, Indian Muslims should ponder over their miserable condition themselves patiently and rationally and find out why they are backward, drawbacked and handicapped. Till yesterday they were considered as equals in every respect but today negative qualities are mostly imputed to them. Many people call them lethargic, fatalist and backward-looking. A few label them as frustrated, emotional and the follower of the dogmatic ulemas. Several consider them devoid of rationalistic, empirical and scientific fervour. There is no dearth of people who call them too much attached to their past, traditions and culture. Superstition, ritualism and fanaticism are imputed to most of them. Their role in the field of games, sports and national and international championships is minimal. In the field of literature, art and architecture they are practically nowhere. Country's political parties consider them as their vote bank and rolling stones that gather no moss. Their depleted dwellings, skeleton-type structures and depressed faces speak volumes of their anger, agony and anguish and the writings on the wall reveal that the future is full of ups and downs for them. As against this, they top in the number of criminals put behind bars, they are found in large numbers in less dignified profession. However, for these ills they should never think that there is something wrong in their social, cultural or religious systems for these systems have already stood the test of time and have provided them grace, glory and distinction. They should not criticize the times for their adverse fate since time always help the braves. They need not fall in the trap of the people who are asking them to come within the mainstream after abandoning their unique characteristics because their distinguishing marks will not only enrich the pluralistic culture of India but would also show them the way out of their malice.

What they have to do is to leave their imprints by letting others know that they are really innovative, dynamic and wise people. They should vehemently compete with their fellow brothers in matters of satisfying their needs rather than the greed for the needs can be fulfilled but the greed can never be satisfied. They have to maintain a balance between material, moral and spiritual development being the followers of Islam which emphasizes on golden mean. They have to show exemplary conduct and they should do what is right and invite others to do what is good and avoid the wrong and stop others from pursuing wrong. They should not judge people by their castes, colours, creeds, place of birth or by their bank balances, mansions, cars, positions and distinctions but by their good moral conducts, piety and righteousness. They should aim at acquiring knowledge and wisdom from whatever sources it may be acquired and propagate free inquiry, large-hearted tolerance and peaceful co-existence. They should emphasize on cleanliness, pollution free environment, better health care and purposeful life. They should strive for the betterment of the poor and the downtrodden and the amelioration of the oppressed and the greatest good of the mankind. They must develop entrepreneurial qualities in them and produce and sell goods and services that are relatively cheaper, adulteration-free, socially desirable and useful. Their high standards of morality, ethics and good moral conducts should be reflected in their business, professions, vocations, industry, trade and commerce. In the field of politics, their accountability, transparency, commitment, honesty and integrity should be reflected at all levels. They should not believe in money, muscle and lung powers to win votes but be above parochial, personal and regional interests and serve people satisfying their genuine needs. They should show concern towards gender justice and suppress the exploitation of women, children, weaker sections and marginalized segments of the society with iron hands. They should develop among the members of the family respect for the elder and love for the younger and will to say what is right. They should transform education system suiting to the cultural heritage, moral values and intellectual and scientific fervor. In a sense they should show by examples that they are useful segments of the society. In this lie their safety, security, progress, contentment and salvation. Sooner they do it, better it is for them.

9

Hindus and Muslims are the Two Sides of the Same Coin

It is regrettable that many people in India are unaware of religious, social and cultural distinctiveness and sensitivities of Muslims and Hindus and harbor misleading notions about them when the fact is that in many respects Hindus and Muslims resemble with each other as Ram resembles with Shyam and Bilal with Hilal. They are the two sides of the same coin. Both have rounded and sharp corners, both have good and bad aspects and dark and bright sides. Both have majority of very good and sterling people and a thin minority of bad and unwanted elements. It is a fact that most of the people from amongst Hindus and Muslims fall under the category of the silent and simple guys. Most of the members of the majority and minority communities do not speak anything on vital national issues in public but believe in what they hear from others. They are clear-hearted and nice people. They are mostly involved in their day-to-day matters and have little time to harm anybody. Likewise, there are intellectuals, elitists and meaningful people among both the communities who are liberal, considerate and excellent part of the society. They never indulge in any untoward activity or communal tangles. Most of the time they too remain silent save discussing national issues within their drawing rooms but when situation demands they take stand and influence the course of events significantly and materially. Besides, both the communities have distinguishing religious, cultural, social and aesthetical similarities as well as differences. Both the communities are governed by their moral codes of conducts, rich heritages and historical perspectives. Both relish their customs, conventions, ethos and practices. Both celebrate their festivals, auspicious occasions and ceremonies with zeal and gaiety. Both believe in some Super Power or God, Accountability and After-life. Both are religious minded, upright and God-fearing. Both revere their religious books, saints and holy men. Both believe in spiritual salvation, moral contentment and physical development. In a sense both the communities are traditional, value-oriented and conservative. There is no conflict of interest among them. As against this, there is a microscopic minority in both the communities which is vocal, fanatic and narrow-minded. Many a time the ingredients of this segment create bloodshed, heart-burning and ill-will between both the communities because of their parochial, communal and narrow perceptions. By systematically exploiting, the contrasting and healthy differences found between the two communities, they incite people on violence and hatred. There is a need to know something about this section of society on both sides of the corridor. We should educate people about these elements rather than concealing them under the debris. Truth can come out only when controversial matters are dealt with rationally without any bias. Whenever and wherever we find the fingers of mutual accusations, incriminations, indictments and denunciation being raised against any section of the majority or minority community they mean mostly the microscopic minority of the narrow-minded Hindus and Muslims and not the general category of majority of Hindus and Muslims. Many Hindus consider these fanatic and vocal sections of Muslim minority as fundamentalist, conservatives and traditionalists. Likewise, several Muslims treat this reactionary part of the vocal minority from amongst Hindus as inward-looking, orthodox and reactionary. The reality, however, is that both the sections of the society are the perverted parts of Indian society and despite differing in many ways they resemble with each other as black resembles with black.

The Perception of Many Hindus about Muslims

It is the misfortune of Indian society that several Muslims know very little about Hindus and most of the Hindus are ignorant about Muslims. Consequently, many segments from the majority community label most of the Muslims as narrow-minded, inward-looking, fundamentalists, conservatives, hot-headed, fanatics and what not. They consider the political, religious, cultural and social struggles of several Muslim organizations as revivalist, communal, separatist, and reactionary rather than reformist, secular, nationalist and progressive. They advise Muslims out of sympathy to shed their uniqueness, distinctiveness and social, cultural and religious identities in order to come within the national main-stream. They often believe that the Muslim mindset and outlook based on a reactionary and communal tendency is primarily designed to create a Muslim identity around Islamic framework with a view to convey their otherness. Many Hindus stresses that Islam is reflected in the scholarly and ordinary parlays of these conservative people as a separatist, communal and neo-fundamentalist paradigm dominated by diehard priestly class. The religious sects among Muslims, in their opinion, mostly try to ask Muslims to follow the obsolete traditions pertaining to their women folk and show their obsessive concern for the protection of Islamic ideology and pan-Islamism. They are generally involved in inviting Muslims towards praying, visiting mosques, shrines and imambaras and observing other religious customs, rituals and practices. One is also led to believe that this conservative structure of Muslim society has a unified structure of consciousness or these people are a community acting in unison that collectively attach importance to their social, cultural and religious practices and institutions and are prone to pan-Islamic rhetoric. These Hindu segments further allege that reactionary Muslims always talk in terms of their religious, cultural, social and distinct identities. They abhor Western culture and Christian ways of living. They want the revivalism of Islamic ideologies and value system. Their maulvis, religious preachers and clergies dauntlessly preach Islamic code of conduct. They cannot tolerate any changes in their lifestyle. They are not willing to accept the common pattern to govern personal matters. They want special privileges for themselves. Their communal sections mostly talk in terms of betterment of Muslims only. They always complain about discrimination and step-motherly treatment to Urdu. Most of their budding poets sarcastically release their frustration at Mushairas held throughout the country. Their most of the press clippings are full of bias against the prevailing system. Most of the Hindus belonging to this category believe that Jamaat-e-Islami aspires for Nizame Shariat, Tabhlighi Jamaat struggles for self-purification. Nadwa strives for puritan form of Islam and Jamitul Ulemae Hind talks of Muslim rights and Muslim empowerment. Muslim League wishes to maintain its own identity and does not hesitate to vent its feelings. Some radical people among this group do not relish when they observe many Muslims proceeding to attend the Urs at Ajmer Sharif, Kalyar Sharif, Fatehpur Sikri, Delhi, Nagaur and Mumbai, Bangalore in large number in India with traditional fervour. They abhor any subsidy or help to be given to Muslims at the time of Hajj or any pilgrimage to holy places. They raise their eye-brows when Muslims observe their Eid festivals with gay and gaiety. They see their mighty processions at the time of Moharram and Holy Prophets' Birthday with suspicion. They do not like the call of the Moazzin and hate Muslim's obsessions for cow slaughter, opposition to the construction of Ram Temple, resistance against Common Personal Law and the abrogation of Article 371.

Moreover, many Hindus firmly believe that Muslims are a distinct lot. They are excessively involved in their religion and mix religion with politics. Their uniqueness is reflected in their dress code, dialect and behavior pattern. They distinguish themselves by decorating their houses with the verses of Holy Qur'an and the pictures of Holy Kabah, Mosque at Madina and the shrines of Holy saints. The way they throng towards the tombs and shrines of their saints and offer chadders and donations with enthusiasm and commitment mark them from others. The enthusiasm with which they greet each other on

Eid festivals, the manner in which they meet their Hajis and the mode in which they celebrate Moharram speak volumes of their exclusive identity. The azan of the moazin from the minarets of the mosques, the sweet melodies of the verses of the Holy Qur'an from Muslim houses and sermons of the maulvis from the podiums manifest their novelty. Their veil system for women, gender bias in favour of males and conservative food habits indicate at their orthodox mindset. They start every auspicious work with the recitation of Holy verses, house warming ceremonies with milad and naming of the children with animal sacrifices. They steadfastly keep the fasts of Ramadan, regularly attend five times prayers and perform Umra with reverence. They pay Zakat, spend on charity and entertain the wayfarers. They blindly follow the dictates of Holy Qur'an, adhere faithfully to the sayings of the Holy Prophet and give extreme regard to the fatwas of their maulvis. The gracious beards on their faces, marks of prostrations on their foreheads and the humbleness in their eyes raise them in the eyes of others. The triple talaq, four marriages and fatwas on sundry matters attract the attention of media. Their hue and cry on minor matters, coming on the roads in the wake of disrespect to their religion and asking for special favours raise the eye brows in the society. Their living in aloofness and ghettos, unclean and unhealthy surrounding and illiterate and depressed environment create aversion. They celebrate their victories, ceremonies and functions with religious ceremonies and try to keep their unique identity intact.

Muslim Mindset about Several Hindus

Likewise, several Muslims too perceive Hindus with extreme bias and coloured glasses. Many Muslims consider Hindu sects like Vaishnavites, the Shaivites, Arya Samajis and Kabir Panthis as revivalists and organizations like Hindu Mahasabha, RSS, Vishwa Hindu Parishad, Bajrang Dal, Shiv Sena as obsessed with Hindu traditions, customs and ethos for they often, in their opinion, express their anxieties over the evangelical threat to Hindu identity and Hindu cultural distinctiveness. It is stressed by a few sections of Muslims that

Arya Samaj reflects the restoration and the glorification of pristine purity and the sacred Vedic culture and ancient Hindu civilization. In the same way, the Tilak School of Maharashtra, the Bengali renaissance and the Swadeshi movement too were mainly concerned with Hindu heritage and the revival of Hindu Sanskriti. The Hindi Urdu controversy and cow question are shown as nothing more than the symbols of Hindu revivalism and resurgence to mobilize the Hinduised religious community to seek access to political power and economic resources. It is further maintained that a section of Hindus not only saw a vindication of their right to assert their dominance in the wake of the demolition of Babri Masjid but many of the Hindus of India also wanted to build a resurgent Hindu nation and revival of Hindu culture and its ideology. It is stressed that they repudiated secularism, denounced the Congress for appeasing Muslims and suggested that Indianisation of Muslims was the only solution to the vex problem of Hindu Muslim conflict. The manner in which there has been the mushroom growth of various Hindu parties of all hues across the country is depicted by this Muslim segment as nothing but Hindu revivalism and aggression. The worship of the bricks of proposed Ram Temple, the shilanyas ceremony, the participation of sadhu sants in mobilization programmes and Advani's Rath Yatra were taken as symptoms to awaken Hindu consciousness and create Hindu militancy which had the predictable results. It is concluded that the religious frenzy aroused by the violent section of Hindu society seized the fanatics and towns after towns fell to communal riots and murders, looting and arson took place on large scale which threatened the very existence of the multi-religious, multi-culture and multi-lingual society. Religion took the centre stage and puja ceremonies, yagnas, chanting of the verses of the Vedas, breaking of coconuts and adoring of tilaks became the symbols of the resurgent Hindutva. This vocal section of Muslims also believes that the Taliban like religious intolerance shown in the wake of Valentine's Day and indignation towards free mixing of boys and girls, show of power against the wrong depiction of Hindu deities, adverse religious utterances in print media and terrorist activities practiced by some fanatic section of Hindu society in response to the Muslim terrorists are the main factors that led to extremism, fundamentalism and communalism among Hindu society.

Muslims too believe that Hindus are a distinct and a unique entity because they have excessive obsession towards their religion which is reflected by the sweet melodies of the verses of Gita, Ramayan, Mahabharat, Hanuman Chalisa and Gayatri Mantra from Hindu houses. One is bound to be charmed by the chanting of bells from Hindu temples, fragrance of flowers from Hindu shrines and echoes of schlock from Vedic Pathshalas. Hindu houses are mostly adored by the pictures and statues of Rama, Krishna, Hanuman and Hindu deities. In many drawing rooms one can see Ganesha in his magnificent forms. The way people gather at religious gathering of saints like Asaram Bapu and others and enjoy their sermons speaks volumes of Hindu's respects and regards for their religion and religious heads. The way elite people throng towards Sai Baba, Shirdi and offer millions of rupees as offerings show that they are the blind followers of their religion. People perform bhumi pujan, house warming ceremonies and inaugurate functions by lighting lamps, chanting Vedic schlock and performing havans. Even the prominent men and women wear stone-studded rings for good luck and good fortune, consult astrologers at the time of fixing marriages, establishing business ventures and going out for a new journey. They consider some days as auspicious and some as inauspicious. The manner in which marriages are solemnized with religious fervour and Holi, Diwali, Dashera, Durga Puja and Rath yatras are carried out reveal that a significant portion of Hindu society is essentially a religious and value-oriented society. One can see the mixture of politics and religion at the time of filling the nomination forms, celebrating victories, getting ministerial births. A beautiful blending of worldly matters and religion can be observed at Baba Ramdev's yogic camps and at the time of burning of Ravana on Dashera celebrations at Ramleela ground. There is gender inequality in Hindu society too. Boys are preferred over girls, women are kept under constrains, dowries are lavishly paid and some unscrupulous burn even the brides for the sake of dowry. Thus, Muslims too believe that Hindus also make it sure that their distinct identity is not diluted.

Actually, both the sections, that is, the majority of simple minded Hindus and majority of clean-hearted Muslims and the minority of vocal and fanatic sections of Hindus and minority of radical and aggressive segment of Muslims are similar and identical in matters of their excessive religious zeal, blind adherence to their customs and extreme passion towards their traditions. They affect one another. What happens to Hindu extremist society affects Muslims' fanatic section and what happens to Muslims' obscurantist influence the Hindus radicals equally. Likewise, the liberal and moderate Muslims and the broad-minded and large-hearted Hindus are identical. They too affect each other. The conflict is not between the silent majority of Hindus and silent majority of Muslims or liberal and the moderates from the majority and the minority but it is between the extremist sections of both the societies.

Religion, piety, value system and conservatism and good moral conducts are not bad in themselves. They are the strengths of Hindus and Muslims. The majority community and the minority communities are proud of them. What is wrong in them is the excessive, pervasive and blind misuse of such healthy and beautiful institutions to harm other sections of the society. Meaningful Hindus and Muslims shall always resist the erosion of their age old customs, traditions, cultures, uses and practices at the hands of pervasive Western culture. It is the Hindu and Muslim societies that have preserved so long India's age old heritage and value system. If they are made weak the whole marriage system, family structure, social and cultural milieu would collapse. It would be replaced by the Western system with disastrous consequences to the country as well as the world. No purpose would be served by blaming them because both of them are committed to their age old and well-tested systems. The rationalists and the Western educated liberals cannot appreciate the sentiments and mindsets of these two great communities for they judge them from the Western standards rather than from the angle of Indian heritage.

Secularism in India is Skin Deep Only

It is an admitted fact that Hindus and Muslims have always respected each others, religion. The kings and emperors despite following their own religions enthusiastically never imposed their religions upon their subjects. People were free to follow their own religions without any hindrance. Likewise, the people of India despite pursuing their own religions with all sincerity never hated other religions or created any trouble for other people merely because they were following other religions. Even today Indian people mostly follow their own religions in their own ways and never hate or abhor any other religion or create any hindrance or problem for the followers of other religions. Indian State too has no religion of its own and it is either neutral to all religions or shows equal respects for all religions. India is secular in the sense that religion is considered purely as a personal matter like ones colour, shape, structure, taste or liking and people have freedom to follow their own religions in their own ways freely without creating any problem for the believers of other religions. Indian State is secular but it cannot play with the religion of its people. It is difficult for it to pursue freely any policy without caring for the religious, cultural and other sensitivities of the people. Indian people are highly concerned about their values, and faith and cultural heritage. They seldom allow the state to play with their religious, moral, aesthetical, social and cultural sensitivities. Thus, Indian secularism for all practical purposes is supposed to have a positive approach towards religions rather than a neutral or negative one. The state is supposed to have no religion of its own. It cannot be neutral to or between religions but has to show equal respects to all religions. It is because of this reason that the state is finding it difficult to frame several laws which are prevalent in many advanced countries but which are contrary to religious practices of the people.

Many a time the critics levy a charge of communalism upon Muslims and ask them to follow the path of secularism when the fact is that secularism in the sense of complete indifference to religious and cultural sentiments of the people is only skin deep in India and even Hindus, Sikhs, Christians, Buddhists, Jains and Parsis are far from such secularism. Actually, secularism was taken in its true spirit by Pandit Jawaharlal Nehru and his colleagues who were supposedly inclined mostly towards communism or who had no specific faith in any particular belief system or dogma, however, they too failed to devise an adequate mechanism with necessary checks and balances for the implementation of secular ideas in their letter and spirit with the result that secularism remained confined to the theory only. In practice people did what suited them most. The cracks in secularism were amply visible during the days of Nehru. The people's aversion with secularism can be gazed from the fact that the Constituent Assembly did not use the word secularism while framing the Preamble of the Constitution. Besides, many Congress leaders during the days of Pandit Nehru were pro-religion and even some of them possessed rightist mentality due to the circumstance prevailing during those times. In addition to this, the older generation had a natural inclination towards their religions due to the compulsions of old age. Thus, Vallabbhai Patel had developed a specific mindset suiting to the Hindu society during the later days of his life, Pandit Govind Ballabh Pant had shown his inclination in favour of Ayodha dispute, Acharya Kirpalani had expressed his disapproval with Nehru's policy towards Kashmir, country's President Rajendra Prashad had presided over a Cow Welfare Conference due to his special passion for the sacred animal, K.M. Munshi never hesitated in revealing his Hindu identity and B.G. Kher, Pattabhi Sitaramayya, Purushotam Das Tandon, Sampurnanand, Govind Das, Kamlapathi Tripathi, Ravi Shankar Shukla and Charan Singh and many Congressmen had spoken in regional and sectarian tones on many occasions. Many revivalist moments had started in various sections of majority community. Several prominent Hindus had adopted a parochial approach. They wanted a Hindu state and Hindu Raj and predominance of Hindu culture. Even Janta Party which was being supported by Muslims whole-heartedly had aligned with Jan Sangh. Indira Gandhi under the compulsions of her old age too had developed soft corner for Hindu deities and Hindu ceremonies.

Rajiv Gandhi, the architect of modern India too had talked in terms of Ram Rajya being an ideal form of governance. Narasimha Rao and many of his colleagues were supposed to be responsible in some ways with the demolition of Babri Masjid. The role of many Congressmen did not remain above board. They had shown their several colours in the wake of foreign policy decisions, elections in Gujarat and canvassing during elections in several Hindi speaking states where elections were due and the Congress Party was facing the challenge posed by Hindutva ideology. During the Ayodhya upsurge the climate of the country was vitiated by the communal atmosphere. It is alleged that even those who were hard-core secularists felt comforts at the fall of Babri Masjid. During 1989-92 when Ayodhya moment was at its peak one could hear some people saying untoward things to Muslims and derogatory slogans were raised by the hard-core fanatics from a section of the majority community in pre-dominantly Muslim localities. Many sensible persons from film industry too did not lag behind in surcharging the communal atmosphere by producing sensitive documentaries.

Similarly, Muslims also did not lag behind. Prominent Muslim leaders like Maulana Azad, Dr. Zakir Husain, Fakhruddin Ali Ahmed and many others were committed Muslims. In their parochial interests many Indian Muslims too were not behind any Hindu radical party or extremist organization. They too had shown their communal colours on various occasions For instance, Jamaat-e-Islami was openly propagating for 'Nizame Mustafa', Muslim League was aspiring for a political space, Dr. Fareedi's Majlis-e-Mushawarat had fought election on Muslim platform, some of the misguided Kashmiri youths had taken to extremism and terrorism. Many Muslims had revolted against forceful family planning methods of Sanjay Gandhi and Muslim masses were not willing to yield on Common Personal Law. They had come on roads in the wake of Shah Bano case and against derogatory remarks made by some rabid radicals. Radical Muslims were planning for revenge and the Babri Masjid protection Committee too had contributed in the polarization of Muslims.

The fiery speeches of some of the members of Babri Masjid Action Committee had created ill-will between different communities in the country. Even the prominent Muslims leaders such as Maulana Hifzur Rehman, Maulana Bukhari, Banatwala and Salahuddin Owaisi and many others were talking in terms of Muslim interests. Actually, several Muslims do not relish secularism of liberal type. They have accepted it as a lesser evil but heart to heart they have affinity to their religious, cultural and value-oriented system. Likewise, many Hindus also did not like the neutral type of secularism. They too have deep-rooted affinities with their age old religious system.

In the opinion of many Muslims, secularism has different meanings for different people. They assert that if Sikhs keep beards and turban they are heralded for maintaining their religious and cultural identities but when Muslims wear beards and skull caps they are looked differently. Likewise, when the nuns adore their full black robe they are revered but when Muslim women wear black burquas they are looked with disapproval. Similarly, when Muslim educational institutions appoint or admit a larger number of Muslim students they are advised to appoint or admit non-Muslim employees or students in respectable number to be called secular but when the non-Muslim educational institutions appoint or admit even hundred per cent non-Muslim employees or students nobody compel them to appoint or admit Muslim employees or students in reasonable number to declare them secular. In the same way, many Muslim officers claim that if they appoint any time a larger number of Muslims being the heads of their organizations or do something for the betterment of Muslims, they are usually branded as communal. As against this, if the heads from the majority community appoint hundred per cent people from their communities and do everything for the uplift of their communities no eye brows are raised. The media often project madrasas adversely for providing religious education and efforts are being made to introduce modern education in madrasas. As against this, no attempt is made to introduce similar measures in Hindu religious institutions imparting

Hindu religious education. For instance, when Muslims fight for their reservations in jobs, educational institutions and legislature, they are called communal but when other communities do the same thing they are not treated likewise. These are the facts of life and are deeply imbibed in history and hence one should accept them as they exist in the society. However, one thing is certain that the posterity of dynamic and emerging Indians would never accept the double standard and these abrasions would soon become the matters of the past. Speaking generally, there is a significant content of admirable as well as deplorable communalism practically in every section of Indian society. Both the segments of the society try to help their communities without harming the interest of other people as well as they try to benefit their own communities at the cost of other communities. Thus, the positive and negative communalism of minorities and majorities strengthen each other and so the process is continuing.

Indians should Practice what They Preach

The need of the hour is to break this vicious circle and create a new awakening among masses based on secularism, humanism and large-hearted tolerance. The present situation demands that people should remain committed to their faiths and belief systems, serve their fellow-citizens with their utmost devotion, cooperate with the state and support broad-minded and enlightened politicians to run the country in the true spirit of Indian Constitution. It is the biggest folly to presume that Hindus and Muslims cannot live permanently in peace and tranquility. When people with so many differences such as colours, shapes, structures, habits, ideas, intelligence levels, wealth, possessions, and areas can unite and live happily with each other then why people of two religions with merely one difference of religion cannot live for ever in accord and harmony. Indian people should know that Muslims are not an exclusive entity separate from others. Save the difference of religion they are similar to them practically in all respects. In matters of language, customs, traditions, eating habits and dress they are nearer to them than the Nigerian Muslims or Arabs, Iranians and Indonesians. Their manners, customs, languages, behaviour patterns and diets resemble with their Indian counterparts. They are not outsiders; they are as much the flesh and blood of India as anyone else and they have every right to share what India offers them. They seek rights but also never falter to share obligations since they know that if the duties and obligations are accepted the rights automatically follow. Being the free citizens of India they are willing to play their constructive role in the building of a progressive and prosperous India and to be sharers, in common, with others in the triumph and setbacks that may come in the way. They too are loyal to the country, respect their motherland and are ready to die for the sake of their country. The present with all its miseries, uncertainties and agonies is destined to pass. It is the future that counts. It is this future that beckons all Indians to answer the call of sanity and piety with courage, fortitude and confidence. Muslims too should not lag behind but come forward and prove their credentials to their fellow beings and highlight the usefulness and relevance of Islam for the betterment of mankind by showing their exemplary conducts to people.

It is the duty of every citizen to prove by his conduct rather than mere preaching that his religion does not harm other belief system as it is most suitable for the betterment of mankind. No one believes in sermons. People want living proofs. Muslims being the followers of Islam too should show by example to the people that that they are the followers of Islam which is broad-minded, liberal, democratic, secular and golden middle path. They should prove by practice that Islam hates extremism, bloodshed and arrogance. They should convince people that their religion is a peaceful, just, equitable and pious religion and preaches love for God, compassion for humanity, care and concern for the downtrodden and respects and regards for fellow beings. They should show it by practice that it believes in non-violence, charity, peaceful co-existence and large-hearted tolerance and does not allow forceful conversion, injustice towards other belief systems and hatred between people of various faiths. They should concentrate on the theme that Islam is truly secular in the sense that it treats the believers of other faiths with compassion and dignity and does not permit any kind of discrimination on the basis of religion and asks its believer not to fight on the basis of religion but depart peacefully by saying, "to me my religion and to you your religion". Their main emphasis should be on the fact that Islam considers the life, honour and dignity of other believers sacred and gives equal protection to their properties, possessions, professions and vocations and it safeguards their cultures, customs, ethos, religious practices and provides sanctity to their temples, monasteries, churches and synagogues. It bestows honour upon the saints, priests, clergies and clerics of other faiths and showers respects to their religious books, religious heads and religious places. Being the followers of such a dynamic, progressive and humanitarian religion, Muslims too should not lag behind in the task of service to mankind and nation building. They should show by their sheer hard work, excellence, good conducts and genius that they are admirable and loyal citizens of India as well as the wonderful human beings.

The Majority and the Minority Communities should Cautiously Watch the Changing Trends

The people of India should watch the changing trends in the country with extreme care and caution. The country is undergoing a sea change. There are chances of unusual happenings on the pattern of Egypt, Tunisia and other Arab countries because of corruption, inflation and poor governance. Fingers are being raised at meaningful people within the corridor of power. Besides, the emergence of political mafia, unscrupulous business magnates and scoundrels and the erosion of democratic and humanistic values, collapse of Nehruvian secularism, ebb and flow of Hindu-Muslim relations, defeat of Marxists, secularists, modernists and post-modernists and the rise of Hindutva and Muslim extremist and the pervasive forces have shaken the faith of the people. The glimpses of pre-marital sex in schools and colleges, the abandoning of aged parents by a few adult children, neglect of infants by some of the sensuous parents, frequent divorces, and infrequent instances of lesbianism, sodomy, gay marriages, group sexes, wife swapping, gigolos, nudity shows, adultery here and there as well as gambling, alcoholism, drug addiction and obscenities are shattering the fundamental structure of the Indian society. The greed for more and more has generally broken families, created cleavages between spouses, made children destitute, shattered joint family system, dented the blood and clan affinities, harmed good neighbourly relations and reduced the friends and colleagues to the lowest of the low. Many girls have discarded their age-old dress code in favour of a thinly dress system; several poor and destitute girls have been exploited as strip teasers, dancers, call girls, sleeping partner and what not.

The Indian people should also resist the call of those priests, clergies, pontiffs, saints, maulanas and molvis who have superficial knowledge of religion as well as those opportunists and reformed ones who are paid by the vested interest to toe the official lines to get government favours and those extremists and fanatic preachers who are crowd pullers and who use religion to get prominence. Mostly these seminaries are either ordinary preachers or high profiled ones or community leaders whose eyes are on government chairs, state gifts, media attention and favours from those who are in power. Sometimes they speak in the tone of nationalism, at other times they become religious bigots and many a time they project themselves as the selfless, pious and sincere saviours of the community. They speak in different voices revealing sharp differences in their ranks and file. Some of them give cheap and irreligious indicts and fatwas and advices; incite ordinary people on agitations, violence, belligerence and militancy; and create hatred between believers of different faiths. They increase the inter-communal heat by their fiery speeches, gestures, postures and body languages and involve innocent people in rituals, trifles and inter-sect conflicts. Many of them are obstinate, hot-headed and diehard parochial and inward-looking beings and generally command respect due to their typical dress code, behavior pattern and traditional outlook.

Muslims have added responsibility to let others know that Indian Muslims are neither anti-feminist nor anti-progress nor anti-humanity. They do not drag themselves into the debris of the past glory but try to evolve an alternative strategy based on wisdom, forbearance and foresight to recoup their past losses. They have a keen desire to fight for their Constitutional rights through peaceful and democratic means and they do not hesitate to demand their genuine rights due to the fear of any backlash. They should convince their fellow brothers that the fundamental ideas of Shariat or Islam are not in any danger in a democratic and secular country like India where people are by and large religious and tolerant towards others religions and the state too considers such principles as pious and sacrosanct. Muslims' main problem is their safety, security and identity; political, social and economic empowerment; educational, cultural and infrastructural development; and peace, progress and prosperity along with enduring relationship with fellow citizens and healthy equation with established political parties. They have to chalk out a dynamic and coherent course for them suiting to their cultural and religious heritage and give it a pragmatic meaning not in isolation from others or confronting other belief systems but through close understanding and interaction with them. They have to give new forms to their expressions in accordance to the secularized and democratic idioms and explore fresh, peaceful and non-violent avenues to articulate their aspirations, anxieties and misgivings and misunderstandings. The misfortune with Muslims is that they come out with purely a quasi-religious agenda in the shape of helping the mosques, madrasas, wakf boards and protecting graveyards, mazars and makbaras as well as safeguarding Urdu and Muslim culture which throw the political parties on back foot due to the fear of backlash of the extremist parties. These issues are certainly important but once Muslims are politically, economically and socially empowered these issues would be solved automatically.

Hindu and Muslim Cultures are Identical in Many Respects

The people of India should know that as Hindus and Muslims are similar in many respects, their cultures too are identical in many ways. The culture of Muslims is not an exclusive entity separate from others. It is as much Indian as other Indian cultures are. Muslim culture has many things in common with the culture of their Hindu brothers but side by side it has its own identity. Despite the fact that Indian Muslims in various parts of the country differ in matters of manners, customs, language, social ceremonies and diet yet there is something like Muslim culture which is in vogue in the country for the last several centuries. Similarly, despite the fact that there is difference between Hindu culture and Muslim culture still there are several commonalities between them. According to Professor Mushirul Hasan, Muslim culture in India has its own history and individuality and distinctiveness. It is obviously Indian and refreshingly different from the culture of many Muslim countries. Muslims have deep roots in Indian society and are the natural inhabitants of this great country. They have much in common with other communities in moral consciousness, family life, religious fervour, economic structure, political awakening and cultural attitudes which can easily fit them in any pattern of regional or national culture. Like any other Indians they have a multiple identities. Sometimes they are peasants at the farms and behave like other farmers and at other times they are voters and vie with each other for the victory of their candidates. Many a time they line up like others for getting railway tickets, get admitted in hospitals for treatment and enjoy along with their Hindu brothers in cinema halls and on playgrounds. In the same way, they stand shoulder to shoulder with their brethren and participate on the occasions of Eid and Diwali.

India is a land of diversities where Parsis, Jews, Marwaris and Gujaratis are distinguished from others by their unique style, dress code and magnificent cultural and social ceremonies. Hindu ladies are perceived by their bindis, sindoors, mangal sutra and saris and Hindu males are differentiated by their kurtas, dhotis, hair locks, tilaks, and sacred threads. Sikhs are identified by their turbans, beards, kirpans and karas and their women are spotted by their shalwar kameez with heads covered with dupattas. In the same way, the nuns and fathers in Christian missionaries and public schools are comprehended by their long robes and the sects of

Jains are understood by their white robes and bare bodies. Similarly, the saints, achariyas, pujaris, sadhus and sants are inferred by their long hair, bald heads, magnificent hair locks, saffron clothes and the villagers, city dwellers and the people from South, East, North and West as well as Srinagar to Kanyakumari and Amritsar to Kolkata are known by their apparels, languages and food habits.

A synthesis of Hindu, Muslim, Christian and other cultures is amply visible within the confines of India. Hindu ladies wear salwar kameez, Muslim women adore saris and blouses, Muslim males and Hindu males frequently use coats and pants. Similarly, many marriage ceremonies of Hindus, Muslims, Sikhs and Jains are common save nikah ceremony and feras. Likewise, several customs observed by different segments of Indian society at the time of births, deaths, house warming, etc. are similar in many respects. Holi, Diwali and Eid millan resemble with each other as Ram resembles with Rahim. In the same way, the pattern of houses, food habits, behavior pattern of different sections of Indian people have become common. People accept the differences between various castes, creeds, religious groups with admiration and seldom raise any finger of doubt considering them as the distinguishing marks of their cultural heritages, social customs and religious practices. However, Muslims lament that when the same people observe Muslim males and females wearing different apparels their reactions are sometimes unpleasant. It appears that the adverse reaction sometimes towards Muslims' cultural identities is partly due to the historical reasons, partly due to terrorist activities committed by some Muslim men and women under the garb of their unique distinctiveness and partly it is the outcome of aversion found among some of the European countries against Muslim veil system. Many of the European countries are asking Muslims to abandon their specific identities with a view to guard their societies from the potential terrorists. As a matter of fact, Europeans are afraid of the spread of Islam due to the past glories of Islam and the present terrorist activities committed by some of the radical Muslims. When they observe minarets and bearded Muslims and burqa clad Muslim women among them, they perceive Islam marching towards them to engulf their irreligious and non-biblical system. In addition to it, the Muslims' dress code and cultural and religious practices pose a challenge to their ultra secular modes of living which too are in variance to their scriptures and religious dogmas. They fear that the simple and the sophisticated code of living of Muslims might impel their young people to follow Islamic code and abandon their ultra modern and irreligious pattern of life.

It is indeed painful to digest discrimination in any field. Even Mahatma Gandhi fell offended in South Africa when he faced the discrimination at the hands of the whites. One should ponder that if one is living in a Christian, Buddhist or Communist country and one is asked to abandon one's distinguishing identity and compel to follow the Christian, Buddhist or Communist ways of living, how one would feel about it? It is certainly difficult for the minorities to survive along with their distinguishing marks in any majority country where their survival largely depends upon the majority community for there is always a pressure upon their minds from mainstream cultural milieu to abandon their distinguishing marks. Since they move, interact and transact mostly with the people of the majority community, there is a tendency among many of them to follow the ways of living of the majority community to minimize the chances of discrimination and acquire acceptability among the dominant community. It is because of this reason that many Indian educated Muslims have adopted the behavior patterns of majority community and call them moderate Muslims when there is nothing like moderate or less moderate Muslims in Islam. They have copied from many Indians who are living in foreign countries and have accepted European and American ways of living just to acquire respectability since they are at their mercy in matters of their livelihood and survival.

Muslims certainly have a unique moral identity which is linked more with their conducts rather than physical outlook and which differs from other cultures materially. One can easily distinguish a Muslim woman from Morocco to

Indonesia by her shyness in the eyes and her blushful face. Similarly, a Muslim can be demarcated from others by his downcast gaze and humility and humbleness on the face. Muslims should wear the robe of piety and piousness. Instead of mainly indulging in distinguishing their cultural and religious differentiations and physical and outward identities such as the skull caps, shirts and trousers, tahmads and sherwanis, they should conduct business, professions, vocations, trade, commerce and industry with transparency, honesty and grace. They should pay taxes sincerely and regularly and be polite in their dealings. They need not indulge in the business of liquor, gambling, games of chance, cornering, profiteering and in all those activities such as corruption in public life, adulteration, immoral advertising campaigns, under weighting and under cutting as prohibited by Islam. They should deal with workers with love and affection rather than with contempt and pay them their due in time. In essence, they should distinguish themselves in every field as the ideal citizens due to their excellence, honesty, piety and good moral conducts. Holy Qur'an too has distinguished them merely by their conducts and not by their outward differentiations. It says, "You are the best of nations raised up for the benefit of mankind; you invite people to that what is right and forbid the wrong and believe in God." Thus, by inviting humanity to all that is good and enjoining what is right and forbidding what is wrong they can carve their own place in the civilized segments of the society.

Indians should also learn from the Western society which imparts significance to the loyalty of family as well as loyalty to society but prefers the loyalty of society over the loyalty of family. According to N.R. Narayana Murthy, the people of advanced nations have tremendous respect for their community, property and look after their parks, gardens and public palaces with care and concern. They also keep their social interest above personal interest and do not allow their personal relations to interfere with their professional interests as a consequence of which nobody can bribe them easily and the meritocracy is not sacrificed at the cost of personal preferences. They do not believe that public projects are the concern of government or the third party but take equal interest in the personal as well as the collective projects. They do not boast of their past or present but have respect for others especially those who have accomplished more than they and try to learn from them. They have dignity of labour and are proud of their jobs and have tremendous respect for transparency and accountability. They seldom become intimate without becoming known and friendly and do not expect undue favours. They are punctual, hard working, devoted and have respect for other people's time. They are strong and confident and independent in thinking and display intellectual honesty. They fulfill contractual and legal obligations and rights and strive for common good achieving the genuine needs of the society rather than running after the greed.

Indian Muslims should also learn from Indians who have made tremendous progress in each and every sector. Our competent businessmen and young entrepreneurs have floated multi-national companies of world fame, they have established a chain of knowledge hub across the country, they have established several franchises in collaboration with the foreigners and they are pioneers in IT sector. Indian scientists, professionals, technocrats, bureaucrats and journalists have left a mark of their excellence at the global level. Muslims too should come in all fields including business, industry, trade and commerce. They should know that there are viable markets where they can succeed by introducing innovated business models in product designs, pricing, financing, production and marketing and selling. Thanks to the impact of globalization and technology that they can sell their products any where in the interconnected global village. Since the demand for goods and services is more in the areas of the bottom of the pyramid, Muslims should concentrate on enhancing efficiency and cost reduction and on the production of such goods and services which may suit the purse of the bottom of the pyramid. They should also create an export sector of their own and develop world class leaders who may demonstrate values through leading by examples. They should create a non-political and non-controversial social and educational foundation by donating a small portion of the profit to address the problem of the poorest of the poor. They should align their interests with the interest of the country and leave a lasting legacy upon the countrymen and the posterity by their honesty, hard work and commitment.

We should recognize and appreciate the diversity in unity and unity in diversity in the Indian context and learn the theology of tolerance, love and peace from Islam, Hinduism, Christianity, Judaism, Confucianism, Sikhism and Buddhism and others. As a plural society we should endeavour to tackle our ethnic, regional and religious problems with compassion, love and grace. If India is to survive as a civilized, democratic and secular state, the fight against injustice, intolerance, hatred, communalism and religious bigotry has to be waged against all fronts. We have to create a climate of harmony and peaceful co-existence in a plural and multi-religious, multi-ethnic and multi-cultural society where people of all segments can walk with their heads high. We have to integrate all the narrow emotional orbits of divergent people into the multi-dimensional harmonious fellow-feeling and strengthen the moral fabric of the Indian state by harmoniously blending Indian traditions in the priceless and glorious heritage of India so that our country can become a gorgeous, vibrant, progressive, prosperous and mighty country. It needs self-less, God-fearing, efficient, committed and large-hearted and enlightened people who are unfortunately dormant but it is hoped that they would rise to the occasion and salvage their beautiful country from the morass in which it has fallen.

Please refer to the facts and figures including the tables provided in the book from Sachar Committee Report entitled "Social, Economic and Educational Status of the Muslim Community of India", a report prepared by Prime Minister's High Level Committee (Cabinet Secretariat) Government of India under the Chairperson Justice Rajindar Sachar.